Storytelli

STORYTELLING

A SORT OF MEMOIR

Andrew Sinclair

Ashgrove Publishing
London

First published in the U.K. by

Ashgrove Publishing

an imprint of:

Hollydata Publishers Ltd
27 John Street
London
WC1N 2BX

ISBN 978 185398 189 0

Book design by Brad Thompson

Printed and bound in the U.K.

CONTENTS

ALSO BY ANDREW SINCLAIR

ACKNOWLEDGMENTS

For various previous printings of parts of some of these episodes, may I record my grateful thanks to *The Atlantic Monthly*, *Granta*, *The London Magazine*, *The Texas Quarterly*, *The New Statesman*, *The New York Times*, *The Spectator*, *The Sunday Telegraph*, *The Sunday Times* and *The Times*; also to the Bodley Head, the Dial Press, Faber & Faber, Harper & Row, Little Brown, Lorrimer Publishing, Macmillan, Sinclair-Stevenson, Weidenfeld & Nicolson, Cape and Constable. All their incomparable editors helped to shape my prose, if not always my life. I am also grateful for quotations from Charles Simic, *Dime-Store Alchemy: The Art of Joseph Cornell*, Philippe Ariès, *The Hour of Our Death* and Robert Pogue Harrison, *The Dominion of the Dead*.

None of my works over the past 25 years would have been finished without the expert assistance of Liz Spicer, consummate at her art.

The cover picture is a painting by Patrick Procktor of the author in the Colony Room, with Muriel Belcher and Francis Bacon in the background.

Unlucky Greeks, are we not dead?
Seeming alive, by dreaming fed?
Or do we live and is life dead?

PALLADAS OF ALEXANDRIA

Further than Guess can gallop
Further than Riddle ride –
Oh for a Disc with the Distance
Between Ourselves and the Dead!

EMILY DICKINSON

INTRODUCTION

Biography is credible fiction. What means are used to a bad end? Intermittent diaries, surviving letters, muddy memories, and the testimony of witnesses, friends or foes or passers-by. Nearly all sources are contradictory and haphazard. From the many facts and records of any life, a selection must be made. The author has a bias, determined by his time. For instance, what were the motives of the subject of the book? Were they before or after the discovery of psychology? Can these modern processes be applied to the actions of those, unaware of analysis, in previous ages? How could Oedipus ever foresee that Freud would be that much after him? Complex it is.

As for autobiographies, from Saint Augustine to Jean-Jacques Rousseau and the ghost writers of celebrities today, these books are prime examples of evasion, excuse and omission. They are rarely more believable than the penny ballads, once sold by hawkers outside Newgate, as the last confessions of a hanged highwayman. To cast the chosen in a good light, episodes from their past are left in shadow and oblivion.

Yet the genre drifts on, and always will. And so it should, as a matter of style and imagination. For Homer in his *The Iliad* about the fall of Troy, mythos was truth. His heroes and demigods were held to be the founders of the Greek cities, which sent out many an Odysseus to conquer and colonize Asia Minor before a long journey home. The warriors were legendary. In the theatre, their exploits created the original supreme tragedies of human beings, battling against their destinies in the chaotic play of human existence. And as Michael Chabon wrote, 'All novels are sequels to *The Odyssey* and *Don Quixote*: influence is bliss.'

Even if I refer to myself as 'I' throughout this memoir, I must try to detach myself from My Self, whatever that may be. I must try to judge fairly my words and actions, as they affected other people. As for my reasons, well, often there were none. And when I seek to speak from another character's point of view, that is the method of a novel, neither more true nor more false than a slew of biographies. I have sometimes hoicked into the text a scene from one of my novels, when these were the contemporary observations of a past period, more accurate in many ways than my memory of it now. I have also worked in the film industry, and so I have used screenplay techniques, which so often convince us of the immediate reality of human actions. My diaries, however, are so sporadic and full of vagaries that my fiction is often superior in matters of fact.

If I also seem to treat myself as a stranger who appears to be me, it is because I never wanted to grow up. I always wished to retain a sense of wonder and surprise. When a child, I never quite knew what I would do or say next. I was often caught out by what I did and said. Yet because I wrote and spoke about these episodes, I found I was meant to believe them. After all, they did come from my pencil and my lips. And then I was no Proustian; I did not wish to live in the mouths of other people. I have ignored my critics and the opinions of others, ever since my flash success with a couple of novels while still a student at Cambridge. I was universally derided, and I resolved to be an original at whatever cost, as long as I did little harm. A career was not for me. Only the life of a free spirit, if I had one, and could live that way.

So there we are. In this minimal personal saga, with the belief of T.S. Eliot and the enduring Homer, that past and present and future are webbed from the same weave. The passage of time, however, creates an autopsy – the judgement of each of us on ourselves as a coroner reaching his verdicts from flawed and variable evidence in the dock. Every reader, if any, must decide what is misleading in this work. Did anything really happen to me in what way, and when? I leave my words to you.

BIRTHING AND MOTHER

⎯⎯⎯⎯

I came into the world in Oxford in slow time and the wrong way down. Or up. Anyway, only one way out. The history of my future life. My head was too big. That has not changed, either. I was pulled out by forceps. The marks are still on my ears. My small and valiant mother, Hillary, was in labour for forty-eight hours. Given the choice of bringing me out in pieces, she chose to push on, an enduring strain against pain, which became a tough streak in me, as a whole. My protracted birth shifted me from Capricorn to Aquarius, the goat to the water-carrier on both shoulders. Not that the Zodiac has any meaning, but my reckless energy was to be balanced by steering through the slop and the swell of words, as I tried to explain what I had done, without ever knowing quite why.

We cannot choose how or where or to whom we are born. We are babies of happenstance. The poet Larkin wrote a notorious and silly poem about our parents fucking us up. They don't. They make love and we are the consequences, willy-nilly. And unlike Tristram Shandy, I cannot conceive of my conception. Although we are said to remember every experience from the foetus to the corpse, our talent for forgetting is essential. We have to select from the evidence presented to us, in order to survive, and even to create a toddler picture of ourselves. My mother nearly died of insisting on having me alive and out of her, despite the doctors' advice. I neither walked nor talked until I was two years old. I shot around at speed on my bottom, sculling with my arms. My favourite food was coal from the bucket by the grate.

As a child, I was not self-conscious. I was a small being in an alien world of adults, who either answered my cries, or did not. So I learned what I could ask for, and what not. A biscuit perhaps, but not the moon, although I thought the moon a new penny until I was four, and I could have asked for it, to put in my piggy bank. I absolutely accepted my little world and all that was in it, for I knew of no bigger or different one. Certainly, other little boys had other mothers, who were also aliens, but my peers all seemed to be much the same as me. In an age before television, there could not be any other possible worlds, except the one right around me. Even when we travelled from London to Oxford by rail to escape the Blitz, the capital and the train and the university city were immediately my whole world, the moment that I was in them, and I had no memory of the worlds before the present one.

I had no identity then. I did what my mother or my school told me to do. Even when I mucked about with my brother Ian in the back garden, there was little intimacy between us, and none on the playground. Yes, I was self-centred, but I was not the centre of my world. I was merely a small piece of a bigger jigsaw, a pleat in a skirt, a knot in a fleece. Yes, my mother made me hold out on my spread arms the skein of wool, while she wound the end into a ball for the darning of the socks and the knitting of the sweaters. Living was a process, which moved one on from day to day. I was a speck in it.

Without being able to compare how other little boys lived, I presumed they all lived the same as I did – the black-out, the rations, fathers away at the front, but away, anyway. We did what we were told. There was a war on, wasn't there? It didn't really matter to small boys, except we could pay sixpence to sit in the cockpit of the stranded Spitfire in St Giles' and jiggle the joystick and prang the Jerries – rat-tat–ratty-tat-tat. Only pretend.

My mother only cried once in all her hardship. And even I didn't blub, when the doctor told me not to, sewing up my thumb with a carpet-needle and saying, 'No pain-killer for you, son. They need it for your dads in the war.' We were not hardened or taught to be Spartans or Stoics. Though it did my brother and me little good, I thought this must be how all the other little boys were treated in the world. Little girls were a total mystery to me.

So I was lonely, but I was not self-conscious yet. Shooting up through my school with an arm upraised and a pat answer to every question, I found myself stranded in the top form, far too young and friendless. Lumpy and unathletic, I held my own on the muddy sports fields by showing no pain and a dogged ploughing on. The only time I was cornered in a 'bait' by a ring of other boys on the playground, I refused to be baited. After striking out with puny fists against a few tormentors, I merely squatted, my arms around my knees, and let them hit me, until they went away, bored and disgusted. How can the mob bear to have no victim?

I became more aware later. With a nearly-photographic memory, I had excelled in all classes, until the age of twelve. After the Sports Day at the Dragon School, I was depleted. In the wish that nobody would personally excel, the headmaster had decreed that all races should be house events, and as the world's slowest red-legged runner, I ensured our team always ended last. Parachuted onto a platform to declaim Shelley's Ode: 'O Wild West Wind, thou Breath of Autumn's Being', I came to a dead stop on the moment when the hectic leaves were being hurried to their dark wintry bed. I burst into tears. There was the audience in front of me, several hundred adults, judging my shame. There was I, called an 'old boy'. Weeping at my own failure, I and them, separate, never to be in one world again.

My elder brother and I were not allowed to go out to the Gold Coast, where my father, Stanley, was a colonial police officer. He was a handsome but limited man, who rigorously did his duty. His nicknames were appropriate – Zinc, because he was as hard as metal, and Boy, because he never grew up into reason. He had met my mother in Basutoland, now Botswana, where she was a school-teacher in the Orange Free State over the Border. Extremely intelligent, she had been chucked out of the family ranch. Eventually, she told me why. After many decades of evasion and silence, the truth came out.

'Back in Ficksburg, my father killed my mother.'

'Was it murder?' I asked.

'I didn't think so then.' My old mother's eyes became an even colder shade of blue. 'Nor did the jury. But I do now.'

'Why?'

'You don't go duck shooting with a rifle. And he married our Boer governess. I was thirteen, but I was sleeping in his bed to stop him killing himself. Sometimes, after she moved in, we had to eat turnips in the barn, my brothers and I, to stay alive. And we were killing an ox a week for the blacks, and a sheep for us. I won a scholarship to Rhodes University, but I never got the fifty pounds to pay the rest. It all went to her and her children.'

I had heard other parts of the story of the Free State spread in South Africa. Both of my grandfathers had fought in the Boer War, one of them from India with Lumsden's Horse. The other had stayed after the Peace of Vereeniging. I still have a photograph of him and his cronies in a wooden cricket pavilion, taken at the signing of the peace. They were bearded men, as was the new King Edward the Seventh and the commandos on their horses in the conflict. My grandfather had acquired a fifty thousand acre ranch on the dry veldt near Bechuanaland, as the spoils of war. Ficksburg was two days' ride away, and there was hardly any communication from farm to farm.

My elder brother Ian and I were some of the later colonial children. We were dumped between tours, particularly to the Gold Coast, now Ghana, because the Foreign Office barred minors, given the death rate from malaria and blackwater fever. In the days before penicillin, the remedies were only quinine and some compound called M & B, which would reduce my mother to a sweating and gibbering wreck with a temperature of 105° in the three days of its recurrences. In a scandalous pre-war affair with my later stepfather, my mother left Ian and me with her relations in South Africa. These are my first memories. I could undo my right shoe, but not my left, to throw over the rails of the P&O liner; so I arrived, hobbling. A young cousin had scarlet fever, so we were put in quarantine in an orchard of apple trees, as in Eden. And in a thunderstorm, an uncle tried to fix a fused electric bulb. Lightning hit the roof of corrugated iron and blew him backwards off the table, outlined in fire.

With the Second World War coming, my mother had to take us back to England. Given the fear of bombing, we moved from London to Oxford, held to be a safer target. She still believed in the values of the empire. Small boys should not be hugged after the age of four, in case they might grow up to be wet or pansies, instead of officers. If we took too much jelly, we were hit over the head with a silver ladle. Sixty years and more passed, until I persuaded my mother to hug me often. She had told me of lying on her Bath lawn in a swimsuit in the sun with her baby grandson Merlin, crawling all over her and pissing happily on her body. 'I brought him up,' she told me firmly, but in his tiny way, he had brought her up, as well.

As she was so small, a little blue tank, always on the charge, and her two husbands and sons were so tall, she used to carry around a wooden stool to stand on and talk to us. Yet, she was not always totally in command of larger men. In a gold mine in Ashanti, she was told that she could have a heavy gold ingot, if she could carry it away. Immediately, she bent and lifted it out of the door. The embarrassed mine manager ran up. 'I didn't quite mean that,' he said, and she had to give up her good fortune.

She always thought men didn't quite mean enough, even her husbands and sons. She was a determined woman, who turned herself from a bush South African rancher's daughter into a true-blue Tory lady. I have always loved the serpent and the chameleon in women. Every year, they may shed a skin and reinvent themselves in another glittering suit, sloughing off the past. My mother did it slowly, grinding off wars and some poverty, to bring up her sons, as best she could. The urge to rear a family is the essence of our society, and my mother was awfully good at that. I truly loved and needed her, and I knew she could do no wrong.

This trust would be reinforced after the death of her second husband, Patrick Eve, in the Gold Coast, the summer before I was drafted to do my National Service for two years in the army. She was demented with grief and rancour, and she elected me as her defender against my father for the next twenty years until he passed away. This was when she was most in error, but I would not discover that until it was almost too late.

My Childhood, if Worth It

War children, we were not the same. The adults remembered peace, they thought the war abnormal. To us, wartime was forever, in Oxford. We listened to a fairy story, often told, but always good to hear. Instead of 'Once upon a time…' the story would begin, 'Before the war when…' I was four years old when it began and I had no memory of peacetime. In those lost and magic days, there were all the toys money could buy; but in the war, our tin and lead soldiers were taken away to make Spitfires, Hurricanes and bullets to shoot the Huns. Before the war, there was all the food we could eat, even chocolate and trifle; but in the war, there was the weekly cake queue at Oliver & Gurden's, where we could buy two shillings' worth of dry Madeira cake off ration, if we hung about the baskets of the waiting housewives for a whole afternoon. When I was six, the first very short story of mine published in the school magazine told the story of a small boy starving to death, nursed in his final illness by his mother in rags. I still remember the last sentence. ''Give me an orange, an orange,'' said the boy, but there was none, and the cottage on the moor fell into silence again.'

There was also the blackout. Before the war, the night streets were as light as day and the skies blazed with fireworks to remember Guy Fawkes on the Fifth of November even more brightly than the searchlights laying grids on the dark after the sirens sounded. But in the war, we felt our way along the pavements by touching the garden walls under the dead street-lamps, and we traced the numbers of strange houses in braille with our fingers. The blackout was for ever, in Oxford.

Rationing was our existence. Coupons set the limits to what we wore and ate. Our desires were cut into coloured squares by the scissors of grocers. Children cannot live in last year nor imagine next year; the present is, is and always will be until they grow up and remember inexactly what their youth was. So we were war children and our world was too dark and too cold, always makeshift and short of things, a world of the fourth-hand, the worn, the patched, and the drab. Our fathers were away fighting and our mothers tried to protect us from the combat, but it squeezed them and us, reaching into every home in khaki gloves to pinch and scrape. We were not victims, struck low by poverty and denial, as so many modern authors claim. Nor was our education cut short by privation. We had to survive, and so we did, as best we could.

We had fled to Oxford when war was declared because there was a rumour that a secret agreement had been reached with Hitler. Although the Führer was no gentleman, we did have the riposte of the Royal Air Force to make him keep his word. The pact was said to be that, if we did not bomb Heidelberg, he would not bomb Oxford and Cambridge. The perfidious British naturally surrounded the university cities with aerodromes and filled the Oxford suburb of Cowley with war factories. But Hitler kept his promise; the nearest bombs fell at Boars Hill and only killed some earthworms. So the war for me did not mean blitz and ruins, but shortages for ten years until rationing ended.

My mother, my elder brother, and I lived in an old brick semi-detached house in Polstead Road, a mile north of the city centre, and a few doors down from where Lawrence of Arabia had spent his youth. He had a hut at the bottom of his family's narrow garden, where he used to dream of a desert empire from his tiny shed. Our garden, a few yards wide and a cricket pitch long, had a hen run behind the stumps. We had eggs for the duration, and the fact that we named each hen individually Whitey or Brownie did not stop us from enjoying them when they finally reached the pot. Eggs, pickled in great pitchers; hundreds of Kilner jars of bottled plums and apples and jams; occasional salt-dried meat biltong from South Africa and Spam from America, these were our luxuries, and Marmite on fried bread.

Almost penniless on the salary of a colonial police officer in the Gold Coast, my mother took to writing historical romances about hardy women and unreliable men. One of them, *I Struggle and I Rise*, about the Dutch resistance to Spanish invasion in the 17th century struck a chord in the war years and became a best-seller in America. Although the tax authorities on both sides of the Atlantic took most of the spoils, and the dollar was then worth only five shillings or four greenbacks to the pound, my mother burst into tears, when a cheque with more than four figures on it arrived through the post. We were solvent, at last. The only other time I had seen her weep before was when she had sent me to the local post-office with a ten-shilling note to buy a tin of beans for six-pence. Overcome by having so much money, I spent another four-and-sixpence on an illustrated paperback of British fighters and bombers. On my return, my mother broke down. For our budget was shot to pieces.

The war made us all pioneers. My mother made and preserved food from scraps and ends, and she darned clothes until jerseys and socks were joined patches. We built whole battle fleets and tank armies out of pins and balsa wood. What we could not make our-selves, we had to do without. So we learned how to fix things and imagine them into what they were not. Deprivation is a great im-proviser.

Memories of war. The androgynes in the ARP in dark blue fat-rumped trousers checking our blinds to see no streak of light showed. The mysterious airmen in lighter blue, flown from nowhere, about to go on their missions. The Yanks stopping me to give me gum, tasting of rubber and peppermint. 'Are you sure you can spare it, sir?' I asked as I was taught to ask, and they laughed from great heights at such odd politeness from a kid with chilblains on his bare knees.

Then we had the lodgers who were billeted on us, and they cried louder than children. They were the wives and parents of the wounded dying in the head hospital in St. Margaret's Road, where my mother visited, and where I used to sneak past four times a day on the way to school in case the nurses pushed out Frankensteins on wheelchairs with only a ball of bandages above their dressing gowns and slits to represent mouth and eyes. They almost always died in there, but the one survivor in ten would be rolled out as a mummy to scare a small boy witless.

Everyone worked and had no time. And when I first became old enough to understand the war, we had begun to win. In fact, we won so often that a sense of fair play made me wish for a few Ger-man victories. My games were filled with tanks and guns, dogfights and flak, convoys and submarines on the battle-map which my mother called her carpet. But there was a private world out of wartime behind the drawn blinds, when the coal fire scorched the grate and blackberry jelly covered the toast and my mother read us

Dickens, *Oliver Twist* and *A Tale of Two Cities*. He and Walter Scott, whose total work I read between the age of ten and eleven, were my interior escape routes under the barbed wire, the first a tunnel to slum and blood and thunder, the second a refuge of chivalry and fair ladies and gentlemen with maces.

Yet I had my little prisoner-of-war camp for eight months of the year, an educational institution called the Dragon School, which taught me admirably, French at six, Latin at eight, Greek at ten, and precious little science. For obvious reasons, German was not then an option on the curriculum. The school fitted me to take a scholarship to Eton, where I decided to go because I lost an argument about the best of schools in the playground. My elder brother had gone to Rugby, so using up the dregs of the family income; so I had to get a scholarship somewhere, or it was state education and out.

My best escape of all was down Polstead Road, across Walton Street, and up a little track called Aristotle Lane. There I ran away every holiday to fish for silver roach with scarlet fins in the onyx canal under the humped brick bridge. From time to time, a red and yellow and black coal barge was pulled past by a clopping Shire horse, on to London, on to London, down to the Thames, and as far as Rio, where did the canal end, how did I know? And why didn't the steersman in the cloth cap call to me, 'Boy, boy, need a hand. Come on board. I'll take you anywhere.' Further up Aristotle Lane was the higher hump of the railway bridge with its sides of corrugated iron, where I could stand in the middle while the steam trains shuddered the boards beneath my feet and sent up smoke on either side to make a cathedral of cloud above me. And beyond was Port Meadow, where the horses and the cows grazed on the common land, rolling away and away to the bright river, with the swans so strong they would break a leg with their beaks or fly away gracefully to the ends of the earth.

Later, I wrote a sonnet about my brother and me; it was called 'Snail racing' and was published by the poet Alan Ross in the *London Magazine*:

> There is no thread to lead us through their maze.
> It has no axis. Their meanderings
> Make tracks of silver slime in spoilt lace ways,
> The snails are weaving in the early mornings.

We pluck them off the slabs and line them close
On cracks we dare not walk on as small boys.
A line of armour at our starting post,
We cry, 'Off! Off!' They cannot hear our noise,
And if they budge, they inch on here and there
Until their horns recoil to touch each other,
Hard-shelled and vulnerable, as once we were
At play in Polstead Road, I and my brother.
So sensitive, so dumb. At snail's pace grew
The subtle jealousies between us two.

The Wall and the Dame

Going back to a Feast of Old Eton Collegers – I don't quite know why – I encountered a dread figure from my Election year. 'Andrew,' the hirsute plump sweating figure jeered, 'we used to call you Redlegs.' Also Cyclops, and the Melancholy Bloodhound, for I was then rather sad and ugly. 'You came with round red legs, and yet you left as our top athlete. How did you do it?'

Indeed, a combination of despair and loneliness, which I countered with Wrath and Pride – the two Principal Boys among my Seven Sins. With slow reactions and small hands and feet, I was a physical shambles. Yet I learned one thing early on the pitches and the perils of Eton. SHOW NO PAIN, AND THOSE SET AGAINST YOU WILL PART AS THE RED SEA.

My parents were divorced and gone to Africa, where my mother had married again, Patrick, a handsome lawyer in the Gold Coast, whom she ran as usual. Many a holiday was spent with step-relations, who did not want to bother with me. So my room at Eton College became my home, with its folding bed and elementary desk. The scholars were set apart from the rest of the private school; in my case, because my family were not rich, my education was free. Indeed, although I appeared to be a gilded youth, I would pay for my own education after the age of thirteen by another scholarship to Trinity, Cambridge, and state grants and later by fellowships at home and to Columbia and Harvard and Stanford universities in America

Eton College had originally been endowed by King Henry the Sixth for seventy poor scholars, and so the strongest and meanest of us were pitted every year in the Wall Game against the best of the Oppidans, the eleven hundred other school members, whose rich parents paid large fees for their sons' exclusive education. What I had learned before at the Dragon School served me well on these fabled playing fields. Remaining slow of movement, I gave up quick ball games like fives and squash for golf and rugby and the Wall Game, that early rendition of the Battle of the Somme. My smiling and grinding attrition of my rich foes – I was called 'a tug and a thug' –

brought me improbable success as a player of games. An odd physical imperturbability gave a momentum to my curious career. I could scrum and boot with the best, while retaining a certain mental agility and detachment.

If the Battle of Waterloo was won on the playing fields of Eton, as the Duke of Wellington claimed, Passchendaele and the Somme were fought to a draw in the Wall Game. Brutish, immobile, nasty, long, and without result, that plodding encounter was a mudbath and a class war each St Andrew's Day between the cleverest youths in the country and the most privileged ones. I ended as the leader of my pack, the Keeper of the Wall, because I showed only endurance and knuckling and no flinching, however much the hurt. The fields of Eton were never played on, for they were rehearsals for killing grounds to come.

Although public schools were meant to be pink hotbeds of passion among the boys, I hardly met it in College, perhaps because of my conspicuous lack of attraction. But the one outrageous person of my time was the brilliant Jeremy Wolfenden, whose father's Report would change the laws against homosexuality, and turn a crime into a pastime. Later famous as a gay journalist and possible double secret agent, Jeremy's experience at the Wall altered his style forever.

In this experience in his No Man's Land, I suppose I saved his life. Treading thick mud, I was knuckling forward as First Wall along the grotty bricks, inching on with my knees the crouching Jeremy as a Second over the small ball. Then, I found my knobbly boots treading on his back, not on the squelchy earth. With his body down, I shouted the salvation cry, 'Air!', but it took a couple of minutes for the Bully to break up. Jeremy was inert, not moving or breathing. As we pulled him up, his face left a deep death-mask in the mud. We thumped his back until he began to choke and cough and tremble back into existence. He never played the Wall Game again, and he was left with an abiding hatred of the class sports and privileges of his school.

So many contemporary writers had been Collegers at Eton that my dreams of becoming one had a track record. Cyril Connolly had written a famous essay, 'Enemies of Promise', to try to prove that an education there was the crippling of literary inspiration, but he was only trying to excuse his own failed promise. George Orwell, then called Eric Blair, was a Colleger. The Sitwells were from Eton, Henry

Green, and Anthony Powell. When Somerset Maugham with his old lizard's face came down to talk to our Literary Society, he declared that one in five of England's leading novelists came from Eton, as high a proportion as sat in the average Conservative cabinet: Harold Macmillan was an old Colleger too. Maugham discouraged us from becoming writers before the age of forty, recommending us only to copy out Swift and Defoe and his own works before then, but we reckoned that he feared our competition.

Our formidable matron was called a Dame. Behind her back, we called her 'Elsie'. To her face, as to The Queen, she was addressed as 'Ma'am'. As well as running the laundry and the cleaners and the bedmaids, she was a minor doctor for our sprains and bruises, and, in my case, a terrible blue boil. Our filthy khaki army trousers for the Wall Game often scratched our legs and left us with sores, as with the trench troops in the First World War. Rather ashamed, I took my horrible pustule to Elsie for treatment, and I stretched out a bare shin towards her, sitting on a stool with her needle and her bandages. She pierced and pressed out the foul mess. Then she burst into tears.

I could not believe it. I had thought her hardly human, as tough as my mother, who hardly ever gave way.

'You don't realise,' Elsie was sobbing. 'I don't want to do this bloody job. There we were – three sisters in the country in Cumberland. And then the war came – and there wasn't a possible young man – we could marry – alive, – you see – in twenty miles of us. Cruel. Who'd want to be a Dame?'

I dared to put my hand on her shoulder, but she shook it off. Those caked khaki trousers had caused the outburst – or did I look like some young Yeomanry officer, too far gone at Wipers.

'Oh, go along,' she said and patted me, as I limped away.

So Elsie and the Wall Game taught me first of the hidden reasons of why people do the jobs they do, and do them as they do, and do them so well.

Eventually, I was in free fall in the abyss between my Etonian appearance and the penury and lack of family in my life. In the Easter break before my last summer half, I was abandoned by every connection I knew, and I had only twenty pounds in my Post Office account. I went to Battersea to stay in cheap lodgings, ready to experience what is miscalled 'real life'. I fell in with a South African music teacher, who made money by playing piano ditties in Mayfair hotels. I sat beside her and collected tips and free drinks. When I spoke of this adventure as a swansong to the Eton Literary Society and left the conclave, the Headmaster opened a weary eyelid and said, 'Oh dear, I see we have George Orwell again.'

What an identification with a fellow Colleger, but I had too little of Orwell's searing integrity and insistence upon the truth. I had been, however, one of the final generation of colonial children, featured in his *Burmese Days*, when he was a District Officer like my father in Africa. Later I read his works, roughly in the disorder of his life, and I was struck by his reactions from his experiences. Curiously, in his 'Shooting an Elephant', he told of how he had to fell a great mad beast, because it was expected of him. He could not look a fool in front of a jeering Burmese crowd. He had already made up his mind that imperialism was an evil thing. He hated his service bitterly. 'In a job like that you see the dirty work of Empire at close quarters.' Later, he had to attend 'A Hanging'. The drop took a long time to strangle the lashed, hooded figure. When it was over, the impulse was 'to sing, to break into a run, to snigger.' So it would be for me in my slight mutiny over the Suez fiasco and my first novel about a rebel in the Guards, a satire on the British far-flung flag.

In utter contradiction, my time in Battersea was hardly as rough as that of Orwell, while *Down and Out in Paris and London*. For my weekends were spent with my Pop friends in their stately homes. At one owned by the Hornby family of WHSmith fame, I was so bewildered by the array of silver prongs on either side of my plate that I could hardly scrape enough food from the butler's gleaming tray to slake my hunger. But I did learn one lesson from the Duke of Marlborough, who was the guest of honour, for his son had married into trade. The very upper class confuse rudeness with wit. His joke was that he had been asked by an American woman at lunch, whether he minded if she smoked between courses. His reply was, 'Not if you mind if I fuck between courses.'

Oddly enough, I had no particular sense of class divisions or warfare at that time. Rather detached and sometimes melancholy, I was not envious and hardly looked inward. Very much under the influence of Homer and the values of ancient Greece, I believed that, as in *The Iliad*, one's acts made one known, and as in *The Odyssey*, one had to be very clever to avoid the tricks and traps of circumstances and society, Perhaps that was why being 'too too clever' was the put down of the shires, where showing any intelligence sent one to Coventry rather than Belgravia.

As for the departed and long gone, I could hear only the faint trumpet calls of memory. In the playing fields of the Dragon School in the November chill of Poppy Day, we children in blue shorts had been drawn up to hear some of the roll-call of the dead in the First World War, while a bugler sounded the Last Post on haunting notes that led my childish fears towards the mysteries of death. Although I was to know two suicides in College at Eton and in my army training for the Brigade of Guards, I would never see a living creature die until our car on leave hit a heifer in Surrey. As I cradled the head of the jerking cow in my arms, it quivered and lay still, and I watched a film close its open eye, that veil between heaven and earth which I would later explore.

Although I lined the route to Windsor Chapel in the scruffy Cadet Corps for the funeral of King George the Sixth, and I would see Winston Churchill in his triumphal catafalque and river voyage to his ceremonial rest in peace, I could never stomach the glory of the warrior dead which stuck in my craw. When I was at Cambridge and had protested against the Suez campaign, I used to go out to visit the American cemetery outside the city along the Madingley Road. To avenge the Blitz on Coventry and London, we had surrounded our university city with airfields for bombers; their crews on their blanket raids often had casualties, a half missing and more. In this graveyard, the thousands of the fliers were buried in arcs, facing the white flagpole of the Stars and Stripes, the curve of the crosses broken by an occasional Star of David, the Muslim crescent nowhere to be seen. In the memorial chapel, mosaics showed angels flying among Liberators and Flying Fortresses, while a strategic map depicted the bombardments inside Germany, which culminated in the fiery holocaust of Dresden. A programme announced that on Poppy Day an RAF Anson would drop five thousand sweet peas on the ungrateful dead.

Where the imperial arteries meet is in London at Hyde Park Corner. There Piccadilly runs into the bronze Duke of Wellington and his Apsley House and the old St George's Hospital, now a luxurious hotel. A huge Memorial Arch stands in a green traffic islet in the middle of a vast roundabout. The last time I was there, a squadron of the mounted Life Guards in armour and glory rode through the Arch towards one of the two First World War monuments on the grass. In front of the cavalry, a stone field mortar was erected above friezes of guns and a dead soldier, at last resting in peace. The legend read out the ledger of the dead:

In Proud Remembrance of the
FORTY-NINE THOUSAND & SEVENTY-SIX
Of All Ranks of the
ROYAL REGIMENT OF ARTILLERY
Who Gave their Lives for King
AND COUNTRY IN THE GREAT WAR
1914-1919

On the far fringe, bombarded by traffic noise, past the Iron Duke on his charger, flanked by four Georgian infantrymen, stands a beautiful naked young David, posing on his broadsword and his lance. He is guarded by two Maxim machine-guns wrapped in laurel wreaths. His requiem is the most startling of all obsequies:

ERECTED TO
COMMEMORATE
THE GLORIOUS
HEROES
OF THE
MACHINE GUN
CORPS
WHO FELL IN
THE GREAT
WAR

Saul hath slain his thousands
but David his tens of thousands

The counting-book of the lost at the back of the plinth numbers some twelve thousand machine-gunners. But then, how many more Huns did they mow down, as a sickle through the wheat?

To endure the horrors of war, soldiers are taught to believe that they will survive the conflict through their courage, or if they are killed, they will progress to another and better life. This is morale, and it is held to be essential to all armies. The cult of the warrior achieving the hereafter by his brave deeds is an inheritance from our tribal past, when the Greek heroes might achieve the Elysian Fields rather than Hades and the Vikings aspired to Valhalla. When I visited the ranked divisions of the headstones of the war dead in Flanders, I thought how neatly were arranged their horrible endings. To sing 'Onward, Christian Soldiers' or to view among the exploding artillery shells the Angel of Mons was a mass delusion obscuring the truth of the trench experience.

There were no rites of passage for these slaughtered lambs without God, many of them as anonymous as the corpse beneath the Parisian Tomb of the Unknown Soldier. Unshriven, they might wail as the sudden dead, forever condemned in Virgil and Dante to an eternity in a purgatory because Charon would not take aboard his ferry those who had not had a proper interment, although on French popular postcards, patriotic angels hovered above the .75, the glorious murderous field gun. Whatever the messages of pulpit or cathedral, there was little consolation for the millions of mothers, who wanted to bury their sons individually, in dignity and respect.

For a lesson in how to die well, I would always remember one hot summer afternoon in an Eton classics form. The Beak was teaching us of the death of Socrates. We wanted to be outside rowing or thwacking cricket balls, Wet or Dry Bobs. He saw one pupil yawning.

'By tomorrow morning, boy,' he said, 'you will write me out a Georgic.'

That was the worst punishment. A sleepless night spent scribbling five hundred lines of Virgil's Latin verses.

'But, sir,' the boy said, 'I haven't done anything.'

'Exactly. But you have not paid attention to the death of Socrates, the wisest man there ever was. And why was he made to drink the poison hemlock? Because injustice rules the world.'

It still does.

Summer and Bamber

The swan dies after many summers. Indians, poetically speaking, spend nostalgic summers. I spent five summers as a Colleger at Eton. My fifth and last summer I remember the best. I sang my swansong then with Bamber Gascoigne.

We had many things in common, which were uncommon to our contemporaries. We were both in Pop, or the Eton Society, a self-electing power-group of social charmers, who had annexed to themselves most of the desirable privileges of our insulated group. Pretty clothes; the right to punish; the prestige of exclusiveness; the moral superiority of belonging to the best club; the sole capacity of wearing a buttonhole all the year round and sealing-wax on the bottom of our tails; a stiff collar to show a stiffer neck and a butterfly-tie to show the freedom gained by knowing the flower of the school; reserved seats on the low wall called Pop Wall, which ran in front of Chapel and God – what more could any peer or power-group desire or get? Only wisdom; and this commodity Bamber and I thought we had particularly earned.

We were Scholars, but socially acceptable; we were intellectuals, but affable ones; we had scholarships to Cambridge, Declamation Prizes, Reading Prizes, even honours at the Wall Game. We edited the 'Eton College Chronicle'; we were congratulated by The Queen Mother and Princess Margaret for our dulcet speeches; we acted the leads in the school production of Julius Caesar.

I remember lying on the coir-matting, underneath black drapes and a flying organ in School Hall, with a snuff of dust in my nostrils. I was Brutus, and I had stabbed myself deeply, until the red toothpaste showed on my fingers; now I lay dead on the mat, breathing heavily. Above me, Bamber's voice stressed, Old Vic and obvious, 'THIS WAS A MAN'. And he was saying it wrong. He should have been saying, THIS IS A MAN. No boy now.

We used to spend a great deal of our time walking round the artful wildernesses and casual kemptness of Luxmoore's Garden, a plot presented to Eton by an old green-fingered Beak. Only the First

Hundred in the school could use its shady paths and proper per-spectives towards Windsor Castle, the Thames and the Chapel. Bamber and I used to pass much of our leisure and lounging-time there. With sophisticated simplicity and calculated childishness to show our youth at heart, we played Pooh-sticks in the stream, racing twigs down the tangled currents. Or we struck charming poses to each other and to the admiring lesser Etonians, who envied us in our seeming independence and neglect of them. I usually wore sponge-bag trousers, a purple waistcoat with silver buttons, and de-liberately-holed shoes, to show that I didn't really care for pomp, but only for circumstance. Bamber normally came out into the sun with 18th-century flowered brocade between the lapels of his morning coat, in this last arrogant summer.

On a final night at school, Bamber and I walked out of College into the graveyard that lay under the Chapel. The time was one in the morning. Moon splashed on the flat tombs and blackened the moss, which blotted and blobbed the stone. A yew-tree, traditional, stood sentry; it was crooked and bent and warped with long duty. Spiked railings were iron sentries before the main road and the Gothic street-light, called the Burning Bush. And, round its prongs, shapes were clustering.

'What's that?' I wondered. 'Down there. Let's go and have a look.'

I squeezed through the railings, but Bamber preferred to stay be-hind. I walked to the metal Bush. The figures, at my coming, ran away. There, festooned among the weaving ironwork that sup-ported the glass lamp, stag's heads gaped at me with mournful eyes, mounted on wooden plaques (inscribed DUMFRIES 1895, DRUMMANDROCHIT 1909) holding up their antlers like bro-ken bones in the perpetuation of their death. The hands of the raiders had lifted their blind-glass gaze from their safe sockets above the tedium of the Beak in the division-room, and had taken them, in ridicule, to perch as dumb cuckoos on the branches of the horned Burning Bush. Seeing one head left on the ground, I picked it up and placed it in position. Decapitated already, I knew I was going from my rutting pride. A mere trophy of time past.

Returning towards the graveyard, I saw that the jokers had taken the statue of the Virgin Bathing from the Drawing Schools, and had left her as a hitch-hiker, lonely, marble, cold, and with her hand stretched out by the Bus Stop. I touched her chilly palm and returned to the graveyard, but Bamber was gone, and my flaunting folly with him. I was alone and ridiculous in the cemetery. Eton Chapel was falling like a crumpled dust-sheet from its wooden towers, cross-stitched by the lines between the blocks of its stones. Round me were yew-trees and tombs and Hill's House, blackly sleeping over the haphazard dead. Tomorrow I was departing as though I had never been. I was only leaving behind me A.A. SINCLAIR carved on Chamber Wall, A.A. SINCLAIR printed on old School Lists. And there was nothing in that name, which would survive. Only in the man going on, into the army, and whatever next. I would not be as would so many of my contemporaries, a youth who never quite left that privileged and inspun school, because there was the best carefree time and place we ever had, or would have again.

Bamber and I rather lost a regular contact with each other. I must have felt, however, that I was still in touch with him, through a higher consciousness or a hidden nostalgia. For I forgot to inform him that I expected him to be my best man at my final enduring marriage to Sonia. He did turn up, but only because he had read about it in the *Evening Standard*. Ah well, print is sometimes even preferable to telepathy.

My stepfather died, and my mother came back to England, dis-traught and needing me. I had to listen all that summer and realize that I had become the only man in my mother's life: my elder brother was wasting out his National Service behind barbed wire by the Suez Canal. My stepfather had been a major in the Cold-stream Guards; his wish was that I should try to join the Brigade of Footguards and his old regiment. By a combination of toughness, risk, and luck, I managed to survive the bloody-minded training camp at Caterham and do well at the Officers Training School at the old ducal home of Eaton Hall. I was accepted as an ensign in the Third Battalion of the Coldstream Guards, then posted on pub-lic duties in London, which meant living in Wellington Barracks by Buckingham Place, and guarding it, St James's Palace, the Tower of London, and the Bank of England in a succession of quaint cer-emonies and military rituals that made us both the security and the chorus line of the London scene and season.

Public Duties

It was a time between times. It was not a war and not a peace, but a cold war. It was not a recovery and not a recession, but a restoration and a rest. It was not prosperity and not poverty, merely the illfare state. It was not so much the time of clubs or of pubs, more of coffee bars. And so, between the champagne and the warm beer, the grounds collected at the bottom of the cup; from them fortunes might be read. It was not the time of Rolls-Royces or of bicycles, rather of motor scooters. There was a median of things, a meridian and a miasma.

Yet it was hardly the golden mean of the ancient Greek philosophers, the correct balance for feeling and action in the midst of extremes. It was the waiting-room at the railway station, the pause over tea and currant buns before the next train came. It was the queue at the post office to pick up the undelivered parcel from persons and points unknown. A dull expectancy pervaded the middle 'fifties. It was a time to see through.

Everything could still be faced without losing too much, even at the ending of an empire. Débutantes danced to the dated music of Tommy Kinsman, and the street gangs dressed exactly like Edwardian gentlemen. The rise of the Teddy Boys appeared to prove that the lower classes were back to aping their betters. These narrow-trousered dandies who coshed and robbed were as proud of their plumage as any aristocratic Mohock who had terrorized Georgian London. The spiv with his flash and criminal ways was gone, the war of the classes was apparently dying out as secretaries began to dress like ladies and thugs like Brigade of Guards officers. Unsocial security seemed to have blunted the worst edges of poverty and inequality, and the Tories were too wise to scrap it for the old class conflict that might destroy their chosen strategy of levelling up rather than breaking down.

My own public duties were inflicted upon me by the state. These consisted of a display of fancy military postures – the fabric of the nation. I described these ceremonials during my first Long Vacation at Cambridge in a tragic novel with the plot of the Gospels, called *The Breaking of Bumbo*. Alas, all its readers fell about laughing, when they came across it; but then, I always had a weird sense of humour. I had served for a couple of years, doing my National Service in the Coldstream Guards, so I knew a little about the drill. And so I wrote about a young lieutenant in the Redston Guards, Bumbo Bailey, strutting his stuff:

At last, in May, Bumbo began Public Duties – the Bank Picquet, Tower Guard, Street Lining, and Ensign of The Queen's Guard. The Bank Picquet would march off in the late afternoons, across the Horse Guards Parade, down to the Embankment, along by Blackfriars Bridge, up through the City into the great doors of the Bank of England. Bumbo led them, his jaw pressing against the chin-strap of his bearskin, to keep the seven-pound wicker-cage steady in the wind. He would feel his scarlet tunic stretching against the swing of his left arm, while he held his sword steady in his right hand, as a point of pride, all the way, four miles to the Bank. Occasionally, two weird middle-aged women would pace them, solemnly marching on the pavement beside them into the City. Nobody ever discovered who they were, or why they did it. They were christened Fortnum & Mason.

As for the Ensign of the Guard, it was a proud morning for the bhoy, to lift up that Colour so high, snide and handsome; and if there weren't two or three thousand Christopher Robins, Alices, Dollar Bills and Old Colonials watching the Changing of the Guard every time he did it. Full House for every performance. And, more satisfactory than applause, respect. Instead of laughter, awe. No boos and catcalls, but oohs and aahs. And the swing of the jerk-step of the slow march in the forecourt of the Palace, with the butt of the Colour sunk in its socket by his crutch, while the Brass Band slams out Figaro,

...Milanol ... lol-lol-lol ... lol-lol-LOLLO,
By the left, by the right, by the CENTRE,
Dee-dah-dah ... dee-dah-dah ... dee-dah-DADDA,
By the right, by the left, by the FRONT...

And there was the occasional Street Lining, when the poor bastards of Guardsmen behind Bumbo had to stand still for five or six hours, spaced regularly as the tarts along Curzon Street, while the Golden Coach rolled out and back again, and the loyal populace huzzaad cheerfully. Bumbo, at least, could walk up and down, pretending to inspect his men; or, stood At Ease, he could rest his hands on his sword, its blade bent with its end jabbing the tarmac, as he leaned forward over his pointed toecaps, set the regulation eighteen inches apart.

To my family, *The Breaking of Bumbo* was beyond the pale. My father wanted it 'scrubbed with Lysol'; my South African uncle lifted it with tongs and put it on the fire. When my mother read the work in proofs, she offered to buy it out of the press from Faber & Faber; but when it became an accredited best-seller, she told me for the next thirty years that it was the best book that I had ever written. So much for the criticism of one's nearest and dearest. But then, I was often to consider most critics as voracious sheep. When my grass was withering, they spat me out. When my meadow was lush, they grazed with high praise.

Philip Larkin was not too wrong, however, when he wrote in a letter: 'Today I bought The Breaking of Bumbo by Andrew Sinclair as a Boots' chuck-out – Good God, every 'new young' writer I read seems worse than the last. John Braine – there couldn't be anyone worse than him. Oh yes, there could: John Osborne. And now Andrew Sinclair: soft-headed hysterical guardee. Like an upper-class John Wain… I've just got to James I's accession to the throne of England. He sounds a terrible ass, rather like Andrew Sinclair actually.' In spite of the reaction of the bilious Larkin, the novel was a great success. It went to many editions, and ended in every country-house lavatory in the land. At the age of twenty-two I found myself second only to William Golding and *Lord of the Flies*, as the best-selling novelist for T. S. Eliot and Charles Monteith and the other editors at Faber & Faber. I was held to be a part of an odd phenomenon called the Angry Young Men, and I was one of the very young among them.

The others seemed to me improbably old, thirty or more. And there was a fundamental difference between us. John Osborne's plays, *Look Back in Anger* and *The Entertainer,* glorified the class war at the kitchen sink and reviled the dream of empire that expired at Suez. Yet in his work and that of Larkin's friend, Kingsley Amis, and John Braine and John Wain, nostalgia bubbled in the pink bottle. I used to declare a difference of direction. I was trying to kick my way out, they were trying to kick their way in. Their radicalism and socialism were red rungs to be climbed on the way up the social ladder to a high Tory heaven. I was on the slippery Odessa steps down to observing a failed revolt, the debacle of a whole generation. I would update my novel as a film about the protests of 1968, starring the young Joanna Lumley and the satirist John Bird, only to be vilified by the Right as anarchic and unpatriotic, and by the Left as a reactionary against Chairman Mao and Che Guevara, even though I was to write books about him, too.

I was never to know which side of the barricades I was on. Only in some reappraisals fifty years later would Bumbo be considered another important attack on imperial Britain as were *Look Back in Anger* and *Room at the Top*, while the film was seen as a paradigm of student revolt, if not in the class of Lindsay Anderson's *If* and Jean Vigo's *Zéro de Conduite*.

So time shifts opinion, as a poacher turns into a hunter. The success of *Bumbo* and of another short novel of mine about Cambridge undergraduates, *My Friend Judas*, made me the most envied and disliked student in town. As I was still only twenty-two years old and in my third year at Trinity, I was too much and too soon. As I knocked the brace of them off in a few holiday weeks, I was told that all novelists should imitate Proust and hide their works in a cork-lined room until late middle age. My literary peer group, dominated by F.R. Leavis with his provincial litanies in *Scrutiny* and by the Movement, decided I was rubbish. Early fame is intolerable to elder critics, especially as my antecedents seemed to be the opposite of what they were. I was hardly working-class and must have inherited places at Eton, in the Brigade of Guards and at Trinity.

The spectre of my apparent background of privilege was to envenom most of the English critics for the rest of my literary life. My riposte was to ignore all of them from campus to terminus. I would never reply or explain myself to them. I would be original. I would write in many styles on a slew of subjects in my own way. I would be a free spirit, if I had one, and if I could live by it.

An improbable encounter, as usual, stitched together my past and present worlds. Slouching towards Magdalene in my has-been outfit, I met the ruddy Major Torquil Matheson in his undress uniform of smart civilian clothes and bowler hat. He had been my battalion commander in the Coldstream Guards in London. Once, I had made him laugh. When asked by him at Morning Orders what I had done the night before, I replied that I was looking, as any visitor, for gold bricks in the Strand. 'Bring me one tomorrow,' he said, 'or you're confined to barracks.' So I sent out my Soldier Servant to find a red brick, and I painted it gold, and I wrapped it in Christmas paper, and the next dawn, I laid it on his desk. When he opened the packet, he guffawed. And I was forgiven, but not this time on a Cambridge street.

'You look terrible, Sinclair,' he said. 'But I suppose I can't send you to the guardroom now.'

'No, sir,' I said 'But what brings you here to this fearsome city?'

Torquil looked more sheepish than a gelded ram.

'I have to take a course,' he grumbled. 'To get into Staff College. Or I'm out.'

I never saw him again. He must have failed his course. For he ended up as the Master of the last Hunt in Kenya. Very appropriate too.

There was a postscript. The first and most exclusive club I ever joined was the Horizontal Officers Club. It only ever had four members, given the qualifications for entry. Its Brigade tie of dark red and blue stripes was crossed with tiny embroidered swords. During a rehearsal for the Trooping the Colour, I had keeled over, with my Sergeant saying, 'Mr Sinclair needs the soles of his boots repaired.' Another Ensign member, wearing his blue winter overcoat, had to sheathe his ceremonial sword in its scabbard, one-two-three, one-two-three, but he missed the slit opening and plunged the point of his weapon into his leg. He stood until his leather Wellington boot filled with blood, and then he fell. To faint on parade was the equivalent, as John Aubrey had noted of the Earl of Oxford, to bowing and farting at the court of Queen Elizabeth the First – never to be forgotten or forgiven.

Satire was the weapon slipped into our hands to assault the Establishment and to incise the last tattoos on the twitching imperial corpse. Philosophically, logical positivism ruled the roost at Cambridge, and we were taught to destroy the meaning of country or glory by asking what they meant. The supreme Wittgenstein had recently been lecturing with a bleak wit as acute and rare as James Joyce's in *Finnegans Wake* or Samuel Beckett's in *Waiting for Godot*, two other piercing texts of that time. Personally I learned, more from one of Wittgenstein's thrusts than from anyone else, that we should never call ourselves a target: when somebody fired an arrow at us, he was usually aiming at another target – himself.

In retrospect, I wonder why we felt so arrogant and self-important, unlike Larkin and his peers, cut down to size by the events of war. Why did we feel we had the right to act out the opinions of our generation, as John Bird and Jonathan Miller and Peter Cook and the rest of the cast of *Beyond the Fringe* and *That Was The Week That Was* and *The Establishment* wanted to do? Or as Timothy Birdsall and Mark Boxer did in caricaturing the powers that were, a few decades before *Spitting Image*? Or as the gnomic and refined Michael Frayn did in his surreal sketches for the *Footlights*? Or the Angry Young Men among whom I was a minor Fury? Who chose us, or did we choose ourselves with the divine right of careless youth?

Certainly, I was not given to introspection. If a door opened, I walked through it and blacked my eye. I had no sense of myself in time or place or priority, and I don't think my contemporaries had. As the actress Eleanor Bron said, if you were any good, things would happen. The odd thing was, however, that we were generally bourgeois and educated, and things were meant to happen in the late 'fifties to the wrathful working classes and the popular arts. But briefly, in that time between times, we attacked the old assumptions without putting on the new. We were the heirs of an established past, which allowed us to become the predators of the present.

Armoured against criticism by logic as well as the egocentric dash of the young, I secured a Double First in history by a long grind and dashed off a second novel about contemporary Cambridge, *My Friend Judas*, which proved to be almost as successful as the first one. Written in a private language that teetered between a parody of *The Catcher in the Rye* and *The Pilgrim's Progress*, I found myself hailed as the Beatle of the upper middle classes. The little amusement in the book was provided by its dedication to a failed love affair – *To another JUDY with whom this book would never have been written.*

I knew myself well enough to appear in the novel as Augustus Clare, as seen through the eyes of my contemporaries. This had already been done at Eton in the Drawing Schools, where I had painted a sad self-portrait. Coming across it, Bamber's mother had said, 'Alas, too true,' although she did have the grace to add, twenty years later, 'How lucky for you, Andrew. At last, you've grown into your face.' Old, when young, and not young enough, when older, I saw myself only too well in Augustus Clare:

As for this pill Augustus, he really needs a prescription for his make-up, but no one ever gave it to him. He looks like a bull-dog with a belly-ache, lives in a garret on top of Trinity, acts as if he were Father and Son and Holy Ghost, and is ugly, bloody, rude and dull. This means he has a reputation for wisdom. He increases the reputation by frequently having nothing to say for himself; he discovered early that silence is usually mistaken for sympathetic understanding, not stupidity: but, sure, the silence of the wise doesn't imply the wisdom of the silent. When Augustus does speak, he makes his short stories so long that he calls himself a novelist. And the worst thing that ever happened to him was that he did have a novel accepted at twenty-two. The strange thing is, the book wasn't all that bad, if you took it by itself and didn't know the old phoney of the author. So he's trailed round the rest of his time here looking for something interesting to provide a sequel. Jeez, what a sorrow-seller. His life's one long pain after another, for him and for us. One long rage in a cage. If he isn't searching for a script, he's searching for a soul-mate. He spends so much time analysing his affairs that he can't live them. I tell you, he only falls in love when he's short of a plot. Why he can't go on a course of learning to be normal like other poor ordinaries, not even Augustus knows.

After *My Friend Judas* came out, young women wrote to me about fleeing their convent schools to liberty in the Fens, while young men consulted on how to escape National Service without a court martial. I appeared to be the apostle of elegant mutiny. But at Cambridge, I dressed *de rigueur* for the period in old corduroy trousers and thick wool polo-necked sweaters and scuffed black suede shoes, so rarely cleaned that I had to be hoovered before entering any drawing-room, which I hardly ever did. My reaction extended to diet and drink. I used to live on a daily egg, boiled in water, which I then used for my instant coffee; stale bread and tins of orange segments made up the fare. As for drink, I followed H.L. Mencken's remark about the Democrats, that they quaffed anything which burned and gave thanks to God.

I had done nothing to pursue the history of my family, until I had a recognition at Muirfield golf course near Edinburgh in Scotland. I was still in the Coldstream Guards, about to leave my term of service, when I was called up to be the fifth and last member of the regimental team in the Army Championships. When I arrived in the club house, the rest of the team, a Major-general, a Colonel and two Majors, hooted at me, a poor Ensign. Over the chimneypiece of the main room hung a portrait of William St Clair of Roslin. Although he wore knee breeches, a red coat and a black hat and carried a wooden baffy, his face was the spitting image of my own, long and hangdog, the four lines of melancholy splitting both of our faces from nose to lower cheek, from mouth to chin.

Later I would find out about him, the last of seven centuries of male St Clairs, who had ruled at Roslin Castle, but then had only daughters to marry off. A member of the Royal Company of Archers, the royal bodyguard for Scotland as I was in England, he was a founder of Muirfield in the late eighteenth century, and also admired by Sir Walter Scott, who wrote of him:

> The last Roslin was a man considerably above six feet, with dark grey locks, a form upright, but gracefully so, thin-flanked and broad-shouldered, built, it would seem, for the business of war or chase, a noble eye of chastened pride and undoubted authority, and features handsome and striking in their general effect, though somewhat harsh and exaggerated when considered in detail. His complexion was dark and grizzled, and as we schoolboys, who crowded to see him perform feats of strength and skill in the old Scottish games of Golf and Archery, used to think and say amongst ourselves, the whole figure resembled the famous founder of the Douglas race... In all the manly sports which require strength and dexterity, Roslin was unrivalled; but his particular delight was in Archery.

Although heredity and genetic luck became more significant in old age, and I was to write books on the Sinclairs and Rosslyn Chapel and the search for the Grail, my Viking resemblance to my ancestor

slipped my mind, when I went out on the tee in the morning. I performed in the Army Scratch Competition in the early hundreds. The
officers in my team were in despair. Yet in the matchplay, erratic Andrew Sinclair struck two rounds in the low seventies. For the first
time since they had marched south to restore Charles the Second to
the throne, the Coldstream Guards had won a coup or a cup in the
north. The Major-general in charge summoned me to a drink that
night, knowing that I was leaving shortly for Cambridge and another
career. Would I stay on for a third year and the next army tournament
with promotion and pay? I admitted I was a reluctant soldier and said
that I had never pulled a trigger once in the last eighteen months: I
had been guarding Her Majesty and fooling around with debutantes
in the Season. The Major-general looked at me with twinkling contempt, and said, 'Whoever joined the army to fight?'

I felt small, very small. Of course, the Coldstream Guards were
the bravest of the brave as well as serving as the royal guardians.
Later, when I refused to fight at Suez and *The Breaking of Bumbo* was
published, I was threatened with a court martial. The scandal, however, would have been a downer for the army's public relations, let
alone its duties. Anathema though I was then to the military, history
would prove me right. In my novel, I had been one of the first to
state that the Suez disaster was the result of a conspiracy between
Britain and France and Israel. Thirty years on, I found myself at a
dinner party, given by Sir Geoffrey Howe, who had been Foreign
Secretary, before he slapped Margaret Thatcher verbally with her
own handbag, so that she also lost office.

When the ladies had left the table and the port was being circu-
lated clockwise, I found the man on my left was a Major-general
Hobbs, who knew of me.

'Sinclair,' he said, 'didn't you write that dreadful Bumbo book?'

'Yes, sir,' I said. 'I'm sorry.'

'You shouldn't be. It did very well, didn't it?'

'I think so, but I don't think the Brigade liked it.'

'We didn't. But you were right. Over Suez. That didn't work.'

'History,' I said. 'It's what I try to do.'

'Talking of that,' he said, 'I am now doing the publicity for all of
the army.' He smiled, at last. 'I think we could use you. As you do
write a bit.'

Forgiveness, at last. All because time moves on, and I had been right about the long gone. I shook my head slightly, and I heard myself say: 'Too late, sir. Too late.'

SUEZ, JACK GALLAGHER AND DENIS BROGAN

As in many moral decisions, there was no immediate decision to be made. Only a small situation ending with a darkly comic failure. My first term at Trinity College had been uneventful; quiet flowed the Cam. Then came the revolt in Budapest and the Israeli attack on Egypt, followed by the British and the French ultimatum. All work stopped at the University of Cambridge; fist-fights broke out in the streets; a Tory student even knocked down his supervisor. A friend of mine got drunk listening to the news bulletins, said he was bored with academic November, didn't want to write his weekly essay for the following day, and set off for Hungary from London Airport with ten pounds of penicillin in a package. 'Do what you can to stop me being sent down,' he said off-handedly to me and departed in an undergraduate odour of irresponsible sanc- tity and heroic unpreparedness, to spend three days wandering around the rubbled city and another three days in the cellar of the British Embassy, before he was evacuated, like a child in the Blitz.

I had promised to follow, committed by the affected light-heart- edness of my friend. I knew that my own name was top of the list for Reservists, who were to be called up next; I knew that my Cold- stream Guards battalion was ready to move off to Suez at twenty- four hours' notice; I also knew that, by moral and political conviction, I should become a conscientious objector against this nonsensical revival of nineteenth-century gun-boat diplomacy. Moreover, emotion for the underdog and denial of my own fear made Budapest the antidote to Ismailia. To fight in one war might excuse my refusal to fight in another. Courage might be the best refuge from cowardice.

I was interviewed by the Master of my College, and my tutor Jack Gallagher. I told them that my object was to set up a refugee camp in Austria. I said nothing of going to Budapest to fight. They told me that, if I went, too many might follow. I replied correctly that other undergraduates would only profit by my example to remain behind. They said I would lose my scholarship, my state grant and perhaps my place at the university; they suggested I was seeking a quick emotional thrill instead of accepting the long-term moral difficulty of staying put. I replied that I would avoid a court martial, a bad conscience and the breaking of trust with a friend; I was making a practical decision and bringing practical help. The Master, my moral tutor and my mother were tacitly or explicitly convinced by my conviction, as I myself was convinced out of my own mouth.

I had arranged to meet two old cars and a quarter of a ton of Red Cross stores in London, after I had seen my mother for the last time. Ten minutes before I was due to leave for Cambridge station to catch the down train, I found a note in my room, asking me to visit Jack Gallagher, in his room. Among the piled books, I felt ridiculous in my army boots and government-surplus flying-jacket.

'I'm going,' I said definitively, selling myself valour. 'It's too late to stop me now.'

'Have a drink,' Gallagher said, offering me a whisky.

'I can't. I'm going in five minutes.'

'Well, if you've made your mind up,' Gallagher said, 'there's nothing I can say. But I warn you, the last sacrificial lambs all got killed in Spain. Only the English poets weren't touched. Heroes are out of date.'

'Perhaps. But I've got to go now.'

'I see. But promise me one thing, will you? Ring me up, before you leave England.'

'All right. If I can. Good-bye.'

Gallagher nodded his head and scowled. I took the train to London, drinking tea in the dining-car, hardly believing that I was implicated in the consequences of my own professions and actions. I met my mother in the buffet at the railway hotel in Victoria. She and I firmly believed that she, as Mussolini, was always right. 'You can't go now,' she said, 'something dreadful has happened in the family.' She told me what it was, the perfect alibi for cowardice, the strong ethical reason for backtracking. 'If you go and get killed,' she said, 'I shall die, too.'

If I took her at face-value, or as my mother, which she was, I did not need to go to Hungary. The road back to Cambridge was the harder road, hidden victory in seeming defeat, family before friends. But if I took her as an emotional woman, who had contradicted her previous acceptance of my departure because of an unlucky accident, I could still continue. Yet Suez looked like being over in a week. America and Russia were going to put an end to the whole sorry mess. Perhaps the entire hooha was an emotional pep-pill, as they had all hinted. Perhaps this was not the occasion, nor I the man. Perhaps this was another moral crisis which was only a joke.

'I won't go,' I said. 'I'll go and tell them.'

'I'm sure it's all for the best, darling,' my mother said, and I felt a guilty ease within me.

I went to meet the others. Four other Cambridge students were there, loading stores into the two old cars.

'I can't come,' I said. And I told them the reason.

'We quite understand,' they said. And they did not, because it was only a reason, and it was not all the truth. So I spoke my reason again more convincingly, and again they said, 'We quite understand.'

I exchanged some boots and army clothes for a sports jacket and a pair of flannels. And I handed over some foreign money. And I went to the flat of a friend, and I telephoned Gallagher.

'I'm not going now,' I said. I hardly recognised the flatness of my own voice, surprised into feeling that I was suffering at not going.

'Good,' Gallagher said. 'How do you feel about it?'

'Not too good.'

'Don't come back for two or three days, then,' Gallagher said. 'I'll fix it all up for you. Go and have a rest. All right?'

'All right. Thank you, Jack. Good-bye.'

'Not at all. Good-bye.'

Not only did Jack Gallagher save me from my idiocy, but he cut the corset strings of my British habit of restraint. He continued to put up with my dramatics and paranoia by entering into my delusions and treating them seriously. Often sleepless and hating imprisonment at night, I used to climb over the walls of Trinity onto the Backs, there to wander in the moonlight across the parks between the colleges. I would return over the spikes and ledges to see Wittgenstein's friend, Piero Sraffa, toiling under his black skull-cap on his monumental edition of the economist Ricardo's work. And Gallagher would always respond to my knock and ask me to help him finish a bottle of Scotch by dawn.

He was a selfless man, who nurtured two or three undergraduates a year through their self-pity. One late night, when I was at my worst, he helped me draw out the defences of Trinity in Bren-gun and mortar positions against the time when *They* came to get *Us*. He told me of visiting André Malraux twice after the war and seeing the map of a capital city on the wall, also ringed with defence weapons. The first time, Malraux was a supporter of the Communists and the city was Moscow; the second time, Malraux was a minister for de Gaulle and the city was Paris. Along with Camus, the writings of Malraux were to have a great influence on me, particularly *La Condition humaine* and *L'Espoir*, in which men were revealed by their actions, while all their many plots and desires as in Stendhal's *Le Rouge et le Noir*, terminated at their death. Life had no post-script. And I liked de Gaulle's comment on the work of his author minister. 'Clouds, clouds – and sometimes, flashes of lightning.'

Gallagher was the best historian of Africa of his generation, tough of mind and incisive of pen. He taught me mental survival and some physical strategies: never to have one's photograph taken, else it might be used to identify one; never to give one's correct identity for the same reason; and only to travel light, preferably with a paper bag containing a toothbrush and a great many small dollar bills.

His example was an inspiration to me when I later became a moral tutor myself: 'You are old enough to deal with your own finances, the police and paternity suits. But if you get into trouble with this College, I will defend you to the death.' He already had been my guardian over the Suez and Hungary business, and he taught a form of self-analysis as well as a structure of historical inquiry. Never say somebody has terrible friends,' he told me. 'You are always somebody's terrible friend.' I certainly was his.

He rose to become Vice-Master of Trinity, and he lost a leg because of drink and diabetes. He made me view my education, not as a national bias, but as an unending inquiry. Every country was my different country: perspective was all. Once he had staggered into my college garret room to deliver the story of both of our lives. These were his words before he left, slamming shut the oak on me: 'Sometimes, Andrew, I can solve the history of all the world, but not my own personal problems. And sometimes I can solve my own personal problems, but not the history of all the world. But, dammit, never at the same time.'

The remarkable Professor Denis Brogan was my tutor in my fourth year, when I decided to read for a doctorate in American History. Both he and Gallagher had come from the same poor

Celtic urban roots that I had, and we shared a certain irreverence and lusty cast of mind. Brogan was a memory man; he could forget nothing; he photographed mentally the pages he read. The British expert on the United States and France and their histories, he had run Intelligence into Vichy during the Second World War.

He told me of an RAF bombing mission sent to devastate the railway stations of Genoa. As any old port in a night raid would do to dump your load, and as navigation may be another form of necromancy, the Lancasters took out the sidings and engines and goods waggons of Marseilles instead. Brogan received a call from Winston Churchill himself, telling him to save the reputation of our Air Force for its pin-point targeting, and also our agreement with Vichy over respecting a sort of neutrality. On the first week of his appointment, Brogan had personally withdrawn all the ugly women spies for more seductive and effective ones. Now the agents on the ground came back with an amazing story. How had London known, when the *maquis* in France was unaware, that a huge smuggled shipment of wolfram, the essential ingredient for toughening the armour of German panzers, had been loaded onto trains to depart for the Führerland that night? The Marseilles raid became a textbook account of precision bombing. Rather like the truth of history, really.

Brogan and I would meet for supervisions on the train to London, both of us heavily engaged in metropolitan activities. He taught me to appreciate the old alliance of the United States and France at the time of the American Revolution, and the longer *vieille alliance* between France and our country Scotland. He appreciated the wit of the records of the past, with their praise for successful errors. Both of us were always interested in women, and Brogan even persuaded me that Britain was the country of tortured love, France of the rational affair. He had once proved this to a fellow French Intelligence officer, when half a dozen operatives from either country had appeared at a post-war drinks party with the current women in their lives. On analysis, each Frenchman proved to be accompanied by his appointed bedfellow, either wife or *maîtresse* or *maîtresse en titre*, while each Briton was accompanied by an inconstant lady of melancholy or perversity.

My favourite tale of wartime romance was the occasion on which Brogan said that he was courting the great-great-grand-niece of the philosopher Jeremy Bentham. They had taken shelter under a theatre awning off Shaftesbury Avenue, as incendiaries rained and blazed from the sky during the Blitz. Tonight was the night to sleep together, Brogan had declared. It might be their last night. But she had replied, 'I would love to, Denis, but you are not the sort of man I could afford to be caught dead in bed with.'

The last time I wanted to see him, I did not. I missed him, and I still do. He left in my Harvard room a crude drawing, which he had bought in the old seedy neon Times Square off 42nd Street in New York. A couple were sketched, as they copulated on the top of the notepad: the caption was: THINGS TO DO TODAY. Would that there were still such moral tutors for the young things of today.

My university was my time of trial, of change, of awakening. In an essay for an unpublished collection written by young Oxbridge contemporaries to be edited by the blind Indian writer Ved Mehta, I analysed what I thought that time had done for me. Two and a half years at Cambridge had taught me that conviction was another name for prejudice, that the closed book of the probable truth was only visible to the open mind, and that Socrates was always right by never saying that he was. I had learned a little of the amused, suspicious, responsible, sceptical tolerance of English humanism. My chief commitment seemed not to be committed, especially to any unseen fiction. Creeds were only for those weak enough to need them; they should not be imposed on others. Even my subject, history, was meaningless except for the meaning that I wanted to give it. I had been taught circumspect doubt and reasoned belief. For a difficult person like myself, who could only envy those cradle-believers, the pure in heart, both doubt and commitment needed to be approached warily. I began to learn this approach at Cambridge.

PAMPLONA

Alongside some Cambridge companions, I relived the American myth of Ernest Hemingway. With an American Fellow Roger Donald, a Polish Countess and Jonathan Spence, a prodigy from Clare College who would become a Professor of Chinese History at Yale, we set off, squashed in a Morris Minor, to begin replaying *The Sun Also Rises* in the Café Le Select in Montparnasse. Our roles were unclear and queasy. We sat there in an edged misunderstanding, Spence and myself opposed to the worldliness of Donald and the Countess. The drive to the Festival of San Fermín at Pamplona and the bull-running was tedious and constipated. We found two rooms over the noisiest bar in town: a single bed in a cupboard for the Countess; three iron mattresses in a larger space for the young men. Then we were caught in a winnowing process of myth and mayhem and sleeplessness. I recorded the reason for our insomnia:

It was the year of the plastic horn.

One hundred thousand of these tiny trumpets, made from set and tinted grease, had been brought into town to tempt the Basques. They had been tempted. Perhaps a thousand Basques had huge drums and brass horns of their own and could join the hundred bands blowing through the streets of the town. But the other ninety-nine thousand brought their own personal plastic horns. They made the sound of a gale blowing through wrapping paper on steel mesh. It was the sound of a mob of fingernails scratching a wallpaper. It was a rude sound.

At College in Oberlin, Hemingway had stood up higher than the trees. He had walked as a giant, wearing clean prose. He had made writing appear in the fist of any sure young man in Ohio. With sweat and grit, treading in the tracks of the master, anyone could write lean. For Hemingway had shown that the sun also rises in the Fens.

There were two cafés in town in the plaza, decorated by plac-ards stating DAMN FINE FIESTA – *Hemingway*. The Café Kutz was one, and there was another one. They were the two sides of the Spanish Civil War. The Republicans went to the Kutz, the boys for Franco to its neighbour. We went to the Kutz. Hemingway would have gone with us. And there we met Jake, a writer from Oxford called Jim Farrell, who was a friend of Roger Donald. He was a lunger and could hardly swim across the waterhole we found outside town, as the good book told us to do. And there in the Kutz was Bud Trillin, a winsome ugly New Yorker journalist who spoke immediately to children as St Francis did to birds. And a Tom figure from The Great Gatsby, Jay van Alen, who treated the local distilled grappa called Chinchon as an overflowing nipple. 'My pee's turned a shade of vino clarete,' Farrell said to Trillin. 'But isn't it inter-esting how cheap European travel is. You just have to lie in the dark in a cheap room and eat nothing.'

We drank all night. The best joke was persuading the Basques that an automatic cigarette lighter dispensed free white wine. It led to a few firefights and broken noses. In the morning we ran in front of the bulls through the streets to the ring. The first time, I capered drunk among their horns. Then they tossed somebody up in the air and trod on him and I ran like shit away.

I met Lady Brett at the other cafe. She arrived in the plaza in a white Rolls-Royce with a chauffeur. She looked like a beautiful pug on long legs, and she knew me vaguely from my Bumbo days. She had been asked to Pamplona by a friend of her tycoon father. Then she found that only one bedroom was booked at the best hotel, and she dumped him in Biarritz and went on alone with his car and reservations to Pamplona. I was the prof-iteer, to the envy of my friends. We had the best seats to the bull-fights, sombra and not sol, and we watched the sickening Hemingway routine day after day, the stabbing down of the proud neck of the beast by the picadors and the missed lunges to the bowed heart by the matadors and the cutting off of the ears for an unmeritable victory. At night, we drank and jived until dawn and ran before the bulls of the next day. About the third night, I was seen to fall off the roof of a car in the plaza onto my head. While I was unconscious, Lady Brett was driven off in the white Rolls back to Biarritz.

So the myth became the fact. Farrell was the incapacitated writer and would die after his masterpiece was done, *The Siege of Krishnapur*, by slipping off the rocks of Ireland into the sea. Lady Brett had come and gone towards Lucian Freud, an elusive transience from a life that none of us could live. At the same time, he was painting a hair-by-pubic hair portrait of the naked Debo Devonshire, which the duke nobly hung in a secluded spot at Chatsworth. When the estate gardener saw the picture he did not think that he was viewing Lady Chatterley, but he did give his opinion.

'Well, I wouldn't be a Duke.'

We would now fall apart after our Hemingway adventure. We fled the Basque festival on to Madrid, where Roger Donald had a row with the Polish Countess, who departed angrily. And then as an affront to the Yank, Spence and myself insisted on a visit to the Merchant Navy Club on the Rock of Gibraltar. We enthused over the dark cardboard steak, mashed lumpy potatoes and dried peas, and especially the creased shorts of the blue Bobbies playing policemen outside.

We split in Torremolinos after spending the night on a hillside, where we were woken by the Spanish police with flashlights. The expedition was hardly the Shangri-La of the aspiring artistic classes. Spence went by train to an *inamorata* in Italy, while Donald drove me back as far as Paris, relentless and unstoppable, determined to be rid of me as soon as possible. In the course of an interminable monologue to keep himself awake, he told me how *jejune* I was. While at Harvard, he had driven logging trucks in the south and had been on massacres in the bayous of Louisiana, where great steel nets trawled in alligators and moccasin snakes as well as tuna fish and crabs, and where massed ducks were blasted from the heavens by pump-action shotguns. This was the real Hemingway, while I was only acting it. He would forgive my gaucheness and become the editor at Little-Brown of some of my books. Preknowledge sometimes leads to later publication, not always to permanent disdain.

TONY RICHARDSON

———∞∞∞———

To make my early notoriety worse, the Royal Court Theatre decided to adapt my first novel into a musical. So I had to meet its gifted artistic director. At a party in December at his penthouse by Putney Bridge, Tony Richardson presented me with a small Madagascar ape with spindly arms and long fingers and brown luminous eyes. This slender loris had committed a crime in Tony's aviary. It had stretched out a paw and plucked against the mesh an Indian nightingale, which it then ate delicately, breast and legs, in morsels. I took the loris home and left it with a friend and returned to America; but the poor little cannibal pined and died of cold and neglect.

I should have taken this episode as a warning lesson about Tony himself. After his culture-changing successes at the Royal Court Theatre with *Look Back in Anger* and *The Entertainer*, given its Suez and end of Empire theme, he decided to make a song and dance show of *The Breaking of Bumbo*, about the folly of opposing the upper classes. Lyrics by Julian More of *Irma la Douce* fame, choreography by Sir Kenneth MacMillan on his way to inventing ballets in Covent Garden, music by John Addison, the lead to be played first by O'Toole and then by Albert Finney, how could we fail? We could, because the failure lay in Tony.

As the slender loris, he was devouring and ruthless, a brilliant picker and chooser of bits of us between the mesh of his infinite manipulations. Because of him, I met his first wife Vanessa Redgrave, herself with a father as ambidextrous as her husband. Indeed, Michael Redgrave's lover, Freddie Sadoff, came bounding in, wearing a white bell-bottomed sailor suit. He persuaded me to adapt and let him direct my Cambridge novel, *My Friend Judas*, as a play. Breaking house records in Brighton, it bombed at the Arts Theatre in London. I never saw it, but news of the catastrophe reached me at Harvard. The detonation was loud enough to bang across the Atlantic, led by all my Cambridge friends cat-calling from the Gods.

In a fatal decision for his career, Tony had decided that he would conquer Hollywood, which would be as easy as shocking Sloane

Square. He went to Los Angeles to direct an appalling version of William Faulkner's novel, *Sanctuary*. We met at breakfast at the Algonquin Hotel in New York. My musical was off his schedule. The problem was that he denounced me to excuse himself. The book of the musical, which I had written, wasn't good enough, although John Osborne had given it his imprimatur, before Tony gave it the boot all over England. I was to blame, not Tony, who never was.

Actually, it was surprising that he put up with my work for so long. When a script-reader for the Royal Court Theatre, John Osborne recorded that Richardson surveyed half-a-dozen submissions, granting a maximum of two minutes to each one, before tossing the paper pieces away with the shrill put-down: 'There, that's how you read a play.' So he had behaved with his slender loris. Fascinating and engaging, repellent and seductive, Tony made a little monkey out of me.

WHAT CAREER?

⁓

I had published a social history of Prohibition in the United States before submitting it as a PhD thesis, and so I had become a Founding Fellow of the new Churchill College in Cambridge. Then I was bitterly reproached by the young wife of a Manchester university graduate and lecturer, after giving a talk there. 'Oh, you're so clever, Andrew Sinclair, you publish two crap comic novels, and then a serious book on American history. So you get all that publicity and those reviews. What an artful planner you are.'

I had hardly ever planned anything in my life. When opportunity knocked, too often I did not knock off the opportunity. A maxim from Machiavelli informed my choices. He reckoned that a career in a man's life was based equally on luck and *vertù*, a word which meant something between skill and quality. Then there was *opportunità*, which involved luck and fate, But when *necessità* came along, it chopped your head off. My progress had been farcically easy, too much so for my own good and awareness. I had never even thought I did not know how to write a novel or a play or a history book. I had done it and the works were mainly successful. My nonchalance and arrogance and the attention of the press had made me a voice of my generation, although I was not at all.

I had not considered whether anyone could describe his or her own time merely by the luck of personal experience and the skill given by God and genetics and education. Like the jesting Pilate, I had preferred to run away from truth into satire, and I was travelling on a grant to America as an answer to staying in Britain. I was, however, one of the last children of the Empire, as Orwell had been, but also I was sailing to the first independent Republic, which had repudiated that Empire in its search for liberty, equality and the pursuit of 'happiness' – later called 'property' in the Constitution, as if these were the same condition.

My Harkness Fellowship took me for nearly two years to Harvard and Columbia universities, where I researched and wrote *Prohibition: The Era of Excess*. At this other Cambridge, France arrived in

America for me. I had given a lecture on young English novelists, reading from my own works in my pride of being out of place. One of my audience was certainly the most beautiful student of her time, Marianne Alexandre. Her auburn hair reached her waist, her grey eyes spilled over into soft lips; she was willow-thin and delightfully alien in every thought and deed. Her mother taught French at Brandeis, a neighbouring and dangerous university, where I was soon going to live with Marianne in a female dormitory, which her mother was meant to supervise. Rather like my moral tutors at Cambridge with their blind Nelson's eye, she turned her myopia on everything she did not wish to see, including my nights spent with her daughter after arriving cautiously with my toothbrush packed in my empty typewriter-case.

Herbert Marcuse was the ruling spirit of Brandeis, and his talk of revolutionary violence was a toxic substance to the heads of the young. The black communist and feminist Angela Davis and the future radical leader Abbie Hoffman were influenced as students by him, and I was pricked by his message in my passing. He seemed a Marx reborn into modernity: the radical fervour of the German Jew translated into the deconstruction of our civilization. He had been active in the revolutionary movement of Rosa Luxemburg, he had helped to found the Frankfurt School of Marxist sociology with Adorno, and he had fled to America in front of the Nazis to preach as scientific history his *Liberation* and also *One Dimensional Man*. His equation of liberalism with fascism in its fight against socialism, the 'comfortable, smooth, reasonable, democratic unfreedom' which prevailed in advanced capitalism as a token of technical progress, appeared to be as convincing as his equation of individual freedom to Marxism was perverse. This ancient call to subversion and uprising was thrilling; to bring down the soft state of things by one swift thrust rather than slow acupuncture.

Set against such regenerative violence was the Parisian decadence of Marianne herself and the elegant French professors at Brandeis and Yale, who were still half in love with easeful death and the romantic nihilism of Baudelaire and Verlaine, Rimbaud and Lautréamont. They posed the question to inchoate and hopeful artists such as I was – How should we fix the vertigos? How reason through the unreason of the senses? Between the red barricades of 1848 and the *déjà vu* of the boulevards and the sane liberation of the

Crimson at Harvard, I was being extricated from my past education and wish ever to return to my own country.

So I was sent further and further from my previous education. The distance was increased by an exaggerated drive across the new continent in an enormous white Buick that was the free gift of my fellowship. We were all under the spell of Jack Kerouac's *On the Road*, which its promise of liberation on wheels; we also could be rolling stones shedding moss and going nowhere except into intense sensation.

Marianne and I were married by a mumbling Massachusetts judge after an obligatory blood test; two strollers on the street were our witnesses, and we set off for San Francisco with Jonathan Spence, now at Yale, as our fellow traveller, sharing the expenses and dangers of the honeymoon.

High in Wyoming, Marianne had a haemorrhage, which became a miscarriage. We were turned away in Spokane in Washington State by a Puritan doctor who wanted nothing to do with poor travellers in such trouble – she might have bled to death – but we found Samaritans in a Jewish hospital in San Francisco. They gave her eight pints of blood, even though I could not pay the bill except by instalments. With that extraordinary combination of greed and generosity, caught between the supermarket and the heart, that characterized the nation, they told us that the blood cost thirty-three dollars a pint, but if we could find eight free donors, it would only cost eight dollars a pint. In the end, strangers bared their veins – Park Rangers and cowboys – on our drive back, the casual and spontaneous giving that told me that I was in a new world of easy acceptance and warm feeling. So we were spared two hundred dollars of blood money.

As I freewheeled all over America from coast to coast and border to border. I was overwhelmed by the energy and scale and opportunity of the land. I wrote a sub-Kerouac picaresque novel about such expeditions. Little of *The Hallelujah Bum* is now readable in its limey Beat lingo. But one passage praises the wonder and the splendour of bridges and cranes and highways, the very works of man that transformed the crossing of the United States, already defined into squares by Thomas Jefferson, that magnificent architect of the grid-iron stamped on the ground that turned North America into a gigantic waffle, when seen from on high as a pie in the sky. I tried to imitate Walt Whitman and Hart Crane in extolling the iron deeds of the pioneers, and to follow the Beats in their distrust of the soft consumer times to come:

Bridges, cranes, highways, take me with you. Walt would have loved you, only he died too soon. But he had people to love, to hosannah in an exult of frontier. Now the people are rotten and patched and only what they built is fine, and the last hope is in the things and in people seeing the last hope in the things they have made.

I sing the body plastic
I believe that you are to stand or fall with the soul of the
New World
Toupee, dark glasses, deaf aid, red-running nose,
Face lift, mask, cream, profile surgically Roman,
False lashes, teeth, teats, smiles, bowels in the purging,
Flesh sweetly firm in Maidenform,
Hips, hip-sockets, hip-strength, supple in sinuous corsets,
Womb, man-root, love-perturbation rising at dirty pictures,
Woman and all that is a woman's vanity-case
I demand that you let my gushing rivers interpenetrate your
Kleenexes
While I bestow upon you fierce and athletic bubblegum,
artistic musical,
popcorn, rude-muscled candybars,
From Spearmint, from Saltwater Taffy,
All the seedpips in the jamjars, all the nipples in the bra bars,
All the mixes, all the cookies, all the fabrics, all synthetic
Pioneers! O pioneers!

Luckily, my Cambridge tutors, my revered American mentors, Oscar Handlin and Richard Hofstadter, who even wrote a preface to *Prohibition*, liked me for my wild side. Each of them had a novel and poems tucked away, but they did not dare to publish these effusions, for fear of compromising their reputation. I dared and I didn't seem to give a damn, however badly my youthful efforts were received. Indeed, Hofstadter taught me the validity and accuracy of our academic craft, which was to pick out 50,000 facts and shreds of contemporary evidence from several million selected pieces, and then to fit these into the skein of our presentation.

'Andrew,' he said, 'I am told that I have written six seminal books. I could have written each of them in ten different ways. And they would still have been called seminal.'

In *The New York Times*, Walter Allen noted that three English novelists had recently written of their American experiences, myself and Pamela Hansford Johnson, once engaged to Dylan Thomas and now married to the scientist and author C.P. Snow, and Kingsley Amis with his *One Fat Englishman*. He preferred my offering as the most 'American', but said that all three of us achieved in light-hearted comedies what we set out to do and were pointers to the future.

Indeed, we were pointed over the Atlantic by the compass needle of fellowships. I roomed with Warren Plath in my first Harvard semester and so met again my known Cambridge poets, his sister Sylvia and Ted Hughes, also back on a grant. I had published one of her husband's first poems in an ephemeral Cambridge magazine. Hughes had always looked and behaved like Heathcliff in the intensity of his love, but Sylvia presented herself as the submissive New England housewife, particularly in the presence of her mother, who lived somewhere in the far suburbs of Boston towards the encircling highway. I was never to understand Sylvia's later reputation compared with his, the supreme poet of nature of our age: it all appeared as dough compared with beak.

Even so, they were the first two of the five genii of our age that I was to encounter. But at the time, there were no indicators of the tragedies to come, so movingly recalled in the belated *Birthday Letters*. Only in retrospect, near our own deaths, can we set out some lost truths of our past loves. *De mortuis nil nisi verum.*

Yoiung Colleger at Eton

Playing Brutus in Eton production

Competing in the Boys' Golf Championship

With the Oppidan Keeper in the Wall Game

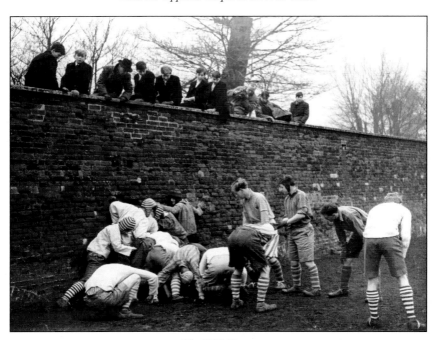

The Wall Game

(right)
In the Coldstream Guards

(below)
Interviewing for BBC TV's
Lost Without Trace

Arrival in New York, cartoon by the author

In New York on Harkness Fellowship

Andrew and Marianne in New York, 1961

JOHN F. KENNEDY

My first smell of death was in the deep delta below New Orleans. In this roadside graveyard, the dead were poor. They had themselves buried as best they could afford. The families with a few dollars had built traditional small houses for coffins above the swamp. The rest did what they could – a small oval of stone, a wooden cross, a mere hump in the ground. All was so wet that, for the first time, there was a scent of human carrion. Yet above, the Spanish moss was light wool on the winter trees; I trod on paths of crushed white sea shells. Only the swamp beneath made even the crosses crooked.

Twice under snow, I visited the grave of John F. Kennedy, two months after his murder and burial, in the Arlington military cemetery near Washington. There had been a queue a mile long to file past the simple mound of pine branches within a small picket fence. By a little cross, five soaking military caps from the armed services and a blue shoulder-strap and a black lamp with a burning flame, sending orange rays into the sleet. This seemed no way to bury a young President of the almighty United States, but it had been his wish to go so simply without the pomp and circumstance of a Mausolus or a Caesar. Already a riddle was circulating from the afterlife:

Knock, knock.
Who's there?
Kennedy.
Kennedy who?
So you've forgotten already.

For lack of persuasion, I myself was almost guilty of the death of America's greatest poet of the time, Robert Lowell. I had met him, when he came to deliver a lecture at Harvard in his grizzled bleak manner. The audience was ten people. At the end of his wayward and laconic address, a determined young lady from Smith College arose to ask:

'Where do you think you stand, Mr Lowell, in the mainstream of American poetry?'

Lowell rocked gently on his heels from side to side and considered his response with true Brahmin finesse:

'Right here,' he said.

It was the best of responses; it was the worst of responses, answering nothing. Later that night, we all got drunk together at a party given by the blind Ved Mehta, for we both were at Harvard. Ved's attraction lay in softly stroking the long hair of women with sensuous fingertips. Lowell, though, was getting too plastered. We left together to lurch towards the poet's automobile.

'Robert,' I said, 'you can't possibly drive back to Boston. Spend the night in my rooms. I'll doss down on the sofa.'

'Never felt better,' Lowell said. 'I'll never drive better.'

I tried to restrain him by the arm, but he shook me off. And unfortunately, he was able to find his car keys. My words were useless. They carried no conviction. On his way home, he drove into a lamp-post. He spent six months in hospital, but he recovered, in his fashion. Later, when he met the pianist Oscar Levant, he boasted that he had been committed to twelve sanitaria.

'How about you?'

Ever discreet, Oscar did not wish to offend the great poet, nor to compete with him. So he replied:

'About ten.'

THREE CULTURES

Chosen as a Founding fellow at Churchill College, rather too young, I discovered that I was on a construction site. My teaching quarters were in a prefabricated hut. I shared a thin wall with George Steiner, whose melodious rant wonderfully instructed me on the literature of the four cultures he knew – German, French, English and American. He and I were the sole representatives of literature and history in a new college of twenty-five Fellows, nearly all of whom were scientists. Some had won the Nobel Prize and most had worked and were working on the three revolutionary inventions by which Cambridge altered the twentieth century – nuclear fission, computer technology and genetic engineering. I had come there to be in the forefront of radical change in the shape of the world. Although I knew nothing about science, at least I would be there.

As most of the young felt, so did I, hating and fearing the atomic and hydrogen bombs and the politics which they spawned. And I was teaching in the heartland of the atomic Establishment. The paradox was that I knew that the forces of destruction and creation were both present. The old could be annihilated just as the new could be remade by machine and gene. After the bombing of Hiroshima and Nagasaki, the leading Australian physicist Mark Oliphant had said, 'This has killed a beautiful subject.' He had been a pupil of the great Lord Rutherford and he had supported the open exchange of scientific knowledge. Theoretical physics were now constrained by secrecy, contorted by military application, and convulsed by moral doubts among the scientists.

Indeed, the British atomic bomb tests in Australia had proved the graveyard of the ideals of the Cavendish physicists. Although some sites for nuclear fission tests were offered in the United States under American supervision, the British government decided to conduct its own independent experiments in a Commonwealth country.

Supervised by Sir William Penney, the first director of the Atomic Weapons Research Establishment, a series of atomic bombs had been exploded. The first device was loaded into an old frigate and blown up offshore. The British navy feared that the Russians might smuggle a bombship into an English port and detonate it as an atomic Trojan horse. The effects of such an attempt were the object of the test. Unfortunately, a large radioactive cloud was carried by the wind over the Australian mainland, contaminating huge areas. This was the first of some hundred explosions of atomic weapons, three more of which led to fall-out on British aircrews and naval personnel, on Australian towns and on Aboriginal settlements, leading to loss of life. In spite of the known results of fall-out on the Japanese survivors of Hiroshima and Nagasaki, the British government allowed the testing of thermonuclear weapons above ground in conditions that led to a deterioration in health and to early deaths of servicemen and civilians.

Scientists working for the government on defence could no longer pretend innocence about the effects of their actions. The weapons they designed would probably be used, even if they were only tested. They did not warn the military well enough about the dire consequences of detonating nuclear weapons. And although they became more important as advisers to governments and general staffs, they still claimed that they had hardly any influence on the employment of their inventions. The more responsible physicists did do something to put pressure on their administrations to cease trying out nuclear weapons in the atmosphere, which could carry clouds of pollution world-wide. Yet no major Cabinet minister or general or admiral came from a scientific background. And the specialist advisers and scientific peers created by the needs of the Second World War did not have the power to change the decisions of their governments. Their terrible inventions were not under their control.

The master of Churchill College, Sir John Cockcroft, was himself in that position, as was another Fellow, the leading apologist for the responsibility of the scientists, C.P. Snow, later created a life peer. Both were heavy men, who made a virtue of their bluffness and their affable bumbling, their disguise for their long understanding of the labyrinths of power. Cockcroft had himself been a pioneer in splitting the atom and had risen through the laboratories to run the British nuclear research establishment at Harwell, while the chemist Snow had also advised many governments on scientific affairs while labouring alongside Anthony Powell in writing a contemporary British Proustian series of a dozen novels, *Strangers and Brothers* as against *A Dance to the Music of Time*. These were the honest furrows of a plough-horse compared to the pirouettes of a pen-master.

In one essay reflecting on the ethics of his own past, Snow wrote about the trouble of getting onto any kind of moral escalator. No one knew whether one would ever be able to get off. When scientists became soldiers, as Snow told me, they gave something imperceptible of the full scientific life. Such was not a matter of intellect, but of morals. This was a moral price which sometimes had to be paid. 'Soldiers have to obey,' Snow finally decided. 'That is the foundation of their morality.' It was not the foundation of scientific morality. 'Scientists have to question and if necessary to rebel.'

Snow was not stating that loyalty was without virtue or that all rebellion was good. He was pointing out that loyalty could become conformity, and that obedience carried to the limit could become destructive. More crimes, as Nazi officialdom proved, could be carried out in the name of obedience than ever were in the name of rebellion. Snow himself had become a government official rather than a wartime scientist, and he had fallen into the moral trap of conformity. He was liable to hide behind an institution and refuse moral choice, and he was painfully aware of it.

Snow had already delivered a memorial lecture on the opposed 'Two Cultures' of science and the arts, which became a book and made him a global name and would shortly fall foul of the invective of the literary critic, who ran the visceral *Scrutiny*, F.R. Leavis. In a criticism of that lecture, the distinguished scientist Michael Yudkin later declared that government ministers probably never had understood properly the hazards of nuclear tests. They could not evaluate scientific evidence because they were not trained scientists. Thus they had to rely on the opinions of their advisers, who usually stated their views with more dogmatism than the evidence warranted. The specialist advisers themselves might distort or fail to mention evidence that might prejudice a chosen policy. The ethics of the Cavendish were often mute in the corridors of Whitehall.

Yet if the splitting of the atom at the Cavendish had finally led to a secret of causing mass death, it also led to a secret of all life. Sir Lawrence Bragg, a founder of crystallography, had become a director of the Cambridge laboratory. He was particularly interested in solving the structures of proteins, then thought to contain the genes which transmitted hereditary traits. But recent research in New York had suggested that deoxyribonucleic acid or DNA molecules might be the carriers of genetic material.

In 1951, a young American biologist, James D. Watson, had come to the Cavendish to work on the structure of proteins in a unit led by the Austrian emigré chemist Max Perutz. He soon developed a partnership with the brilliant and temperamental physicist Francis Crick, whom Watson said was rarely in a modest mood. Using the patient work of the London physicist Maurice Wilkins on the DNA molecule, Watson and Crick began to speculate on the genetic origins of life. The great American chemist Linus Pauling was also experimenting in California. Three groups were competing to discover the primary secret of human biology, a discovery which would be as momentous as splitting the atom. The front runner, Wilkins, would be a loser. As Watson observed, Wilkins had escaped into biology only to find it as unpleasant 'as physics, with its atomic consequences'.

There were important differences in understanding between biologists and geneticists, chemists and crystallographers and physicists. The Cavendish unit managed to bridge these gaps. Using the shape of a double helix, the form that Leonardo da Vinci himself had created in his staircase at the Château de Chambord, Watson and Crick solved the problem of the structure of the DNA molecule. In a letter written from the Cavendish on the twelfth of March 1953, Watson outlined the discovery in crude diagrams. This was the beginning of all genetic engineering and the biochemical changing of human society, twenty-one years after nuclear fission was performed at Cambridge, a dozen years after the seminal work of Turing on computers that cracked the code, eight years after the dropping of the atomic bomb on Hiroshima, simultaneous with the making of hydrogen bombs and the poisoning of the atmosphere with radioactive fall-out.

As Percy Bysshe Shelley wrote of the West wind, so the Cavendish Laboratory was destroyer and preserver. Even the finding of the structure of the genes could have terrible consequences. Since fundamental changes in the shape of living things could now be developed, Mary Shelley's fantasy of Frankenstein approached reality. We could not only alter the plants and animals on the earth, but also ourselves. James D. Watson himself was horrified by the probability of cloning and the reproduction of identical human beings. Great controversies and legal measures would arise about scientific meddling with ordinary human reproduction. Sperm could be frozen and banked, babies conceived in test-tubes. We could, indeed, begin to remake ourselves, for better or for worse. Meeting him later on the road to Washington rather than Damascus, I asked him about these awesome possibilities. He said that cloning must never happen.

Francis Crick was also a Founding Fellow at Churchill College, which turned out to be more conservative than Winston had been. When China briefly invaded northern India and withdrew, the talk at the high table was not of the merits of Mao and Nehru, but of how much money the college would have made in investing in tea-plantations in Assam; their share-price had plummeted, only to bob up again. John Maynard Keynes, who had made the fortune of King's College with similar plunges on the stock market, was rubbing his dry finger-bones in his grave with glee. At the dons' dinners, we never solved the problems of the world or even our own. We talked of building the college and money – I suppose, the important things right there and right then. But for a young radical with a foot on the accelerator, it was a red light on Global Street.

I was more and more aware that my Cambridge years of satire were not revolutionary. They were incapable of replacing the Establishment except with its heirs or with themselves, blunted by the process of easy inclusion into the right ranks. Those who were actually changing human society – the Fellows of Churchill College – were far older and wholly impervious to our assault. They ignored the cause of nuclear disarmament, which served as another chance for the arts graduates to attack the technocrats who had invented the monstrous atomic weaponry. The new *Frankenstein* was Stanley Kubrick's *Dr. Strangelove*, subtitled *How I Learned to Stop Worrying and Love the Bomb*.

The original atomic fission had been performed in the Cavendish Laboratory, and the literary puritans of Downing College did not allow the physicists to forget it. Their attack was on the Cavendish's chief interpreter and only major novelist, C.P. Snow. By charging him and denying his premise of the 'two cultures', F.R. Leavis only proved that the 'Two Cultures' were more antagonistic than ever.

In his previous lecture of 1959, C.P. Snow had made some simple, but important statements that reflected on his experience and widely influenced his time. By training he was a chemist; by vocation, a writer. He had a ringside view of one of the most creative periods in all physics. He had intimate friends among both scientists and writers, but the two groups kept apart. In his lecture he had pinpointed their different little societies as two cultures. To him, 'culture' meant a group living in the same environment, linked by common habits and assumptions and way of life, and a development of the mind. He thought that the literary cultures of Chelsea and Greenwich Village shared a common language, but to them, the scientists at the Massachusetts Institute of Technology might have been talking Tibetan. The intellectual and practical life of the whole of western society was being split. As far as the new scientific revolution was concerned, literary intellectuals were 'natural Luddites'.

Exaggerating his case, Snow dismissed most leading writers of the nineteenth and twentieth centuries as pessimists without the social hope of the scientists, who had the future in their bones. Snow here equated literary culture with 'traditional culture', which did not wish the future to exist. The gap between these two cultures, scientific and literary-traditional, was growing wider in England, where there was early educational specialization and where social forms were crystallized. In Victorian times, Lord Salisbury had his own laboratory at Hatfield; the prime minister, Arthur Balfour, was interested in natural science; and the leading civil servant, Sir John Anderson, had done research in inorganic chemistry at Leipzig. 'None of that degree of interchange at the top of the Establishment is likely, or indeed, thinkable, now.'

The separation between the scientists and the non-scientists was greater than ever. Academics at Cambridge had ignored the Industrial Revolution, which had enriched them and had separated Disraeli's 'Two Nations' of the rich and the poor into Snow's 'Two Cultures'. Yet even more significant was the new scientific revolution, which Snow dated from the 'thirties and the use of atomic particles in industry, largely the creation of the Cavendish Laboratory. The innovative industrial society of electronics, atomic energy and automation would make society cardinally different and enable the western nations not only to benefit their own populations, but also to bridge the abyss between the rich and the poor nations by exporting their technology.

The danger lay in the split of the 'Two Cultures', both at the universities and in the government. The scientists, who managed the new revolution, could not communicate their social hope to the administrators. According to Snow, time was running out for western societies to close the gap between their cultures. History was merciless to failure, nor would we in the West write it. But Snow failed to foresee the coming to power of a prime minister with scientific training, Margaret Thatcher, and the collapse of socialism in Marxist Eastern Europe in the face of superior western technology.

Yet at that time, Snow's plain language and simple dialectic had a global appeal, which provoked a vicious assault at Cambridge from the self-elected guardian of the university's essential values, F.R. Leavis. As provincial and rigorous and condemnatory as any regicide in the Civil War, Leavis hated Snow for his international success, his loose definitions, and even his literary reputation. To Leavis, Snow was portentously ignorant – but a portent of an ignorant time, in which Leavis was considered a sage and a mastermind and a guardian of the values of the heart of England.

At another memorial lecture in 1962, attended by a crowd of hundreds of undergraduates and dons, Leavis claimed that he was not enjoying the murderous field-day. In fact, his words breathed envy; his tongue was malice incarnate. He demeaned the university traditions that he claimed to be defending. He talked of Snow as an intellectual nullity, as undistinguished as it was possible to be, incapable of posing or answering problems. As a novelist, let alone as a scientist or thinker, Snow did not exist. In Snow's major novel, *The Affair*, science was a mere word, the vocation merely postulated. Snow's lecture on the 'Two Cultures' was a document in the study of the *cliché*. Snow was as ignorant of history as of literature.

Leavis used the minor tools of a Wittgenstein to brand Snow's statement about scientists having the future in their bones as not a meaningful proposition; he forgot that most of his vilifications of Snow were meaningless. He rightly pointed out that Snow had not defined 'culture' exactly and had slid from 'literary' to 'traditional culture', as well as dismissing the worth of the major literary figures of the previous hundred and fifty years. Leavis concluded in vainglory. He was not a Luddite. Human intelligence was needed to respond to the challenges of the new technology. The proper study of Cambridge was language. The centre of the university should be a vital English school. Twenty years of running the critical magazine *Scrutiny* had taught him that the academic was the enemy and the academic could be beaten. He and his disciples were, as they knew they were, 'the essential Cambridge in spite of Cambridge.'

The most astute of the comments on the controversy that acutely exposed the many little rival 'cultures' and traditions at Cambridge was written by a research biochemist, Michael Yudkin, for the *Cambridge Review*. Although praised by Leavis for denigrating the use of the phrase 'two cultures' when there were many 'cultures', Yudkin agreed with two of Snow's theses. There was a failure of contact between scientists and non-scientists. This failure was unfortunate and probably dangerous. But Yudkin did not think any significant improvement was possible. With his claim that society's hope now lay with the scientists, Snow was pursuing the falsely optimistic idea of a new Renaissance. There would be no bridge across the gap between science and the arts. There would only be the atrophy of Snow's traditional culture, which would be gradually annexed by the scientific one until only a single culture remained. In his last words on this commentary, Snow seemed to accept some of Yudkin's criticism and pessimism, saying that Renaissance man was no longer possible; England had lost even the pretence of a common culture.

For good or ill, Britain persisted in the pursuit of independence through nuclear deterrence. Yet nuclear power could not change British society by itself, nor finally preserve it. The well-being of the country depended on an economic revolution based on scientific invention, the computers and biotechnology also developed at Cambridge. This did not depend on a military solution. If C.P. Snow exaggerated the gap between the 'two cultures', he was correct that electronics, the peaceful use of atomic energy, and automation would make society radically different.

Further inventions in electronics would spawn the computer revolution which would make Cambridge itself the Silicon Fen of England, with digital companies setting up shop around the abilities of the scientists of the ancient university. The third industrial metamorphosis had begun, and it had begun largely at Cambridge. That revolution, which the Cavendish had helped to start, was so awesome in its application that no arts professor, no master of the media, and certainly no politician could gauge its consequences or adequately describe its future. It could only be attacked and misunderstood in its significance, as F.R. Leavis did in his deadly personal assault on C.P. Snow. For lethal it nearly was. Shortly after the appalling lecture, Snow had a minor operation. As he was suffering from great stress and distress, his heart stopped under the effect of the anaesthetic. He was clinically dead for five minutes, until his heart was massaged back to life. He and his wife, the novelist Pamela Hansford Johnson, ascribed this setback to the Leavis vituperation. When he told me of it, his anguish and his wife's loving concern touched me.

George Steiner and myself were two of the few dons at Cambridge to speak out and write on behalf of Snow's integrity and honesty, and against this slow death by a thousand envies. The result was that George Steiner was never given even a mere lectureship in English at the university, although he was to become Professor of Comparative Literature at Geneva and he was incomparably the most brilliant speaker at Cambridge with the greatest knowledge of western literature. My own works were to incur the distaste of the Leavisite literary editors during the decades to come. Such was a Lilliputian war about greater matters than which end of an egg to break, a microscopic squabble about a macrocosm. But then, as solitary human beings, we can only understand well what personally happens to us. One thing was proven: how unforgiving Cambridge was.

At the end of the 'fifties and at the beginning of the new decade, C.P. Snow had postulated that there had been a rupture between two cultures, science and the arts. In point of fact, three cultures were already dividing like an amoeba. Not only was there a split between a scientific and an artistic culture, but both of these cultures were considered elitist in an age of spreading mass democracy which had its own standards – particularly in popular music and in art – and where advertising techniques on television were changing the perception of images. The leading patrons of culture, the government departments and committees in charge of distributing funds for education or research, the British and the Arts Councils and the local authorities, pursued what Keynes had advocated after the war – standards of excellence which might educate a larger audience. But there was a searching of souls among the governors that this policy of excellence, which Lord Reith had also advocated at the British Broadcasting Corporation and which his successors were steadily eroding, might be wrong for the times. Perhaps there was a lower common denominator in the cultures of Britain – and this should be patronized. This was precisely the fear of T.S. Eliot in his *Notes towards the Definition of Culture*: that mass education would adulterate and degrade culture, preparing the ground for the barbarian nomads of the future – an accurate prediction of the pop art and music of the youth 'culture' of the next decade.

For the riches bred by the new technology were granting a vast spending power to the young, who had been taught to be consumers, not to be patrons. The incessant barrage of advertisements on American television had educated the new generation in spending on various appealing products, particularly on gramophone records and musical tapes. This vast and immediate power of consumption was creating fresh arbiters of taste, semi-literate pop stars and artists, who used the devices of mass production to produce works of 'art' that had the quality of instant recognition. Thorstein Veblen had accused the Gilded Age of the American moguls of conspicuous consumption; this modern age was guilty of spontaneous consumption. And the existing standards of culture and art were to be the victims of that. From the snob to the yob.

Abstract expressionism was the first schism between American and European culture. The considered drips of Jackson Pollock appeared to have no meaning and no content. The viewer interpreted the splodges and brushstrokes as he wished. Lack of beauty was in the eye of the beholder. The pop art which followed attracted the new consumer culture of the young with its superimposition of advertising images on those of art, with its insistence that brand names were also tides of aesthetics. When its extreme practitioner, Andy Warhol, said that he wanted to be a machine, he seemed to resolve the conflict between the sciences and the arts, between the technology that made the young so rich and the pictures they wished to consume with their money. He asserted the triumph of mechanical art and the destruction of the values of the fine arts.

Such a resolution appeared to be a final solution to the conflict between the three cultures with their differing patrons and consumers. Yet the permanent remained the enemy of the instant, the abiding was the foe of the non-existent. Charles Snow still lived, and I never forgot what he told me about the afterlife. When his heart had stopped and he was clinically dead, he said that he had left his body and looked down upon it. His spirit or soul, in which he hardly believed, left his warm corpse before returning to its place. Possibly there was some resolution in things through the reconciliation of the spirits of mankind.

My thoughts about our three societies and cultures at the time reflected a growing pragmatism and a reluctance to make a drama out of a minor moral crisis. This was reflected in the affair of the Churchill College chapel. There are probably more Anglican chapels to the square mile in Cambridge than in any other town in England. The bigoted history of the university towards Roman Catholics and those of other faiths was notorious until recent times. We had opted for an inter-denominational chapel in our new college, where those of various faiths could wheel in the Cross or the sacramental symbol of their choice. A certain Anglican clergyman gave £25,000 towards the construction of a Church of England chapel, and the gift was accepted by the Master.

At a special meeting of the twenty-five Fellows, the two doyens of the scientific Establishment, the agnostic Charles Snow and the embattled John Cockcroft, challenged each other. The speeches were those of another age and might have been spoken in the controversy over Charles Darwin's *The Origin of Species*. Eventually, the vote went by 13 to 12 against the Anglican chapel. But within twenty-four hours, Cockcroft had broken the opposition, approaching each of the rebellious thirteen with the statement that he might resign as Master and destroy the nascent College unless we altered our vote. Eleven did so, but Francis Crick and myself would not. This was a matter of principle. Either the Fellows ran our policy by our votes or the Master did as an autocracy. And both of us soon resigned our Fellowships, although Cockcroft assured me that I could come back when I changed my mind. I don't think he was so ready about Crick, who was already more notorious for giving parties with nude models and very exotic drinks, and so was more poised to go. Sir Winston Churchill even wrote to Crick, asking him to change his mind. But the irrepressible Crick sent back a tenner for the Churchill Foundation to use for the supply of heteira or tarts, to service even agnostic or atheistic Fellows. The cheque was returned.

At the same time, an intense friend of mine and another novelist and historian, John Caute, decided to resign from his sinecure at All Souls at Oxford in protest against its refusal to reform itself into a teaching institution. We discussed our strategy: to dramatize our decision and attack our institutions; or to stay mum. He published an article in *Encounter*, 'Crisis in All Souls'. I did not speak a word, any more than Iago had after the death of Othello. Seven years before, I would have rushed into print as I had over the Suez crisis, sure of my rebellion and my righteousness. But I had been offered another travelling fellowship to America, which would take me back to Stanford and San Francisco, there to write about Women's Rights.

I was finding it impossible to do what my fellow novelists and teachers of Americana, Malcolm Bradbury and David Lodge, managed to do, to accommodate an artist's life with an academic one. In all, the opportunity outweighed the morality, and decency and discretion overcame publicity.

Later, I was to write a book, *The Red and the Blue*, about the 'three cultures' at Cambridge. This analysis was subtitled, *Intelligence, Treason and the Universities*. In the 1930s, there were the 'two cultures' of C.P. Snow, and two traditions, one of which dated back to medieval times, the free exchange of all knowledge and ideas between every country. Before the nuclear age, scientists at the Cavendish Laboratory believed in the open exchange of research, even with Soviet Russia after the leading physicist Peter Kapitsa was held in Moscow by Stalin to head research that was to culminate in the hydrogen bomb. From Trinity, Kapitsa had established a superior group of scientists, and at his request, the Council of the Senate actually sent all the contents of his Mond Laboratory to his enforced homeland.

The arts, however, had another tradition epitomized by the Apostles, a tight-lipped and secret society of intellectuals, masterminded from King's and seeking to influence academies and politics nationwide. A leader and later life peer, Noel Annan, would even call British society in the mid-20th century in a book, *Our Age: Portrait of a Generation*. In terms of treason, of the hundred or so clandestine members of the Apostles, three were convicted as traitors for passing on classified material to the Kremlin, three others were probable traitors, and another twelve of Marxist or homosexual persuasion served as occasional conduits of intelligence. Too literally did they prove in their lives the meaning of the novelist E.M. Forster's Apostolic fiat, that it was better to betray one's country than one's friend.

Yet even when I was at Churchill College, the old 'culture' of the Apostles was a dying duck. With its longlasting tradition, it could not cling any longer to male bonding or recruitment from one country, one sex, one class, and two Cambridge colleges. The other 'culture' of C.P. Snow was also moribund, losing its noble Cavendish tradition of free trade in pure research and of the community of like minds to the necessity of secrecy. Political and military considerations led to the allocation of scientific resources and to restrictions on the spread of information. Where there had been contact, there was now a closet. In a real sense, the physicists of the Cavendish could say, 'We are all Apostles now'.

That was the wrong university tradition. The scientific revolution pioneered at Cambridge was not confined to discoveries in nuclear energy, but included electronics and computers, biochemistry and genetics, crystallography and radio astronomy. The scientists of Cambridge in collaboration, where possible, with the scientists of the world, did change the communications and the perceptions of mankind, and threatened to question and alter the very structure of the human body, of plant and animal life, and perhaps of the universe itself.

Thus a 'third culture' began to be born. There is now little limit to the inquiry of the free mind, and there should be none to the free trade of the fruits of such research outside military and diplomatic use. The digital age would make this ideal even more inevitable. Our Age was proven to be an illusion of the technocrats. It was not Their Age. It had passed them by. Lord Annan had assumed that a few hundred like-minded Oxbridge graduates had run the country and its culture for the past twenty-five years. The arrogance of this mandarin élite was matched by its tolerance. It regarded itself as an Immoral Front. 'If someone said, 'People should be stopped from doing that,' the Immoral Front insisted that authority should justify its laws and conventions. If the young wanted to demonstrate, or utter absurd views, or do disgusting and disobliging things, or make love with their own sex or in heaps, we might think they were idiotic or ill-mannered; but, if they were entitled to do so, we saw no reason to stop them; or if a law did exist to stop them we asked: was it wise and humane and on what grounds did society issue this prohibition?'

What the Immoral Front never did was ask itself whether disgusting and disobliging young people cared at all about these elderly opinions. They did not. Their age was hardly Our Age. There was no communication between the generations. The professors and the civil servants knew next to nothing of the revolutionaries and the pop singers and the artists, who had tried and failed to change the powers of that time. Proudly, Lord Annan could write that no government had ever contained so many former dons and intellectuals as the Labour administrations of the 'sixties; but among them, there was no leader who could arrest the decline of Britain from the superpower of the 'fifties to the sick man of Europe twenty years on. And there were few or none among Our Age who might stop this, either. There was certainly no populist, who would understand the many alternative strategies of government propounded by those excluded from Our Age, that self-appointed group who never considered the old Roman question, *Quis custodiet custodes?*, 'Who shall guard the guardians?' They knew they were the right guardians. There could be no others. They did not see that it was not *Our Age* but another age, the years of the heedless young.

Whatever government could still do, the audience was drifting off. As in the American Declaration of Rights, 'We, the People' were stirring and would never again be put in straitjackets in any bag. The cats had fled. The great escape had started with the satirists of the 'fifties; it had been inspired by the Beats and The Beatles and The Rolling Stones of the 'sixties. Then the digital revolution would come, when everybody might have a say in the new democracy of the word. Anyone could be interactive and Twitter more than the birds in the trees, even if he or she wanted to chop them down. Instant communication meant incipient revolution. No more carrier pigeons needed in the age of Broadband. Governments had to beware. Mass protest was as possible as a plague of fleas or of locusts.

As for my own Cambridge career, the exposure of the Apostles prevented any possible return to the Fens as a lecturer. I was doomed, anyway, by having agreed to serve as the attack dog for my old Trinity tutor Peter Laslett, who was trying to introduce Sociology as a discipline into the university curriculum. This meant diminishing the History Faculty, controlled by Professor Geoffrey Elton, who had stuffed it half full with Tudor and Stuart constitutional historians.

At my first Council meeting, I found myself by far the youngest Director of Historical Studies there. Elton rose to his feet, declaring that he was the most popular lecturer on his courses; his classes were jam-packed, or words to that effect. Without warning me, Laslett called on me to reply. As usual, I was unprepared and did not know what I was going to say. The volley that came out of my mouth was lethal, and also suicidal. I stated that, unlike other recent undergraduates, I had never gone to Elton's lectures, because I didn't agree with him. Indeed, Laslett had told me that I had only got my Double First over Elton's dead body. Anyway, I declared that his classes were only crammed tight because everyone knew that he marked all the Tripos examination papers and ploughed anybody who did not hold his particular point of view.

Sociology was voted in. High time, but another career path for me was kaput for the third time.

ANNIHILATION BLUES

The consequence of Suez was, indeed, that the Empire went, under the astute direction of the British prime minister, Harold Macmillan. The winds of change that he released to blow across the last of the British colonies confirmed the doldrums of the Suez invasion and, at the personal level, the futility of my father's life as a Colonial Police commissioner, who was soon forced into early retirement. America and Russia were the only great powers now: yet the new Conservative defence policy of increased reliance on nuclear weapons stimulated the just cause of the Campaign for Nuclear Disarmament, which concluded at Trafalgar Square an annual march of forty miles from the Atomic Weapons Research Centre at Aldermaston. Although the government hardly altered because of the Suez debacle or the protest marches, a process of change was begun. The children of the last Just War were breaking down the gates of the Establishment.

I joined an Aldermaston march more from personal grief than political conviction. My flatmate Timothy Birdsall had died of leukaemia, and we held it to be the result of overground nuclear testing. He was the most amiable and funny of men. His cartoons for the *Spectator* and *That Was The Week That Was* showed a deft and immediate originality that was as spontaneous as his humour. Looking through his memorial volume Timothy, edited by Michael Frayn and Bamber Gascoigne, I am still struck by the piercing sympathy of his satire. A graduate squats in the street, his upturned mortar board as a begging-bowl: behind him, a placard:

AFFLUENT SOCIETY TO SUPPORT

A wife looks at her City husband over his breakfast newspaper and says, 'Darling, where is the Free World exactly?' Two schoolboys in shorts and blazers pass an evening newspaper poster scrawled with K.'S BIG BOMB, and one says to the other, 'What are you going to be if you grow up?' Timothy had two small children who did grow up and a marvellous actress wife, who played in *Look Back in Anger* at the Royal Court Theatre. His loss turned our satire into sympathy, our mockery of politics and society into a terrible urge to change them.

He was already dying when the Cuban missile crisis had wonderfully clarified our minds. The yeast of the 'sixties was not pop music or sexual liberation, but the conviction of the young after the Cuban threat that they were living on borrowed time. As much as sex and drugs and rock music, the fear of mass death defined the decade. There were many ways to go – heat and blast and the slow poisoning of radiation. Historians argued about whether the menace of nuclear missiles in the Caribbean led to the most dangerous clash of the Cold War, or the did Berlin airlift in a power play between the young god Kennedy and the shoe-banging peasant Khrushchev. The worst was that the Cuba crisis was only about atomic war, beginning with intermediate-range nuclear weapons in clearings in the island. Conventional weapons had nothing to do with it. If the standoff had gone wrong, there would have been an apocalypse.

This prescience of instant annihilation was summed up in the acronym M.A.D. – Mutually Assured Destruction. The strategists of the major powers had made the use of nuclear weapons appear inevitable at one time or another. This had been the subject of my third novel, *The Project*, in which a nihilist physicist set off the terminal rocket as a war game. Making Marianne and myself say that we refused to have a child in the circumstances, but would only adopt an orphan from the Third World. And the dying of a friend from the polluted and irradiated atmosphere confirmed our darkest suspicions and sent us marching from Aldermaston towards Trafalgar Square.

Yet the leaders of the Campaign for Nuclear Disarmament were increasingly moving from one just cause, which could attract anyone who did not want to die, into the many panaceas of the Left. They edged the whole organization towards protest not only against the bomb, but against hunger, old age pensions and the whole gamut of socialist grievances. So they destroyed its universal appeal, and that pure protest seemed to us to reside only with the Anarchists. Just as George Orwell had supported the democratic Left in Spain against the totalitarian Socialists, we felt that our commitment was to freedom of speech against the bomb above all.

As it was, we were attacked by the police in front of Westminster Abbey and the Houses of Parliament, our flags were ripped down, our guitars were broken, and in a confrontation of extreme absurdity, I found myself pulling up a red and black banner from under a police boot like a rebellious American colonist feeling his liberties had been trampled on. I was then struck a blow in the chest by the police officer, who announced, 'I'll put you inside.' I hit him back in the chest with the brilliant riposte, "I'll put you inside." We glared at each other, the free-for-all drove us apart, and I found myself running across Parliament Square and up The Mall, waving a tattered banner of freedom for all the world, like Pudovkin's Mother or Charlie Chaplin picking up the wrong flag.

My recklessness was part of my political incoherence. I worked by passionate instinct, not by party politics. As a Fellow of Churchill College, I was in the heart of the atomic Establishment. Yet here was I running with the Anarchists, whom I suspected were the last of the free. I knew their history, that they were far greater in numbers than the Bolsheviks and should have taken over in the Russian Revolution. But, of course, true to their principles, they could never organize.

I also knew that they were not a party so much as a contradiction of all parties. President Kennedy and the United States had kindled my hope or memory of the future, and if something was to be done to change Britain, only the Labour Party appeared able to do it. So I wrote to its leader, Hugh Gaitskell, out of the blue, even though he had routed the unilateral nuclear disarmers within the party. I told him that the style of his speeches was terrible. I said that I would act as his speech-writer without pay and try to give him the style of a Kennedy, who had inspired us with the products of his script-writers. I was a historian of America; I thought I could do that for the Labour leader.

Incredibly, Gaitskell replied and accepted. The gall of my Cambridge contemporaries made us offer ourselves, and if we were any good, things happened. Gaitskell was only receiving two thousand pounds a year to aid his expenses as the Leader of the Opposition, and he could hardly afford a secretary. He had expensive tastes and depended on hostesses such as Ann Fleming to run his social life for him. He may have responded to my mixture of social awareness and youthful radicalism, but what he wanted was the Kennedy jokes and apt quotations from the classic writers. These I did provide, particularly in an article designed to save the Euston Arch from destruction. But then he threw away my speech on joining the Common Market at the Labour Party Conference and turned against it, evoking a thousand years of history as an excuse for staying out. In my hoity-toity way, I told him that I would not write his speeches any more if he ignored my efforts. But when his ratings slipped again in the polls, he recalled me, and I realized in my ignorance that I was working for a great man, a true lost statesman.

On that occasion, the shadow cabinet had been meeting in the leader's office in the House of Commons, while I waited outside. As they filed out, their salute to the alien youngster was characteristic – George Brown's jocular 'Hello, comrade'; James Callaghan's polite 'Good morning'; and Harold Wilson's suspicious glare. But when I was called inside, Gaitskell disarmed and shamed me. He said that he knew from his daughters, who had recommended me to him, that my generation spent their holidays in Europe and supported entry into the Common Market, but that the members of his generation felt a guilt about the Empire, and that they could never fulfil our remaining obligations towards the Commonwealth after an entry into Europe. As he spoke, I thought of my father and his imperial service that I had repudiated. And yet, Gaitskell continued, he could be convinced that he was wrong. He might well be so, and, if the circumstances were different, he would have the courage to change his mind.

His argument and his decency and his frankness made me feel ashamed of my superior lack of understanding. So I composed his speeches once more. He even offered me a safe seat in Parliament, but I refused to run, knowing my inability to sit on committees or supervise the local problems of a constituency. His last letter to me of 4th December, 1962, before a planned trip to Moscow, lies in front of me. 'I wonder if I might seek your help in the following please? Each year I have to send a New Year Message to the Party and I should be most grateful if you could do a draft for me.'

The opening paragraph of my draft and his undelivered message still stares me in the face:

We do not want to ring out the Old Year. 1962 deserves no bells. There is no cause for rejoicing. This past year only stands as a witness for the prosecution. The Tories have let muddle slide into trouble, incompetence into injustice. Unemployment rises, industry sags, education is choked, Britain declines. I accuse the Tories. They will answer for it in 1963.

Before Christmas and the Moscow visit, Gaitskell caught pneumonia. He was taken to hospital, where he was stricken fatally by another infection, what we now call an infirmary bug. There were the usual conspiracy theories about his sudden end, particularly as he was to go to the Kremlin. In fact, the wards of the National Health Service were no cleaner then than they are now, and deadly microbes lurk in healing places. And so, the best post-war Prime Minister the Labour Party never had expired in the care of its greatest bequest to the nation.

Hope died with him – the hope of changing things within the Labour Party and the country. He was the first revisionist Labour shadow Prime Minister, and the little man who would follow him, Harold Wilson, would weasel and widdle away the election victory which he inherited. Gaitskell looked to the Democrats and to Kennedy in America for his inspiration in turning his party into the natural majority party of Great Britain. Many of us were then under the influence of things American except for the Marxist left wing, and Gaitskell was trying to eliminate their influence in the party.

After the murder of Kennedy, this second dying and killing of hope affected us even more. Satire seemed a blunt instrument, a cosh for caring. Even on that vehicle of deflation, *That Was The Week That Was*, my friend Bernard Levin delivered a eulogy on the dead Labour leader: 'That he *did* save the party he loved was not the least of his achievements. The tragedy is that it was to be the last. And the tragedy is not his alone, but the tragedy of all those involved in, or even affected by, the struggle for freedom and social justice, those twin causes in which he so devoutly believed, and in the selfless service of which he lived and died. The ideals of democratic socialism,' he said, as he conceded defeat on election night in 1959, 'have never shone so brightly'. If they shine less brightly today than yesterday, it is because of his passing.'

My political career as an *eminence d'écrire* was not quite over. Roy Jenkins intended to make a series of six speeches across the country, defining his policies, if he were to lead the Party. I was assigned to embellish his policy on transport, particularly on future highways. Conjuring with history, I added two blunt sentences. 'In Tudor times, it was said that sheep ate men. Now cars eat men.' Unfortunately, when *The Observer* reported the speech, the headline was: NOW CARS EAT MEN. This was not Roy's phrase. I was never again asked to aid his elegant prose. In the theatre and in Westminster, never, never upstage your leader.

When not in Cambridge, Marianne and I were living in a rare attic flat on the top of a Georgian brick terrace house in Soho Square. The very name of the onetime London village was a hurrah for killing, originally a call to the hunting dogs pursuing a hare to its death. Many of the old Fitzrovian painters and composers and poets had been hounded to their graves after the war, the victims of booze and fags – Nina Hamnett and John Minton, the two Roberts Colquhoun and MacBryde, Constant Lambert and Dylan Thomas, who had already foreseen his end in his last poem, calling himself 'an old ramrod dying of strangers' – and pints and chasers. There were still Francis Bacon and Lucian Freud to be seen at their lunches in Wheeler's in Old Compton Street; but we could rarely afford to get beyond the bar, where they would serve half a dozen oysters and a glass of Chablis and free olives and brown bread and mayonnaise for twenty-one shillings, a guinea a head. And there was the French Pub, that last hangout of the Soho bohemians, the poets and the plastered artists, pissing their lives away.

Already the conditions for writing poetry in Fitzrovia were in decline. George Barker saw that young poets could no longer create and eat at the same time. 'It is already impossible for them to drink and write as they wish: the beer is no longer singing beer.' For economic and social reasons, artists had begun to move from Soho by the early 'fifties, because of the rise of crime and rents, which could be afforded only by strip-tease shows and pornographic bookshops. The Fitzrovians who stayed in the area had to be able to pay for it – or so George Melly found when Lucian Freud took him on the occasional binge to the Stork Club where the hostesses served whisky in teapots outside licensing hours. The sting of war and bohemia was already blunted. The future of writing and the arts would be less concentrated, yet more restricted and overly cautious after the middle 'fifties, the suburban celebrations of John Betjeman, the provincial pastorals of Philip Larkin. State patronage would increasingly make for safe production for subsidy. Some noble and unfashionable romantics would continue to laud the lost past and intermittently try to live as they had then; but even they were aware that their peers had departed and that modern times were replacing the beery universities of their fledgling days.

As literature fled from the garrets and pubs of Soho, music entered by the cellars and the clubs. This was the first youth culture that Britain had ever seen, and it grew from the protest songs of the exploited. I had heard Joan Baez sing in a voice more piercing than a bleeding nightingale in a coffee house off Harvard Square in 1960, and Pete Seeger a year later in Greenwich Village. And now Ewan MacColl, who was separated from Joan Littlewood and her Theatre Workshop in the East End, was bringing the folk songs of the Depression 'thirties to the jazz and skiffle players of the 'fifties. Tennessee Ernie Ford's 'Shotgun Boogie' and 'Sixteen Tons', the blues of Muddy Waters and Bo Diddley and Chuck Berry, the rock of Buddy Holly and Elvis Presley, and the cool sound of Charlie Mingus and Thelonious Monk – these galvanized the traditional jazz bands of Humphrey Lyttleton and Chris Barber from a homage to Louis Armstrong and Charlie Parker into another beat. We would go to their clubs off Oxford Street and Cy Laurie's in the basement of Mac's Rehearsal Rooms in Windmill Street; then we would progress to Ronnie Scott's in Gerrard Street and later in Frith Street, where his club still endures.

The pessimism of that borrowed time, the feeling that we were living under the dark nuclear umbrella, put Marianne and me under the influence of the blackest wit of his post-war Oxford generation. Known as Deacon to the other undergraduates such as Kenneth Tynan because of his solemn style and utterance, Derek Lindsay dominated his friends as Larkin had, but through his magnificent pessimism and bleak vision. 'I was not laughing,' he once said to me when I took him to a comedy in the theatre. 'The sound you heard was a glottal spasm or premonitory death rattle.' He never elided a syllable nor used an apostrophe, every phrase considered to each dead stop. His conversation was usually about himself and his survival in his Mayfair maisonette, which was decorated as his own *memento mori*. 'I died many years ago,' he used to say to us. 'My subsequent activity has been to maintain this status quo.' A sufferer from tuberculosis, he had been operated upon. 'They removed a lung and whatever other organ they could reach. I recovered sufficiently to participate in my diurnal death throes. I must go back to isolation. It has its horrors, but the horrors of knowing one is not alone in this world are incomparably worse.'

We had met him at a drinks party – he swore it was the only he had ever attended. My book on Prohibition and his only novel *The Rack* on his Swiss sanatorium years – hailed by Graham Greene as one of the greater books of the century – had been printed by the same American publisher. At the gathering in William Sansom's garden in St. John's Wood, Deacon was smitten by the beauty of Marianne, although he praised my own novel, *The Breaking of Bumbo*. When he gave us his address and telephone number, the erratic poet and publisher James Michie almost had a seizure: how had we penetrated into the hermitage of the most solitary recluse in London?

We became two of the few people that Deacon ever saw. We were entranced by the long dark pain of his body, the brown melancholy of his eyes and his sonorous prophecies of woe. 'The world is a vast concentration camp,' he told us, 'each generation of prisoners handing on its torch of suffering to the next.'

Yet Deacon himself, who always said he was born to die as early as his mother and father had, applied a fierce discipline, so as to linger on here. After he had lost a lung through tuberculosis and was condemned to an excess of pills and a daily routine for the rest of his life, he never deviated in his gloom about his future nor in his wish that the rest of the human race join in his witty misery. When Michie declared to Deacon at midnight that he was committing suicide before dawn, he woke at breakfast to find a fantasy postcard of kissing lovers' skulls pushed through his letterbox, with the message, 'Why did you not?'

Both Scottish and Venetian, and as handsome as Lucifer, Deacon was orphaned at the age of three, because of a car crash. He was brought up by a conventional aunt as a lonely child. The Second World War intervened with his public schooling, and he rose to become a captain and an adjutant in the conflict, without seeing too much fighting in the front line. At post-war Oxford University, he seemed the ultimate Oscar Wilde crossed with Jonathan Swift, the acme of elegant pessimism. He hunted and drank and crackled with nervous scepticism: he published a short story and married for six weeks a lady who would become the Governor of Holloway Prison.

Then tuberculosis eroded his laconic strength. Sent to an Alpine hospital for the mountain air, he endured a regime worse than that of his regiment. And he fell in love, or apparently so, his first escape from his obsessions. The years of his slow cure were the subject of *The Rack*. The torment inflicted on the body to achieve health, the agony of hovering between living and dying, and even the pain of feeling for another person were recorded in prose worthy of Marcel Proust or Thomas Mann. To me and Graham Greene, indeed, *The Rack* was superior to *The Magic Mountain*. The book was a cry from a soul under torture, from a writer who did not believe that he had a soul.

Deacon was nearly a hermit, inhabiting his own special and premature mausoleum in Mount Street. Its white walls and drawn thick grey curtains embalmed a fantasy and Surrealist collection. There were primitive Staffordshire pieces of skeletons and judges, highwaymen and painted china clocks without faces. There was an Arcimboldo of a man with a face made up of vegetables, also many turn-of-the-century small French posters and automates showing the beginnings of aerial transport and the cinema. And then, there was the great entrapment, the albums of exotic French postcards that ended in the carnage of the First World War. Dozens of babies burst out of balloons or flowerpots or artillery, the hours were flowers and moustaches were the measures of love, mysterious men in their flying machines out of Jules Verne ogled bathing beauties from above. All of this stuff was a rare choice.

And there was the ant colony with its glass front in the bedroom. The workers scurried up and down the exposed channels to their bloated queen, forever on their errands to feed their indolent mistress. This was a microcosm of Deacon's view of life. We were not different from ants. We toiled uselessly in the service of the wrong motives. We were liable at any moment to extinction from some giant boot from the sky. As this was the time of our friends lost to leukaemia through atomic radiation and of marches from Aldermaston to stop nuclear testing, such philosophy, expounded with persuasive brilliance, fell on sprouting ears.

To him, nature was injustice. We should not go blind into creation, which was the first sabotage, as Cioran had said. For Deacon, everything which moved or wriggled was wrongly condemned. If he saw a photograph of the vivisection of a monkey, he spent a sleepless night. Nothing could help to cure our ills. When I heard him give a rare laugh at the black farce, Frank Marcus's *The Killing of Sister George*, he replied, 'No, Andrew, it was the rictus of despair.'

He was a great raconteur of death gone wrong. He told me a story of leaving his Swiss sanatorium to buy a revolver and kill himself. It was hard to buy the weapon. He had to pledge the gunsmith not to kill anyone but himself. He went back to his hotel suite and decided that it was too grand to stain with his gore. He progressed to a night-club with a friend, became drunk, went to sleep in the bath, nearly drowned, but was saved by switching on the shower in his last convulsions. Then he put the revolver in his mouth, was too weak to press the trigger, hated the taste of the gun barrel and ordered coffee and croissants instead. With his breakfast came the hotel manager, who insisted that he left the suite immediately because a dignitary wanted it. To him, suicide was a form of slapstick. Deacon often took his temperature with the gun instead of a thermometer – he could not tell the difference. He had probably breathed so much down the barrel that it was clogged with rust.

Deacon's attraction to Marianne was through French and Edwardian Decadent literature, particularly Rimbaud and Verlaine, Lautréamont and Oscar Wilde. One of the few people capable of writing flawlessly in two languages, she published two elegant novels in English, *Paradox Lost* and *Watcher in the Park*, The first was an account of a lesbian affair in Paris with a café singer: the heroine was only seventeen. The second was about a twelve-year-old girl enticing and then condemning to prison a retarded male exhibitionist, so that she was more sinning than sinned against. These perverse texts alienated the wives of the last of my conventional friends from Eton and Cambridge. The words were far too far from Leavisite puritanism. They marked the distance I had travelled from our old common ground and the new byways I was exploring.

My own next novel, *The Raker,* was a dance of love and death. Shown on the cover, which was one of Deacon's collection of Edwardian fantasy postcards, was Pierrot talking to Pierrette, their heads the sockets of a skull, their champagne glasses its teeth. The epigraph was Emily Dickinson's poem 'The Lost Gentleman':

Because I would not stop for death
He kindly stopped for me

The carriage held but just ourselves
And immortality
We slowly drove, he knew no haste
And I had put away
My labour, and my leisure too
For his civility

The novel ended with the Raker's suicide. His last note was meant to be that of Socrates, after he had drunk the hemlock. 'We owe a cock to Asclepius,' Socrates had said, referring to the God of Healing. The Raker died at the point of writing, 'We owe a cock to ass.' His hand then failed.

Such pessimism and perversity appeared to us to suit the temper of the times under the mushroom cloud. Soho itself seemed to be cocking a snook at death and trying to recreate the Berlin days of the 'twenties, while life still lasted and homosexuality was still criminal. At the Huntsman, the gays danced together to rock records in the cellar, convivial on cappuccino. At The Fitzroy Tavern and the Golden Lion, the boys flounced to meet the older men over a pint or two of bitter. At the French Pub and Muriel Belcher's Colony Room, we could find Francis Bacon and Lucian Freud. And there was the Marquee, where the new Rhythm and Blues groups were playing, and there The Rolling Stones made their West End opening.

The war was within us as much as it was without us. In Paris, where we had bought a ground-floor apartment in the *rue Campagne-Première*, the images of the past and present were exploding. On a side-street by the Coupole and the Dôme, a new film bar had opened, the Rosebud. Named after Citizen Kane's boyhood sledge and dying word, the place played cool jazz and attracted the generation formed by the American cinema, now translated into the French *nouvelle vague*. Our gods at the time were Godard and Alain Resnais, whose *Hiroshima Mon Amour* and *L'Année Dernière à Marienbad* seemed to have done what T.S. Eliot had achieved in poetry, to have created a contiguous past and present and future, a confusion of the years by screen cutting that mocked the steady running of the hours. And Godard made us see each moment afresh. The master of the unexpected, he altered our vision of what we thought we already knew.

These heady cries from the Rosebud were echoed at Shakespeare & Co., a bookshop named in honour of Sylvia Beach, who had published Joyce's *Ulysses*. The place was now run by two Americans, Mary and George Whitman, from premises in the *rue de la Bûcherie* on the Left Bank facing Notre-Dame across the Seine. Here most of the visiting British and American writers flopped or congregated, including Ferlinghetti, who had found in its relaxed welcome an inspiration for his own City Lights bookstore in San Francisco. Otherwise, the American travellers went to the cheap and tolerant Beat Hotel in *rue Gît-le-Coeur* off the Place Saint-Michel, where the aged Madame Rachou would clear up nearly everything that Ginsberg and Corso and Burroughs and their associates left in a mess behind them.

The Coupole was our usual restaurant, however, and most of Paris passed through its doors, looking for one another. The 'thirties paintings on its pillars, the paper tablecloths and the first-come, first-served principle of seating made it a democratic magnet for the artists. The tide was flowing away from Saint-Germain, where the tourists far outnumbered the old *habitués* and the Deux Magots was already printing on its napkins and bills – RENDEZ-VOUS DES INTELLECTUELS. Jean-Paul Sartre himself had already fled to the Dôme beside our cafe, and we would pass him, blinking with grey myopia through his glasses at Simone de Beauvoir or a visiting girl of the sort that de Beauvoir had characterized in *L'Invitée*. There were fewer literary and artistic groupies left in Montparnasse than in Saint-Germain, which had surpassed its neighbour on the Left Bank in the 'fifties, but now was surrendering the tricolour of the arts again. A rare excitement, a whiff of revolution, a sureness of culture, pervaded the crossroads of the four great cafés on the Boulevard du Montparnasse, the Select and the Rotonde, the Coupole and the Dôme. There, was the scent of caramel-coated roasted nuts and crêpes with calvados at this best encounter-ground of all the world.

The personal, alas, so often is the victim of the general. We could not escape Deacon, who often followed us to Paris, not on a cultural pilgrimage, but to embellish his collection of surreal postcards. Or so he told us. For four years, Marianne and I saw him twice a week, enthralled by his sombre oratory. Then one day in our French apartment, she told me that she was in love with Deacon as well.

She wanted to leave me in Paris and live with him for a while in his new house in north London. Curiously, I had forecast this very situation in my novel *The Raker*, a triangle between the Deacon figure and a brash writer of obituaries and a young woman, while Denis Brogan had long before told me of *L'ami de famille*, the accepted lover in French triangular relationships. I first knew of the affair when Marianne suddenly dropped her opposition to my going on my Gog walk over the Borders from Edinburgh to York without any money, sleeping rough. She no longer cared quite enough to prevent me. There was now an alternative.

Influenced by sagas and anarchism, I had long intended to write the whole mythical history of Albion, the visionary Britain of William Blake, within the body and mind of a single amnesiac outcast, walking to London at the end of the Second World War. He would be called Gog and represent the never-ending revolt of the people and the provinces against the power and the rule of London, represented by his half-brother Magog – the two names of the traditional giants of ancient England. Gog would conjure up the historical unconsciousness of the island as well as his own past life, although his recollections and impulses would be questioned by the attacks of his wife Maire. A cartoon of Albion, drawn in the eighteenth century and in my possession, already showed England and Wales and part of Scotland as a giant drinking a mug of ale astride a dragon fish. The whole history of a nation might be contained in the form of one body walking at one time – past and present and future all occurring to his mind in the now, in the eternal struggle between the country and the city.

At any rate, that had been my vast idea far beyond my experience or capacity. I had not dared do it; but in my pride, confronting the news that Marianne wanted to share me with Deacon, I told her that it would release me to act out and write my grand design alone on the open moors and in the urban wilderness of Limehouse, when I would move to the docks. In the last analysis, my trade was solitary and could not admit the close love of a woman; we had hardly been separated for the past five years, day and night.

In my cold anger, I did not count the cost to my heart, the amputation of my emotions. Vainly I believed I should and could sacrifice my love to my art. And in a way, I was escaping from outward commitment and politics into an interior journey to the very essence and matter of my heritage, cutting free from present ties to explore the violence of the past in paranoia and ancient myth. We are what we were, I thought. I was, therefore I am, and so I will be. Equally, I began to learn the meaning of a *ménage à trois*, until then a mere Gallic bedroom farce. Instead, Marianne and I might still leave together on our Journies to the End of Night.For my other tutor in the art of racked survival was now Louis-Ferdinand Céline, the tortured Rabelais of the French defeat by the Nazis.

LOUIS-FERDINAND CÉLINE

The French writer I had learned to admire was Céline. Becoming more proficient in the French language, I discovered that, by introducing the argot of the streets, he had confounded the strictures of l'Académie française and increased the lingo by as many new words as Rabelais.

'You certainly know P. Brueghel's huge 'Madmen's Fair',' Louis-Ferdinand Céline wrote in 1932 to Léon Daudet. 'The whole problem is nowhere else... I only rejoice in the grotesque on the borders of death.' So the new sensation of French literature wrote to a right-wing leader, who had just praised his masterpiece, *Journey to the End of the Night*. Its publication had been a fantastic success; it was hailed by the press of all political parties. To Daudet's voice, Trotsky added his, praising Céline for his understanding of the psychology of despair – 'its filthy, bloody and nightmarish absurdity'. Then a curious mixture between Communist and Catholic, the critic James Agee lumped Céline along with Whitman, Blake, Beethoven, Christ and Tolstoy as one of his six heroes 'with so much in common'. Yet no one quite knew what a monster and genius had been elevated in the 'thirties as the Jeremiah of French society.

The supporters of the Left presumed Céline was theirs. Clawing his way up from the *petite bourgeoisie*, hating the rich and the bosses because of his mother's humiliations as a lace-seller and his father's as an insurance clerk, Céline's raving assaults on the corruption of France continued through his second novel, published in 1936, *Death on the Instalment Plan*. He had been wounded in the skull in the First World War. 'What other more romantic writers sought, Wilde, Proust, Rimbaud, Verlaine, in the forcing-house of buggery and the hard labour of alcoholism, I, I got it served up on a plate defending my country! ... Like that! neat!.' In a torrent of gutter slang, this insomniac night-wandering doctor of the poor called down the destruction of Paris and the world by flood, fire and apocalypse. In his vehemence, the French Left saw a prophet denouncing the rot of capitalism with the invective of the people. 'It's hate which makes argot,' Céline explained later. 'Argot is made to express the true feelings of misery … to allow the workman to tell his boss that he loathes him.'

With his sliced phrases of poetry and muck, his choppy punctuation of exclamation marks and triple dots, Céline succeeded in his attempt to make print gurgle to the inner ear, to set down the language of guts and tripes and deep festering hates. He once described his revolution in the French language as one which took his readers through the Métro, the bowels of the earth, instead of through the false trivialities of the light of day. 'It's my genius,' he claimed, 'my stroke of genius! not thirty-six possible ways! … I put all my world on the Métro, sorry! … and I rush on: I lead the whole world! … willy-nilly! with me! … the Métro of the emotions, mine! … without all the claptrap, the lumber! in a dream! … no stop anywhere! no! to the end! the end! direct!'

While *Journey to the End of the Night* dealt with Céline's life after he volunteered as a cavalryman, *Death on the Instalment Plan* was a record of his first eighteen years after 1894, the year of his birth. Céline never wrote about anyone except himself and those he met, whom he involved in the fantasies and annihilations within his own skull. There is no careful Proustian resurrection of the past in his second novel; there is a violent and lusty and filthy scramble after the ultimate scatological and poetical sensations of childhood and youth. The legend of King Krogold plays the role of the *madeleine* in acting as a thread that binds the present to the recollections of the past. But Céline's bloody, authoritarian and romantic legend has little more than technique in common with Proust's use of an exquisite taste as a link to nostalgia.

Céline's second novel drops the skirt from the dirty rump of the *Belle Époque* and the years before the First World War. In almost a parody of Proust and his society world, he writes, 'I know something about last century, I saw it depart. It disappeared along the road beyond Orly,' where his old aunt lived in a smelly cottage, the fruit of fifty years' savings as a toilet attendant. Céline describes the desperate struggle of the small shopkeepers and artisans and clerks to survive against the competition of the new machines and large firms. Their world is a tooth-and-claw effort to stave off poverty and to fulfil the demands of the rich and indifferent. The well-off grind the shabby genteel, who in turn beat their children, who in turn torture their pets. There is a chain of suffering which is handed down from class to class and generation to generation and species to species.

In the running war between him and his father, Céline confesses that they both had a heart, but that 'life isn't a question of heart.' He admits that his limping, whining mother did everything possible for him, but 'it was having been born that was such a mistake.' He takes up a position of stubborn silence against both cruelty and kindness; 'to confess things is asking for trouble.' Survival is all, by any means. There is no question of right or wrong, merely of stopping people from bothering you. Utter hatred is reserved for all bosses – 'another name for plain scum whose one idea is to fling you out into the street.' So much for the backside of the gay and glittering Proustian world, which has never produced a better scavenger. 'The existence of the lesser people of the *Belle Époque*,' Céline himself wrote, 'had more to do with a nightmare than a dream.'

Another of Céline's obsessive theories was developed in his second novel, the theme of dying and the role of the corpse in the life of the living. As a doctor in the Paris suburbs, one of Céline's daily tasks was to examine corpses and write out their death certificates. Like a monk in the Middle Ages, he seemed to demand the presence of the cadaver at the feast. In *Journey to the End of the Night*, the remains of Robinson were praised as going further on the journey than Céline himself; in *Death on the Instalment Plan*, Courtial's suicide and the disposal of the corpse provided the occasion for Céline's collapse and contrition, when he decided to join up in a fit of sobbing, because he realised that his horrible calamity was 'always to cause everyone pain.' Again, a gangster's remains was the arbiter between existing or not in a later London novel.

Only one of Céline's fixations was not developed in his second novel, the dance of death. This concept of people drinking and whoring round a coffin came to dominate Céline's work more and more; Courtial's headless corpse was merely trundled off on a wheelbarrow. The novel was Céline's second acknowledged masterpiece, only a little inferior to his first because of a restriction of place and a milking of comedy, which often made the bucket of ribaldry overflow and waste itself. The horrors and jokes of Paris and the French countryside and the Channel coast were not quite as profound as the previous journey through Africa and America and Europe.

Yet to say that the second book is slightly worse than the first is to say that *Finnegans Wake* is not as good as *Ulysses*, or *The Trial* as good as *The Castle*. In my opinion, Céline joins Joyce and Kafka as one of the three writers of the last century whose perception and style have most changed our literature. Céline's political aberrations still withhold due recognition from him. In 1936, he was invited to Russia to spend his royalties from his first novel, as these could not be taken out of the country. He came back with a loathing of Stalin's state and published a bitter attack upon it, *Mea Culpa*. He followed up his anti-Communism with an odious, disgusting and insane assault on the Jews, *Bagatelle for a Massacre*. With Jews, he lumped together the Communists, the Freemasons and democrats in general, as idiotically as his father had done. The right wing in France opened its arms to this new champion, who sold his delirious prose and unbridled envy in hundreds of thousands of copies.

In *Bagatelle* and its successor, *The School of Corpses*, Céline's denunciation of the Jews bypassed the pseudo-scientific anathemas of the Nazis and reached absurdity. As Gide pointed out in an excuse for Céline, how could anyone take seriously a man who accused Cézanne, Picasso, Maupassant, Racine, Stendhal and Zola of being Jews? And Céline did not stop there; he even accused the kings of France of Jewishness. His madness against the Jews – later apologists were to claim – was like Swift's proposal to eat Irish babies, a supreme irony, a *reductio ad absurdum* of racism.

Yet it was not. Céline never wrote about anyone but himself and he wrote seriously; he was obsessed by his own life and influences. He came from the traditional Jew-hating class of France, the small shopkeepers and clerks, those who were once anti-Dreyfus and who then would back Poujade and Le Pen. If Céline mocked his father's anti-Semitism in his second novel, it was only because he feared an imagined Jewish conspiracy and thought he should disguise his true feelings. But in 1937, he saw fascism triumphing in Europe, he felt his power as an established author, and he vomited into print.

The left-wingers dropped Céline, now revealed as a *petit bourgeois*, who equated monopolies and inflation with Jewish banking. They saw only and rightly that his hysteria and huge sales had spread the defeatism and pro-Nazism, which were to lead France to disaster. He called for an alliance with Hitler and denounced Britain and

America as pro-Semitic stooges. And when the war and defeat came in 1940, he said that he had told France of the disaster to come.

Yet Céline was too dangerous for the French Right. His rage exceeded sense. He was the only author to have articles refused by the Fascist French press for 'racist delirium'. He loathed Pétain and wanted all of 'negroid' Vichy and the South of France to be eliminated, or at least severed permanently from the north. His books were even banned in Germany. He was too extreme for professional Jew-baiters among the Nazis. As early as the Vichy régime, Céline saw that the Germans had lost the war. Thus he began to trim. His only wartime novel, *Guignol's Band*, was an incantation in which his *alter ego*, Bardamu, had strange adventures during the war of 1917 in Soho and the East End. England became a wonderland, anti-Semitism had gone underground.

As the war ended, Céline fled to the collaborator's castle of Sigmaringen, then on to a Danish prison. This exile was chronicled in *Castle to Castle* and *North* in his charged and breathless prose. The French authorities tried to extradite and execute him; but they failed. Until the amnesty of 1951, he lived in misery with his wife and his old cat in Denmark. His last ten years were spent in Paris at Meudon, where occasionally – a friend of his told me – he played at being half-Lear and half-Genet, with rare lapses when he was caught in *flagrante delicto* of pleasure. His death was announced on the same day as Hemingway's suicide. Thus the most original French writer of the mid-century received a few paragraphs while the headlines went to a famed foreign author, who (as Céline's friend Marcel Aymé wrote) may well have been a better hunter than writer.

Politics die, however, and style remains – even if the death of six million Jews will always remain to make an obscenity of Céline's reputation. He is a writer beyond pardon; but, then, he never asked for pardon. He slandered everyone he knew, his editors, his friends; no one was spared from his ravings except his wives, his cats and the occasional dancing girl. He ended his life bitter against the stupidity of the Germans; the cleverness of the Jews had been proved to him by their victory. His new hope lay in the Chinese. 'Luckily the Chinese are coming,' he screamed in 1955, 'to put an end to it! this ripe mess! to make you construct the Canal 'Somme-Yangtse-Kiang!' '

In Denmark, Céline, begging for amnesty, claimed that he should be judged not by his politics, but by his style. And, indeed, history in the long term makes such a judgment. Who cares, when reading the novels of Dostoevsky, about his reactionary politics? Céline is, undoubtedly, the father of the French literature of despair, while such writers as Henry Miller have confessed that they have learned all from Céline. This is not to deny that Céline was vain, mean, detestable and downright murderous towards the Jewish people and the French nation. And yet he suffered for his crimes; without his shattered skull, he would not have been delirious, insomniac and paranoiac; without his anti-Semitism, he would not have had to wander through burning Germany or waste in a Danish cell.

Céline said to an American-Jewish professor, who went to visit him in exile, that he had more in common with a Jew, who had actually suffered in Buchenwald, than with a thousand who spoke *in the name* of the sufferers but had suffered nothing themselves. The tortured had no need of introductions. To those critics, who cannot see the genius of Céline because of his repellent anti-Semitism, I can only state that he mightily increased the constricted French language with his argot, as only Rabelais had done before him. Moreover, neither Beckett nor Pinter would have written as they did without his example of the three dots ... between his phrases. He was the prophet of the pause, the chronicler of the cough, the Homer of the lacuna, with every gasp between a few words another gulp for breath in the intermittence of our existence.

ALBERT CAMUS

Camus was to me the apostle and instructor of my university days. His Algerian mother and my South African one never caressed either of us; they did not know how, or thought it was bad for a son. We had a shared colonial background, and we could not come to terms with an imperial heritage. We both appeared to believe that by our actions we were known. We existed without motive, rather at the mercy of sun and circumstance, feeling alien in our borrowed societies. Yet we felt responsible for what we did, even if we did not always know why we had done it. The thing was, as in *La Peste*, to have a *métier*, a reason to live. This could be less than a cause; even the love of one woman was enough. That, too, was a job and a reason for existence.

As I often did, Camus also found living absurd. Such a feeling was not the nausea of Sartre, who thought that the past did not exist, and behind the appearance of things, there was nothingness. Both Frenchmen agreed that all our survival was a mere series of moments; the Marxist Sartre wrote that he 'could no longer distinguish present from future and yet it lasts, little by little.' Yet Camus saw the existential process, not as an excuse for inaction and withdrawal, but as an opportunity for 'my revolt, my freedom and my passion.' For him, 'the present and the succession of presents before a constantly conscious soul is the ideal of the absurd man.'

Given a world so contrary as to allow the Algerian war in his homeland with its interminable massacres and betrayals, Camus rejected violence and terror and all persecuting systems. He was forced to find a reason for the divine in the black farce of the doings of the world. We had a need for God, as we looked for the impossible. Men could reach the possible on their own. God was beyond any rational category, and a belief in Him demanded Ignatius of Loyola's 'Sacrifice of the Intellect'. Even if He was cruel and indifferent, the only escape from absurdity was a feeling for a Being in charge of some sort of man's fate, for good or ill.

In imitation of Camus, I have kept a belief in the soul or spirit, and

I have lived by circumstance rather than in the pursuit of a career. I have left many safe houses and walked through many wrong doors, which have slammed shut behind me. I have suspected all institutions, and I have revolted from some of them. I have always struck out for my freedom, and so I have had the liberty to do almost everything I wished to do. And I have been obsessive about what I was doing at the time, with a reckless passion for action and a few women.

My difference with Camus lay in his reaction against the worth of history, although he valued myth. His home city of Oran appeared to him as the Minotaur, the muffled call of inhuman and glittering forces. For me, the past was a trajectory through time. Solitary, at Delphi or Stonehenge, my eye became the site, one with the ancient ruins and the land. These trances were a long moment of being in time past. And in the writing of my researches, I excluded our wayward society in order to try and experience what was and still is. Unlike Sartre's Antoine Roquentin, I would never give up the biography of the Marquis de Rollebon, because nothing could ever be proved. Causes and strands might be woven into the characters of the dead and their periods of long-gone shuffling on. For retrospect allowed the making of a Penelope's web to put off the critics of my anarchy. And Ulysses did finally come back to Ithaca after all his improbable adventures, before leaving for his end. For all that, I cherished Camus for one of his final statements. 'I am no one's guide. I don't know, or know only dimly, where I am going.' Sartre, alas, saw every sentence of his as an *Oriflamme* and a red flag, or a guillotine.

Other than Camus and Malraux, my French hero was Jean Biche, the code-name he took, when he was in the French *maquis*. Married to my literary agent in Paris, Marie Shebeko, he had served as a fighter pilot in both world wars. When Marshal Pétain surrendered, Jean had commandeered a French destroyer at Bordeaux and had the vessel sailed to Gibraltar, the first craft in the Free French fleet. Dropped back into his homeland to join the Resistance, he was captured by the Gestapo and tortured, but he survived to become a leading representative of Dassault, which made the warplanes to defend the nation. His most haunting story was having to execute a comrade in the *maquis*, because he was betraying the group to the *Fifis*, the Vichy police. Jean shot him in the back of the head, while his friend was pissing. Evidence from his clothing proved his treachery. But was there any? Or did Jean just do his duty?

Jean and Marie used to meet Marianne and myself in the Coupole near the Dôme. He changed my life, not through his courage, but through his manners. One of those old ladies, living on a prayer and no baguette, came to the table, trying to sell three fading yellow roses. Jean took them and gave her a thousand franc note.

'*Impossible, m'sieu,*' she said and began to weep.

'Madame,' he said, 'if I were in your situation, I could not sell my roses with your grace.'

Since then, on many travels round in poor countries, I tried to buy things I did not need from people, who were very much in need. And Jean Biche told me another story about having dinner in the 'twenties in the Coupole. A starving young Italian would come up to him, as he was dining, and show him some sketches of nudes, and ask him to buy one or two. So Jean would give him a bank note and invite him to a meal. Once the artist had gone, Jean would scrunch up the drawings, with his napkin. He did not notice that they were signed by Modigliani.

This same loss of artworks occurred at the little restaurant in our road, Chez Rosalie, in the rue Campagne-Première. For forty years, painters on their uppers thronged the place, from Picasso to Foujita, from Utrillo to Van Dongen. When they could not pay their bills, Rosalie took a picture from them and put them in trunks in her cellars. On her death, everybody expected a hoard of masterpieces. Yet as nearly all the *caves* in Paris were damp and full of rats, all that remained were coloured nests of rodents and wormcasts.

Some of the old artists still survived. I remember meeting the celebrated sculptor Zadkine, who looked like an ancient grounded eagle with his golden eyes flashing with genius, as those of Picasso. In an age before ubiquitous television, he only went to the cinema to see documentaries about nature. When I asked why, he replied, 'I come out with a leaf sticking to my nose.' He also told me about his friend, the emaciated sculptor Giacometti.

'He was also too thin. Like his works. And he never smiled. He said he was bored, bored. The *ennui* did him in. Then one day he breaks his ankle in the gutter in Rome. A little smile, at last. And he says, '*Enfin*, something has happened to me'.'

Of course, Camus was right. Only as we fulfil our *métier* may we have a reason to exist and forget the interminable days.

Haiti, Ho

My head lay on two raised boards. It had already been sliced from my shoulders by some guillotine. Monsieur Dimanche was cutting off my forehead with his axe. White chips of skull, pale shavings of skin stood up under the blade and flew away as distant gulls.

'My hatchet is my paintbrush.'

Each time the axe fell on my forehead, I died a little death. I was sitting five feet away from my own face, which was laid out ceremoniously as the stone mask of a knight on a medieval tomb. My stiff hair seemed a helmet on my brow. My cheeks were drained of blood. I felt myself to be the soul let free from the flesh. I was my own spirit, watching Monsieur Dimanche try to mould the white oak of my death into a decent likeness of my life, good enough to persuade my mourners that my descent into the beyond had not been too unprepared.

Monsieur Dimanche put down his axe. His words had been locked in the log, which he was shaping into my head. Now they poured out of him like the babble of splinters from under a mechanical saw. 'Before you came,' he said, 'I had a dream. I was in despair. Then this monk appears to me, this Eastern monk. There is a great fire in him. He says, "Fly with me." I know I cannot fly. But he takes me by the hand, and I am flying. And the same fire shines out of me.' Monsieur Dimanche laughed. Then he said with great seriousness, 'You are the monk.' Then he picked up his axe again.

Outside the studio, black children in bare feet were begging a brief stay to their hunger. They parroted the mystic phrase, 'Five cents, Joe,' to the passing tourists. Outside, women carried straw hats full of hens and mangos. They squatted, knees akimbo, on the edge of the gutters of Port-au-Prince, to make their few cents of profit on their petty trading each day. Outside, one man in ten could find work in the capital of Haiti – this was depression. When one man in three could find work, it was prosperity.

Marianne and I were staying at the Gingerbread Palace above the city, where Graham Greene also stayed when he wrote about the damnéd island. We were living like a king and queen, dining hugely to the sound of dances called merengues, in the glow of candles set among plucked poinsettias with their bleeding open palms. I was in luxury among poverty. My fasting was an endless gorging. If I was a monk, then my monastery was in the centre of Sybaris. But, in fact, it was set on the rim of the slums.

'I am no monk,' I said. And, as if to prove my words, the axe in the hand of Monsieur Dimanche stuck in the wood. He chipped away two or three times. He was worried. I saw a large knot appear on my left temple. 'I told you I was no monk,' I went on. 'That flaw in the wood is the hole for the left horn of the Devil.'

Monsieur Dimanche shook his head, and continued to chip with his axe. The black blade hacked through the white oak, as arrogant in its sure attack as the victories of the liberators, Toussaint L'Ouverture and Christophe and Dessalines, against the enslaving French one hundred and fifty years before.

'Ah,' Monsieur Dimanche said, appalled. He was cutting back my right temple to the level of the left. As he cut, he uncovered another dark knot in the wood. It was the slot for the second horn of the Devil. There were no other flaws in all the bleach of my face. Only the two blobs high on my forehead, the marks of the Evil One.

'I am a white Devil,' I said. 'Or else my wife is being unfaithful to me in the hotel. Those knots are definitely the places for horns.'

'No, your wife is not unfaithful,' Monsieur Dimanche said.

'Then I am a white Devil,' I said, thinking of Deacon and Marianne.

'No, the monk.'

Monsieur Dimanche put down his axe and lifted my head onto its base. Above my polished nose and cheeks, great troughs of roughness had been hacked into my forehead. Thought seemed to have scratched out my brow with its fingernails. 'Come back tomorrow. I will have smoothed it,' Monsieur Dimanche said.

He had, indeed, made my head. Only there was something about the eyes. They were white blind eggs that could hatch nothing. They did not perceive.

'The eyes,' I said. 'Perhaps they should be more deep-set.'

Monsieur Dimanche took my chin in his right hand and turned my face toward the electric light bulb in the ceiling. 'Yes,' he said. He let go of my head, and began to draw on my wooden eyes with a red pencil. The oak bled with false pink wounds. 'Tomorrow we will finish that.'

As I reached the veranda of the Gingerbread Palace, I heard a commotion behind me. There was a threat of song. There was the grunt of a conch shell, rhythmically blowing. There were lights, the flowing torches of revolt. A long column of shaking men was coming up the drive, like the battalions of slaves from the Bois Caï-man, where the ceremony of the severed pig had sent them out, avenging gods from Guinea, to break their brothers' gyves and to burn the sugar plantations of France. Were they risen again, sick of the slavery of want? I felt myself alone, ridiculous, imperialist, damned by skin and mind and income to misunderstanding unto death.

A waiter went out to meet the column. Uncle Tom to the dark tower came. And the column unexpectedly turned away, obedient as a crocodile of schoolchildren, and honked its jigging way down the drive. The waiter returned. He explained that the whole thing was merely a Rara procession. Each year groups danced to chase away the evil voodoo spirits, the *loas*. There was nothing to the whole thing.

Yet throughout the night-time city, voodoo priests were drinking the blood of a headless cock, as it flapped its wings in a last spasm while the priest drained it dry. There were five thousand shamans in Port-au-Prince alone, more in the plains outside. Each dawn, the cocks crowed the day awake. Each night, their bodies were ceremonial bottles, burned after use. At this frequent blood sacrifice, the murder at the heart of Haiti was appeased. The machetes that hung at every belt needed no further victim. The rest of life was in the hands of *le ton Dieu bon*. The voodoo and Roman Catholic priests assured men so. Thus, the gnawing anger of the land was eased by the ritual killing of fowls, by the resigned belief that God would provide, and by the laughter that can outface despair. Only the daily labour, or the search for it and for food, was not to be escaped. As they worked, the men reminded each other of the Creole proverb, 'If work were really such a good thing, the rich would have taken it all long ago.'

I thought of these things on the veranda of the Gingerbread Palace, and I could see only revolution ahead. A sudden spatter of rain fired a volley on the roof. The repeating rifles of the drops stuttered their requiems. Haiti has only two seasons, the season of dust and the season of mud. This was the muddy season, and it rained each evening for one hour. Somewhere beyond the horizon, real rifles were coughing out men's lives, and corpses lay along the beaches of Cuba. Revolution and counterrevolution, rich and poor, each for each and all against all – must that be the way of the Caribbean? Only the Dimanches of the world were excused from these considerations. To him, I was a monk and Haiti was a heaven.

The next morning, Monsieur Dimanche took Marianne and me up to his studio in the mountains. His head bobbed at the level of our shoulders. He shook with the ecstasy of showing his secret place to strangers. We walked up the hill, past the careful villas that aped in stucco and tile the kempt Rivieras that girdle the beaches of the world.

After a quarter of an hour we reached a mountain village, where mud huts with roofs made from the dried heads of sugarcane brought Africa a step away from suburbia. Below us, men were working in the fields, at the sugar harvest. They moved in a long line, swinging their machetes against the stilts of their giant enemies.

- One sweep of the machete clears the tangle about the cane
- Another cuts the cane eight feet from the ground
- A third amputates the cane at the ankle
- Two stripping rips, one up and one down
- Flay the cane alive from the scabs of dead leaves
- Flick the left hand, holding the long spear
- Swing the right hand and cut with the machete
- Economy of motion that is all of grace

Behind the cutters, women and boys tied the cane in bundles and gathered the heads. The incredible industry of the hacking men in front left no room for pause. Each man should cut two tons of cane in a day. For this, he might earn the small fortune of a quarter of a dollar. Indeed, *le ton Dieu bon*.

Monsieur Dimanche took me gently by the arm. 'Always our great thinker,' he said, laughing. 'Please come in.' He led us into a hut that was narrow and long. It was divided into two partitions. The first was piled with logs and roots, some roughly shaped into

Madonnas, loas, serpents, grotesques, and Devils. Yellow almond wood, brown wood, white wood, red wood all lay together waiting for the finishing of his hand. Only his final choice would discriminate among them.

On our return, Monsieur Dimanche finished his work on my head. He began to gouge at my eyes, as they lay on the boards beneath him. But he did not like the position. So he called in one of his many sons and apprentices, who were always at their carving, the finished ebony of their bodies a reproach to the rough logs in their hands.

My head was stood on its base and tilted backward. Dimanche's son put his two palms in front of his forehead, and used this living stay to support the back of my skull at the angle needed for his father's work. The line of his body made one side of a Gothic arch, such as points the way to the scrolled heavens of the roofs of medieval cathedrals. The other side of the arch was made by the leg of the table and my head, joined by the whiteness of their wood. Ebony and oak, the living bearing up the dead, both equal and necessary – the miracle of the visual symbol was too apt. I smiled, while Monsieur Dimanche gouged at my wooden eyes that I might see.

'Monsieur Dimanche,' I said, 'in this land where all the colours are so bright and ready, is there no colour problem?'

'There are some who would have it so,' Monsieur Dimanche said. 'They would stir up the blacks against the mulattos for political reasons. They are sick in their minds and see things so. But it is not true. *Mon cher*, we are all here to help each other. You come to me. You bring me luck. Should I believe such silly things? We are all men.'

He dug the pits of my eyes deeper. His knife seemed to be searching for a canker in my mind. Small cysts of wood were falling down my cheeks onto the floor.

'You are right,' I said. 'We are all men.' With this admission, I entered the world of Monsieur Dimanche. I was baptized in the simplicity and the strength of his art and his beliefs. The sympathy of his opinions was a surprise and a shock. And now he was scraping and shaping my reborn eyes. The point of his gouge was tracing the ridge of my eyelids, was digging the holes of my pupils. He worked for half an hour. Nothing was said. I basked in the easy answers of the faith of Monsieur Dimanche. At last, he stood back.

My eyes were defined now, two ash leaves of peace under the branch of my brow. The face which Monsieur Dimanche saw in me, the face of the monk, the face of still melancholy and quiet acceptance, this face I could imagine as the perfect mask of my own. My flesh was at fault. My wooden face was more truly myself. Yet it was still dead in its white oak. 'It is a wonderful resemblance,' I said to Monsieur Dimanche. For the statue at last seemed to be me.

Of course, I was not what he saw in me or sculpted: I was merely giving him the dollars he had to have to live at all. Yet it was a truly testing time. We met an opposition family of the old Creole aristocracy, which had ruled Haiti before Duvalier and his slogan: *LE NOIR DUVALIER AU POUVOIR*. I had boasted that I knew people in the new Kennedy Administration in the United States. I was given some two hundred detailed pages of the recent tortures and killings of the dissidents in the island, and I was told that the old Eisenhower Administration still maintained a detachment of Marines at Port-au-Prince to bolster the regime. I put this evidence among the leaves of my papers, prepared to saunter with it through Haitian Customs, in the blitheness of my folly.

Then the Berlin crisis came upon us. The rains dripped down, long and silver, on the thatch restaurant of the Gingerbread Palace. There were southern planters there as well as the killer security *Tonton Macoute* spies. I was gloomily considering how far the two hundred dollars in my pocket would take us towards South America, before the nuclear rain began the following day. Could we beat this fall-out to another tropic? But as the Suez crisis, it ended in a farce. Khrushchev blustered; Kennedy saw him out; the Berlin Wall went up; the air-lift to the besieged city soared in. Another necessity became a jest of decision. We flew back to Miami, and the thorough Haitian Customs officials, searching my baggage, did not look through the pages of my manuscript. After all, they spoke French, and why the hell should they leaf through this nonsense in a lesser language?

We returned to the United States without a fuss, and I went to see Arthur Schlesinger, one of my professors at Harvard who had a niche within the Kennedy circle. We met at a safe house in Massachusetts, and I showed him my evidence from Haiti. I asked him to withdraw the American Marines, until there was some social justice there. And incredibly, it happened. My foolish and presumptuous voice may have changed American policy in a tiny way. Then I believed that we still lived in a time where a Lone Ranger could have an infinitesimal influence on global policy, at least in America. Democracy might work.

We sailed home on a French liner, the old *Liberté*. To us, the ship appeared to be well named after the freedom of the radical spirit. We could do things that might change things. Many years later, I said to the poet Christopher Logue that the American Revolution was the first of all European revolutions. No, he insisted, it happened after the French Revolution. All the history books in the world, I said, would prove that it happened ten years before the French experiment. 'I'm interested in the truth,' he said, deflating me, 'not the facts.' At that time, the truth seemed to be that Kennedy had rekindled the radical hope in the world, and that France, with its extraordinary historians and philosophers of youth and existentialism, was not far behind. The American President, however, was on his way to be murdered, and France to another undone urban revolution. The facts were that they failed, while the truth, whatever it might be, still had to be found.

THE BEATS AND A CONTINENT

Following my grant to Stanford University to write a book on the early decades of the struggle for the rights of American women, Marianne and I sailed for New York. There, on New Year's Eve, we were asked by the writer Joyce Carol Oates to a party in a block of apartments with a plate-glass shatter-proof door near Columbia University.

While I was chatting to a cadaverous actress, who was playing the whorehouse madam in Genet's *The Balcony* and was introduced as a whorehouse madam and looked like a whorehouse madam – nature imitating artifice – Norman Mailer made an entrance with a Brooklyn minder and the second of his serial wives, Adele Morales, whom he had stabbed a week before, missing her heart by inches. He had been committed to the Bellevue mental wards, she had not preferred charges, and now she was egging him on to a challenge to fisticuffs or arm-wrestling with cries of, 'Why don't you give 'em a lecture on murder, Normie?'

The minder propositioned every unavailable woman with four-letter invitations, Mailer failed to get into a fight, and when the trio left, we all heard the splintering of the indestructible door, and the siren song of Mailer's wife, 'Normie didn't do it, I swear, Normie didn't do it.' Normie said he didn't and the minder swore blind that nobody had done nothing, so they walked off into the night, leaving our Southern hostess to pick up the pieces. I was quite cured of my previous admiration for Mailer's invitations to take on the American dream.

Another assault by Mailer was at a later party in New York. The epicene Gore Vidal had insulted Norman in some review or chat show, and so the aggrieved one used a fist to make his point and dotted Vidal smartly on the nose. Blood now flowed where hearts then bled. Kneeling and staunching the wound in his nostrils with a silk handkerchief, Vidal fell back on a chintzy sofa. Then Truman Capote pranced up and plucked the claret trophy from the fallen author, and he waved the crimson rag in front of all of us, shrilling,

'Gore's gore! Gore's gore!' But the bleeding victim had the last laugh with the riposte: 'Words fail Norman Mailer yet again.'

Vidal later claimed to have been at a dinner party with Greta Garbo. She was wearing trousers and a blue blazer with brass buttons, and she asked if she might visit 'The Boys' Room'. When she returned, the awed spectators visited the lavatory, and indeed, the seat was raised. This episode reminded me of the extravagant bohemian painter Waldo Peirce, who had to relieve himself in a winter wood near the Bois de Boulogne, in the company of two dykes. In the snow, he inscribed his signature with the flourish of his piss. 'I bet you can't do that,' he told the ladies. Perhaps Garbo could.

Thirty years on, at dinner at the Garrick Club, Norman Mailer appeared as avuncular, dressed in a three-piece suit and a weskit and watch chain across his expansive tummy. He had survived six wives and their alimony along with nine children, although he had to make a million dollars yearly to service their demands. And so he had given up rebellion, as older men often must. Past lust becomes present dust. So genius may founder in the blood payment of old misapprehensions. As he finally declared, 'What you didn't succeed in doing, you didn't succeed in doing. So fuck it.'

As for considering his past, Mailer admired Günther Grass for finally admitting in *Peeling the Onion* to have been a member of the Waffen-SS during the Second World War. Yet he, too, had held onto something for so long that he might never record it. 'It seems to me that stabbing my wife, Adele, is probably what I will never write about.'

I had found in Manhattan the most brilliant and critical minds that I had met, even at Harvard. Higher education seemed to sharpen the wits. The professors and their assistants at Columbia University, the New York publishers and museum curators, the artists and the actors, appeared to be able to temper an intense Americanism with a certain worldliness and regret from Central Europe, as though their tongues were full of old honey scraped from the bottom of a new jar with a switchblade. But they were all under the extreme pressure of life in this insane metropolis. Although Hemingway had defined genius as grace under pressure, this forced display of intelligence under the stress of earning enough to live well threatened to burst the cooker and blow the lid.

Our best friend there had killed himself, because of the corruption of his success, with sleeping-pills in front of his ten-year-old daughter who became my ward. As her guardian I advised her mother to pull the child out of her school in Central Park, where drug pushers already besieged the gates, and to return to England, if she wanted her daughter to survive the appalling trauma which her father had inflicted on her.

Of my two principles in life, the first is the most important: *Never harm the innocent*. The second follows from it: *κινέι ως 'ερώμενον*, Aristotle's words: *Move towards what you love*, and so encourage society to give all its citizens the opportunity to move towards what they love. The young were doing that, anyway, without the helping hand of the authorities in the 'sixties. But our leaders and our friends were still being struck down, as if we lived in plague years. Both of my editors and friends in New York, Roger Klein and Peter Ritner, were soon to commit suicide from metropolitan pressure and the judgement of an age, in which a publisher could hardly come out of the closet or the loss of his Gold Credit Card. Death still seemed to be our cloud.

We bought a green-and-white ancient Pontiac, and we began to wander free and slightly afraid. 'The pleasure and horror of living in the trunk of a car,' my diary also stated, 'is to find out that we can shrug off things, dear things, all possessions. We can live in no-time and no-place without dead-lines – in the past of research or in the infinite present – and we discover that all we miss are five or six people we have left in Europe. We would blow over the earth, dirt in the wind, if love of friends did not make us mud.' The rolling wheels and unravelling highways did reel the spools of our minds, until we came to the Mardi Gras in New Orleans. As the fifteen flamboyant floats of the Krewes came by, the capering shapes on them were dressed as Greek gods, with masked faces. We, the people, howled at them, 'Throw me something, mister,' stretching our imploring arms. And the gods of the Krewes threw down beads and necklaces and plastic alligators and purple rabbits with winking eyes – baubles for their screeching beseechers. Behind them, the drum majorettes swaggered their Lolita bums and the brass bands played and the motor-cycles sang their sirens to the crowd, and the last of the lost of the old jazz bands played, little old men blowing their horns and banging their drums in black suits, like the Scots tribesmen I came from, with only two tunes – a celebration or a lament, a stomp or a blues.

Driving across America was to sew together a continent by road-signs. How many more miles to El Paso or Albuquerque, to Reno or San Francisco? The numbers dwindled, the Rockies loomed. When once more, it was proved that the east coast did connect to the west, I thought dear old Bishop Berkeley was proved right. Maps were no good. I had to affirm the flip seaside of the United States personally, otherwise it might only exist in the mind of God. It was my good luck that in that other Berkeley to the east of the Bay Bridge, there were new beginnings, in the revolt of free speech, and the search for the liberty of the spirit through psychedelic drugs.

— On the go thru Texas it's the oil embargo
— I have forgot the national speed limit double nickels
— No cars for miles so its 75 I'm doin
— Out of a mesquite bush, the black Lone Ranger
— Seven foot tall and hardface under his Stetson bonnet
— The turquoise winks on the bonegrip of Colt revolver
— Walk over to the flash lights of the patrol car
— Approach the bear before he comes to you and smile
— Show him my British licence and my New York plates
— Maybe not a fine but I'll get a warnin
— Now sure he smiling and sayin to me Sir
— Your pants are split way down to your back legs
— Sudden breeze up my bum and I know it's fright
— Shrieking at him Oh my God indecent exposure
— Big bear begin to laugh and I won't be busted
— Back to the station to tell of bareass limey
— Ahm turnin you loose sayin and he does so

Further along the route, we saw the Apocalypse, or a fair idea of it, towards Montana. We went in under twin black cyclones arching darkly over the highway with their pillars of cloud on either side and the sun shining towards the west. But when we were approaching the place of Custer's Last Stand at the Little Big Horn, we ran into the tail of a thunderhead coming down a pass. It was like being in the beard of a giant grey buffalo with lightning forking the fringes of the sky beast's hanging hair.

Then we reached the flat and the rain stopped and the low sun stood to the right, balancing itself beneath the cloud and the low hills. It threw a lurid tiger-skin across the land, until the screes and the buttes were livid yellow against the black rearing sky, the sage-brush was luminous green and strips of coal backed the outcrops lying between us and the sun.

Just before reaching San Francisco, we heard of a mass sit-in at Berkeley, followed by many arrests and the surrender of the faculty, which declared that free speech on any topic including revolution was tolerable on campus. With these constitutional rights won, the students there were beginning to demand power, just as the con-stricted Beat movement was starting to expand into the global cult of the Hippies. Our guide was the thin and wise, wide-eyed and yellow-brushmopped Stewart Brand, whom we had first met as a GI photographer in Soho Square through a mutual friend. He had told us of sky-diving, 'like the first cold separation at birth, a free fall into being alone with another free fall near, an even colder sep-aration into death.'

We set up shop in an empty apartment on Vallejo Street off North Beach and under Telegraph Hill, furnished for a hundred dollars with a bed and a table and chairs from the Salvation Army, all painted white. The second-hand cost nothing in the United States, which only wanted the new; food and wine were half the price they were in Europe; this land was a cut-price paradise. Among the metal jams of the tailfins of the automobiles in the adjoining car park, an old Chinaman denied his age with precise callisthenics.

Across the street was a commune, and there was living again our friend Stewart Brand, who was to become one of Ken Kesey's Merry Pranksters and the founder and the undertaker of *The Whole Earth Catalog*. But now he was experimenting in the future with a young Ottawa Indian woman called Lois, who wore a silver disc in the middle of her forehead, and Tom, who had played in the Atomic Band of the US Army before nuclear explosions and dropping out, also a Pre-Raphaelite Jesus Christ, who could fix the third gear of your truck quicker than your head.

The use of hallucinogenic drugs to achieve a further reality had already spread from Timothy Leary's pioneering psychological experiments at Harvard, and LSD and marijuana had reached the Beats through Allen Ginsberg and others of the City Lights Book-shop congregation. The Californian poets had experimented before Leary: Michael McClure, in *Scratching the Beat Surface*, recalled Francis

Crick from Churchill College buying one of the hundred-and-fifty copies of his *Peyote Poem* in 1958 and including two lines from it in his book about discovering biogenetics, *Of Molecules and Men*:

THIS IS THE POWERFUL KNOWLEDGE
we smile with it

To McClure, the use of this verse showed the important reaching out from science to poetry and from poetry to science that was part of the Beat movement and would be part of the Hippie surge. As a Christmas card, Stewart Brand was to send me a drawing of the starry night sky with a round hole in the middle and the query, 'Why haven't we seen a photograph of the whole Earth yet?'

So I would in the future, but my first introduction to his new culture was a commemoration of the death of Aldous Huxley, when I was assured by the local commune and its Berkeley friends that dozens of them had accompanied the British prophet of science and magic mushrooms on his last trip beyond the moon by the use of hallucinogens that he had recommended. Later, beside an extraordinary night bonfire on Stinson Beach, the spirits of the Shamans were called up by Carlos Castaneda and various Indian friends with green shapelessnesses appearing from the flames as banshees, reminding me of the old Scottish inscription:

All is botgastis and eldritch fantasies:
Of brownies and bogillis full this buke.

To recover, the Beats used to congregate in the Co-Existence Bagel Café down the hill towards Chinatown, where a double-bill was always playing in the family cinema. Gazelle-footed Chinese maidens kicked the hell out of sorcerers and assorted thugs, while the main item was a wicked Emperor torturing a peasant hero, looking for his kidnapped love, and saved by the intervention of a divine warrior. Best was the City Lights Bookshop, from where the lanky poet Lawrence Ferlinghetti orchestrated the whole Beat movement, though unable to keep the bearded Allen Ginsberg from screeching his 'Howl' all over the city. An enchanted year, really, before all would be trashed by the Hippies and the drug culture, and Haight-Ashbury become the poor kids' slow killing-ground. Where smack and crack go in, crime follows, and Utopia and Shangri-La are puffed into Bedlam and Newgate and the charnel house.

I had no time to take psychedelic drugs and lose my mind. I had two books to write – a biography of America's least and worst President, Warren Gamaliel Harding, as well as the book on women's rights. The study of Harding was called *The Available Man* and showed how the insignificant and the incompetent could rise to the greatest office on earth by being the chosen compromise and the glad-hander without enemies. It added to my growing disillusion about the power of anyone to put into effect political reform.

The book on women's rights, *The Better Half*, also seemed to show that the long Victorian battle for the vote had lost its ideals when emancipation was achieved. Its success was the failure of its hope. But I did prophesy that just as the first struggle for feminism was begun by women supporting the rights of black men in the south, so the new women upholding the freedom riders and Martin Luther King's campaign for black equality would end by demanding their own fulfilment. Certainly, the politics of protest were livelier at Berkeley than they were on the Aldermaston marches. How could mediocre politicians change anything that was in doubt? With our young leaders dead in their prime, what would we hope to achieve?

Even our fear of nuclear death seemed to induce a creeping detachment. In the commune over the way, Tom told me the strange story of how he had become a drop-out, the prototype of the hippies, many of whom adopted their new style of life as he had in a protest against the wealthy conformity of their middle-class homes. Drafted into the army, he had found himself in a special military band in Nevada, because of his ability to play the horn. Their detail was to march out onto the white desert flats and line up facing a row of empty gilt seats, as in the opening of the Ionesco play *The Chairs*. Generals and Pentagon officials would appear from Jeeps and nowhere to provide an audience, while the band played 'The Star-Spangled Banner'. Then an almighty blast would detonate from behind their backs, and the bandsmen would drop their instruments one by one, in spite of orders to play on and never turn to view what blew to the rear. Yet they would look backward to see a vast mushroom of smoke spreading across the blue heaven.

An alternative to political responsibility was being offered in California as the Situationists would suggest in Paris and Huizinga had written in *Homo Ludens*. The power of play might alter society. South of San Francisco, in Perry Lane, in Palo Alto and then in a log cabin in a redwood forest gorge near La Honda, Ken Kesey was gathering his Pranksters together before setting out on his rainbow-painted Hieronymus Bosch of an International Harvester school bus. Theirs was a continental trip of the mind and the body, fuelled more by psychedelic drugs than gasoline, travelling across the frontiers of the senses and the states. They played games with the cops and the laws; they mocked authority and pissed on probity; and they were to find their dandy scribe in Tom Wolfe's *The Electric Kool-Aid Acid Test*, which was like Heisenberg's Uncertainty Principle in trying to describe a phenomenon after it had already moved on.

Seeking such an inner journey and a serene detachment as we left San Francisco, Marianne and I accepted a gift of an LSD solution in a tiny glass bottle with a cork stopper in return for all our Salvation Army furniture. We intended to take the drug in the Arizona desert, in Navajo or Hopi country, to see whether we might enter their ancient dreams. I had already set myself what I called the hardest question in my diary. Should I gratify my urge to live and develop myself or should I try to help others in general? 'The crippling egotism of wishing to write or the sense of continued failure of trying to do some good. To be proud or to lose – is there another choice?' A refuge in detachment was being offered. As a new Candide, I was being told to cultivate my karma rather than my garden. But when we reached the unearthly and solitary dream landscape of a dry creek near Monument Valley, we found that the cork had blown and the volatile genie had fled the bottle.

We lay down anyway and apart. And without a drug, both of us had our first trip through time. With our heads pillowed on bleached rocks, we were – or seemed to be – the split and curved and weathered shapes about us. We were sky, dust, stone. Hours were minutes or no time at all. And afterwards, since we were sleeping most nights in the Pontiac, looking through the car windows at mesas and stars to wake in the silence and sun, we were reaching a new understanding at last, which we found at the Bandelier National Monument. We looked through tall trees and over a stream at the large ruins of an ancient pueblo of cliff-dwellers. This time, as we lounged on the grass in the sun, we were both conscious of our flesh. I peered forward and saw the tip of my nose. I framed the cliff dwellings with a crooked arm to block the brightness. I was seeing pictures logically. I felt myself a pipe of food and shit with the mind separate. Only the inward closed eye saw no flesh. Here the Indian symbols were the essence of things: cloud, deer, rain, thunder, life.

And beyond the cliffs we knew was Los Alamos, where the atomic revolution had plotted its primary explosions. We had visited the White Sands by Alamogordo. These were under snow, white on whiteness. The gypsum dunes were a lost and solitary world, but on each side of them was a Missile Range – 'the largest testing ground in the free world', in the words of the local advertisements. By Alamogordo, the first atom bomb had been detonated to begin our age, pale cloud over mineral waste. 'The sands advance,' I had written, 'the era recedes, by inches.' While we stood alone on a dune, a rocket had been launched beyond the crested mountains. A long roar, a reverberate clapping, no noise, a bleach of space, an end of the world.

Remembering this, we went on to the San Ildefonso Pueblo. Among these log and adobe cabins, we found the studio of Maria Martinez and her son, a noble and sure man. We talked of art, of how the toy canoe with the water painted on its side was a canoe in water, of how the celebrated blue Egyptian hippopotamus with lilies painted on his flanks was a hippopotamus in a lily pool by the Nile. We bought a silver box with the essence or symbol of a turquoise deer in a forest on the outside. I still did not understand. We visited the museums of Santa Fe, and then we drove out to the Great Sand Dunes. It was cold and night. We were alone in the campground in early May. We lit a fire. The dry wood flared. I looked into the flames. I saw red deer skulls with branched antlers of yellow. The fire was not like red deer skulls with antlers of yellow; the fire was red deer skulls with antlers of yellow. The thing seen with the inward eye through the outward eye was the thing. A great bird with forked wing and tail was black in the blue night sky. Wonder was sight.

If I emphasize these experiences, it is because they did change my awareness and my diary still tells me that I felt it there and then. T.S. Eliot's understanding had come true. Time past and present and future were all the same. In that flow, competition was as meaningless as destiny. There was still opportunity, but that was a question of chance, not of will. This applied even to the possibility of political change. Necessity had struck down our leaders of hope. God only knew if and when any others might take their place.

And so we drove back from the American West to take a French liner back to England. I had been offered another job before my insight, teaching American history and political philosophy at University College in London. And Deacon had his craving for Marianne on the far side of the ocean. Before casting off across the Atlantic, we visited Rockport in Maine, where I had my last lesson about the interplay between humanity and nature.

I met a fisherman, who thought the folks were selfish there, because of his friend, a seal, which would sleep on the cushions of their pleasure boats.

'I went diving undersea,' he explained. 'And then this seal pup follows me up on shore. Thought I was her mother. She had lost her own. So I become her mother, feed her on a bottle. Then we go diving together. What a diver! Better than any man. Then we play water basket-ball together. And she hits the hoop five times I do. How can folks hate her because she likes a warm sleep like we all do?'

He was silent for a while, but I said nothing, for it was his story.

'We go swimming one day,' the Rockport man said, 'and I lose her. Where has she gone? How could she leave me? Maybe she had to go back to her own, even though she had me. Then two weeks on, I read in a paper, all the way from Connecticut, that's two hundred miles from hereabouts, a seal comes out of the water on a play beach, and she sits there, and she claps her flippers, and she wants fish to be given her. So I know it's her, and I go down there and I bring her home. She is badly bit all over, the wild seals don't like her being with me, but she heals good, and we're back on the diving and the ball games. And what do you know? After the fall, she has a daughter, so we raise her between us. And it's a better ball game. I got my daughter to help me against Mother.'

The Rockport man fell silent again. I said nothing. Then he said: 'Folks say to me, why aren't you married? And I say, I got Mother and baby seal. And they say it's not natural. And I say, what's natural? They sure are better company than some.'

YOUNG MAN RIVER

Fading from *Kind Hearts and Coronets*, which I later published among a series of classic screenplays, Robert Hamer made *The Long Memory*. Beautifully photographed by the Kent Marshes, where Derek Jarman would meet his end with his waste garden, the film starred John Mills, a man imprisoned for twelve years and seeking revenge on his grasses, but finding that vengeance was not worth it, when it came to the point of the knife.

The strange and scuttling film producer Théodora Olembert asked me, as an introduction to the film industry, to write a script for the alcoholic director Hamer. We were then living in Limehouse on the Thames as well as living in an attic in Soho Square, so I concocted another Thames thriller, called *Fog on the River*, my first professional screenplay, although, as I was to learn, I would not be paid for it. I only remember its theme song:

Fog on the river
Fog on the sea
The fog forever
Lies on me.

Theodora did, however, introduce me to the jovial John Terry of the National Film Finance Corporation, and without his later help, I would never have been able to make my best film, *Under Milk Wood*.

Broke and drunk, Hamer was directed by Theodora to my top flat at 17 Soho Square. Could I look after him for a few days? Meeting a balding noble wreck, rolling around outside, Hamer told me he was being divorced and made bankrupt. He dropped a last half-crown, which rolled in the gutter. 'Leave it,' he said grandly. 'It's no use now.' Moving into one of our four little rooms, he drank everything down to *eau de cologne* without giving any thanks to us. His favourite story was how he had been best man at a society wedding, and his speech opened with the words: 'I am unique. I have slept with both the bride and the groom.' A failed pitiful assault on my wife Marianne, while I was away teaching at Cambridge, made me throw him out. I never saw him again. He was dead some weeks later. At the end of his tether, as others on the river.

Where the cranes are tall and fine
And the lamp-light doesn't shine
Where the docks are dark and wet
And the mud will never set
Where a dream is dark as sin
And you'd rather lose than win
Let me in – Let me in –

Jacky Stocking, waiting in the night
Jacky Stocking, keeping out of sight
Careful how you go, dear
'Cos you never know, dear
Someone's just behind, dear
Never you mind, dear
There's nothing you can do,
Jacky Stocking will take good care of you.

Because of romantic feelings about the incredible city of London, I had always wanted to live in Soho and the docks and the Parks, by a Bohemia and the river and the green. Owned by Mrs Fisher, a bargee Queen with cheroot and pin-striped suit and monocle, I discovered in 1964 an abandoned terrace in Narrow Street on the Thames in Limehouse. Blitzed in the Second World War, the dwellings had been built in the eighteenth century by brick and beam, mortar and timber.

I was seduced by the view from the six derelict houses, which still had the barge-builders operating from the remains. The buildings were set on a wharf on an outer bend of the Thames, so that the eye was carried by the sweep of river towards Greenwich on the left and Tower Bridge on the right. Facing me across the Thames, two factory chimneys made a rifle's foresight to aim the view, while day-and-night sounds of machinery and wreaths of smoke flew with the gulls and the swans over the water from the working of ENTHOVEN and ESSO on Lavender Wharf. Around them, gutted ruins from the blitz, and a rubbish tip, where trucks emptied wastes down canvas chutes into lighters to be towed away.

On either side of the river, warehouses squatted and bulked below the arms and torsos of the cranes, which were spiders in the blue fog of the morning or else were dragonflies in the low slant of the evening sun. Below, on the north foreshore, the long coffins of the Thames barges had slats over their maws and red-painted decks, still the same size as the galleons, which had been made there in the first Queen Elizabeth's time, when Walter Raleigh had sent ships off to found Roanoke, and when the whole of North American history had been a dream of adventurers seeking El Dorado from this East End of London town.

Scrubby tugs also lay on the gravel bank, their hatches lime-green, navy-blue-funnelled, rust-arsed and ready for reconditioning to leave a cleaner wake. At the end of the buildings, the back of a pub called *The Grapes* (Charles Dickens drank here) and beyond, another great chimney of a power station, smutting the air so that black rain fell on the twin giant cranes that walked away downriver into the last light, two red lamps shining at the edge of their platform. To the west, the river crooked its vein into the heart of the City, with a Wren church spire pushing up its white bill in the midst of a nest of the iron-boned cranes. On the rim, Tower Bridge held up its two manacled wrists, while the street-lamps dressed themselves in single file to confine the water o'nights.

Such mystery and brutality of place, such stark demand of beauty, such harsh vision, made me decide to keep a hidden place there for my writing. And when the long narrow studio was finished, with its white-painted pine walls leading out to a balcony that jutted over the tidal Limehouse Reach, I could stand on my rope-caulked deck of beams and steer like Captain Ahab towards the two chimneys across the river, when the storms hammered at the skylights and the barges banged against the wooden watergate of the house, trembling like HMS *Victory* at anchor before Trafalgar.

Then I knew why I was there, playing the sea-dog at the muddy ditch from where England had grown to Empire, black factories, coal-dark bricks, iron ships, the docks of London, where any sailor could drop down in the fo'c'sle in a cone of yellow light from the deck lamps and begin as Conrad's Marlow to say: 'A funny thing happened to me on my way to Penang last voyage...'

I would watch the great cargo ships from the four corners of the world, as they were towed beside the wharves by the tugs. Sometimes I saw a couple of floating cranes move slowly past, hanging the low sun on the gibbets of their frame, the *London Hercules* and the *London Titan*, as Lady Life-in-Death's skeletal ship in *The Ancient Mariner*. Once I saw a red-sailed Thames lugger, drifting a bloody patch towards Greenwich; once a four-masted clipper training ship; once even a painted galleon, again as the craft of Samuel Taylor Coleridge, mysteriously making towards the sea without noise or sails, by opening the air in front and closing it behind, presumably set on course for the new silvermines of film sets in Spain.

Most evenings, in the decay of trade and night and main, there were just some bumping tugs, pulling strings of barges loaded with bales of old paper, or a few lighters croaking their way across to France, or some navy cadets toiling at the oars in whalers on water too dirty even for a shrimp to survive in, or perhaps cold youths in racing-sculls, which made a plaything of this foul river that had once floated counter-Armadas. For the little diesel freighters of rebuilt Rotterdam were now taking most of the trade of the continent away from the London docks, as Europe slowly began to unite and Britain stayed in her cold island, waiting for destiny to visit again, giving her another opportunity, or else carrying her away.

Limehouse was, indeed, the finale of the imperial theatre, its docks deserted, half its houses fallen into a wasteland of bomb-sites, a whole generation of dockers neglected by even Labour governments, which knew what a safe seat it was for Clement Attlee in the House of Commons. If violence was the theme of the time, this slum certainly was rich in aggressions, with memories of the Chinese gang wars and Jack the Ripper's murders and now the bully-boys of Cable Street and the Kray brothers, still terrorizing the turf of rubble. The local version of shooting grouse on moors was potting rats with air-rifles on the gravel foreshore or cornering them with terriers in the barges, where the excitement of the bloodbath led to one famous docker biting off the heads of the rodents – until his false teeth slipped.

There was none of the proletarian nostalgia of Arnold Wesker's plays in the East End. The dockers all marched for Enoch Powell, when he warned against the rising tide of immigration to Britain. 'What, Andrew,' they said to me in the pub, 'you never shared a toilet with them?' I had not often, but when I pointed out there must be only three or four immigrants among the ten thousand registered London dockers, many of whom had worked on unloading ships for generations, they thought I had missed the point. They wanted to have no competition, to keep things as they were. And I knew that the word 'comrade' did not always extend beyond the White Cliffs of Dover.

Narrow Street was the first riverside private development in the East End of London and would prophesy the regeneration of the docklands, which began twenty years later to produce the giant cigar cases of Canary Wharf. One of my neighbours, a young doctor named David Owen, would become a politician and a peer and split the Labour Party, which had denied Limehouse for so long. But this beginning of a move from the middle of London to the peripheries and the world of the working classes was being paralleled all over the country. I was, however, not a property developer. I believed in co-operative housing. Keeping one of the six houses in Narrow Street for myself, I gave away the other five ruins at cost price to young professionals. The price then was £3,000 pounds each, for premises now worth a cool two million quid, as they turn their sheeted glass fronts on the reflecting river.

When, however, there was a planning objection, Owen disappeared over the horizon from his obligation. After I had solved the problem, Owen returned.

'How much will it cost now, Andrew?'

'Still, three thousand,' I said – and he was a Foreign Secretary to come, responsible for taking us into wars and such. 'But, David, I will never serve in a trench with you.'

More remarkable and a bonny fighter was another doctor from St Thomas' Hospital. As I had, so Michael Barraclough had an insane passion for rebuilding ruins; I was to do so three times more, he twice. Writing my mythical novel *Gog*, I heard rather a clatter below. I went down to find that Michael had demolished much of the party wall beneath. He stood, grinning, in the gap, among the dust and the fallen bricks.

'Michael,' I said, 'you've knocked down the wall. You didn't even ask me.'

'No,' he said. 'But I was saving you.'

'Saving? Now the whole house will fall down.'

'Ah, there's the point. The wall was falling. And now I can repair it for you.'

What can you do, except love a man like that, with his impeccable logic? A journalist, called Carole d'Albiac, came to interview me at the time. Her description was most accurate.

He lives in a flat in Soho Square and a house in Limehouse, which he is converting, surrounded by the Belle Époque; toy Japanese soldiers, busts of famous feminists, Lautrec posters, musical boxes and instruments, a black mobile paper bird, old watches that he is making into a musical box, horses from fairgrounds, more posters. He wears old clothes in sombre colours, doesn't always bother to shave, drives an old mini-van, drinks whisky. His conversation is scattered with quotations – within a few hours from Plato, Simone de Beauvoir, Sartre, Freud, Kennedy, Mary Wollstonecraft, Conrad, Proust, Marx. He needs to eat and sleep less frequently than most people. He likes to be alone and discover his natural rhythm. When he is tired of sitting in one room writing, watching ships go by and the light on the water, he knocks down a wall, moves earth or plans a room. He listens intently to what people are saying, looks very mournful if the conversation is not intelligent, and very cross if, at the end of an argument, his opponent says he doesn't believe in argument, anyway.

At that time, a Cambridge friend, the playwright Michael Frayn, said of me, 'He's craggy. His long, rather sad face, lights up and becomes animated. He's very telegenic. I always thought that, like Jonathan Miller, he had the power, when you were discussing something, to make it romantic.' I doubt any small screen presence, but I am incurably romantic. And I have always tried to make a practical matter of my reveries.

My wife Marianne also said that of me. 'He isn't satisfied to leave hopes, projects and ambitions at the dream stage. Sooner or later, when someone tells him that their secret dream is to make films, climb Mount Everest, go back to law school or become a Bedouin, Andrew very sincerely asks, 'Why don't you?' and proceeds to demonstrate that it's perfectly feasible, and offers help. And he really does convince people sometimes to try again, that it's not too late.'

Alas, I have tried too often to prove that only the impossible ever happens. And yet, without that belief, how may we ever achieve more than we are capable of doing?

FRANCIS BACON

⸺◦⸺

The painter Francis Bacon once said that he only had two regrets in life – twice more than Édith Piaf, who sang that she regretted nothing. He was sad about giving up a couple of places: Millais' old studio in Cromwell Place in Kensington and a renovated Georgian terrace house on the Thames River in Narrow Street, Limehouse. That was when I was his waterfront neighbour, where the barges at their moorings bumped against the back doors at high tide and made the old brick walls tremble on their clay foundations. The setting sun turned the river bend into the burning golden bow of William Blake, pulled towards the west between the cranes and warehouses of the trading waterway.

Bacon found this glare too bright for him to paint there, as he had also found at Monte Carlo and at Tangier. 'When the tide was in and the sun was out,' he told David Sylvester, 'there was a continual glitter inside the place.' Such a shrine made it too difficult for him to work: he needed a flat light. He made of his studio 'an almost bare show-piece, used only very occasionally for entertaining'. An attraction of Limehouse lay in its fierce privacy with an antagonism to the law that had lured Verlaine, when he had fled to London with Rimbaud. They had found themselves least persecuted in Soho and the East End, where most forms of human behaviour were practised and tolerated. By their trade and lack of an alternative choice at sea, sailors were used to homosexuality and to providing favours to gentlemen, when they ran out of money on their shore leaves. Nobody talked to the police, because the lethal sin of the community was to nark or grass, to rat or tell tales. Even the Kray brothers never descended to homosexual blackmail, as the journalist Daniel Farson testified in his evocative, but impersonal *Limehouse Days*, perhaps because one of the twins preferred boys, saying, 'Little angel faces, less evil-minded than girls.' The point was that no sexual inclination was taboo in Limehouse, unless the police got an ill wind of it; but the breeze rarely blew that way.

To his outpost in Limehouse, Farson invited his Soho friends, especially Francis Bacon and the fellow members of the Colony Room, a louche Soho drinking club. When I, at last, got to live in 88 Narrow Street, I could walk across two terraces facing the river and hop over a low wall to find myself outside the back of Farson's home. Alone and immersed in writing *Gog*, I was invited by him to a party one night. I arrived rather late, and I found there were only men there, Farson and his Soho friends, a few East Enders and more sailors. Rather shy and heterosexual, I was embarrassed, but pleased to talk to Francis Bacon for the first time. I had previously lived in Soho Square and had often seen him in Wheeler's and the French Pub without daring to approach him. We talked a little of our mutual love of the Greek dramatists. On a second approach from another man, I cast off. These were not quite my moorings.

A month later, there was more of a drama. Early in the morning, a banging at my terrace window woke me. A bleeding and naked sailor from the Regent's Canal Docks was demanding to get in. I opened the terrace door, patched up his cuts, gave him some old clothes and a little money, and sent him back to his ship through the Limehouse dark. I never said a word, but obviously there was some rough business down the street. A month later, I was woken by thumping and running on the higher terrace above my head. This time I did telephone the police, who rushed round immediately to catch some burglars, already reported by Farson for breaking into his premises. The police surrounded the terrace from pavement and foreshore, believing that the thieves could not escape. Then they conferred with me. The noises off that I had heard were the boots of the coppers themselves. They had disturbed me during their previous inquiries. They had come to put the handcuffs on their own wrists.

Life at Narrow Street was never without the incident and accident and chance that Bacon loved. Daniel Farson solved his problems of theft by importing a minder recommended by the Krays to live in his attic with a ferocious Doberman. Such a remedy appeared to me to be worse than the malady. I went to the landlord of another local community pub, *The Black Horse*, and made it known that I would sign job references for any Limehouse criminal on his release from gaol on the condition and his oath that he would not steal from his honest job, whatever he stole elsewhere. I would also represent the neighbourhood to the local Council in any just demand for better schooling and lighting and pedestrian crossings, though not policing. In return, I expected total protection from burglary and arson for the six houses in Narrow Street, which were being occupied by me and my friends. We both kept our side of the bargain for a decade, until I left my home.

There is a deal of honour among East Enders. Farson recalled that Francis Bacon found it out, when he was talking to a young friend of Ronnie Kray's, who listed the charity and benevolence of his criminal patron. In the end, Bacon could not bear the litany of praise, and exclaimed: 'Fair touches the heart!' 'It does, doesn't it!' said the delighted wide-eyed boy. In fact, the actor Stanley Baker had already introduced Bacon to the Kray twins in Tangier, and Ronnie Kray and two of his henchmen visited Bacon one Sunday morning in his studio to deter him from suing a friend of theirs for paintings that had not been paid for. Bacon was soon persuaded.

True to the culture of his place in London before he left for the countryside, Farson ran a singing pub on the Isle of Dogs, which he renamed the *Watermans Arms*. He revived a version of the Music Hall there with occasional turns by George Melly and Annie Ross. Francis Bacon brought along his Tangier friend, William Burroughs, and the Beat English writer Alexander Trocchi. Many in film and show business came, Jacques Tati and Claudette Colbert, Groucho Marx and Trevor Howard, Lord Delfont and David Merrick, Tony Bennett and Shirley Bassey, Joan Littlewood and even Judy Garland and Clint Eastwood. In a way, Farson was destroying the culture which he loved by introducing into it the glamour and power of other parts of other cities. Finally, the *Watermans Arms* was killed by its own success. The more crowded it became, the more Farson lost the money, which ended in his opinion in the pockets of his employees and his associates. Running a profitable club or a pub in the East End needed the techniques of the Kray brothers, not of an illuminating photographer and a good writer, whom even the acerbic Colin Macinnes recognised as 'realizing his own dream'.

As the last survivor of the authors and artists in Narrow Street, until the film director David Lean was to live at an old banana wharf further down the road and the consummate actor, Sir Ian McKellen was to move in, Bacon used his studio occasionally as a place to receive and entertain. In a hilarious story he used to tell to his friends such as John Richardson, he even claimed to have encountered there the next love of his life.. He said that he was asleep and alone one night, when he woke to the noise of a burglar in his bedroom. He did not behave like the Edwardian lady in her mansion in the same situation, who announced, 'I am the only thing of value in this room, and I am removing it immediately' – which she did. Bacon's tactics were contrary. 'Take all your clothes off,' he said to the burglar, 'and get into bed with me. Then you can have *all* you want.'

That is how Francis Bacon used to tease George Dyer about their first encounter in 1964. The story may have been just a funny one; but Dyer had served time for breaking and entering in Borstal and in Pentonville – a fact which emerged in court when Dyer committed the ultimate sin of his background and set up Bacon on drugs charges at the end of the decade. However they did meet in reality, the choice of Dyer as a habitual lover marked Bacon's descent from the older educated mentor to the younger rough trader. And at the end of his life, he was to repeat his choice of a young East Ender to see out his fortune and his days. No more the raffish genteel for Bacon, but the feckless prole. In a way, it was back to the grooms and the stable-lads of his adolescence in Ireland.

Yet there was to be a sea-change in the law and in the attitude to homosexuality during the 'sixties. With the Sexual Offences Act of 1967, homosexual acts between consenting adults ceased to be criminal. The Obscenity and Theatre Acts were reformed the following year, leaving the only weapon of attack against works of art or public performances, deemed by some to be offensive, to be private prosecutions for blasphemy or for procuring acts of gross indecency. Bacon's paintings of men coupling like dogs had never been prosecuted nor his Crucifixions of gruesome reptilian mangled shapes. But his private sexual life had made him vulnerable to a gaol sentence for more than forty years of his adulthood. It was almost perverse of him to be liberated from the threat of the law and enter of his own will into the daily menace of the criminal mind. Yet, forced to act as a potential outlaw for so long, he had come to find, as Oscar Wilde had, the company of wide boys and grafters more interesting than of social climbers and scholars. He could not kick the habit of his low life.

A school friend of mine, 'Grey' Lord Gowrie, who had been the Minister for the Arts as well as deriving from the same part of County

Kildare as Bacon, wrote a trenchant tribute to him. Since the death of Picasso and more than any other painter, Bacon had provided the age with the image of Ezra Pound's accelerated grimace. He did not record the past and was the least narcissistic of artists. He used a present preoccupation or recollection to prompt any act of painting. He was a man of great but narrow erudition, because he was impatient of anything less than masterpieces that he could use for his art. His bleak view of human life did not stop his joy in it. He was good company and generous with money, because he had been a hustler and now had more than he needed. 'Politically, he is an old-fashioned aristocratic liberal with a low threshold of boredom.' Nevertheless, Bacon was the greatest living painter and the most important British one since Turner. He shared the aloof intuition of French romantics like Baudelaire. He had the nihilism and gaiety of certain eighteenth-century minds. Nature was threatening and monotonous; noctambular urban life was his territory. Like Samuel Beckett, Bacon was 'an artist of endgame'.

The last time I saw Francis was at Groucho's club, when he had refused to go to Moscow to see an exhibition of his works there. He read to me a letter sent to the Russians that the remarkable visual imagery of Eisenstein's films of *Strike* and *The Battleship Potemkin* had much influenced his paintings, particularly those of screaming faces, especially those of the Popes. We discussed Aeschylus. He quoted to me a favourite line of his which I misheard. 'The Reek of Human Blood *smiles* out of me.' A letter from him rebuked me for writing in my book, *War Like a Wasp*, on the culture of the 1940s, that he had actually said, 'The Reek of Human Blood spills out of me.' And he added, 'Spills is so weak and it ruins the metaphor.' Very well educated, he, however much he tried to disguise it.

Although eighty years old, he looked like a pantomime Principal Boy. His spiky hair was brown with Kiwi bootpolish; a little rouge touched up his smooth pale cheeks; he wore a loose shirt and britches, tucked into high glossy boots. We drank four bottles of champagne in four hours, mostly paid by him from a roll of fifty-pound notes, his weekly allowance from the Marlborough Gallery. He despised money and only used it for lovers, friends and gambling. Paralysed in my chair, I watched him leap upright, as if on spring heels. He asked me, 'Can you think of a bad cause, Andrew?'

I had the temerity to reply, 'What about yourself, Francis.' He laughed and said, 'That's *too* bad a cause.' He had to make a will to leave his millions to someone or something. Eventually, they ended invested, through a close friend, in brothels in Thailand. Francis would have been amused by that. Wealth is worthless. Art abides.

SCREENPLAYS

—◦◦◦—

Ah, Lorrimer years, and many of them. Lorrimer was the middle name of Peter Whitehead, the mythomaniac of our age. As blue-eyed beautiful as David Hemmings and as charismatic as Casanova, he was as mirror-conscious as Narcissus. As a movie buff, I fell under his spell in Soho. I had money, he did not. He sucked me into his screenplay editions: he began with Jean-Luc Godard's *Alphaville*, and into his film productions, one with The Rolling Stones, *Tonite, Let's Make Love In London*. Always in love with himself, Peter had to produce, direct, write and star in his own movies. At certain times, some of us believed that his circular bed in a Soho garret was the hub of the Hippie universe. O tempora, O Peter, O morass.

I have a practical insanity within me. I like to turn my obsessions into going concerns. Peter wanted to sell out to me, I wanted to print classic screenplays. I knew nothing about how publishing worked, and I still know very little. Anyway, I was making too much money, rewriting film scripts in Hollywood. I used to hate myself out there in Beverly Hills and Bel Air – those plush rooms, that mortal loneliness, the death-dealing in the Polo Lounge. All the while, I creaked out the words, which were slowly read and hardly approved. Over the weeks, I felt futile, corrupt and isolated. These appalling episodes would culminate in a restaurant called the Brown Derby. It was 1968, the blacks were burning down the ghetto of Watts, I was on the only hotline between Hollywood and Havana, where my wife Marianne had gone to present a baby to Castro's Revolution, and I had had quite enough. Rather like Graham Greene's *Our Man in Havana*, the monitored telephone presumed 'baby' meant 'bomb', and I was already being followed by a CIA football squad. The snickering Vice-President of some studio or another informed me that George Raft owned the restaurant. If I didn't get my words right, I would be knee-capped.

'How much do I owe you?' I said.

Surprised, he said, 'Twenty-five thousand dollars.'

I wrote him out a cheque and handed it to him.

'Twenty-five thousand dollars,' I said. 'And now I will tell you what I think of you.'

He looked at the cheque in wonder. 'Writers don't return money,' he said.

'This one does,' I said. And then I told him that I hoped the blacks would not only burn down Watts, but the whole of bloody Los Angeles. This had something to do with free speech. The VP smiled, and he folded up my cheque and put it in his pocket.

'You'll never work here again,' he said.

'I don't want to,' I said. And left. And never did.

I was, indeed, blacklisted soon for my Cuban connections. Whatever rash choices I have made have spurted from my two main sins, wrath and pride. I watch with astonishment the results of my actions. As Dylan Thomas said, 'Temperamental? It's ninety per cent temper and ten per cent mental.'

I used to say I wrote bad screenplays, in order to print good ones. Over twenty years, we quite invented the genre in the English language and published some seventy-five scenarios filmed by directors such as Orson Welles and Kurosawa, Eisenstein and Lang, Bergman and Buñuel, Carné and Vigo, Hitchcock and Ford, Antonioni and Pasolini, Erich von Stroheim and Pabst, W.C. Fields and the Marx Brothers and Satyajit Ray. All the major directors and screenwriters of the Spielberg generation had our classic scripts stacked on their shelves. We were teaching film grammar to the better makers of movies as well as to the younger tyros, who now could learn the art of cinema from the supreme texts of the past.

I met Jean Renoir, tubby in a check suit; Truffaut, as subtle as a dissolve between night and day; and Roman Polanski, whom Kenneth Tynan rightly described as 'the five-foot Pole you wouldn't touch a barge with.' The two, who stick in my memory, were Josef von Sternberg and Jean-Luc Godard. On my scripting safaris to Hollywood, I worked with Sternberg on *The Blue Angel*. Bald and short and authoritarian, he told me exactly what to do and what he had done. His favourite exhibit was a cartoon of himself, manipulating a wooden doll of Marlene Dietrich on wires. As he wrote in the introduction to the screenplay:

Film actors, as all students of film history know, are nothing more than glorified marionettes. But unlike a real puppet-master, the director of a film does not manipulate strings on expressionless puppets. For him the dolls are extraordinary personalities who are prone to move every muscle of face and figure to demonstrate every awkward emotion. And when the strings are manoeuvred to present acceptable masks, there is dismay and rebellion. What to reveal and what to conceal is the function of the director.

In a letter, Sternberg said he liked me very much and advised not too much furious work. 'Don't. It is unwise. Your perspective vanishes. Your energy with it.' In his simple contract, he bequeathed to us the stage rights of *The Blue Angel*, which he claimed to own. Indeed, I wrote the book for a musical of it, orchestrated in a haunting way by Colin Towns and mounted in Liverpool and Bristol and Brighton, without reaching London. And as for Lola-Lola, singing about herself.

> Looking at me
> What do you see?
> Nothing I can do about it.
> Take me as I am
> I don't give a damn
> Nothing I can do about it.

Occasionally, I believed I was in somebody else's movie. We were to publish seven films by Jean-Luc Godard, beginning with *Alphaville*. The last two would be *Weekend* and the revolutionary *Wind from the East*. Over these, I met him. He was back to filming with an Arriflex on his shoulder in London, and he had run out of money. He was making a movie about continual rebels, which starred Mao and Guevara and The Rolling Stones, recording *Sympathy for the Devil*. In a surreal ending, he acted as a deranged director, sending off a black man and a blood-painted white woman with guns on a cinematic dolly into the air. As I was sitting in my Soho office, a small man in an old brown mackintosh emerged through the door. Announcing himself as Godard, he asked me how much money we had in the bank. I looked at a statement. For once it was more black than red.

'Eleven hundred pounds,' I said.

'Next Wednesday,' he said. 'I want it all. Used five pound notes. In a brown paper bag. What films do you want of mine?'

I took the two previous insurrectionary ones, and I went to my branch. When I asked for all the money we had in used fivers, I was regarded with deep suspicion. I was photographed in case I was a drug-dealer. Or was it money laundering? Only Godard was taking me to the cleaners. I knew the story of him, cracking the safe of his French producer, who would not come up with the necessary. I drew up our simple two-page contract, for that was all it was in those days of trust, and I waited for his appearance.

Looking extremely seedy, Godard sidled through the door. I handed him the paper bag full of fivers. '*Ici le fric*,' I said. 'Would you like to count it, *m'sieu* Godard?' I asked.

He shook his head. Revolutionary honour was at stake.

'What do I have to sign?'

I gave him the short terms of agreement.

'Would you like to read it?'

Again he shook his head. He signed the second page, and he turned to go.

'*Pardon, m'sieu Godard*,' I said. 'But I feel as if I am in one of your films. A bank robbery, I believe. Probably the wrong target.'

At last, I achieved a smile from the great man on his way out.

'*Exactement*,' was his last line, although I was reminded of Willie Sutton's reply when asked why he had robbed so many banks, 'Because that's where the money is.'

My other highlight was working with Graham Greene on the publication of the script of *The Third Man*, with all its cuts and emendations. The film called on the genius of an extraordinary quartet, Graham Greene and Carol Reed and Orson Welles and Alexander Korda. It set a particular style for British films, a combination of realism of background and penetration of character, based on the two main qualities of the British wartime cinema, a feeling for documentary detail and social purpose. Carol Reed explained the success of the film, shot in 1949, by saying that it was one of the first British films allowed to be made chiefly on location. Until that time, making films in studios had falsified and glamorised all.

In this film, the wet, brooding labyrinths of ruined and occupied Vienna express the traps and ambiguities facing people there, the harsh and shifting choices forced on the survivors of the war. Men plot out their little schemes in front of an arras of urban disaster. Harry Lime scuttling across the bomb-sites, the small operator trying to get rich on the surface of a total waste, is the symbol of the futility of shrewdness in the face of devastation. Lime tries to exploit war and shortages; he dilutes the life-giving penicillin until it gives death. But he is caught in the same vicious circle and in a closed city; as the British Military Policeman Calloway says, 'A rat would have more chance in a closed room without a hole and a pack of terriers loose'. War and its aftermath crushes all individuals, however clever they may be. And Orson Welles invented his most famous view on history on the Big Wheel:

> In Italy for thirty years under the Borgias they had warfare, terror, murder, bloodshed – they produced Michelangelo, Leonardo da Vinci and the Renaissance. In Switzerland they had brotherly love, five hundred years of democracy and peace, and what did that produce...? The cuckoo clock. So long, Holly.

In the course of printing *The Third Man*, I was told a splendid story about one of Korda's screenwriters, entering the office of the maestro and demanding to be paid. 'We had a gentleman's agreement,' the offended author said. 'Looking round this room,' Korda replied, 'I see only one gentleman in it.' This tale was capped by the actress Beatrice Lillie, knocking on the boudoir door of Nöel Coward at his Blue Harbour house in Jamaica. 'Do you have a gentleman in your bed?' she inquired politely. 'Just a minute,' he replied. 'I'll ask him.' But then, he was not speaking only for himself.

Ever since publishing the film script of *Les Enfants du Paradis*, I had been in love with Arletty. Along with *Casablanca*, this was the greater of all the romantic films ever made. The American movie dealt at the distance of an ocean with the German occupation of North Africa, while *Les Enfants* was made during the brutal Nazi seizure of Paris. At that grisly time, a certain latitude was allowed for French comedians. One of them would nightly raise his arm in a Hitler salute in a cabaret, while shouting, 'In the shit! In the shit! That high.' The laughter was even higher, and he did not end in Buchenwald. Even the Gestapo guffawed.

As a period piece, *Les Enfants* was allowed to be made during the occupation. The enigmatic and seductive performance of Arletty turned mime into anguish, and acting into tears. Yet she was living under a foreign régime of particular nastiness. She had her admirers; sometimes she succumbed. When put on trial as a *collaboratrice* after the end of the Second World War, she gave to the tribunal an immortal line in defence of the feminine necessities of a reasonable survival:

'While my *cul* may be international, my *coeur* has always been French.'

Her judges did not break into applause, but she was forgiven. I was understanding, for the mother of my French first wife Marianne had fallen in love with a German officer before the outbreak of hostilities. Although she had married another Parisian husband, Arsène Alexandre, and had two small daughters, her previous lover came to occupy her city, while her spouse was in prison camp, where he died. What was she to do? Collaboration or emotion or getting by with a brace of little girls? Unlike Arletty, she could not put it together with her lover in Bavaria, after the German defeat. So she had to flee to the provinces, and then to America to escape the consequences of what she had done at home.

Many of the more accommodating French women were shaven and stripped and driven out of their communities. As for the divine Arletty, I saw her in Paris in her last queenly stage performance in Cocteau's *Les Parents Terribles*. Soon after that, reaching for eye lotion in her bedroom, she put acid on her peepers and went blind. I don't believe in retribution. I know that her image will always be the temptress of my soul.

Although dealing with the most litigious protectors of copyright in the world, the film lawyers, Lorrimer was only threatened once with a many million-dollar suit. Under a false name, I had written an illustrated book on the fantasy cinema, called CINEFANTAS-TIC: on its cover was a thirties' school lunch tin, featuring Superman, which I had picked up in a junk shop on Long Beach. A New Yorker walked through my office door, who turned out to be the head of the future Marvel Comics. He waved a copy of CINE-FANTASTIC at me.

'Don't you realize,' he said, 'this is copyright?'

'No,' I said. 'It's just an old lunch tin.'

'Can.'

'Can, then.'

'It's going to cost you a few million.'

I looked on rather a sympathetic face, who was looking at an object on my desk. It was a Mustang fighter, carved out of an engine block as an ashtray by a bored maintenance airman in the Second World War

'Have the whole company,' I said. 'I'm rather bored with it, and we're broke. What a good way to go.'

He was still considering the ashtray.

'I used to fly one of them,' he said. 'Over here.'

We settled for the ashtray and a hundred buckshee copies of CINEFANTASTIC. And every time I visited his offices in New York, I was met by a sign in neon letters:

DISTINGUISHED VISITOR TODAY
ANDREW SINCLAIR

Another New York publishing friend was Joe Reiner, who, at Crown Publishers, saved most small publishers every weekend by paying cash for their unsaleable stock, which was then turned around in Outlet stores. He told me that if the books really had no market, such as volumes of old sermons, Crown would sell them to the proprietors of shooting galleries near 42nd Street or on Coney Island. These editions were hollowed out and presented as prizes. On the cover, the legend: IF YOUR HAIR IS FALLING OUT, and in the cache where the text was within, PUT IT IN HERE. And if there was a glut of buckshee books, there were always the Lampstand Tomes, shellacked together to weigh down the bases of the lights.

Once Joe took me to see a miracle, that Borges might have imagined. This was the desk of the boss, Nat Wartels. For forty years, he had piled his correspondence in a great paper ziggurat, which almost reached the ceiling, the letters and bills stacked indiscriminately. Yet his memory and retrieval were better than a multiple of magpies. Asked for a reference, his hand would dart in and pluck out the very missive, sent to him several years before, as a cock pecking at a heap of grain. He did not trust discs and files. Documents were lost in them, he said, or shredded, or went down.

He was right, of course, particularly in this age of the computer virus and malfunction. The point of Nat's pyramid, as was that of Cheops, was to preserve the necessary and give us inscrutable, if mortal, means of communication. Inherent in this plan was also a convenient forgetfulness of what had gone wrong in the past. For oblivion is as important as cognition. The waters of Lethe took Dante from the Inferno to Paradiso. To be remaindered by Nat Wartels was not to prove the ephemera of paper, but the permanence of the word.

My drinking friend was the head of Macmillan, Jerry Kaplan. After some misdemeanour, he was demoted to limbo, the Thirteenth Floor of the Chrysler Building. Because of superstition, no elevator in New York recognizes or stops there, because it does not exist. There is No Being and Nothingness of Sartre between the Twelfth and the Fourteenth Floor. Finding my way with difficulty to Jerry, he asked me to dinner with Edward Albee. 'I have to take a young man, Andrew. Or we're not allowed in.' On the way, we had a few drinks. Jerry ordered, 'A vodka martini on the rocks. Without the martini.' When I asked why, he replied, 'You get more vodka that way,' with the martini as missing as the Thirteenth Floor. At the Albee dinner of eight men, I didn't pass muster as Jerry's intimate friend. And yet, I heard an illuminating thing. *Who's Afraid of Virginia Woolf?* was perhaps written for two male couples. If Albee ever allowed it to be put on, what a bitch-fest.

Outed and broke, my closest publishing friend, the huge Peter Ritner, had hurled a chess set through the seventh-floor window of his apartment, when I beat him at the game. Alas, he followed it one night with his body. To lose your gold Credit Card in New York is a likely suicide. Or the sheriff will knock at your door when you can't pay your bills. Not knowing this, at another dinner, I went cold all over, and I could barely move or speak, hardly a heart attack or hypothermia on such a sweltering summer evening. Peter Ritner was walking across my spine to his grave, as those you love may do, at their end. The heels of ghosts are very cold. For it was the partner of my guest that evening, who first came upon Peter's corpse the next morning. I could never explain the accident without meeting looks of incredulity. Yet it was just so.

GOG AND GOLDING

—∞∞∞—

Until I wrote my first long novel, *Gog*, I thought that experience was something that happened casually to me. The material for my fiction would come from my normal life. But gradually, as I felt more in command of my style in the novel, and as I grew more to recognize my obsessions, I realized that I did not have to wait around for experience to occur. I could go out and find on the ground what I wished for the themes that I needed for my novel. *Gog* took three years in gestation and another two to write. The work demanded a great deal of research into the byways of mythology and the details of popular revolt in Britain; it also demanded a huge grubbing into the facts of being alive in 1945, something which I had largely forgotten. But it made me do another thing, which I began in terror and ended in gratitude. I had to tramp some four hundred miles without any money along the old right-of-ways in England and Scotland.

This lurch of rambling, which gave me all the details I needed about season and sight and hunger and cold and just moving, was not a real experience of being a tramp, as George Orwell's was, when he described his years of poverty in *Down and Out in Paris and London*. I was trudging towards a perfectly good house on the Thames and a perfectly secure income from academics and writing. I was only playing at being a vagrant, with my shorn hair and assumed accent. Yet the sensations, which I experienced, were all true enough. An empty belly is no forgery, sleeping on a moor, soaked to the skin, is no lie. Lying out in a gale all night on the site of an old camp by Hadrian's Wall gave me a better picture of the feelings of a Roman sentry on guard duty nineteen hundred years ago than I could reach in my imaginings or gleanings in London.

Approaching somewhere with the same physical sensations as one's hero makes all the difference in the description of a place. York Minster does not look the same to a fat man after a good night as it looks to a hungry man after a week out. People do not behave the same towards a dirty stubbled hiker as they do towards a car driver with a crease in his trousers. These are all simple observations, but vital ones. Until I had condemned myself out of my own mouth to a host of friends, and until shame drove me out to trudge as I had boasted that I would, I was one of the complacent authors who claimed that memory or plagiarism or inspiration could provide a far better description of a thing than the thing itself. How convenient if this were true, and far more comfortable. But it is not so.

The fatigue and hunger of the seven nights and days of my first pilgrimage over the Borders granted me an ecstatic vision in York Minster, as I tottered in front of the Five Sisters, the grisaille glass windows given by a Crusader to this ancient holy shrine. In the setting sun, the windows spoke in their blinding grey diamonds of the virtues of humility and mercy, which I did not have. In my spinning head were the voices of angels; in my ears, an organ sounded the music of the spheres. I trembled, and almost, I fainted. Then I went to the police station to try and borrow a fiver for the train home; a friend would pay the banknote into a London police station. The coppers were red with rage. What? I had no identity papers. What if I had died on the Moors? How could they know where to send my body? Very inconsiderate of me. Anyway, the fiver arrived, as I waited outside in the rain, and I was dismissed.

I arranged my second wandering from the prehistoric and broken circle of monoliths at Avebury along the Hard Way over the downs to Canterbury Cathedral, so that I would coincide with the Summer Solstice at Stonehenge, and be couched down on stubble in a field among the hares and the grass tumuli to the south of the mighty standing stones and the army camp at Larkhill, where no birds sang, only bullets and barrages. At dawn, as the sun rose over that ancient observatory, I viewed the Druids at their ceremonies. And later, I had a cup of tea with the Chief of the Order in his white robes. He appeared to be more wily than holy, but then, as my book attempted to say, how else might I understand the myths of Albion without such unending artifice?

Good novelists may make bad newspaper reporters, and good reporters may make bad novelists. Yet the novelist has to stir his stumps and become something of the reporter. There are two lines of W.H. Auden's, which long ago influenced me before I had written my first novel. Auden wrote that the novelist:

…in his own weak person, if he can
Must suffer dully all the wrongs of Man.

The gifted may, perhaps, suffer all these wrongs by a process of telepathy, a sympathetic transference of themselves into the condition of other men. All novelists have to do this in some small degree; it is the necessary trick of their trade. Joyce Cary could not have been further in character from Gulley Jimson in *The Horse's Mouth* or the protagonist of *Mister Johnson*; but his characters breathe, as if the author had puffed the air of their paper mouths. Yet without his detailed knowledge of Africa and of the life of the failed artist, would Cary have convinced us about the flesh and blood of his two major creations?

Fine it is, if a writer can suffer at a distance for others; but it is better and more sure if he suffers close. Fine it is, if the ordinary course of life brings the happenings and material, which are necessary for writing novels; but it is more sure if the writer goes out to take the road and gather material on the theme that he has chosen. The deluge of suburban and university and business and young-married novels that flood the book stores with what Benjamin Franklin once called 'happy mediocrity' would be channelled into more original pools, if writers looked out for the detail needed to describe their dreams, rather than submerged themselves under the flotsam of their rutted lives.

Hard it is to plan a novel on an original and curious theme, and then to find the time and money and energy to pursue that theme to the limits of mind and body. But it is that very difficulty, which forces the writer into more originality; it is the *chosen* experience that becomes the different undergoing and distinguishes one particular novel from all others. The will to write should dominate everything, even a way of normal life; it did mine, only when I wrote *Gog*. During the two years of its walking and writing, hardness was all, and a vision as blinkered as the Blackwall Tunnel under the Thames river.

I ended the book to find myself losing my wife to my best friend, a long slow sharing that seemed to have no turning. She always used to reproach me because I did not fight for her. That was just. I was too proud, and I wanted to be forced to do my *Gog* walks by wrath, my other great sin, which I try to suppress. I used to say that every woman needed two men to give her enough time and conversation, while every author needed half a woman to give himself enough time to write alone. My statement was only a defence, which did not even convince me. For company, I had an Abyssinian cat called Mishkin, which used to sit on my lap while I typed, until she decided to join in with her paws, making my manuscript rather surreal. She would also sleep in my bed with her head on my pillow, waking me in the small hours by walking across my face as she left on her nightly errands and me to my interminable solitude.

I knew well a spirit of England and genius of the place, as the Greeks and Romans used to call them. William Golding would not say that of himself, although he had been a classics master at Bishop Wordsworth's School. One of his pupils and models for *Lord of the Flies*, Derek Dawkins, remembered him teaching after his return from duty as a rocket-ship captain during the war. 'When 'Scruff' Golding read poetry, all the angels in heaven stopped to listen – it was pure music.' Another schoolboy, Malcolm Cooper, who was ordained into the Church of England, believed that Golding's sufferings and loneliness at sea brought him to the point where the knowledge of God's presence was sufficient. He developed 'a living spirituality.'

He never told me that, though at our many meetings, I was always conscious of a dark power, a brooding intensity which would burst out in a torrent of eloquence. To hear him speak of the myths and mysteries of existence for hours late at night after bottles of red wine was to hear tongues of fire, almost pentecostal from heaven. As Ted Hughes, he knew of the ordeal of the spirit. He hardly spoke of his own trials, although once he did tell me of the lethal choice, which inspired the irony and black wit of his works. On his rocket-ship chugging across the English Channel on D-Day, he went to sleep and his first mate lost the whole armada of seven thousand ships. He woke, and he changed course across a minefield marked on his chart. He wrote that he was afraid less of being blown up than of being late for the great Normandy encounter. But to me, he added that he lived in fear of his ship, in the nagging knowledge that one spark, one tracer-bullet would explode his floating fireworks factory to blazes.

He was also haunted by his decision to risk the lives of his crew by sailing over the minefield so that he would not be mocked for missing the largest fleet in the history of invasion. Only later did he discover that the minefield on the chart was a decoy to deter enemy destroyers. There had been no moral choice, no risk at all.

He also told me of the terrible job which he had to do. He could not clear it from his conscience, even when he conjured up his blitzed redeeming child Matty from a 'burning bush' in his novel, *Darkness Visible*. The rockets, which Captain Golding fired from his floating platform were called 'bricks'. His job was twice to lay 50 'bricks' over a hellish half-acre, laying waste to Proust's beach in Normandy, even as Sodom and Gomorrah, in pillars of fire. At the invasion of Walcheren, he had to do his duty again, creating his little infernos before the troops landed. That grey morning, the Royal Air Force did not appear to cover the landing, so that most of the other rocket ships and landing-craft were destroyed by shells and phosphorus and bombs. His own ship was one of the few to be spared.

As a war child, I was no Matty. Yet I did know of burns. The fighter pilots who survived being shot down in flames would end up in the Oxford hospital I had to pass four times a day on my way to school. My mother used to leave at nights to sit beside their beds. And sometimes I would see these mummies emerge in wheelchairs, bandages from head to feet, with only dark holes for nostrils and mouth. Occasionally, a nurse would put a cigarette in the lower hole, as New York cops still do to stiffs carried out from Broadway hotels, to show they are alive.

So I could understand a little the scorching and the fear of it. I had met 'Bill' Golding by the good luck of having our first two novels both published by the same house at the same time, along with the early poems of Ted Hughes. My trivial attempts, written while still an undergraduate, were meant to be petty moral tragedies, but everybody fell about laughing. There was no comparison to *Lord of the Flies* and *The Inheritors*, that masterpiece of prehistory and the birth of the human spirit, which Ted Hughes would chose to read on November 20th, 1993, at the Service of Thanksgiving for the life and work of Sir William Golding at the Cathedral Church of the Blessed Virgin Mary in Salisbury.

One memorial service does recall the others, particularly to those who have passed through the same ordeals and wars, and who cannot forget them. Ted was also a charismatic reader on themes of cosmic doubt and grandeur. He forgot time in his tribute to the other illu-minating spirit of his age, and he appeared to read the whole of *The Inheritors*. Millennia passed before his last cadence. Yet the magnifi-cent obsession of both of these genii of the land deserved such a farewell, as rushing as the river of life, which had also saved in Bill's novel the progenitors of humankind. 'We've had Neanderthal Man and *Homo Sapiens*,' he once said. 'Perhaps one day we'll get to *Homo moralis*. Perhaps we're like the ants – ' he paused to smile – 'damned to produce a perfect society.'

Bill was the only writer I had ever stalked. He was most kind when I wrote to him. Visit me by the watercress beds at Bower Chalke halfway between Salisbury Cathedral and Stonehenge – that was his invitation. His house might be found in mid-passage be-tween the new and the ancient faiths. He told me mischievously that his mind also lay halfway between them.

On my second long Gog trudge, I was walking from Glastonbury to Canterbury along the Hard Way on a blasted heath in thunder and rain after Avebury with only a pound in my pocket, when the deluge from the heavens became too much. Towards dinner and suddenly sodden, I knocked on the door of Ebble Thatch. Bill and Ann Golding let me in and dried me out; two bottles of red wine, chess with Bill, then his gifted Liszt and Beethoven on the piano. The next morning, he drove me back to the hill forts on the downs to complete my journey, sleeping out and hardly eating, trying to change my perceptions. Later, Bill liked the published *Gog* because of its passion for the *Matter of Britain*. ''The lie of the land' does give it an organic quality, which I think is what you were after, organic in a Goggish kind of way, ungainly, thumping, outrageous, arcane, savaging, the land's history seen – there's no help for it I have to purloin Hazlitt or is it Kean's Lear? – seen by flashes of lightning!'

I had learned the feel of the land from him, the harshness of the place, the ravage of time. He always told me that his favourite novel was *The Inheritors* about the Stone Age, while I had preferred *Pincher Martin* – 'You would, Andrew, all that survival and lust for life.' For him, his obsession was more with the sea than the earth. A teacher of classics and a seeker after God, he found in the struggle of men against the deep his Odysseys and his Leviathans. 'I was born by it,' he said. 'I've sailed on it, fought on it, swum in it, photographed under it, been frightened by it and done most things you can do apart from drowning in it.' Golding kept on writing about grace and mercy, chance and fate, struggle and survival for those who live upon the sea, culminating in his trilogy of *Rites of Passage* to Australia, which won him the Nobel Prize.

He himself gave up commanding any boat when his private yacht, the 23-ton *Tenace*, hit a cargo ship in a Channel mist and went to the bottom. He and his family did not sink in long revelation and revolt like Pincher Martin, but they were saved. He sailed no more except in his writing. 'I never again wanted to be responsible for other people's lives at sea.'

These experiences afloat infused the flow and currents of many of Golding's novels. They charted the rocks, suggested the reefs, confronted ambiguous men with sightings and tackings, tempests and doldrums. To him, the sea was protean, including and reflecting the various appetites and contradictions of human beings. The primal water was involved in birth and baptism, endeavour and death. In *The Inheritors*, the Neanderthal Lok, upside down over the river, sees the world reversed, watching the murdered body of the Old Woman in the weed-tail and the deep water, the bottom hidden with no trace of life or speculation. *Homo Sapiens* had come in rafts from the waters to destroy the innocence of the old life. In his new head, Lok knows that 'certain things were gone and done with like a wave of the sea.'

The Neanderthalers had never come to the Fall of Man – here physically represented as the waterfall, which is the limit of their summer home. Lok's woman, Fa, finally drops over the rim on a tree as branched as the Cross and is sent rolling towards the sea, picturing the end of the life of the Neanderthal community. *Homo Sapiens* with its stolen savage baby sails a craft from the tree-darkness towards such a flashing of water that it cannot be seen if the line of darkness has an ending.

Yet in this Stone Age, where the idea of the divine and the hereafter begins to dawn, Lok in his sanctuary and icy cave meets an old woman Nil, who is tending to the dying Mai. 'Lok digested this. As long as there was a woman there was life. But what use was a man save for smelling things and having pictures.' With animal bones, Lok is made to dig a grave for Mai's corpse, tucked into a foetal position. Lok reaches other cave burials with crushed heads. The body is lowered into the pit, given water for his journey and covered with soil. And Nil says that the earth mother 'Oa has taken Mai into her belly.' This was a convincing explanation of primitive cave burials, as a regression to the fertile womb of the underground.

Bill even wrote a good review of some attempts I made at translations from the Greek Anthology. I was living then on the river at Limehouse. But as he asked, what had I actually done to deserve to translate these ancient epigrams? He contributed another one to mock me:

You laugh. Would had you been my crew –
A china lifeboat's fit for you!
How lubberly that soul condemns
Who merely sits beside the Thames!

On one trip to Greece, he wrote that he did once address a wall, like Bottom the Weaver in *A Midsummer Night's Dream*.

O well, oh sweet and lovely wall
Show me thy chink –

'And the wall *did* fall down. It sounds incredible, but it is so.' And so it was with Bill. Only the incredible ever happened. He had nine bad years when his *psyche* and his past stopped him from writing until *Darkness Visible* cast the devils out of his soul. Anne and he would stay with me for a week a year in a large and lonely house I had in Hanover Terrace in Regent's Park. I was rather off my head, but then, so was he. Bad patches became later spaces. I would give parties for him, whom I still thought our greatest writer, and neither of us cared about our critics, anyway. I remember one dinner with Gregory Peck and my neighbour Harold Pinter, when Bill entranced us all with tales for several hours over more bottles of red wine. At that period, as with Oscar Wilde, his genius lay in his conversation, not in his works. After the dinner, he destroyed a rubber effigy I had of Bob Dylan, saying it was Satan. But I resurrected the singer to put him in one of my Boxes, rather as a mummy is a memorial of lost times.

Later, at his publishers, Bill told me that the Devil smote him in Saqqara in Egypt, pelting him in the back, trying to kill him. Yet the sand was good, wiping out all the traces except the bones of Cambyses and the Eighth Army. And again at a Faber party, Tom Stoppard came to me and said, 'I would like to meet Bill Golding.' And so I introduced the two of them. But Bill turned his back in a rare discourtesy, and he said: 'And where were you in all the bad years?'

These sorties of his into the alien and hostile world of London literature taught me about loyalty. He only loved those who stood by him in the arid decade of his life between the two periods of his triumphs. And at the Services of Thanksgiving to him and Ted Hughes, I understood what we all have to understand. We are here to honour those who have illuminated us and gone. The true reasons for the death of Ted's Sylvia or of Bill's despair, they need not be said. There is a great chain of the living and the dead. It should not be broken. The past and the present and the future are the same. Never ruffle that river of wisdom. As men sleep in graves, skeletons sleep better in locked closets.

For me, indeed, the Services of Thanksgiving for Bill and Ted were as in *Pincher Martin*, which agreed with the fable that a drowning man before his extinction might watch his whole life unreel before his eyes. This had happened to Bill once, when he had been torpedoed and had woken in a steel and briny coffin some fathoms deep. The pressure of the sea squashed his lungs. God only knew how he burst as a cork to the surface of the water. And so he knew how to write his novel, for he had reviewed all his life on that fathom down.

Unlike most of my old friends, I suppose I have always preferred loyalty to integrity, whatever that means. And so it was with Bill, the Cornishman in him meeting the Highlander. At his 75th Birthday Party at Brown's Hotel, our old and omniscient editor Charles Monteith was still there to keep us in order. As Bill remarked, when he had shown Charles *The Inheritors*, our guide had said, 'Not Cavemen!' On another occasion, Bill remarked, 'God exists outside time. He goes on forever. But I don't have to. Good heavens! I'd die of boredom.' But when he died, he left a gap in the love of nature, which cannot be fulfilled.

At his Memorial Service in the Cathedral Church at Salisbury, I hardly listened to the words, for I was entranced by the stonework of *The Spire*, the subject of another Golding novel. He had the art to put in sentences, the sea and the land and the rock, and man's attempts to fail to change the elements. Yet he had faith in endeavour, and we miss him sorely, now we need him once more.

To end, I bought a watercolour of his in an art gallery in Oxford, *Lord of the Flies*. This showed the little black pests whizzing around some French dustbins. I shall never get the sound of him outside my skull nor the inquiry and the grace of him out of my spirit. But enough. Bill and Ted Hughes are dead, and I will always have joy in them. Their works are the great testimonials of the second half of the twentieth century. They understood England and the endurance of its people. They knew its myths and prophecies, which they tested with hard wits. They went through their own ordeals by calumny and fire. Their spirits left the scorch-marks on their bodies. Yes, we should always give our thanks for Bill Golding and Ted Hughes, who still tell us what we were and may yet be.

In the Beginning, Dylan

There was one voice, who sang like the waking dawn to us in the early years of the 'fifties. As the owls, which were bearing the farm away, the words of Dylan Thomas carried our hopes and our dreams on brown wings somewhere beyond sense and halfway to heaven. There was really not much imagination or incitement in those doldrums of postwar time and his wild words, so carefully wrought in the caches of verse, were our bards and minstrels. He was a funny curly fellow, too, beer-brightness and belly-laughter with his tales of Welsh innocents in the bad pubs of the city, and a regret for the lost wonder of the hills and the spinneys and the fields.

Roistering and raving, chasing his vertigos like another Baudelaire, Dylan was for us a release and a delight, an earthly spirit, both Bottom and Ariel. We were an inhibited generation of war children, rationed and deprived; then Dylan deluged us with all the treasures of Myfanwy Price's general store, gumstoppers, jellybabies, hundreds and thousands for the mouth and the mind. When we heard his poems, we knew that there was much living to be had.

Dylan was the best speaker of himself, with his rich voice enjoying hugely what he had written. After him, Richard Burton and Emlyn Williams were the magic tongues of those incantations that seem to haunt many of us, the more we heard them.

There was a Saviour
Rarer than radium
Commoner than water, crueller than truth...

Dylan was not religious, yet he could not escape from God. He was a Swansea boy, who was the best limner that the Welsh valleys and seas ever had. He boozed his life away, because he found too many friends and parasites at the bar – dying of strangers, he discovered that the seven virtues were deadly, too. A creature of opposites, he could never put together his contrary nature and divided wants without the healing labour of his craft or sullen art. What drove him to his early dying was not writing enough poetry, the damned waste of it all.

On no work of words now for three lean months in the bloody
Belly of the rich year and the big purse of my body
I bitterly take to task my poverty and craft...

Yet, prodigal as he was of his speech and his flesh and the hours of his days, Dylan was no Oscar Wilde, to devote his genius to his life, leaving only his talent for his art. His gift has been sufficient fine poems to stock a memory, enough marvellous tales and plays about Wales to create a comic nostalgia for a country, where most of us were never young. The quality of his prose is so hypnotic that it transports us to his childhood, while we are oblivious of our own. We were all at that Christmas over there with the fat uncles and the fierce aunts. Only the greater writers can make their remembrances more significant than our own. After listening to Dylan, I am almost sure that I spent my boyhood Mumbles, not in the wartime suburbs of Oxford and Port Meadow.

That offer of making his experience universal turned Dylan into a people's poet. I would see *AND DEATH SHALL HAVE NO DOMINION* and *DO NOT GO GENTLE INTO THAT GOOD NIGHT* carved on many a tombstone near Aberystwyth and Caernarvon. When I was to make the film of *Under Milk Wood* and play it at Venice and in Madrid, I could see the common warm humanity of village life, tickling and moving the audiences, who could only take in the music of the words without understanding them. They would laugh and weep, because Dylan's images of Llareggyb reminded them of the Sicily of Verga and the Spain of Lorca. A proud moment for me would be Dylan's widow Caitlin, saying at the London *première*: 'That is exactly as Dylan would want to show it.'

At Dylan's dying in New York with the quotation, 'I've had eighteen straight whiskies, is that a record?', Caitlin had gone off her head. She had to take his embalmed body in a check suit with a red bow tie, contained in a glass-topped coffin back to Laugharne. When Wynford Vaughan-Thomas saw the dressy poet, he said, 'Dylan wouldn't be seen dead in that.' Evans the Death had driven his hearse down from Wales to collect the cargo from Portsmouth docks. Late for the funeral ceremony, a call was received from Cornwall. Evans was complaining. 'I headed west,' he said, 'but nobody told me this bloody country was forked.'

In death as well as life, Dylan mixed comedy with tragedy. Richard Burton would tell me that Dylan had insisted on reciting to him the finest poem in the English language. It ran:

I Am
Thou Art
He, She, It Is
We Are
You Are
They Are

Dylan was the bard of our being. We were allies in what he wrote. When I tried to catch his complexity in a biography, Caitlin would be kind about the lack of success of my writing: 'You have picked the plums and touched the living quick of the Dylan situation with penetrating insight... What baffles me is from whence first did your passion and your understanding come?' I do not know, but I only know this. By Dylan's own words shall we know him, and perhaps ourselves, a little more, for better and worse?

Because of my Dylanesque prose in my Cambridge novel, *My Friend Judas*, I was chosen by the poet's Estate to adapt for the stage his unfinished novel, *Adventures in the Skin Trade*. My collaborator was John Davenport, a heavyweight literary patron, who had lost his fortune and lived on boiled potatoes in the Fens, in a bare house, because he had sold all the furniture. He had written a novel with Dylan, *The Death of the King's Canary*; in its pages, the pair managed to murder off most of the prewar literary establishment. Unfortunately, I invited John to the High Table at Churchill College. He emptied and refilled every glass within reach, then he rolled after me into the Senior Common Room, for a coffee and a brandy.

There was George Steiner, who was teaching English, while I was teaching History. Only a membrane separated us in a temporary Portakabin, so that I would overhear George talking interminably on the telephone about himself. For the College was not yet completed. When Davenport saw Steiner in his black gown among the other Fellows, he squared up to him and demanded: 'Why should a bloody German Jew like you be teaching English here? I should.' I caught John's fist as he drew it back to strike George, who bravely thrust out his withered arm and said, 'How dare you, you cad?' On this Victorian riposte, I bundled Davenport from the room. This was the worst moment in my academic life.

Davenport died shortly afterwards, but not of shame. I had to write the play alone, inventing a Second Act, which concentrated on Dylan's *alter ego*, Sam Bennet, stripping off the seven sins in seven scenes in his Surreal and picaresque years, also shaking off the shackles of Swansea. Dylan himself called the piece 'a mixture of Oliver Twist, Kafka, Beachcomber and good old three-adjectives a penny, belly-churning Thomas, 'the Rimbaud of Cwmdonkin Drive.' James Roose-Evans, who picked up my adaptation to present at the Hampstead Theatre, was kind about my ability to rewrite. 'He's marvellously objective and professional. Even if he has spent days working on an idea, if I ever say I don't like it, he just grins and tears it up. You can have a really creative relationship with him. He has steeped himself in everything Dylan ever wrote or said. He's really got inside the skins.'

In the case of *Adventures in the Skin Trade*, by choice and happenstance, one actor stopped treading the boards to star in the movies, while another was consigned to parts that never revealed his full potential. The first was David Hemmings, the second was Terence Stamp, who turned down my leading role. Hemmings was broke and came to lodge with me in Limehouse. He was dynamic and hilarious and irrepressible, as beautiful as a fallen angel, as rackety as Punch-and-Judy on the pier. Because we couldn't stage the first scene, when Sam Bennet smashes up his Swansea home and leaves for London, I shot it as a Keystone comedy in black-and-white on my 16mm Bolex, with Hemmings cavorting and his agent John Daley – later of Hemdale production fame – carrying the camera legs for two pounds from his client's twenty pounds a week. And while filming an East End whore against the brick wall of my riverside cellar, Clare Peploe walked in with a mysterious Italian gentleman. 'Too busy,' I said, 'go upstairs. I am filming.'

I should try to explain about Clare Peploe, although no explanation would ever be able to elucidate that enigma variation. Her grandfather was a renowned Scots painter, her father ran an art gallery, while her quick quirk of a smile and withdrawn passion made her so elusive that she was pursued by many a hunter. I lost her once on too long a walk over the Borders in order to write *Gog*, before returning to find her gone. We had grappled briefly on a *chaise-longue* among the running rats in an unbuilt corner of Narrow Street.

Sweet Thames, run softly, till I end my song.

Now, exquisitely beautiful with green-wide eyes that glanced away in evasion, another Monica Vitti of mystery, she had brought Michelangelo Antonioni to see me. For him, she was scouting the sets for *Blow-Up*. When I found out who the handsome man was with her, I blushed. I had told him to wait – I was filming. He was charming and murmured something about Dylan and *'certezza d'amore'*. Looking at him and Clare, I didn't think I had much hope of that.

'Translate, Clare,' he said. 'Translate.' She danced on the bare caulked boards, and then she clawed at his sleeve, and said: 'It is better not to love at all, than to love without certainty.'

I never went for introspection and self-analysis, nor did I describe the motives of the characters in my novels. I have always been a sort of existentialist. By our behaviour and our deeds are we known. I was most fortunate that David Hemmings described me before he died, in those days of *Adventures in the Skin Trade*:

Although the play was based on works by Dylan Thomas, it was adapted for the stage by Andrew Sinclair, a man of great singularity who was to have a profound influence on my future. He was also one of the most eccentric people I've ever met.

Andrew was an Old Etonian, a dour academic who gave the impression of being in a permanent state of mental trauma, as if the world might collapse under the weight of his thoughts. He was a highly regarded historian who'd published much fine work, but he dressed like an extra in a Spaghetti Western with that sort of studied rumpledness which only a top wardrobe designer could have concocted. His suits, when he wore them, looked like rejects from the Fifty Shilling Tailor, and his shirts had wide, unbuttoned collars, loosely held together by drab ties in vast Windsor knots.

His extraordinary, triangular brow, furrowed like an ill-ploughed field, seemed to stretch several feet up to a great pink dome, topped by a few dark strands of hair, cascading, wildly. Below, a glorious hooter swept in a great Gothic curve from brow to lower lip. From the depths beneath when he spoke, there emerged a grumbling murmur, like a volcano with a sore throat, while a floppy lower lip burbled in harmony, as if plucked from the point of his chin.

It was an amazing visage, but believe me, I couldn't have written the last couple of paragraphs if I hadn't adored him. He was an utterly unique man in whose Hindenburg head lay seams of knowledge I could only dream of. His adaptation of Dylan Thomas is a stunning work. Not only because it translates Thomas so well to the stage, but also because it does this with elegance, and a patina of nonsense the poet himself would have recognised and admired.

I invited Clare to the First Night at the Hampstead Theatre. As usual, she hardly spoke, certainly not of what was happening in her life, and then she rapidly disappeared. David Hemmings was incandescent in what I believe was the greatest performance of his career – glittering as the comet he would become with a comic timing almost worthy of Chaplin. The reviews were good, and we looked forward to a transfer after three weeks to the West End. In the *Guardian*, 'The poet comes to London, bewildered, over-articulate, shock-headed with a beer-bottle hopelessly stuck on his finger. His encounters are farcical, raucous and touching.' In the *Financial Times*, 'A superb piece of effervescent writing, pullulating with anecdote, caricature and life lived at a pace that would lay most men flat after an hour or two.' And in the *Telegraph*, 'Based on Lewis Carroll – Dylan in Blunderland – deliciously funny, a faithful blend of ribald sadness and unconventional good cheer.'

Without telling me, Clare took Antonioni to the Second Night. He was thunderstruck by the lightning and the gall of the Hemmings performance. That night, David was summoned to Claridge's, where

Clare stood behind a red curtain to hear the audition for *Blow-Up*. Terence Stamp was fired, Hemmings was hired. The moral was, if there was one: – always take a good part, even at four fivers a week. You never know who will come and see you at the theatre. As it was, the producer Carlo Ponti bought the penniless David a white Rolls-Royce coupé, and he drove away from Limehouse with more pomp than the neighbouring gangster Kray brothers. And, as we had lost our star, we never did reach the West End. Yet David was also to give his best film performance as the hip photographer in *Blow-Up*; while Vanessa Redgrave played Clare's indecipherable self, saying to Hemmings with his camera: 'My private life's already in a mess. It would be a disaster if…', only to hear his reply, 'So what – nothing like a little disaster for sorting things out.'

Years later, when I reached Hollywood, and Antonioni was filming *Zabriskie Point* in Death Valley, I read in the *Los Angeles Times* that, between takes, the Italian Director would climb a salt hill to talk to an alone and anonymous blonde, watching the climax, the explosion that shattered a ranch-house. I thought I knew who she might be. And on seeing Clare again for lunch on her rare return to London, I asked her about Death Valley. For once, in her coming and going, she would talk about Michelangelo. 'Yes, it was I. He had twenty cameras ready to record that big blow-up. He said, Was I satisfied? No, I said. I wanted him to blow up all America.'

He could not hold Clare. She quit him for another director, Bernardo Bertolucci. Freud once wrote that, after analysing women for thirty years, he still did not know what they wanted. Clare would always search for some perfection that she could never attain. But in leaving me and going off with Antonioni and taking David Hemmings with them after the run of *Adventures in the Skin Trade*, she was not aware that others had seen the play, and I would be translated elsewhere. And indeed I would be, by the redoubtable Lester Persky, a film mogul in the making, and unmaking.

- 'Now you've signed,' Lester Persky said to me, 'let's renegotiate.'
- This was a new proposition to me. I had thought a contract was a contract.
- 'But we have agreed, Lester,' I said.
- 'You have agreed,' Lester said. 'But I have not yet signed.'

    – 'And once you have agreed and signed, I still have to pay you. So let's renegotiate.'

So we dealt again over a lunch table in New York. I took less money over a longer period of time for writing a screenplay of my stage adaptation of *Adventures in the Skin Trade*. Although Antonioni had taken David Hemmings away from me, Tennessee Williams had also seen the play and had pronounced it the best one in London. He probably only fell for David's beauty and charisma, as we all did. Lester Persky had been backing Tennessee theatrically at that time and had decided to expand into making films. He bought an option on my property for very little and also my services as a screenwriter for not much more. And after a hard day's night in a bar, he got David to sign a paper napkin saying that he would play the lead in the film for a few silver peanuts. All without reference to our agents, of course.

When I had finished my screenplay, I took it at noon to Lester, who was staying at Claridge's. I found him lying on the floor on his back, his legs upstretched on a soft chair. 'It's my spine,' he said. 'But I have ordered breakfast.' At a knock, I opened the door of the suite, so that a waiter could totter forward with a silver platter, holding a cornucopia of goodies, and lay the vast metal dish on the marble table by the bedside. A wail of anguish rose from Lester's lips, and he sat bolt upright. 'Goddamit,' he said. 'You've put it on my contact lenses.' So when I presented my script to him, he said he obviously couldn't read it. And when I asked him for my advance money on delivery, he told me to wait. And as he had warned me before, I would have to renegotiate yet again. For he still had not paid me.

Such was a valuable lesson in how to secure a property, a screenplay and a star for a few thousand dollars. Watch the fringe theatre, pick up the rising writer and the future star, sign them cheaply out of reach of their advisers. Insist on personal negotiations. If not, no deal. Something signed on a serviette is perfectly binding in a court of law. You can wipe an agent's nose on it. Actually, Lester lost on the deal, because he never made the film of *Adventures in the Skin Trade*. Doubtless, he wrote off his expenses, for he went on to become an expert at tax-loss investments in films and produced many good movies through his company, Persky-Bright.

He had though, like Lord Nelson, a blind eye in picking out the signals of the stars to be. When we were trying to put the stage version of Dylan's novel on at The Circle in the Square in Greenwich Village, Lester took me to see another little-known young American actor, then playing the lead in Henry Livings's *Eh!* It was a fine performance, but Lester and Ted Mann, the theatrical manager, shook their heads. 'He's not big enough,' they agreed. 'Not big enough to carry a Broadway show.' The actor's name was Dustin Hoffman. His stage act was just before he was chosen to play in the film of *The Graduate*. If Lester had signed him up on a Babe Ruth candybar wrapping paper to play the lead in our film, we could have set our terms for making it, after a year or two.

The hopeful film producer with a little to spend in mounting a movie must have a nose like a truffle pig and a touch like a fly fisherman. The scent of the right property, the feel for the coming writer and the future star is a deal in store. With instinct and flair – and twenty thousand dollars or less – a producer can put together a package wrapped in gold gift-paper, worth a ten million dollar budget or more.

THEY PROFIT

The faint far whiff of writing screenplays in Hollywood began to change my solitary choices. It had long been the temptation and ruin of writers – Scott Fitzgerald and William Faulkner, Christopher Isherwood and even Bertolt Brecht. I was also from a generation weaned on the screen. Our very language was made spare by one-liners from the stars, John Wayne saying 'That'll be the day,' or the last line of *Some Like It Hot*, 'Nobody's perfect.' Above all, we had learned to write without blatant motivation; the dialogue and the acting and the background had to express all. While scribbling for the cinema meant an almost inevitable corruption in the process, a refinement of a gross of words into a residue of action led to the *reductio ad absurdum* of Hemingway, a sort of grace and censure under producer pressure.

Of one hundred scripts commissioned for the cinema, ten reach some stage of pre-production, and one is finally filmed, usually after rewriting by many hands. My first screenplay for Columbia Pictures, *Before Winter Comes*, was blessed as my first novel had been, by an improbable instant acceptance. I was the sole screenwriter and the stars who were offered the roles instantly took them – David Niven as the British Army officer who was handed back to the Russians, the refugee Topol, an admirable administrator of an intractable camp, with Godard's girl Anna Karina playing the love interest and the young John Hurt in his first screen role as the good lieutenant. This story of loyalty and treachery, duty and betrayal, was set in the occupied zones of Austria at the end of the Second World War and it described the crimes of the British in handing whole divisions of Ukrainians, who had fought for the Germans, back to the untender mercies of Stalin. It was also an echo of the Allies' behaviour over failing to save the Jews from the concentration camps, sticking to the letter of the military law rather than reading the book of justice.

In Bolivia the army, helped by American CIA agents and detector helicopters, killed Che Guevara. In certain radical circles, it was equivalent to the killing of Christ, and the iconography of the posters of the student world treated Che's death in that way. His beret as a halo round his head, his beard as an aureole, sometimes clutching the rifle of revolution in his hand, Che's martyred countenance was displayed on the walls of a million university rooms. Although the authorities required his body to be burned and his ashes scattered so that there could be no shrine to him, Marianne later learned that his two forearms were severed and these holy relics of the liberation struggle were returned to Cuba. Herself torn between Deacon and myself, seeking a cause to resolve the divisions of her life, she begged me to send her to Cuba to do a book for my new cinema press – *Viva Che!* – in tribute to the fallen hero. Her faith and need and conviction were so great that I sent her away. Her absence, at least, postponed a conclusion at home.

Cuba had become the darling of the new Left, an island that could cock a snook, if not a missile, at the almighty Uncle Sam only a hundred sea miles away. In a model contemporary revolution, a small band of guerrillas operating from the countryside had destroyed an urban dictator in Havana and had brought equality and literacy to an oppressed people. The tens of thousands of political prisoners, held by Castro and his ubiquitous informers on every block and in each village, were as invisible to the foreign radicals as the Gulag had been to the fellow-travellers in Stalin's heyday.

Marianne arrived in Cuba to be met by what she called a wave of love, a baptism into revolution. Politically naive, she never saw that she was the consenting victim of an intelligent secret service, which wished to extend its influence and its sources of information. She went to the Havana Cultural Congress in the January of 1968, which attracted nearly four hundred intellectuals from Latin and North America and Europe. Many of them were members of the Fair Play for Cuba Committee, which had been formed eight years previously, and which boasted leading authorities such as Sartre with his Marxist and blinkered anti-Americanism. In a parody of John F. Kennedy's inauguration speech, the imperative was 'Ask not what Cuba can do for you, ask what you can do for Cuba'. So asked, the decadent, romantic Marianne was converted into a fanatic.

My increasing involvement in writing screenplays in Hollywood, the huge income I would earn from acting as a script doctor on a dozen films, and my development of Lorrimer Publishing into printing the illustrated classic screenplays of Renoir and Carné, Bergman and Wajda, Kurosawa and Welles, all collided to divide me from radical activities, even though I was earning the funds to support them. I had sent Marianne to Cuba to commemorate Che, I had not gone. I used to justify myself by saying that I was polishing bad screenplays in order to publish good ones. And indeed, the half million copies of the seveny-five classic screenplays which Lorrimer was to produce over the next twenty years was to teach a whole generation the grammar of the cinema, as it taught me. I also had the privilege of meeting and working with many of the world's leading directors and actors, who tutored me in the film trade by their example.

Marianne returned from Cuba and stayed briefly in my house on the river; we were still, in our fashion, together. She spoke phrases that I had never heard and could hardly understand. This was the jargon of late street socialism, even more meaningless than the sloppy slang of flower power. When she said of the civil war in Nigeria, 'Biafra is a bastion of Portuguese-Rothschild imperialism,' I replied that the statement was in an incomprehensible language. Nigeria was in the British Commonwealth, neither the Portuguese nor the Jews had anything to do with what was essentially mere tribal strife, and the whole vocabulary of Marxism would have to be rewritten as it was meaningless, because its rhetoric was stuck in the nineteenth century and no longer applied to the modern age.

Russia itself held the last great empire in Eastern Europe, after the colonial powers had given up their possessions overseas. The imperialism which it saw in others was its own practice. And it would collapse inevitably from its own colonialism over Catholic Slavs and Muslim Central Asians, if it did not adapt as capitalism had, and speak in terms that had some relevance and sense. My prophecy proved correct, but at the time, I appeared to be a ghastly reactionary. Marianne left for Paris to work for the Cubans in soliciting eulogies from great names for *Viva Che!*, as well as for the student revolt of 1968, which would swell that May to bursting point.

I was to learn more about the truth of the divisions in the Black Power movement and of colonialism, when I tried to stage a *Black Beowulf* in the Roundhouse. I brought over from Ghana a diplomat called Desmond Tay, who was also the leading hand drummer in West Africa. When I confessed to him that my father had served in the Gold Coast Police, Tay recalled being one of his constables and said he was the best officer they ever had, fair and just and true. So much for my guilt about the old Empire. Tay and his troupe beat their drums for our recording for eight hours until blood came out of their fingernails, while a motley work-bag of actors from Africa and the Caribbean chanted my Anglo-Saxon lyrics to the beat of the tom-toms. This ill-starred venture collapsed when the Africans in the cast went to war against those from the West Indies, calling them slaves and Uncle Toms, while the West Indians called the Africans tribesmen and savages. I called it a day when three large gentlemen from Jamaica and Trinidad demanded all the money I had, to make a film of their oppression in fascist Britain by the Grendels of the fuzz, as the police were then known. I never again thought that the blacks would combine better than the Scottish clans had, and so present a united front to English power before they were ground down.

I had driven to Austria to stay on the lake at Hallstadt because the director of *Before Winter Comes*, the old terrier J. Lee Thompson, had wanted me available for rewriting during the shooting of the film. So I could not be present at the student insurrection in New York any more than in Paris at the beginning of that May. My screenplay for Columbia Pictures was also being shot to pieces – with all the compromises of commercial considerations. The script was not allowed to say that a Jew was returned to the Russians by the British, so Topol had to become a gypsy, rather reducing the impact of the film. When the action was to begin, David Niven would have me banned from the set because he always changed his lines and did not like the author present when he did so. A gift of two trout he had caught would be enough to mollify me. The high moment would be Topol's Sedah, given in a Salzburg hotel, with bald neo-Nazi waiters bringing in the unleavened bread, all the lamentations irrelevant because Israel had just recaptured Jerusalem, with myself assigned to read the role of the Wicked or Sceptical Man. I would make my peace with Topol by coaching his English for his best speech, about fleas living for only twenty-four hours as they were performing tricks in a flea circus; under the brute lights, they only lived an hour in a minimalist concentration camp.

For me, there was one revelation, the word made flesh or carved in wood. For the curious thing about being a writer is that the most concrete object you can produce is a word, if you write 'black' the word is there, but only as a suggestive adjective; only the accident of black print may indeed turn the adjective 'black' into a word that is also visibly black. But that is merely luck. What if the printing ink is green or purple or red? Or what if black print is used to describe your colourful adjective, 'many-splendoured' or 'wine-dark' or 'incarnadine'? Such a dullness of ink is enough to make the writer drop his pen and seek the Joseph's coat of blowing his mind.

There is another way out. That is to write the script for a colour film. When I had worked on *Before Winter Comes*, my script allowed for seasonal change, progressing from the snow through the spring and summer to the autumn of post-war Austria. Its various drafts were bound in marvellous colours, crimson and turquoise and heliotrope; but the words of the script remained black and dull, despite the fact that they could jink around like men running for their lives, when the film stars put on the pressure for a change of lines to help their images. On the whole, the words would settle back again into their proper places after the pressure had been eased, due to admirable diplomacy by the producer and director. But the colour of the words stayed obstinately flat and unreal. Far more real were the stars, David Niven and Topol and Anna Karina and John Hurt, who visibly sprawled and smiled several times daily across wide and wonderful screens:

Twinkle, twinkle, mighty star,
How I wonder what you are?
Up above the world so high,
Like a screenplay in the sky ...

I was awed by their company, because stardust was literally scattered in their wake, so that strangers popped eyes and buttons, dropped mouths and parcels at their passing. I felt the mere attribute of the other's attention, the vacuum through which brightness was falling through the air. Then the final draft of the script was done, and the film was set up on location in Austria. The shooting began. And I flew out to Salzburg to see the first scenes in the April snow. When I arrived, the producer met me, a man of sterling and dollar worth, Robert Emmett Ginna. We drove off to the set through mountain scenery that imitated picture postcards more glossily than the postcards imitated it. We needed a nice bit of gloom for the opening sequence, and all we were getting was the background for *The Sound of Music*. Nature's colour really has nothing to do with art.

When I actually reached the set, however, I began to feel for the first time that my dull trade had its own hidden glory. For the words were becoming actual. A tank, albeit made of canvas, lay in a ditch, grey and green and full of false menace as refugees plodded past; it would have been a real tank, too, if the railways could have got one there from a German Panzer graveyard. An elegant Niven still bestrode his jeep like a colossus; but he was now wearing the trench coat and major's crown, glittering brilliantly because the script had stated so. A whole farmhouse had been translated into a Displaced Persons Camp; crossroads bristled with military emplacements and the mobile barbers'-poles that are used by the military to check traffic.

Yet the moment that I, too, felt like a small constellation, the butt end of Cassiopeia, was when I saw the actual adjective. A summerhouse was to be built for the heroine, Anna Karina, the most enchanting screen actress in all Europe. For no reason I can remember, I had specified that this summerhouse should be 'octagonal'. And lo and behold, there in front of me on the green hillside among the pines stood an octagonal summerhouse, so real and wooden and solid that it had already been presented to the Mayor of the local village of Abtenau for use as a Boys' Club, once the film should be over.

I walked to the summerhouse and touched my adjective. I walked round the summerhouse and touched all eight sides of my adjective. I looked through the window of the summerhouse, and inside in a blue embroidered dress stood Anna Karina inside my adjective. Inside the space of nine-letter word with eight sides, I had captured alive, flesh and blood and breathing, the dream image of my young manhood. And I knew for the first time that it still might be true – in the beginning was the word.

On set, I was actually given a role for one day as an American military policeman asking for official papers, a caricature of my father's life. I was desperately worried about Marianne as the news of the ferocious street fighting in Paris spread, with the tear gas and the batons and the mass arrests; so was Anna Karina with her broken connection with Godard, whose chief action was to put an end to the Cannes Film Festival, along with François Truffaut, in support of the national strikes in France. Later at the première of the film in London, Anna Karina would say to me, 'Andrew, you look sad.' And I would say, 'Yes, I was also married to a French revolutionary for too long. She has gone to Cuba.' And she would say, 'I know, the revolution is good, it is good to feel for it – but not a hundred and fifty times a day.'

I drove to Paris before the shooting finished, at the end of May. I had four jerry-cans of petrol on my roof-rack because there was none to be had in France. On the roads outside the provincial towns, the gates of the factories were barred and red flags flew from the machine shops, while men stood idle, peering through the wire and the grilles at the future. They shouted 'profiteer' at me because of the gasoline on the car roof. On television Prime Minister Pompidou appeared beaten, giving huge concessions to the workers – more than nine of twenty million were on strike. President Charles de Gaulle had flown to Germany to check on the loyalty of the seventy thousand troops in the French Zone; their tanks were said to be rolling towards the embattled capital.

When I reached our apartment in Paris, Marianne was lost in the Sorbonne, so I went to the Theatre of the Revolution at l'Odéon, which had been taken over as a night-and-day debating chamber by the rebels. Drama had become real, the *Marat/Sade* play was a street event, the halls being made into parliaments. Stephen Spender was there, and he found it like the sixth act in a Theatre of Cruelty. Although the performances were chaotic, they seemed to the audience more entertaining than Ionesco or Beckett. Spender noted that the Paris students were like hippies without a drug culture; they wished to live the life of the revolution even while they were taking action to bring it to be. They did not wish to hear of the downfall of the anarchists in the Spanish Republic, who had also wanted democracy. Their revolution was thought to be new and unprecedented. The others might have failed, but theirs would succeed. As three of their slogans went:

I TAKE WHAT I WANT AS REALITY BECAUSE I BE-
LIEVE IN THE REALITY OF WHAT I WANT, and: BE
REALISTS, DEMAND THE IMPOSSIBLE, and: RUN,
COMRADE, THE OLD WORLD IS BEHIND YOU.

Although I thought I knew that the failure of the student revolt was certain, there was a contagion of hope at the barricaded Sorbonne, where more slogans were scrawled on the walls: HERE ALIEN-ATION BEGINS – RATHER LIFE! and: YOUTH IS ETERNAL

DRUNKENNESS, IT IS THE FEVER OF REASON, a phrase that Rimbaud could have written. Already new authoritarian groups were taking over from the free-style fighting students, hurling their cobblestones at the riot police, the fearsome CRS with black helmets and plastic shields. Ex-mercenaries from the troubles in Africa, the Katangais, were introducing the methods of their opponents into the revolutionary cause: extortion and beating and rape. As another graffito read: LIBERTY IS THE CRIME THAT CONTAINS ALL CRIMES. IT IS OUR ABSOLUTE WEAPON. While the forces of repression and the state grouped for a showdown, the students seemed to shift from demands for reform to the desire for an apocalypse.

Sinister scrawls on the walls such as: AND IF WE BURNED THE SORBONNE? caused a shift of Parisian feeling from favouring the rebel cause to vilifying it. Too many cars had been torched or made into barricades, private property was under threat. Noam Chomsky had told the occupation squads at Columbia that they would rather Karl Marx had burned down the British Museum than worked on *Das Kapital* in it, and Stephen Spender echoed the thoughts, coming to the conclusion that however much the university needed a revolution, and the society needed a revolution, these were separate issues for the Sorbonne activists, who might still use the weapons of the trained mind. 'For the university, even if it does not conform to their wishes, is an arsenal from which they can draw the arms which can change society.'

Marianne, too, saw the change in conditions in the Sorbonne, although she would not come back with me to England. She would fight on to the bitter end. Her worst experience had been when she was swept to the front of a mob trying to storm the Senate. Two iron barriers secured by a chain held back the press, and through the chink between them, she saw machine-gunners waiting behind their weapons for the charge and the inevitable massacre. But government *agents déprovocateurs* dressed in students' clothing had shouted to the crowd to attack another government target, the *doppelgängers* of Danny Cohn-Bendit who had started the whole revolt in the concrete jungle of isolated Nanterre, one of the new French universities like the concrete ziggurats which I had visited in England.

Marianne also saw the writing on the wall with the reaction of the right wing to de Gaulle's deal with the Communists, who hated this explosion of anarchism and radicalism outside their Stalinist control of the faithful in France. The president promised general elections and gave the unions great concessions, their leaders could return to the workers with more wages and less factory hours, the students were now isolated. The Champs-Élysées was packed with the cars of the bourgeoisie hooting the five-note slogan, *Al-gé-rie Fran-çaise*', for the Algerian war had divided French society as the Vietnam strife had America. This display was 'the triumphant bacchanal of the Social World of Conspicuous Consumption, shameless, crowing, and more vulgar' than any crowd that Spender had ever seen on Broadway or in Chicago.

For it was the consumer and manipulative society that the revolt had attacked – and the workers and their leaders had now sold out and adopted it. Most of the slogans on the walls bore the same message:

THE MORE YOU CONSUME, THE LESS YOU LIVE

SOCIETY IS A CARNIVOROUS FLOWER

MAN MAKES LOVE WITH THINGS

MERCHANDISE IS THE OPIUM OF THE PEOPLE

HIDE YOURSELF, OBJECT!

HAPPINESS IS BOUGHT – STEAL IT

THE IMAGINATION TO POWER

And on one of the dozens of street posters manufactured at the occupied École des Beaux-Arts, a radical conjugation:

I PARTICIPATE
YOU PARTICIPATE
HE PARTICIPATES
WE PARTICIPATE
YOU PARTICIPATE
THEY PROFIT

The Beaux Arts was almost the last of the occupied buildings to fall, and under attack Marianne was given the original of its most famous poster to take away to safety, the blue-black shape of a riot policeman looking like a space terminator with his truncheon raised, and CRS = SS blazoned on his shield. She gave it to me to carry away to England to commemorate the failing rebellion, along with two other significant posters, one of de Gaulle's shadow holding a hand over a young man's mouth: BE YOUNG AND SHUT UP, and the other of the radicals' defiance of anodyne democracy, de Gaulle hitting France with a tricoloured baton and saying: KEEP VOTING – I'LL DO THE REST.

As I left Paris for Calais and the ferry, I picked up three battered students from Rouen and Boulogne, who had come into the capital to protest, and now were going home, because they were frightened and beaten. They were very young and had no ideology; they had joined in the struggle for the excitement and for the attack on all authority, particularly their *lycées* and their parents and the dreaded *bac*, the universal examination. If there was any slogan that took their fancy, it was: THE MORE I MAKE LOVE, THE MORE I WANT TO MAKE A REVOLUTION, THE MORE I WANT TO MAKE A REVOLUTION, THE MORE I WANT TO MAKE LOVE.

The defeat of the students in Paris did not lose their war across the world, although it was an unsettling example, as the defeat of the Commune had been in 1848, when most of the cities of Europe had exploded in rebellion before they were repressed. A map of contemporary outbreaks of urban violence printed in *L'Événement* with its graffito on the cover: WHY IT ISN'T FINISHED YET, showed six revolts in Japan, one in South Korea, one each in Indonesia and Malaya, regular uprisings in China, two outbursts in India, five in the Middle East and another five in Africa, five again in Eastern Europe and five in Italy, many in Germany where the Berlin student leader Rudi Dutschke had been shot in the head, some in Spain and the Low Countries and Scandinavia and Britain, eleven in South America and two only in the United States. The examples of Columbia and Paris had ignited the students of the globe, who had nothing to lose but their final examinations. Massively repressed in every country, the scattered fires still spluttered in England, as always a little behind the times and never knowing when it was beaten.

In Hungary at the time of Suez, which had started my personal rebellion, Russia again was forfeiting all pretence to be the backer of socialist revolutions across the world by intervening in Czechoslovakia to conserve its Eastern European empire. The Prague Spring had been the only successful urban revolution in 1968, but the rise of the Dubcek régime to power was a middle-class uprising of the intelligentsia, resenting Soviet and socialist control over economic activity and political life. At the end of August, a quarter of a million troops crossed the frontiers to crush the reforms. Russian tanks surrounded Wenceslas Square and united the Czech nation by their act of aggression.

Although the Czech leadership was summoned to Moscow and bullied into submission, Soviet power was revealed as a gun barrel behind a brazen mask. Two thousand workers at the CKD factory in Prague described the Russia of Chairman Brezhnev as it was, 'an imperialist state with all its characteristic attributes ... neither the homeland of socialism nor a shield of socialism'. The Tsars had put out the last lights of rebellion in 1848, and now, one hundred and twenty years later, that final extinction was the act of a politburo in the Kremlin. Refusing to adapt, the Communist leaders doomed the Union of Soviet Socialist Republics to future disintegration.

Lyndon Johnson had already dug the grave of his political career during the Vietnamese War and his refusal to run again led to the Democratic Convention ending in sad farce and despair rather than street drama and hope. His fall and the preoccupation of most of the western nations with their own domestic riots had made Brezhnev feel secure enough to invade Czechoslovakia, just as the involvement of the West in the Suez affair had permitted the Hungarian invasion. But that disaster had begun for me the full serpentine cycle of failed protest, which ended by biting its own tail in 1968 on the Paris streets. As John Lennon was to sing in 'Revolution': 'Don't you know that you can count me out.'

Because of an incident at Limehouse, I found I was already known in Hollywood. In a rare stint as a film producer, Frank Sinatra had come to Britain to make a picture. One scene was set on the Rhine; but opposite my river house on the Thames was a factory sign, ENTHOVEN. By cheating a shot from my balcony, a small fortune could be saved from the budget. I was insanely writing *Gog* when a front man hammered on my door, interrupting me. 'Would

I accept a hundred pounds from Sinatra to shoot from my house?'
I swore, and said I was writing. Never taking no for an answer and
presuming that my poverty was greater than my pride, the Sinatra
gang returned a week later with several movie vans and set up shop
in the nearby pub, *The Black Horse*. Again the front man hammered
at my door. 'Would two hundred pounds …?'

'Get out – I'm writing.'

The landlord of the pub later told me a furious discussion broke
out in *The Black Horse* about what to do. Teach me a lesson? Or go
to the Rhine? That would be at least another hundred thousand
pounds on the budget. There was only one solution. Protesting and
livid with anger, Frank Sinatra himself walked across Narrow Street
and banged on my dusty door. Furious at a second intervention that
morning, I ran down the stairs to open up. Hardly noticing the
small shape in front of me and barely hearing his words, 'I'm Frank
Sinatra, and I would like to…', I screamed at him, 'I'm writing. I
never heard of you.' And I banged the door shut.

There was fury in *The Black Horse*. Sinatra's goons, an Italian mob
of brethren, were ordered expletively to do something about me
immediately. The landlord said that I was insane, being a writer,
and anyway this was the turf of Jack the Ripper and the Kray Brothers. Perhaps they were protecting me. And Sinatra would certainly
be deported, if he began a gang war here. Reason prevailed over revenge, and I had the last laugh. In the film dictionaries, after *SINA-
TRA, Frank* would appear the name of *SINCLAIR, Andrew*.

So, when I would reach Tinseltown two years later, I was the man
who had never heard of Frank Sinatra. Where celebrity was all, my
ignorance amused them. I was to become a leading script doctor
for Columbia and CBS Films, and in whatever palace I stayed, at
the Beverly-Wilshire or the Beverly Hills Hotel or on Malibu
Beach, I would always feel an enervating mixture of excitement and
envy, isolation and degradation. There was no question that screenwriters were the serfs of the industry. But in the beginning was the
Word, and without the right words in the script, the leads would
not come down from their Bel Air Mansions and play.

Rewriting scripts for stars in Hollywood such as Jack Lemmon
and Gregory Peck, I learned two vital lessons. Firstly, never give
celebrities a query. They answer, they never ask. If a script had more
than two questions for the star to deliver, it flew out of the window

into my hands for another draft. The other necessity was the topper. The star had to leave each scene with a memorable phrase; preferably monosyllabic, to top the action. Then CUT to the next scene. These quips could become folklore. 'Make my day.' For the star was the star was the star, and had to have the last word, as long as it was curt before the cut.

So the scenario writers were pampered and overpaid, abused and ignored once all the relevant phrases had been squeezed from their fingernails by the torture of the Hollywood writing process, treatment after treatment and draft after draft, the mutilation of the original plot by a thousand slashes until only a twitching corpse was left with the right reflex actions for the great names of the business. It was little fun while it lasted, but it was fabulously profitable. I certainly could write faster than the Hollywood moguls could read. And I could still put out classic screenplays and revolutionary books, which made sense, although I was lashed to the mast as Odysseus when he heard the Sirens, steeped in blood, singing on their clashing rocks.

COUNT ME OUT

I did not know that I was flying back from Hollywood towards England to meet two of the greater recognitions and resolutions of my life. My father had suffered his first stroke and my mother thought I was becoming a revolutionary idiot. I went to see my father in the little bungalow which he had bought near Hastings and called the Matchbox. In spite of his age and his condition, he retained all of that stern immaturity that gave him the nicknames of 'Zinc' and 'Boy' throughout his life. I learned how much I had hurt him and my stepmother by playing out my mother's wars against them, respecting her commands and refusing to see them. In the face of dying, all prohibitions are irrelevant. And so I began to make it up with my father before his end, and I am forever thankful that I did. In their last little place in the twilight of the British Empire, among the carved Ashanti stools and Arab teak chests from Zanzibar, these two old Africa hands had found a private peace, and I was allowed a little understanding and forgiveness from the straightjacket of my radical prejudices and hardness of heart.

I learned that they had met after an extraordinary act of bravery by my father, who had ended his career as the Assistant Commissioner of Police in newly independent Tanzania. He had received a decoration as a Commander of the British Empire for sticking to his duties, and he deserved the medal. There had been a riot in the docks of Dar es Salaam. Wading in alone with his lead-tipped truncheon, my father found his under-officer John with bloody matter oozing from his shattered skull. Pointing at random at six screaming local dockers, he said: 'You, you and you four, you'll hang for murder, unless you save this man.'

My father knelt and wrapped his puttee round John's smashed head to bind in his brains, seeping through the broken cranium. Reinforcements arrived with a hospital van, there were half a dozen arrests and justice or injustice was done. And my stepmother, the matron Phyllis, who had earned her keep from the age of thirteen as a nurse, met my father standing nightly beside John's bed, a vigil in hope of a recovery. John did live, and my father and Phyllis were married to look after each other in their retirement. Although my mother forbade me and my brother from ever seeing them, I did from time to time, especially when they were proudly going to get their gong at Buckingham Palace, which I had once guarded in my public duties.

My mother, in her house at Falmouth, was furious at my visit to my father, although she did concede that a stroke might make a difference. She still venerated my dead step-father and took any deviation by me from her side as a betrayal. And then occurred the only time that I have ever lifted a hand against a woman, a scene from a minimal Hedda Gabler, which was also a laying to rest of the imperial past. We had never referred for fourteen years to what had happened at my crisis of conscience over Suez. That day, I happened to say to my mother that she had changed my life and had caused me great embarrassment among my friends by making me turn back from going to Hungary, after sending me a letter praising my desire to leave Cambridge and telling me to follow my convictions at all costs.

'I never wrote you that letter,' she said.

'You did,' l said. 'I have kept it in a box in the attic.'

I left her sitting by the Aga cooker in the large kitchen of the Cornish house, as I went up to the loft to retrieve the letter. I knew that it was an occasion. Until then, I had presumed that my mother, like a little Mussolini, was always right. I had followed her dictates without question or in silence. But I had crossed her by seeing my father, and now this second proof of her error was upon us. We loved each other dearly, but here I had questioned her veracity as well as her authority.

I found her old letter to me, the beginning of my career as a writer. And I brought it down to her, sitting in the kitchen, and I put it into her hand. She read the first of the five pages of notepaper, opened the door of the Aga and pushed the letter towards the glowing coals. I caught her wrist and took the letter from her fingers.

'You can't burn the truth,' I said.

We never talked of the matter again. But there was something broken between us. She knew that I knew that she was not always correct. The code of the Empire had a fallacy in its righteousness. But it made for more humanity. Although she had hardly touched me since the age of four – contact was bad for boys, especially kissing, in case they became cissies – now we began to embrace and hug, until we ended in that power of love that was the message of the day.

With the publication of *Viva Che!*, I did appear to be waving a red flag for the Cuban revolution. These tributes to Guevara, collected by Marianne from leading sympathetic writers over the world, viewed him as a cultural as well as a revolutionary hero. To Italo Calvino, Che demanded the greatest spirit of sacrifice; he would continue to be more and more right by dying in order to set in motion a struggle which could not stop. To David Mercer, the myth-making about the already legendary Che did not cloak his counter-violence, miscalled 'terrorism', against that of entrenched reactionary authorities with their crimes, tortures and suppressions of popular resistance in Latin America. To Susan Sontag, Che should not be consigned to the pantheon of rebel martyrs or romantic adventurers like Lord Byron, but he should be remembered for his mission in spreading the socialist Cuban experiment across the globe. To Graham Greene, 'he represented the idea of gallantry, chivalry and adventure in a world given up to business arrangements between the great powers.' As for myself, I did not believe that Che's example could succeed outside Latin America, but I was an admirer of his asthmatic courage in taking to the jungle with thirty men to capture a continent, the ultimate in reckless commitment.

The young would find new heroes, but none more inspiring When the general in the film of *Viva Zapata!* looks down at the riddled corpse of the people's leader, he says, 'Sometimes a dead man can be a terrible enemy.' For the rich nations of the earth, and for the corrupt governments that still rule many of the poor nations, the dead Che would remain a terrible and a beautiful enemy.

The success of *Viva Che!*, the first tribute to him to appear in the West, was followed by a political struggle over the publication of his *Bolivian Diary*, smuggled back to Havana and published there after his execution in a free edition of quarter of a million copies. A doctored version, backed by the CIA, appeared in the United States of America. Marianne secured from the Cuban embassy in London a true copy. I translated it with an Argentine student, and then it was published to acclaim; major houses across Europe took it up, and it remains in print as a seminal account of guerrilla warfare, along with the reminiscences of Von Lettow in Africa and of Mao himself in China. My action made Lorrimer seem to be a revolutionary as well as a cinematic press, and so the secret services of four countries put us under surveillance: those of America and Britain, France and Cuba. It was, however, invaluable in gaining me a Cuban visa, when I had to go there in 1969 to extricate Marianne from her revolutionary folly.

The style of the *Bolivian Diary* then seemed to me as flat and necessary as that of *Robinson Crusoe*, yet its cumulative effect was even more powerful and moving than Daniel Defoe's masterpiece, because the reader knew in advance that the hero would be captured and executed when the pages of the diary went blank, following the entry that the army had claimed to have located his hide-out and the news seemed to be a red herring. As clear and understated as the *Commentaries* by Julius Caesar about his campaigns in Gaul, Che was quoted in an introduction to his last work by Fidel Castro. Guevara said to his comrades in the jungles of Bolivia: 'This form of struggle gives us the opportunity to turn ourselves into revolutionaries, the highest state a man can reach; but it also allows us to graduate as men; those who cannot reach either of these two states must say so and give up the struggle.'

Because of these two books, I was asked by the distinguished professor of English Literature of University College London, Frank Kermode, to contribute a biography of Guevara to his Modern Masters collection. In his words, the series meant 'the men who have changed and are changing the life and thought of our age'. So at that time, Guevara was held to be as significant as Albert Camus and James Joyce, Sigmund Freud and Trotsky and Ludwig Wittgenstein. No longer, but my work on Che was received well and translated into fourteen languages. An accolade came from Alberto Granado, who had accompanied Guevara as a student on a long motorcycle trip across Latin America, later made into a film rather more important than *Easy Rider*. The Argentine voyager said that my short book on Che was the most understanding of his character amidst all the many biographies on him. Perhaps, but I was acting as a mere referee between the ruthless terrorist image of him in the eyes of the critics of the Right, and the revolutionary saint, seen by Left Wing commentators. Liberal Pig in the Middle I was, once again. The irony was that this radical publishing was being subsidized by the major studios in Hollywood. I was still acting as a script-doctor for them on rewriting screenplays that were never to be made, a series of exercises in well-paid futility which sapped my self-belief in my powers as a scribe. I seemed to be selling out, as so many of the radicals were, to the seductions of the Mammon of DeMille, although the rapturous reception of *Gog* on both sides of the Atlantic still persuaded some people that I was a good writer. But now I refused to reforge the Hollywood scripts in Los Angeles; instead, I returned to type them in the best suites in the old hotels of Mediterranean Europe, chiefly in Nice and Venice. And there I took Marianne in the October of 1968 to the Grand Hotel on the anniversary of Guevara's death.

Our sitting-room was a vast cube on the Grand Canal opposite San Salute, the church built in thanksgiving to God for saving the lagoon city from the plague. Napoleon had slept in the suite, as had Mussolini and Hitler and Pope John. The faded silk on the walls, the greening gilt frames and the black glass of the wrinkled mirrors that reflected the marble floor suggested that we were in a mausoleum, not only of the famous dead who had been there, but of those we mourned and of our buried ideals and passion. On the anniversary of Guevara's murder, I had huge candles brought in with the special dinner, and their flames made fractured spirals of lights in the obscure reflections of the ancient mirrors, as much ghosts as little funeral pyres. When the feast was over, we made love in melancholy. But we did make love, not revolution.

I did not know that Marianne was desperate to have a child. She flew back from Venice to live again with Deacon. Within a few weeks, she found herself pregnant. Torn between both of us, remembering what had seemed to be the communal love of explosive Cuba, she bought a single air ticket to the island and left. Two letters were sent to Deacon and myself, announcing that she intended to give the child to the revolution. If it was a boy, it would be called Che, if it was a girl, it would be called Tania, la Guerrillera. To my chagrin, she also sent a telegram to Deacon which stated: YOU FIRST, REVOLUTION SECOND. This left me a bad third, although she had always sworn to me that she loved me the best. I was still her legal husband and the only person who could get her out of Cuba, if her nerve failed and she wanted to leave. That would not be a facile matter, for the authorities took away passports when strangers entered. As usual, arriving was far easier than departing. Hot water is fine for a plunge, but it scalds after a dip.

I have never looked for drama nor danger. They were wished upon me, as they were wished upon Graham Greene's hero in *Our Man in Havana*. My telephone calls to Cuba from Hollywood were so heavily monitored that my wife might have been Mata Hari. 'Baby' to the eavesdroppers seemed the code for 'bomb.' In the event, baby meant baby, and I had to bring him out of there in the womb, or he would be born a Cuban citizen, perhaps for his good, certainly for our ill.

My chief concern, however, was how to reach Cuba and return with Marianne before she gave birth to a child given to the system of Cuban Intelligence. My rival and friend Deacon was also disturbed. Every night he railed at me about the faithlessness of women, or a woman, while I wallowed in a grandiose self-pity. He swore the child was mine and ranted at her deception and broken promises to return to him. He slung down two suitcases of her clothes in my Limehouse garage and said he would marry a Guinness lady. Of course, he did not.

I carried a small copy of *Timon of Athens* round in my pocket for a year, until its covers fell off. I identified wholly with the misjudged man, ostracized for his reckless generosity and turned into a human animal. I was to give his name to my film company and the unborn child. The Greek Senator had been right about him, as my old friends were right about me:

Still in motion
Of raging waste? It cannot hold; it will not.

It had not in my own case, as I wasted all I had painstakingly earned, particularly the intimacy of love. I had always quoted Reverdy, that I did not need liberty so much, but only to be chained by what I loved. But I had broken my chain with Marianne and had allowed the affair with Deacon, in order to regain my liberty to write. So I decided I had to write *Magog*, the sequel to *Gog*, about the suffering of *l'homme raisonnable de pouvoir,* whose logical exercise of power led inexorably to the decline of Britain through wrong choice. 'There is a third alternative to pain or inhumanity – work, good work.'

Now Deacon changed his mind and begged to go to Cuba in my place. I laughed at him. I had my plan, I said. Only Marianne's official husband could get her out, and I was still that. I no longer knew whether I was betraying my friend or he was betraying me. I might be betraying my country to excise Marianne from Cuban Intelligence. 'Anyway, it would destroy Marianne's credibility! It would not allow her to leave the revolution with honour, and she has none.' Even for her, the child-to-be was more important than cutting sugar cane.

On a flight back from Hollywood to London, it was the turn of a French intelligence agent to sit next to me. My interrogator was absolutely charming. He gave me a friendly grin and offered me a *cognac*. So I smiled back and accepted and said how bored I was at being followed by members of the secret services, when they were so bloody obvious. What was *his* cover story?

'First, I was Che Guevara's astrologer in Havana,' he told me most seriously. 'And then I was his acupuncturist in Pyongyang in North Korea.'

I laughed until I choked. A spook with wit. Incredible.

'I will tell you all you want to know,' I said. 'The truth. We'll drink a bottle of brandy, and I will tell you the whole truth.'

As the truth was that the affair was about a baby and not a bomb, I had the chance, at the very least, of getting the French secret service off Marianne's back. I could also excuse her revolutionary actions and Intelligence work for Cuba as a matter of self-drama, the old sin of my English generation of the 'fifties, and now the aberration of her Parisian one at the end of the 'sixties. I told the French agent that she came from a family of the Left, which had been present during the Spanish Civil War, and that her attachment to the Cuban Revolution was romantic rather than reasoned.

She had told Deacon that her vision was of dying on the barricades, waving the red flag like a new and true symbol of Marianne. I told this to the agent without mentioning Deacon's name, but I added that I had assured Marianne she was more likely to end up serving twenty years' time in an unspeakable Latin-American jail. I also told him that I was going to get her out of Havana within a few weeks so the child would be born in Paris and be a good citizen of the next French revolution. This made him laugh, we drank a lot and played chess, he filled his dossier on us, and the French secret service bothered Marianne no more.

Because of these books on Guevara, I acquired an MI6 dossier as thick as my arm. Suspected of subversive activities before I could leave Limehouse, I found myself burgled and the telephone tapped during my return to London. But all was bungled: far more Groucho than Karl Marx, or Charlie Chaplin booting the globe in *The Great Dictator*. The loft rented by two women next door to me in Narrow Street was pillaged with every paper taken, even from the wastepaper baskets, but the whisky and the television set were ignored. The Limehouse police were puzzled: it was not a local crime. I knew the solution. The spycatchers had merely struck at the wrong terrace house.

I decided to save them the trouble of playing the next act of the farce. I picked up my telephone and asked for the security services to telephone me back. I wished to denounce a foreign agent. When the call was duly returned from the unknown, I accused myself of earning all the money used to finance the revolutionary books of Lorrimer Publishing – such as *Viva Che*! and Guevara's *Bolivian Diary* – from major American studios rather than Cuban slush funds. There was no need to steal my bank accounts from my home. The accounts were at the Midland Bank in Great Portland Street, and doubtless they would be available to spies with credentials. My paymasters were known radical organizations such as Columbia Pictures and CBS Films, which would be glad to hear that they were supporting a dangerous fellow of my calibre. But really, Hollywood was my nipple, not Havana.

My confession had two good results. My house was not burgled and Hollywood stopped employing me. While my case was not comparable to the Hollywood Ten standing up to the House Un-American Activities Committee in the bad times of Senator McCarthy, certainly the CIA would inform Tinseltown to stop using someone who might turn the profit of his pen into bombs against capitalism. I was never asked again to write for a major studio, a resolution that was best for all of us.

I was, however, left with a cabin on Malibu Lake, where I had found myself on that night of the supremacy of American endeavour and imagination. The clouds covered the whole earth, except over California. And to a croaking of bullfrogs as to Aristophanes, I could walk out from the television pictures of an astronaut taking a first great step for mankind to watching the diffuse orange of the moon in the night sky, signalling that it was there, and that humans had arrived on those far volcanic rocks, and it was not mere science fiction from the sprawling city of dream manufacture, which I would hardly visit again.

There was no sacrifice in giving up such a rich source of my self-despair. And as I submerged in an emotional Slough of Despond in London and tried to think how to extricate Marianne and the baby from Deacon's dominance, this parody of international conspiracy became a skid onto a squeaky series of banana-skins. The telephone men, who appeared to set their bugs on the Lorrimer Publishing telephones, grinned about their entrapment; they would be called 'plumbers' in the Watergate affair which would bring down President Nixon. The right term scuppers each wrong use.

'The telephones are not out of order,' I said.

'They will be soon,' they cried, 'just fitting new equipment, squire.'

"Will you have bugs on every telephone?' I asked. 'Everyone here is innocent except for me. You'll just be wasting your time listening to calls about meeting boyfriends and office supplies.'

'We'll hear only what we want to hear,' the chief plumber said, tapping his nose. 'Modern technology.'

That modern technology consisted of a *bel canto* of whistles and flat notes every time that a particular name was mentioned. The actual contact and spy I was forced to use at the Cuban embassy in the negotiations to rejoin Marianne was called Guido. My old friend from Cambridge, Michael Frayn, rang me to say that he was going to Cuba to write a play called by the ambiguous name of *Clouds* – rather a better assignment than extracting a pregnant wife. Did I have any advice? Little to say at the moment, I said, but I did tell him about the trilling telephones and warn him that his system would now be tapped because he had called me. He laughed, thinking he was still talking to the young paranoiac he had known from his Cambridge days.

A week later, Frayn dialled again in a wild panic. He was hearing strange noises every time that he picked up his receiver. I could not be right, could I? They were bugging his telephone, too. It contravened all his liberal rights, and he had really believed he was living in a Blackheath or Hampstead *in excelsis*, as most of my old friends believed, where our democratic rights and freedom were respected. I asked if I might play him a minor aria, using only one name from the Cuban embassy.

With his permission, I sang in my tuneless but variable fashion the name of Guido *presto* and *molto lento*. In whistles and squeaks, the telephone wires delivered the performance of a Tito Gobbi with flatulence. ''They don't have enough surveillance men,' I said. 'There's a budget cut even on eavesdroppers. So they automatically record the conversation on our tapped machines only when a key name is mentioned. Guido, Guido, Guido, Guido, Guido, Guido,' I sang, murdering the scale in an impromptu *arpeggio*. His eardrum smarting, Frayn hung up, almost persuaded that I was not the victim of a delusion of persecution. But these were the salad days of surveillance. Silent now the digital spy and drone.

Havana Libre

Cuba had no pacifiers. The pregnant Marianne had told me to fly to Havana to get her out. I had to bring pacifiers, she said. None of the mothers on the island could sleep because of the squalling infants. They were using rags soaked in coconut milk to hush the brats. They were desperate.

Sometimes, to arrive is to travel without hope. I suffered a long flight from Madrid, but I did have the time to prepare my lines. The secret policeman who met me off the aeroplane in Havana was charming, black and experienced. His declared name was Carlos.

'We are so glad that you are giving your son to the Revolution, Doctor Sinclair.'

'If it is a son.'

'He will be. And he will fight for the Revolution.'

'Yes,' I said. 'For the revolution. The revolution in my country, which needs it even more than yours. We are still capitalists, you see.'

Carlos looked at me with some amusement.

'Let us take your passport,' he said. 'I will attend to all the formalities. You are our honoured guest for all the time you will stay here.'

Surrendering my passport, I was taken by black limousine to the Havana Libre. When I met Marianne in the lobby, she was with a woman friend, carrying a baby. They both looked at me with silent hope. My heart sank. I did not know what to say, either. I had brought many things, but I had forgotten the pacifiers. The Cuban baby began to bawl. The mother looked at me with such reproach that I winced. Then she put her thumb in the baby's mouth. And I had come to Cuba about a baby. To pacify, indeed. Or no way back.

Revolution does not stir anger. Deprivation does. Particularly when the children are hurt. In Cuba, the parents were meant to go out to cut sugar cane voluntarily, not as in Haiti, where the machete men were paid a pittance for the massacre of the sweet pithy stalks. Propaganda posters for bringing in the *zafra* harvest dominated the hoardings –

huge red numbers in the shape of a train, 10,000,000, that tonnage pulling along coaches marked VAN VAN VAN, presumably for the vanguard of the proletariat. There was even an element of play in the state effort to get office workers back to farm production – a pair of cows on their hind legs juggling with hearts. A line of Havana women in green fatigues fired their rifles vainly out to sea, where only Russian freighters lay, and not a Yankee battleship such as the *Maine* to start another invasion of the island. Yet an American spy ship was monitoring everything and lying just outside territorial waters, as if looking for a landing place and another Bay of Pigs.

The luxury shops in the old Hilton arcade of the Havana Libre had empty shelves except for coloured water in strange bottles and some wooden toys. 'No tips, *companero.*' I was told in the lobby, seething with agents and undercover men and the swelling Marianne, surprised that I had reached her. She was very friendly with Carlos and told me that he was only a guide and host to visitors. All was open and free here, although we could not leave Cuba, of course. She was nearly eight months pregnant, and no airline would accept her as a passenger. The baby would be born in Cuba.

We were already in trouble, because of her friendship with the Black Panthers. Whenever one of them hijacked an aeroplane from the United States and forced it to land in Havana, the Cuban police put the kidnapper into a work camp for six months to interrogate him and evaluate whether he was a planted American agent or a genuine black radical as well as a criminal. One of these Panthers had broken out and reached his leader Eldridge Cleaver's apartment in Havana. When the authorities demanded his surrender, they were met by wild black revolutionaries, flourishing automatics and accusing them of racism and exploitation and treating their fellow freedom fighters like slaves.

In return, the Panthers were now being threatened with deportation. What a good way out of Cuba, I thought, saying nothing to Marianne. To be thrown out might be the only solution, if we could provoke the government into it. Yet Marianne was confident that she could solve the immediate problem, moving heavily between the Panthers and the *commandantes* and Carlos with the birth of the child only weeks away.

Marianne took me to meet the Panthers in their barricaded rooms. Eldridge Cleaver was a natural in his role as an urban guerrilla. He contained the extremes of behaviour without achieving the golden mean. The internal wars needed to overthrow American society had polarized his contradictions. Cool and explosive, large and light on his feet, slow-moving and quick in riposte, deadly serious and very funny, lucid and fantastical, sympathetic and lethal, he dominated without diplomacy.

His misunderstandings with the Cubans were more a matter of street wit than substance. They understood his asides as true statements. Given an old crone to act as a cook and a spy on the apartment, he said, 'If I got to have a cook, make her young, white and willing.' This was reported as, WANTS A YOUNG WHITE SLAVE. When he saw a black Cadillac in the street, he observed, 'I want to get me a big black Caddie for this big black ass.' This was reported as, WANTS BIG AMERICAN CAR. When he bought some grass to smoke in Oriente province and was asked his source, he said, 'Fidel gave it to me.' This was put down as, SAYS HE GOT MARIJUANA FROM CASTRO. And when he sang in the lobby of the Havana Libre, 'I guess I'll have a ball with Haydée Santamaría,' his dossier read, WANTS ALSO TO RAPE CUBAN OFFICIAL WOMEN.

Actually, the behaviour of the Black Muslims and the Panthers to their women was worse than that of any White Male Pig. With his dangerous wit, Cleaver was hilarious about their efforts as Muslims to reduce women to kitchen slaves behind a veil. He told of a time in Oakland, when the men had gone out with their black berets and truncheons on the streets, and their women had taken over their armoury in their absence. When they returned, they found their wives and lovers with their automatics and hunting-rifles, yelling that they would blow the men apart unless they got their equality. Women's rights before black male dominance. 'Honey, honey,' Cleaver had begged his wife, who had actually followed him to Havana, 'don't shoot me! You'll be free and equal. Just take your pretty finger off that there trigger.' And so she did, and most of the Muslims left the faith and became socialist Panthers instead. One of Cleaver's companions was still a Black Muslim, but this failing was dismissed lightly. 'You see, Andrew, he only eats pork *between* meals.'

Trying to broker a peace with the Panthers, Marianne and I had dinner with Carlos in the Havana Libre, where the huge menus now had only a lack of choice to offer. Through the windows, summer lightning flickered over the peeling stucco colonnades of the Malecon, facing the scimitar of the bay. Carlos was indignant and accused the Panthers of being counter-revolutionary. He was black, he had risen from the cane-fields, he was the living proof that there was no racism in modern Cuba. 'All the Panthers want from the whites,' he declared, 'is their women.' Cleaver had, indeed, called Carlos a white nigger, and perhaps that remark had been reported to him as well. Sexual jealousy about the Panthers had been compounded by one of them taking a radical French journalist off a *commandante*. This was no way to respect rank and the Revolution on the island.

The great nightclub of the old regime, the Tropicana, was still kept open. On another night, Carlos took us there to prove how tolerant the Revolution was. Eight overweight white naked marble nymphs still cavorted round a raised fountain bowl, from which water jets sprang into different colours of red and green, purple and blue. The restaurant was in a tropical garden and faced a floor-show on many levels, where dancers and singers and drummers and big bands were crammed into frills and tight pants, performed on rising and falling giant toadstools, and were illuminated by mad rainbows of violent spot-lights. The extravaganza had fossilized into a tawdry vulgarity, as if it were a wake to Carmen Miranda and Busby Berkeley. 'You see how we keep places like this from before the Revolution,' Carlos said, 'But now all the people can come here.'

Looking around the other tables, I saw a noisy Italian baseball team, delegations of Russians and North Koreans, other party functionaries in dark suits like Carlos – those sort of people. And I glanced down at the roast pheasant on my dinner dish.

'I am sure all the people can come here now,' 'I said. 'But they do have to pay for it. And isn't this pheasant on my plate?'

Carlos was not put out, and said, 'But pheasant is the ration this week for *all* Cubans.'

His cold gaze told me this was no joke. Briefly, visions of factory pheasant farms flitted across my mind. Perhaps it was true in a country where, as the American traitor Aaron Burr had once declared, truth was what was boldly presented and plausibly maintained.

'Lucky for you,' I said. 'When we had rationing even after the end of the Second World War, the best we got was corned beef.'

In spite of the entertainment, Carlos did not avoid the matter of our meeting at the Tropicana. His words were a threat and a warning to us as much as to the Black Panthers.

'We are such good internationalists,' Carlos said, 'the only true ones. So no one will blame us if we keep order here.'

'But keeping people here,' I said. 'Is that the same as keeping order?'

'Sometimes,' Carlos said. 'But you are happy here?'

'Very happy,' Marianne said.

'Until we go,' I said.

'Until you go,' Carlos said, 'after you have given your son to our Revolution.'

We were given a grand tour of Cuba to show off some of the triumphs of Fidel Castro's régime. While the mothers and fathers chose to work in the cane fields, their little ones were left behind in *crèches*, provided for free by the government. 'Look at us,' we were told, 'we see to our children in nurseries, which you do not.'

I turned out to be the pacifier in the *crèches*. In those airless rooms with thirty small ones to each nurse, they loved the coming of large people. They would rush up and want to be swung round and round by their arm. '*Cuidado*', I was told. 'If you swing one, you must swing all.' This was the terrible law of the equality of children, let alone socialism. I swung them all until I felt my arms might drop off. But they always wanted more, and I had to leave them howling.

The temple of the island was the ejaculation block of the breeding bulls. There the great Rosafé Signet had given his life to Cuba, so that his progeny would pull the cane carts and provide the beef and the milk of his adopted country. Bought at the age of nine from Canada, he had died in service at twelve years old, jerked off electrically into the false vagina of a cow while straddling his wooden mount in his last throes, his semen frozen into insemination pills that might produce another three hundred calves from those departed loins. 'The Revolution does not sacrifice unnecessarily,' the farm manager said about his bovine hero. 'All cattle are sacrificed in the end.' When I eventually was to get out of the island, I slopped along in my slippers. An old Cuban poet needed my soft boots, which I was happy to leave him, as they did cover his sore feet.

After our grand tour, we returned to visit the beleaguered Panthers. They were adamant that the Cubans were bigots. They just wanted to stay long enough in Cuba to arm themselves and invade Mississippi in a rubber boat, five of them to conquer a continent, rather fewer than even Cortès or Che had used. Their attitude put me finally face to face with reverse racism. While I was younger, I had believed in biting the hand that fed me, in case it might pat me on the head. But this was ridiculous. To flee the homeland of America and condemn it as a racist, to arrive in socialist Cuba and assert it was more racist, what did this say about the accusers? Perhaps it was better to go back to Wittgenstein and ask who was the target. Were the Panthers accusing themselves? Might even I be freed from being a necessary racist by virtue of my heredity?

If Marianne gave birth in Cuba, the child would become a Cuban citizen. He might end working on a sugar plantation, the victim of his mother's revolutionary delusions. So I went back to the Panther apartment, feeling that provocation was the only solution. The Cubans could kill us or deport us. Either was better than detention and later blackmail through the baby. Cleaver was compelling and paranoiac and under pressure from the other Panthers to storm into the streets and shoot it out with the militia. 'There'll be tanks coming down those avenues soon,' Cleaver said. 'I heard they're coming in from Oriente to get us.'

'You would be better off here,' I said. 'Do you mind if I join you? I know how to work those.' I was looking at the old Bren-guns and bolt-action rifles that littered the floor, out-of-date British Army issue, which had somehow turned up here. 'I can strip and use them,' I said. 'I also know the right fire positions when the Cuban army comes to get us. I used to be an officer in the Coldstream Guards. I was very good at guarding Buckingham Palace. Though we didn't expect an attack from Fidel and the boys.'

Cleaver began to laugh, and his cackle set off his dour friends. They fell about to find the company they kept, and they thrust their weapons at me. This was far out for Cleaver, but as he said, he couldn't always choose his comrades. And as I knew, we were only in the same trench, because we had a common enemy. There is nothing like shared hostility to bring East and West together, when never the twain shall meet.

'Marianne tells me you used to teach history too,' Cleaver said. 'American history. So tell this convict here –' his happy name for his soul brothers –' just why he shouldn't have landed in Haiti on his way to Cuba. You know what he did? Get off that hijacked Boeing, kiss the runway and say, 'This be a free black republic for two hundred years. This been free since the American Revolution, where we're going back to have a proper one.' So those local cops, what do they call them?'

'*Tontons Macoutes,*' I said.

'They take him to a quiet place and they reckon to shoot him. But he says he's crazy, so they send him on here. I say he don't know no history. You tell him.'

So I found myself teaching American and African history in that apartment in Havana, while we waited for the attack of the *comman-dantes*. I explained, or I tried to explain, why Haiti had become a black dictatorship and why so many African republics had done the same, although Nkrumah in Ghana and Nyerere in Tanzania were still heroes to them. And then we stripped the Bren-guns and put them together again. And I assigned fire-positions from the windows and the balcony, choosing one for myself. I might have been back in Cambridge with my old tutor Gallagher, working out deep into the night where we would put the mortars and the Maxims when they came to get us. And I might have been teaching my students there about imperialism, what a bad thing it may well have been, but worse might take its place. As it was, such youthful fantasies and concepts had become the realities and the concrete rooms of this dead end in a city, where I found myself willy-nilly.

News of our preparations for armed resistance; a personal letter from Cleaver to Castro, carried by Marianne; the fact that we were more trouble than we were worth; the fear by Castro of provoking another Bay of Pigs if the Panthers were allowed to invade Mississippi in their rubber boat; the damage to the Cuban image, if a few foreigners were eliminated in a fire-fight: all or none of these may have produced a repetition of my denouement over Suez, a drama that had ended not in a bang, but a damp squib. Instead, our passports were restored to us. Places were found on the Cuban airline to Madrid for Marianne and myself, although she was only a couple of weeks from giving birth; and also the Panthers were booked to Algeria, which had agreed to accept them, rather too far away for them to mount any invasion of the United States overnight. We were all taken for a last day on the beach at Santa María del Mar, the perfect finale to our Cuban excursion.

Eldridge Cleaver joked as usual, as he looked towards distant Miami beyond the horizon. 'Guess I'll swim across,' he said. He spoke of the last Panther to join him. 'There he was in jail, breaks out at eight at night, hijacks a plane at twelve, and at three he's back in jail again in Cuba. It's like travelling from Folsom to San Quentin.' He also told of how a clever warder had broken a strike by some of the harder prisoners, when he had been inside. The 'girls' among the men were separated from their dissident lovers and were put on the grass outside, where they could pair off with other prisoners under the eyes of their regular guys, who could not stand the sight and surrendered. Cleaver himself had found solitary confinement very peaceful, as long as he did not feel persecuted about it. The Bible was the only reading there, and he read the good book, 'so I could preach better later.' That was a curious prophecy of what he was to do, in the end.

Not having to invade America was, I suspect, a relief for him. He was no longer condemned by his own declarations. Deportation by Cuba was the answer to his commitments, as it was to my prayers. Before our permitted flight, I affirmed to Carlos that we would continue the Revolution in our own countries. Lorrimer Publishing would print the trials of Fidel Castro and Régis Debray and a book against the American war in Vietnam. I kept my bargain. My small experience with secret policemen is that they do not do you in, as long as you refuse to take their money. There was no question of a Cuban subsidy for what we did, and my Hollywood one had almost ended.

Marianne did not go into labour on the turbulent journey across the air currents above the Atlantic. Deacon was to meet us for the last time at the London Airport. She would then proceed to Paris to have the child in France with her mother to help her. She made one concession to my feelings. If it were a boy, it would not be called Che or Inti, one of Guevara's lieutenants. He would be called Timon, the character from Shakespeare who obsessed me now. Yet Timon had become a recluse because of the faithlessness of those he trusted. I saw no moral in that play in my present case. Yet I should have remembered his words:

All is oblique;
There's nothing level in our cursed natures
But direct villany ... Destruction fang mankind!

When we did land in London, Deacon was there to meet us. He

drove off with Marianne, although I still had all her dumped stuff at Limehouse. When I went back to my office at Lorrimer Publishing and found two lines in pencil in the round handwriting of Marianne, scrawled on the back of a brown envelope: *Gone to Oxford for weekend with Deacon. I love YOU best, you silly boy.*

Hardly a justification, it was the destruction of my life. I went back to Limehouse, took all the suitcases returned by Deacon, packed the things which she had from me, and I sent them by carrier to his house in London. I added a brief note to the effects, quoting Timon of Athens in his view of the human race and of the value of words. Then I telephoned two people who desperately wanted my house on the river and told them that they could have it. I wanted no roots, no love, no ties. I wanted hardly to live, but then, life does go on, as they say.

I was still at Limehouse, when I felt a burning pain in my vitals. I thought I was dying, but I was not. A clot of blood passed through my penis. It had not happened before, and I felt gutted. I telephoned the good doctor next door, and he told me not to worry. 'It's only a gallstone, Andrew,' he said. 'But go along to St. Thomas's in the morning, have an X-ray, they'll find you're fine.' And so I was, except for one fact. At the time that I passed the clot, a baby was born in Paris who was to bear the name of Timon. These two issues of blood happened simultaneously. Of course, a man cannot give birth. But goodness only knows what inducement of the mind can create such a painful reproduction of the act of giving life to another being. I cannot explain it, I can only recount the fact. To this day, I believe in the strange correspondence of mind and body, and I do not know to what extremity that influence will extend.

France is a legal society, as England is, even if the Code Napoléon and case law compound the differences. A birth certificate had to be signed by the father. I had a telephone call from my French mother-in-law. The baby was certainly mine and would be called Timon. He had blue eyes, while the eyes of Deacon were brown. I should not doubt, I must come to Paris and sign. And so I flew over and signed the certificate, and I am always glad that I did. As he was a wonderful baby, so he turned out a wonderful boy and young man. I have consistently believed that all children are innocent: only their parents are guilty. And the fact which I did not then know and discovered later – that *all* European babies are born with blue eyes –

did not shake my belief in him, when he turned out to have brown eyes.

This is not an account of my feelings, but rather of the excesses of the times. Within a month of Timon's birth, Marianne flew out on a free ticket to Pyongyang, where Eldridge Cleaver and the Black Panthers were also invited. In a way, we were all paying the price of our deportation from Cuba. We were being honourable revolutionaries, if that is no contradiction in terms. It was to depress my political future as Cleaver was now travelling under my name; Algeria was soon to deport him to France, finding him as unwelcome a guest as Cuba had. But briefly, as Andy Sinclair, he was roaming with Marianne to Pyongyang, which I termed the Acapulco of the revolutionary classes.

I had to put paid to Hollywood as I was doing to the East End of London. I sold the cabin on the Malibu Lake, where the sets for the original film of King Kong still provided grottoes of fantasy on the arid hills. It was a withdrawal, a coming home. The friends I had known in California were also pulling back from the dream of creating an alternative culture to conserving their different way of life. It was a reverse route in American history, which had always praised the conquest of the savage and the forests and the mountains by the civilized and the frontier and the city. But as early as the works of Jack London and Upton Sinclair, violence had become the condition of the people of the urban abyss and the industrial slums. And now, there were concurrent and opposed popular visions of future disintegration. In one version, world wars and the brutalization of life would reduce every metropolis to a ruined nightmare, in which the thought police of *Nineteen Eighty-Four* or the droog gangs of *A Clockwork Orange* would rule the streets. Already in these dark prophecies, Calcutta was a prototype of the ungovernable and starving slum of the future. The other vision of the *Brave New World* by Aldous Huxley saw it as a society controlled by eugenics and the pursuit of pleasure through a drug called soma. Better in such a Utopia to be a pig satisfied than a savage dissatisfied.

ENDGAME OR NOT

⸻

I had always wanted to live in the parks of London, if I could not live in Soho or by the docks. Bohemia and the river and greenery, these were the attractions of this metropolis. Unfortunately, I discovered in Regent's Park a mansion in Hanover Terrace with a separate mews for very little money down. That it was a short and full-repairing lease and a national monument did not deter my appreciation of the proportions of the Georgian rooms and the sheer size of it all. It was financial suicide, but I did not care. William Golding had always told me that I needed a great deal of room to write inside, as I spread my research papers in widening circles across the floor. So I did not count the cost, although I should have known that the sublime Nash with his stucco fronts was a jerry- builder. At least, the place was suitable for Magog's residence. Now I was disillusioned with my radical past, I was freed to write the antithesis of *Gog*, that anarchist hero. This would be the story of the man of power, the civil servant who had led Britain into its irreversible decline after the end of the Second World War. His sin was his failure. As his epigraph to the book would read: POWER CORRUPTS. POWERLESSNESS CORRUPTS ABSOLUTELY.

For the next ten years, I would live alone in my vast inward spaces, tended by an extraordinary Cornish-Breton adventuress called Jacquemine, and a hippie named Nigel, who I found sleeping rough in the Park. He finally told me what the working class really thought, after he put down Ken Tynan at a dinner that I was giving for William Golding. In one of his apocalyptic moods, the dandy Tynan was upholding the vision of Chairman Mao and claiming that in the rotten British state, all the workers would rather be Chinese peasants. It was too much for Nigel, who rose and said that he was the only worker among us all, and that all his mates wanted to be middle class like us. Tynan was fazed and left asking why I was living with a skinhead.

These years were extraordinary for their dull pain and slow understanding. My rival Deacon turned out to be a superior Svengali with such a concentration of inescapable passion that anyone in his power was a bird of paradise in a gilt wrought cage. Derek Lindsay read deeply, but not widely. He hated a miscarriage of justice. His pen name of A. E. Ellis was taken from the tragic death of Ruth Ellis, the last woman to be hanged in England for murder. Now he concentrated on the Dreyfus case, the Jewish officer in the French Army sent to Devil's Island for an act of treason engineered by other people. Through the good offices of his Oxford friend Tynan, now the dramaturge to Olivier, a Dreyfus play, *Grand Manoeuvres*, was staged at the National Theatre, but it flopped, confirming Deacon's darkest fears of how mismanaged were all the institutions of our country.

He included in his obsessions those very few who tried to be close to him. Marianne would refer to him as her *homme fatal*. He was not fatal, even to himself, but like another genius I knew, Ted Hughes, he would suck his lover into the vortex of his creativity, and there was no swim up. Inside his sphere was to be a fly or two in amber. Time was still, fascination was all, we were stuck, and we wanted to be so.

The birth of baby Timon changed his life. Until then, he had sworn that so bad was the world and so rotten our future, if any woman dared have a baby by him, he would bash its brains out against the wall. He would not condemn anyone of his malign blood to an existence as horrible as his own. Of course, his hidden humanity denied his fearsome philosophy. No Titus Andronicus he, but rather an Aristotle to this young Alexander. Until his death, Deacon cared for this being, whom he had failed to forswear. Although he would become estranged from Timon's mother, he was devoted to the child, who learned nothing at the Lycée or at his English university, but everything from his father. He was instructed particularly that we cannot be indifferent to any living thing which suffers, though all things do. Deacon taught himself German merely to comprehend Goethe more on the wholeness of existence. And he had laboured for thirty years to write a sequel to *The Rack*. In a weak and rare moment, he once gave me the first seventy pages to read, but I never saw more. The chief image in the work was of a duck trying to cross a road, but run over by an army convoy. Successive tyres printed pictures of its bloody and crushed body further along the tarmac. Living was a succession of serial deaths.

Lindsay destroyed almost more than he wrote. His wastepaper basket was full of paper shrapnel. As he told me, 'To write of the torture of the body is easy. To write of the torture of the mind is impossible.' In a way, however, he was trying to write not of a mental breakdown, but of the reconstruction of a whole anatomy of melancholy, now that he had a son to follow him. When Timon would be mainly settled below him in his house in Chalcot Square, he would become more determined in his habits and his solitude. After drugged nights on prescription pills, he would toil on his novel and destroy his efforts, although the whole book advanced insidiously through many drafts over the decades. While in his conversation, he could make the hours pass like minutes; in his writing, he made the words pass like months. This was his search for perfection. What phrase to describe such a spasm, what exact sentence to set down a blind rage? In a sense, precision is the enemy of inspiration; but yet Deacon inched on.

He did not measure out his life in coffee-spoons, but in the intervals of lucidity and relief between insomnia and tension and the pricks of pain. I threatened to kidnap him for a lunch, but by then, he would not open the door to anyone except his doctor. At one of one of our last fond meetings, we played our only game of chess, which ended, as it had to do, in Perpetual Check. Deacon always believed he would die daily, but nobody battled more to preserve a long life on one lung. We used to joke that he would bury us all. Yet one morning in a July, crossing the road towards Primrose Hill, he would be clipped on the head by the wing mirror of a wayward bus. He fell back, suffered an internal haemorrhage and soon died in a coma. The verdict was Accidental Death. This would have amused him, for only the Natural Causes, which he believed doomed us all, should have brought him finally down. He wished that no service would be held over his remains, and that they would be destroyed. From nothing, he came. To nothing, he returned. Yet his work and his son would remain, and a few friends. He desired to be extinct. He is not yet, and perhaps never will be.

As for another epilogue on someone from my past and in my future, Eldridge Cleaver would continue to use the name of Andrew Sinclair on a forged passport to voyage to various revolutionary hotspots, and so plough me with the security services over the years to come. In order to show off his male prowess, he tried to market globally a brand of jeans called 'Cleavers', which emphasised the balls and more of the wearer. In the end, his reading of the Bible when in prison gave him a deal with the prosecuting American authorities. He was allowed to return to the United States as a born-again Baptist preacher. He saved from their sins whole schools of converts, rather than convicts, by dunking them in swimming pools in the Southern states. Redemption and Revolution are strange bedfellows; but the one tends to follow the other.

American experience again broke up the film world in Britain and affected me, returning my career to where it had started, but from the new perspective of more than a decade later. The failure of several block-busters and the success of the low-budget *Easy Rider* revolutionized the expectations of the studio bosses. Cheap was good, small was beautiful, stars were unnecessary if they cost too much for their little light. Such was the proof that the alternative culture of the hippies could be commercialized, while another comet was born from it, Jack Nicholson. The musical of *Hair* would be yet further proof of how Wall Street might exploit Haight-Ashbury, and the dollar became the stem of flower power. Asked by Kenneth Tynan to do a sketch for the equally commercial *Oh! Calcutta!* with its simulated sex and nudity pretending to be codpiece art, I refused. I did not think that royalties should derive from the freedom of the love generation.

For my part, a programme of ten inexpensive films was announced to be made at Elstree under the guidance of Bryan Forbes. As a screenwriter become director himself, Forbes could accept me as the director of my own material, in this case *The Breaking of Bumbo*. But he did not want a historical novel or film. He wanted to reflect the protest of the 'sixties. And I was happy to oblige, as I thought I knew something about radical chic and what had gone wrong during the fourteen years after I had staged my first failed revolt against the system.

There were scenes in the film which succeeded and still have the capacity to wound, particularly the night when the chic revolutionaries led by the radical university professor break into Madame Tussauds, and he holds a blow-torch to the waxwork face of Winston Churchill until the glass eyes pop, and he says, 'So much for Dresden.' Filming this shot made some of the technicians walk out, until I explained to them that Churchill had killed more civilians and refugees in the one mighty fire-raid on Dresden as a burnt offering to Stalin or in revenge for the Blitz, than had been killed in the two nuclear attacks on Hiroshima and Nagasaki. They did not know that, and they came back to work particularly for the naked love scene with a discarded scarlet tunic and black bearskin and Joanna Lumley in her first screen role, playing herself as admirably as always with her swagger and her beauty and her style.

We had gone out to dinner during the shoot. We had recognized something in each other. She invited me up to her Kensington flat for a last drink. She took me into a bedroom, where a small baby lay in a cradle. All was said, and unsaid, in terms of *Winnie the Pooh*. There was another man in her life.

'This is piglet,' she said.

I kissed her hand and I left.

In her naked love scene with Richard Warwick, who had discarded his bearskin for a bare skin to loom ineffectually above her, I was instructed by Joanna, appearing flat in profile on her back on the bed. 'Shoot me, Andrew,' she said, 'when I breathe out. Otherwise, when I breathe in, my ribs stick up. So I look like if I have two pairs of bosoms.' So I did, but the movie was lost. There was no sexual chemistry in the scene. The irony was now slumber. Selected because of Lindsay Anderson's film of *If*, Richard was happier playing public schoolboys than pretending with women.

When the film was over, Joanna wrote to me as a headmaster:

> Don't forget to take your cough mixture and WILL THE BOY WHO IS RESPONSIBLE FOR BREAKING THE BUMBO IN THE NORTH CORRIDOR REPORT TO ME AFTER PREP. Dear heart, take care. Piglet is divine. You are *devilishly* divine.
> All love and XX's
> Jo

Given some withdrawal symptoms on my part, she confirmed a principle, to which I always clung with my fingernails. Power corrupted love and recognitions – those instant attractions when you lock eyes across a room and know in thirty seconds that all is probable. You should only walk away, if you are otherwise engaged. I walked away that time, and I barely managed throughout the rest of my life never to have an affair with any of my students in universities or with my actresses in film-making. Vain of me, perhaps, to wish to be wanted for my craggy charms alone. Yet equally, what a way to avoid the sexual mistakes than ruin people in public.

Oddly enough, I was also never attracted to the available 'free love' of the 'sixties and the 'seventies. The Pill failed to liberate me. I could never sleep with anyone, to whom I could not talk at breakfast. And even when they were supremely intelligent feminists such as Germaine Greer, I discovered that they preferred good behaviour to a brief fling.

I first met the lanky astute Aussie Germaine off the Portobello Road. Later she would describe me as 'an intellectual lumberjack'. She took me to her pad, and told me that she had 'flu. I did not pounce, but I treated her as a Victorian lady. She liked that, although she had not yet written *The Female Eunuch*. I made her a whisky toddy with cinnamon, and in those hippie days when she was columnist 'Earth Rose' for *Suck and. Screw*, I tucked her up in bed, and I departed.

The next time I ran into her was in New York on Riverside Drive near Columbia, at some literary party. She had come to New York to stay with a home-country friend, Lillian Roxon, who was the rock scribe of Max's Kansas City near Union Square, the party place of Andy Warhol and the Velvet Underground. She had thrown Germaine out of her apartment, because she was trying to finish her *Rock Encyclopedia*. All Germaine could afford was three dollars a night at the Broadway Central, then a dosser place, where the rogue tycoon Jim Fisk had been murdered in 1872, by a swindled partner.

At the party, I find Germaine quivering at the thought of going back to the Broadway hotel. I offer her a couch at my New York publisher's, where I am staying. Bold woman, she insists, as General MacArthur, that she will return to her cockroach centre.

'Not without me,' I say, although both of us are nearly penniless. Arriving by the subway, we find two members of the New York Police Department, wheeling out a stiff on a wheelchair. 'How do you know he is a stiff?' Germaine says. 'Because they can't light the cigarette in his mouth,' I say, imitating Mickey Spillane.

Treading warily upstairs to Germaine's hotel room, we encounter a young drag queen, mascara running from his eyes. 'Give me twenty bucks,' he says, 'or they'll bust me.' I take out my last two dollars and give it to him. 'Best I can do,' I say. He kisses lipstick on my hand. At Germaine's cubby hole, I show her how to jam a chair and wardrobe behind her door handle to deter intruders. I do not barricade myself within, but without her.

I was too late for another rendezvous with her in Umbria, where she was trying to reform Italian courting habits. She seemed to switch from a form of discerning Free Love to a wary chastity and husbanding of the earth, waiting for some later flowering. Her restless inquiries about her own nature were translated into generalities about human behaviour, which a scattershot of personal experience represented as sociology, somewhat in the way that Bergson misinformed Proust that there could be rules of getting on with each other. And yet, she was always an original and witty bushranger, who could shoot her mouth off in controversy as accurately as Ned Kelly in his showdown in his armour.

In one way, I joined in the refusal to commit of the time. I had long affairs with two of the more remarkable and beautiful women in London. Carrie spoke seven languages including Japanese and played a mean game of chess, but she had the habit of leaving me for all my best friends, both in the literary and music trades. Her defence was that my friends were so much better than hers. Cat was an aspiring actress, turned into literary agent, of unparalleled poise and grace. Yet all three of us could not engage for many years, nor could we wholly leave each other. In spite of our infidelities, we craved security, but we could not admit to it. To this day, I do not know why. The currents of that free-flowing age never eddied into a pond. That was how it was.

Andrew in Limehouse

Marianne and Andrew in Limehouse

Planning the renovations in Limehouse

With Joanna Lumley on … Bumbo *set*

During the research for Gog

Derek Lindsay a.k.a. A.E. Ellis and Deacon

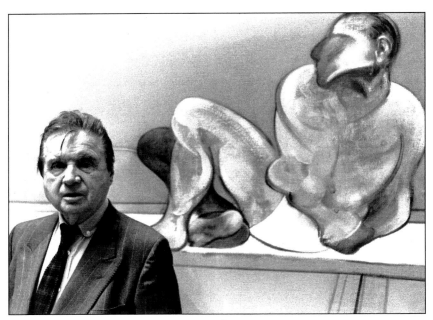

Francis Bacon

Timon and Marianne

SOMEHOW UNDER MILK WOOD

The ancient oracle of the Western world is at Delphi. Near Mount Parnassus, which the Greek gods loved, stood the shrine of the Pythian Apollo. Above it, tawny cliffs as sheer as gravity, below it a green crevasse stretching down to a river through olive groves. Religious games were held here as at Olympia, but some mystery in the place made the oracle the most famous in ancient Greece. The priests who delivered the prophecies were diplomatic and more gnomic than Zurich bankers. The answers were like presidential tapes, capable of many interpretations dependent on one's political beliefs.

For Delphi and its oracle stood for Greek unity, although most of the Greek cities fought each other. The priestess would not commit herself to any one side, although she did actually say that Socrates was the wisest man in the world just before the Athenians put him to death for subverting the state. In general, however, the Greeks did not go to Delphi to invent or direct their policies. They sought its confirmation of what they already meant to do.

So, in my time of great risk and hope and confusion, I went to Delphi. The month was January, three weeks before the start of the film of *Under Milk Wood*. Richard Burton and Peter O'Toole and Elizabeth Taylor were meant to play, if the film could be made in the February storms of winter Wales, even though Dylan Thomas had written it for one fine spring day. Nobody had committed, especially not the money. Anyway, the radio play was impossible to film. But I held all the bills and I cared too much for Dylan's ghost. So on an instinct, because ancient Greece has always mattered to me, I flew to Athens to ask the oracle's blessing on what I wanted and feared to do. Yet I had to make that movie.

Rain was soaking Attica. I hired a Volkswagen and drove off over slippery mountain roads. On one bend, I skidded on a patch of oil. Three times widdershins, and up the bank rather than over the gorge. A man on a cart to pull me back onto the road. A spice of fear to send me on my way. Then Delphi.

The clouds had parted above the oracle. The sun shone down from a hole in the grey heavens that hid the snows of Parnassus. The cliffs that hung above the ruins of the temples and the treasures were almost summer-white and blinding to contemplate. Down by the three standing pillars below the road, which flank the old site of the oracle, the two huge warning boulders were hot to the hand. Warning, I say, because they fell from the cliffs on either side of the oracle at the turn of the century when foreign tourists first arrived in great numbers to consult Apollo. As presumptuous as any tripper, I had come for my answer. But I did not find it at the site of the oracle itself, where the ambiguous answers had derived from the Pythia priestess, high on a vent of methane gas and on the scent of crushed bay and laurel leaves.

So I climbed up the mute slope. The steps and the track to the theatre led past the ruined treasuries of the Achaeans and the Athenians, past strewn stones that were once shrines and temples. The theatre itself in its semicircle of stone seats looked down to the valley, but I sat in the left rows to scan the cliffs. And as I watched the overhang in the sun, I felt some peace, some stillness, some answer forming. But not there.

Finally, I walked between the pine-trees to the stadium near the hill-top. I was alone, for nobody else was there that one fine January day. I remembered that running was part of the Apollonic rite, that the god insisted on his Pythian Games. So I ran up the horseshoe of the stadium and round the curve and back along the straight. The high mountain air was wine in my lungs, my breaths were spirits. In front of me, the cliffs danced for joy. The hills moved in the sun. And the oracle spoke and I understood.

If I had courage and ran on, the sun would part the clouds over Fishguard in winter Wales. And if I risked myself in making *Under Milk Wood*, it was worth the risk. What any man could do was as trivial as the ruined stones of the temples below the cliffs that haunted the place. Yet it was enough for a man to make, in trial and honour, his one small offering. All the shrines would fall, the mountains would abide. But one shaped pebble was sufficient, as a record of a life. Better than nothing, no sign of passing.

So I went back and made the film. I never doubted it would now happen, and it did. The clouds even parted over Fishguard and the sun shone all that February and March. It hadn't been like that in thirty years of bad weather. The locals crossed themselves. 'Aren't you the lucky one,' they said. 'I knew it would happen,' I said, and they said, 'Complacent sod.'

The impossible always happened in making *Under Milk Wood*. At times, its luck exceeded incredulity and vanished into Celtic mist. Like a necromancer juggling the elements, any Merlin of the screen has to mix the gold of the backers with the stars in their courses and come up with a horoscope that promises fair heavens and a safe return. To go at all, the Dylan film had to find a time when Richard Burton, Elizabeth Taylor, and Peter O'Toole were all available to work and in England, which was rather like fixing a weekend between Howard Hughes, Elizabeth the Third and Puck. Then the gold had to be conjured in double-quick time from the state and a merchant bank, both of whom were rightly foolish enough to buck the wisdom of Wardour Street and think there could be profit as well as art in the wild warm words of that people's poet, Dylan Thomas. Then there had to be hayfield sun in March in Fishguard, which would be a blessing not seen in thirty years. '*Wales* in winter!' said the drenched warriors streaming home from Polanski's protracted *Macbeth*. 'Jesus! Not only did Banquo blow off his horse, but the bloody horse blew away too.'

Moreover, we had a forty days' budget about as fat as Our Lord's, when he had the same schedule in the wilderness. What with sixty sets and seventy actors, we had to spend a quarter of our time just shifting from scene to scene; we shot on the run, with the mighty heroes of Lee Electrics humping the hundredweight brute lights as casually as kittens on their shoulders. Everything and everyone had to work too well, beyond normal and halfway to dream. The technicians would mutter about 'Andrew the Luck.' And I would answer, 'Miracles happen daily.' Frankly they had to, so they did.

There is a necessity in a film, once it has begun, which matches the resignation in a Celt, once he has decided to go for broke. There are so many shots to be taken each day, so many actors to play their scenes while they are still available, so many seconds of film to be put successfully in the can each week – or else, the boot. Considerations of art come a bad second to sheer endurance. One makes the script and hopes it works. Any improvisation on the set is a dangerous gift that may save the part, but throw the whole. The important thing, as Beckett once wrote, is to be done, to have done. And to have done well. For there are no excuses. A film-maker is judged by the final film. He can plead none of his troubles on the way, too little time, bad weather, fractious actors, intervention from the money, accident. The fine cut is all.

Yet endurance and luck are not enough to make a good film. There has to be magic as well. And magic is not on call. For me *Under Milk Wood* has always been the supreme incantation of my life. However many hundred times I heard the words during the tedious repetitions of editing and dubbing and viewing the film, the phrases still reverberated in a tease of meanings as only the great sentences do. Richard Burton would complain of being woken o'nights by voices haunting him with Dylan's words; but his own voice with its fits and starts, graduations and gravels, choirs and harmonies was the midnight speech of the lost Bards of Wales. The spell began when he recorded the sullen craft of his dead friend's words all in two hours in a Soho cellar before the picture started. We always had that incantation to play back to ourselves during the bad days, and every time we heard it, the magic came again and we thought that Dylan's masterpiece might work after all.

Daring to make a classic film of the best 'play for voices' ever recorded was a fool's leap into the dark wood. The arrogance of setting forth my own visual imagination with actors on a screen to compete with the dreams of the many followers of the poet with their own night-bright visions from the words alone invited divine destruction. Yet our insolence somehow seemed to amuse the Welsh gods. If they did not forgive us, they played with us obscurely, and through their fatal nudging, they brought the wizardry into the film. If I can try to describe what was beyond sense ...

The problem of making Dylan's radio play into a film lay in its bittiness, cross-cutting from voice to voice all the time without knowing whose voice it was. Seventy little stories to tell in ninety minutes in the life of a small fishing-port. The connecting link was Two Voices, their characters and connection with the town unexplained, Voices with the power to conjure up dreams, knowing intimately the private lives of all the sleepers in Cockle Row and Coronation Street, as Druids in their comprehension and devilish in their mockery. How to make this counterpoint of words into one visual whole, while being faithful to the text ... It was daunting.

I had only half-solved the problem when we began shooting the film. I had given the Two Voices faces and characters, predominance to the powerful, brooding visage and pale-piercing eyes of Richard Burton, foolery to the thin, playful, melancholic skull's head of Ryan Davies, the beloved clown of Welsh television, playing the jester to Burton's King, the imp to Lucifer. I had gone back to an early experience of Dylan's, when he had spent a weekend with a friend in Gower, and the friend's girl with a loose red mouth had swapped beds. I had also gone back to Dylan's other great radio play, *Return Journey,* in which the old Dylan travels home to look for the young Dylan, and the final refrain is the same as in Polly Garter's song … 'dead, dead, dead.' There was also a story of his called 'Just Like Little Dogs', where two men take out two sisters on the beach and the girls change partners in the night. So I made the reason for the two Voices going back to Llarregyb their quest for a girl, Norma Jane Jenkins, whom they had met way back in the war, and had shared; it made for nice intercutting with the children's kissing games, Billy and Johnnie Cristo and Dicky kissing Gwennie, and with Polly Garter's song as she scrubs the floor of the Welfare Hall:

Tom, Dick, and Harry were three fine men
And I'll never have such loving again…

Then Norma Jane walks away into a graveyard and the men leave town in their khaki coats, and it is revealed that Norma Jane had been dead a long time, and that these two visible spirits from the sea and the dark wood have come back to relive their life in the timeless town and resurrect their lost love.

This device gave a unity to the film, a visual reason for all the marvellous speeches of the Voices, that orchestration of words which makes *Under Milk Wood* as binding as a spell. But it did not solve the problem of the final coming together of the townspeople, nor did it help the dying fall of the picture, which trailed away into nothing.

We were filming the night shot of Evans the Death, the under-taker, asleep by an open coffin, laughing in his dreams. The shop for the dead had been built by us in front of two lavatories on the quayside of Lower Fishguard, which otherwise served naturally as Cockle Row. We had set up the shot through the window of the store on the first three letters FUN from FUNERALS – beyond the glass, the end of the bed, with Evans the Death's toes curling through a hole in his purple socks. Then a coastguard siren wailed behind us, meaning trouble at sea. And policemen hurried up the quayside, and we stopped work, and a boat set out across the bay. And we looked at the cliffs opposite until the boat came back. In it, the body of a drowned boy. One of our electricians thought it was the body of his child, and he broke down. The father of the boy turned out to be a local freelance cameraman, who normally worked for television. But in the dead child, we all saw our own deaths and the deaths of our children. So we packed up and went home till the morning.

The funeral was two days later. So I and the Associate Producer left the scene of Polly Garter singing, 'Little Willy Wee is dead, dead, dead …', to pay our respects to the family of the boy and leave wreaths from the company. The father met us, a brave and good man. He said he would not find it easy to leave overnight his wife and her family and his home for some weeks now. So we offered him work in getting us some shots of seals, which we might need. For he knew where the seals were at this time of year. What we did not know was that the seals lay at the bottom of a thousand foot cliff. Putting his Arriflex on his back, the brave cameraman and two of our party got down that cliff, risking their lives and losing the top of a finger. The father came back with some spectacular shots, including one of a group of seals humping away into the foam.

We went back next week and did the shot of the undertaker laughing by the coffin, although nobody wanted to think of it. Dylan had written it, and it still had to be done. But when I saw the rushes of the seals and I re-read *Under Milk Wood* for the hundredth time, I saw where the magic and the end of the picture lay. Celtic myths are full of seals coming back from the sea; their singing voices are meant to be the drowned dead, like the five sailors who come back to Captain Cat in his dreams. 'I lost my step in Nantucket,' says Dancing Williams, now down salt deep into the Davy dark. And endlessly, Dylan refers to dreams coming from the black sea:

Only you can hear and see, behind the eyes of the sleepers, the … flight and fall and despairs and big seas of their dreams …
Now behind the eyes and secrets of the dreamers in the streets rocked to

sleep by the sea, see the ... wrecks and sprats and shells and fishbones, whalejuice and moonshine and small salt fry dished up by the hidden sea.

So I filmed a night dream dance in the pouring rain, with a gale blowing the roofs away, while the actors playing the people of Llarregyb caracoled around the town pump and danced away into the sea, and they were dissolved into seals, and Satan's jester walked back from the wild drowned caper he had led from the back of a squealing pig to the black Milk Wood, where the Devil of Richard Burton was waiting, crossing himself and smiling darkly, with his last incantation sounding, that begins:

The Wood, whose every tree – foot's cloven in the black glad sight of the hunters of lovers...

And so the film had an end, a magical end, that had grown out of its words and its making, out of the life of the welcoming town and the death of the boy that had its sad meaning to us all, out of the rich deep words of the Welsh poet of poets and the tears in Captain Cat's eyes as he remembers Rosie Probert and his lost sailoring days:

Seas barking like seals,
Blue seas and green,
Seas covered with eels
And mermen and whales.

Richard Burton had said to me that Dylan's play was all about religion, sex and death, and darkly comic, too. I did not understand his words until the film was over. My preacher and teacher was not the fond-foolish Reverend Eli Jenkins nor the dark Puritan Jack Black from Dylan's text, but my dandy-dark cameraman Bob Huke, who made me watch the twilights away in his quest for that one shot at evening which he called 'the magic hour.' And in that 'dusk and ceremonial dust, and night's first darkening snow,' I sensed the timeless powers of the Gwaun Valley, where the pagan stones still stand at the doorways and the mistletoe hangs from the wind-bent oaks, the powers of light and night, wind and water, stone and hill, crow and cromlech, Celtic cross and bleeding yew, which are still the old gods in that Pembrokeshire where the ancient Celts quarried rocks to drag all the way to Stonehenge. And I knew that we only had to resign ourselves to the place and its doings to recapture the spell of Dylan's words and describe Milk waking Wood. We were all the servants of the dead Dylan Thomas, who caught the essence of all Welsh sea-towns and made an incantation of them. The film was the making of us. We were not making the film.

The shooting of a movie outside a studio is much like a guerrilla campaign. For Che, read *ciné verité*. The crew descends as bandits upon the chosen terrain. The locations manager lies about the budget and wheedles shooting sites for minimal fees from star-struck owners. The heavy brigade, in this case the Lee Electrics ex-sergeants, who could hump a hundredweight of Brute lights up a cliff as if a web of gossamer, tried to dominate – certainly myself, an unproven young director on *Under Milk Wood*. But as I was also the hidden producer and the money, I could call on some obedience. The paymaster calls the tune, even if off-key. Most dissident was the hard-bitten crew, who never believed I could direct the poetic film or cut it together or get it sold. For my way was a weird and wonderful maze of shooting, all short takes and darting cameras as difficult to chart as a labyrinth.

The delivery of words by Richard Burton enriched the language, particularly in his reading of Under Milk Wood, written for him to play the Second Voice to Dylan Thomas's own First Voice. The Welsh poet's early death gave Burton the leading role in the famous radio version. He told me that Dylan had begged three hundred pounds of him, to avoid the last fatal lecture tour to America. But Burton didn't have the money then, although he felt guilty about his refusal thereafter. He was always conscious of the opportunity in his life, of the help of others, of the love of women, but not of the waste of himself. He was a generous man, dying like Thomas of giving too much to strangers. As a young actor, he was poor. He told me how sad it was at a party to need to court the richest woman in the room, not the most beautiful. Later on, when he was famous, he could choose the most beautiful, and did. In the excess of his nature and the extravagance of his talent, he craved all that love and life could grant to him, from Elizabeth Taylor to the Hollywood style that had ruined so many and made so few.

To work with, he was a supreme professional. His drinking was legendary, but controlled. 'I am not drinking for your film,' he told me. 'That means only one bottle of vodka a day. I am sober on two. But when I am drinking, it is three or more.' He was not driven to drink, but used it to escape from melancholy to sociability. Giving so much of himself so often, he needed the stimulus. Yet his genius was more than the infinite capacity for imbibing shots. It lay in a voice that seemed to contain all the passion and powers, wearinesses and weaknesses of our kind. To hear him speak was to listen to the human condition.

He always seemed to me like the Scots doctor in the Border legend. The doctor dreams of meeting the Faery Queen. One night, walking on the moors, he does. The Queen falls in love with him and snatches him away to join her glittering court and live in a world of fantasy. The doctor forgets his trade. One day, the Queen tires of him. He returns to Edinburgh, an older man, unable to practise his calling, forever longing for what he has lost and never really wanted.

If Burton seemed to squander his great talents, it was from an expanse of spirit. His Shakespearean roles remain in the memory as equal to those of Laurence Olivier and John Gielgud. He told me of his Jenkins brothers from Wales, visiting him at the Old Vic, and saying, 'Give us the long words, Richard,' and he would say, 'The multitudinous seas incarnadine, making the green one red.' Then his family would fall on the dressing-room floor in fond laughter.

For all his love of Dylan, Richard never meant to make my film. 'You have to schedule me back one week,' Peter O'Toole said to me. 'I have to prepare my part. I never thought the film would happen. Richard Burton never meant to play. But you fixed it so he had to. The greatest actor of Wales going back home to appear in the greatest Welsh bard's greatest work. And four television crews waiting to cover him shooting. He had to go. You're a clever bastard, fixing all that publicity.'

I had fixed nothing at all. In fact, I wanted minimal publicity and no television crews covering the shooting. We had far too little time as it was. Already a miracle, getting the three biggest stars in the world then to agree to play in *Under Milk Wood* for a mere ten thousand pounds apiece, for Burton insisted that Elizabeth Taylor play as well, for tax reasons. We had to shoot in February and March, when the weather in Wales usually made the Deluge look like a drizzle. Carting around a bit of moveable dingle, however, a piece of purple heather in bloom and a plastic flowering cherry-tree would give the right illusion and block off any far telegraph pole from view.

I did own the property and nominate myself as director and pro-ducer. With the three star names and a small budget of only £300,000, the money was readily available from the National Film Finance Corporation and a merchant bank, although I do remem-ber one moment in the negotiations, which might have come from Mel Brooks's film, *The Producers*. Each of the three stars wanted fifty per cent of the profits to play for peanuts instead of a million dollars, and the financiers wanted fifty per cent as well. That meant giving away two hundred per cent with no points left for me.

'Give them two hundred per cent,' I said. 'I won't count. And I will go to gaol.'

'You want to make the film too much, Andrew,' they said. And I did, leaving the room with the words, 'I'll sign any contract you put in front of me.'

Eventually, the three stars took control of the world distribution of the film instead of large percentages. He who sells a film and col-lects the money for it can ensure he gets paid his share. I had thought all was agreed and would be signed. I knew that the money was there. I had only three weeks to prepare for shooting in Fish-guard at the western edge of the Welsh coast. False fronts had to be built on quayside cottages and a whole whaler's ship side con-structed on the first floor of Captain Cat's home. My production company was fully liable for everything, but I knew or thought I knew, that all was *pukka*. Richard Burton was coming back to Wales for the first time in ten years, and all the press and television was waiting for him.

And come he did, because they were waiting for him. He could not disappoint them. He could never raise his head in Wales again, if he did not go, because everyone knew he was coming. Yet it was not my doing. It was the doing of his own publicity machine. And by the time he thought he might back out, it was too late. His pub-licity made him appear. He was hoist by his own PR, not mine.

He did put me to one final test. He had arrived in Fishguard at four o'clock in the afternoon. I begged him to appear by the dockside to perform the opening sequence, coming from the sea during the ten minutes of twilight, when the dusk can be shot. The whole crew was there, examining the credentials of an untried young director. A black car rolled down the hill. Richard Burton was indisposed. My film looked like being over before it began. With forty experienced pairs of eyes as gimlets on my back, I walked forward and considered the sea. Then I turned and said, 'Same place. Time. Eight o'clock tomorrow morning.' And so, all would be done, however unlikely that was.

From my reputation, Elizabeth Taylor disliked me on sight. She felt undereducated, her husband had wanted to become a don, and I had been an academic. In her Shepperton studio dressing-room, while making her previous film, she appeared rather dishevelled, if that was possible. She gave me three orders. Firstly, her back was too bad to take the train to Wales; I would have to film her two-day shoot in London. Secondly, it had to be at the end of the schedule, as her movie was a long way from a wrap. And although she was only playing the small part of a Welsh whore called Rosie Probert, she would require three Parisian nightdresses, at the cost of six hundred pounds – half of our total costume budget.

The next time I met her was the *coup-de-grâce*. Richard had invited myself and the comic Ryan Davies, who played the Second Voice, for a drunken evening in his Camden house. After a few bottles, Richard decided we were his two best friends, and he presented each of us with a silver goblet, given by the Rotary clubs of Wales in grateful memory to their favourite son and daughter, Elizabeth and Richard Burton, *alias* Jenkins. 'I have to cut all the jewellery advertisements out of the glossy magazines,' Richard was confiding in us, 'or I would be ruined. She loves the rocks.' But he was unable to forestall the apparition that burst through the door – Elizabeth, in a yellow hot-pants wool suit, covered by a wild mink coat, the tails of the little beasts twirling on the floor. 'Taraah!', she cried, and then she saw the silverware in the hands of Ryan and me. 'What are you doing with *my* goblet?' Elizabeth screeched in the tones of the Three Bears, objecting to Goldilocks. I handed one silver cup back to Richard, Ryan handed him the other, and we left hotfoot into the London night. Behind us, a voice like a police siren rent the black air.

At Lee studios, we waited all morning for Elizabeth to appear. We only had two days to shoot her. For if she and Richard did not leave British shores by tomorrow midnight, their back taxes would have settled much of the National Debt. I went to her dressing-room, and I put down a costly gold Egyptian serpent bracelet, as a peace offering from my pocket. Unfortunately, she was making up herself as Cleopatra, all *kohl* and rouge and peacock eyelids. 'That won't do,' I heard myself daring to say. 'You're a Welsh sailor's whore of the 'fifties. You can't look like that.'

'I always look like Cleopatra,' she said, and dismissed me.

She did not come on set until noon. I decided to turn her into Captain Cat's wet dream, as in the text. 'Grease the lens,' I told my cameraman, Bob Huke, who asked, 'Do I make her look beautiful, or like the back end of a bus?' I swallowed and gulped out, 'Beautiful, please. She has picture approval.'

We laid her on the brass bed and bunged in three shots before lunch on the incredible violet eyes. I noticed that Bob was performing in front of the Brute lights, as the conductor of an orchestra. Only his baton was a black ruler. When she was gone, I asked Bob what he was doing. 'Hiding her three chins,' he said, 'even when she moves. The thingy throws a shadow across her neck. We call it a Charliebar. Any Charlie can use it.' And indeed, for the solo stills, because of her low-slung figure, Elizabeth insisted on being shot upwards by a photographer lying on the floor. On such a take from a worm's eye view, she looked far taller and thinner, and a *bouffant* hairdo made her head a decent size.

After O'Toole had saved the picture by getting Elizabeth back on the bed after lunch, I made my only personal appearance and comment. I was the pair of hands in black globes putting two old pennies on the defunct Rosie Probert's eyes. I had solved the problem of having five different cemeteries in various locations, all pretending to be one at Llareggyb, by travelling with a moveable gravestone as a cornerpiece in the shot; it bore the Probert name. I must say, Elizabeth left without saying good-bye, although she did write in Burton's screen play, which he gave to me, that it had been a fantastic experience. Indeed, for both of us.

At lunch with Tony Curtis some time later, I complained about Elizabeth's behaviour, only to be sharply reproved by Roddy McDowell. She was no Shirley Temple, but one of the few child actresses after her *National Velvet*, who had grown and matured. At the age of fifteen, Roddy had worked with her in Hollywood on a movie. By Californian state law, such minors had to receive four hours' tuition daily between takes. Roddy came out of a lesson to meet Elizabeth, running into class.

'You're late,' he cried.

'Wouldn't you be,' she said, 'if you had just had Robert Taylor sticking his tongue down your throat?'

'You must forgive her,' Roddy told me at the end of his story. 'She has lost all sense of reality. But child star to real star. That is a wonderful and rare thing to do.'

Among the stars, O'Toole was the meteor. Witty and irrepressible, unpredictable and beautiful, he taught me that life is mostly coincidence, and action is all. I had first met him, when he was cast by Tony Richardson to play the lead at the Royal Court in the musical version of my novel, *The Breaking of Bumbo*. He came up with Siân Phillips to visit me and that satiric owl, John Bird, my sharer in a grotty flat over the Coffee Pot in Green Street in Cambridge. He sang songs all night in Gaelic, or thereabouts, she in Welsh. When a policeman came up the stairs towards dawn to stop us disturbing the peace, O'Toole persuaded him to drink whisky from his helmet and join in the choruses. He always had enough charm to steal the brass off a bobby's badge. I would try to reproduce the scene, when I made the film of *Under Milk Wood*; I had PC Attila Rees pissing into the chamberpot of his headgear, while Dylan's words sounded: 'You'll be sorry for that in the morning.'

Dylan's extraordinary radio play would never have been shot without O'Toole's commitment. He had played Captain Cat at RADA, the London actors' academy, and he was committed for little pay to the part. He claimed then to have met Elizabeth Taylor; this led to another meeting, while he was playing with Richard Burton in *Becket*; they swapped roles as King and Archbishop. O'Toole said that, after *Cleopatra*, Elizabeth was stalking Richard, wanting a wedding ring. Eddie Fisher, the previous husband, was after Elizabeth, wanting a reconciliation.

All of them were crammed into the back of a limousine, heading from the studio back to London. And O'Toole said, nodding towards the chauffeur, 'He is the only one, who hasn't had her.' And then he added to me, 'I was thrown out of the car, somewhere towards Maidenhead.' Pause. 'Not that she has hers.'

Later, Richard Burton told me that one morning, on the set of *Becket*, O'Toole had come in, bearing a whole open bottle of Irish whiskey in his hand. He offered it to Burton, who declined and asked what was the particular occasion for celebration.

'It's an Irish birthday,' O'Toole said.

'And what day is that?'

'Any day I say it is.'

And at that, O'Toole drained the bottle in ten swigs, and fell flat on his back. Shooting resumed twenty-four hours later. Twenty years on, he and Richard asked to see again the film of Becket, and Burton, commenting on his own waste of himself, declared, 'We went to watch the disintegration of our own flesh.' Hardly, in the case of O'Toole who was once asked what he knew about the many women in his life. 'They decide,' he said. 'We just turn up.'

Peter once defined love and caring for me, in the mode of Samuel Beckett. Sitting opposite him in the buffet in Leeds station were two old tramps, an old man and an old woman. They were sharing one bun and one cup of tea. The man took a bite out of the bun and passed it over to the woman. The woman took a sip of the tea and passed it over to the man, who then took out his false teeth and passed them to the woman, so that she could bite into the bun. 'There's compassion,' O'Toole said. 'True love.'

In making *Under Milk Wood*, Peter briefly gave up the drink, because he might lose his sight in the part he played. But as that ultimate professional, which he was, he insisted on wearing milky-blue contact lenses that covered his whole eye-ball to play the blind Captain Cat. The trouble was that he could only stand the lenses in his eyes for half-an-hour at a whack, and then he was really going blind after four days of it. If he had not been such a superb performer, capable of five-minute takes hitting an unseen mark without a wrong word, we could never have completed his shots on schedule with him still seeing. As it was, the courage of the man lasted far beyond the good of his eyes until the last four longish shots, which we took from the back or with his lids closed.

Because of Elizabeth Taylor's loathing of me for seeming too clever, O'Toole saved the picture, too. In her two days of shooting at the end of the film, she had only appeared by the first noon for three close-ups of her goo-goo violet eyes, lying on a brass bed. Slumped in despair, I was in my Lee studio room, when O'Toole intruded.

'You've lost your fillum, Andrew,' he said 'Liz is not appearing after lunch. But – what I am about to do for you, I deserve the Victoria Cross and bloody Bar.' He then disappeared. After a long and boozy lunch, he and Burton, who liked me and had coached her, held her up between their shoulders while she read off her lines. And the consummate O'Toole, who always told me 'Get this shot,' when he did something unexpected, conjured a real laugh out of that immaculate and uncreasable face. Playing Captain Cat as a young sailor, he leapt into bed with her, and hitched up his shirt. Tattooed in biro on his tummy was, *I Love You, Rosie Probert*, the part she was playing. She collapsed in a gale of mirth. She wasn't aware, I wasn't told, the result, a miracle of spontaneity.

O'Toole had wanted to play *Gog*, the lumbering hero of a mytho-logical novel of mine. On the cover were the backs of my hands; I was tattooed in ink on one paw with the word *LOVE*; on the other, with *HATE*. 'All those fights,' he said to me at lunch. 'I see you have broken knuckles, too.' I saw little of him after that, except when sending up a portentous *Macbeth* and playing *Jeffrey Bernard is Unwell* to the Soho drunk born. Frail and austere, he came to the theatrical memorial tribute to his other Irish actor friend, Richard Harris. Both of them, Peter had told me, had lost their gizzard, their spleen and their lights, because of the gargle, and they had to give it up. 'A lot of my plumbing,' he said, 'is gone.' Harris, famously, when carried out of Claridge's *in extremis*, had shouted to the other guests, 'It's the food.'

Actually, it was the drink. At a memorial celebration in the Piccadilly Theatre, a Harris son described the effort of the Irish roisterers to survive. Before his end, Harris had emerged into Brook Street, to find O'Toole weaving along the pavement. 'O'Toole,' Harris said, 'look at you. Are we not new members of Alcoholics Anonymous?'

'Indeed,' O'Toole said. 'I am trying to find my way to the next meeting.'

'But are you observing the rules?'

'It is very difficult,' O'Toole agreed. 'You see, every bar I enter, I have to give a false name.'

What a lovely wit! Curiously enough, O'Toole remained reli-gious, as only the irreverent can be. The medieval Mystery Plays seemed to him the basis of English drama. 'It's fortunate for the Church,' he told me, 'that I chose the theatre.' Even more fortu-nate, too, for the theatre was O'Toole's choice of it, to play there instead of the pulpit.

ACTS AND ILLUSIONS

My next voyages of American discovery were in pursuit of two writers, who were South and North Poles apart – Edgar Allan Poe and Jack London. Their sole longitude lay in prolific writing careers and early deaths. They also taught me of the flaws in trying to discern any account of anyone's existence, dead or alive. There have been admirable works of imaginative biography, in which the search for the truth by the biographer is almost as significant as the subject of the biography. The voyage in *The Odyssey* fascinates me more than the historical accuracy of Ulysses, king of Ithaca: Boswell is almost more intriguing than Dr Johnson. *The Road to Xanadu*, *The Quest for Corvo*, and *The Man Who Was B.Traven* illuminate the inquirer, who comes like Childe Harold to the dark tower, or knocks like the traveller on the moonlit door, asking, 'Is there anybody there?' This is essentially a journey to all the places and people who can answer the right questions. And it is an imaginative quest in which the biographer can try to stand and stare, look and hear with the same eyes and ears as the person he seeks to describe.

My wanderings, while writing on my chosen victims, were a discovery of America as well as of my subject and myself. As if he were a fox, I had to burrow into all the holes of the doomed poet in order to write a short novel, *The Facts in the Case of E. A. Poe*, for it contained a short biography of him, apparently written by a modern man who identified himself totally with Poe. His therapy was to go to all the places where Poe had been and to write a biography of his quarry, so as to separate himself from his *alter ego*. The act of visiting all the areas of Poe's life gave me personally as well as my antihero Pons an exact opportunity to compare ancient and modern sensibility as well as historical awareness. A black comedy, the novel itself mocked psychiatric techniques applied in the analysis of the great dead, but contained a valid method of writing historical and literary accounts by the description of place and the comparison of time.

Autobiography is notorious as a method of whitewash and blindfold. The memoirs of Bismarck, for instance, rival those of Gypsy

Rose Lee in hiding more than they reveal. The proper study of mankind may be man, but not myself. Even the writer of a secret diary such as Samuel Pepys hoped for its posthumous discovery, or else he would have destroyed it before his death; he too wrote not only for himself, but for the eyes of others and possible publication. And as for the quintessential John Aubrey in his *Brief Lives*, he wrote in code, but he did not destroy his works. These were deciphered by a barrister three centuries after Aubrey was gone from us. If there were no biographers, the writers of diaries and autobiographies would have to invent them. Or who would ask the right questions and set their records straight?

I do not distinguish overmuch between the writing of political or literary or artistic material. These all depend on the evidence available, the approach to those testimonies, the ordering of them, and the nature of the seeker and his time. A biography is, after all, never finished. It exists only to be rewritten. From lack of other documentation and competition, the lives recorded by Plutarch and Tacitus will always remain seminal and basic to Roman studies. But their judgements have been questioned by playwrights and historians, from William Shakespeare onwards. No biographer can escape from the sensibilities and values of his age. We are caught in the same ticktock of time, from which we seek to rescue our subjects. As we explain others to our contemporaries within their terms of reference, so we date ourselves in front of our sons and daughters. For when they become adults, they will demand that the accounts of the past are written in the terms they understand.

In my novel, set in modern Manhattan, a man called Ernest Albert Pons believes he is Edgar Allan Poe born again. He chooses a psychiatrist by the name of Dupin, Poe's French detective in three of his mystery stories. His analysis is to search out the truth about Poe's career – and so separate the poet's personality from his own. His quest takes him through the disturbances and changes that have overtaken America and Europe until his journey becomes as much a commentary on modern life as a hunt for the elusive nature of his subject. In fact, in order to escape from his heritage of the Holocaust, Pons seeks refuge in the macabre horrors of the Southern genius in his tales.

Poe could be a conformist, but also a charlatan. He swung between the pit of despair and the pendulum of evading dire circumstances by flight. Anywhere might be better than where he was now. For he always felt himself an outcast, capable of any ruse to survive, but also a victim of the greedy money-changers of New York. If he flipped his nature, it was not to deceive, but to escape, as Hans Pfaall to the Moon or Arthur Gordon Pym to the shrouded final figure at the Pole. He was perverse. Although the creator of a French sleuth of piercing insight, he committed his own crimes. He was a cryptographer and a hoaxer. He confessed of 'The Raven' and 'The Gold-Bug': 'The bird beat the bug, though, all hollow.' And in his essay on 'Diddling', he stated that man's destiny was to diddle. He himself had all the ingredients – 'minuteness, interest, perseverance, ingenuity, audacity, *nonchalance*, originality, impertinence, grin.'

Poe did pioneer modern science and detective fiction, the thriller and the horror story. The only other American writer in the nineteenth century to alter literature in such a staggering and magnificent way was Walt Whitman. Yet Poe's greater capacity to conjure up new genres lay in his paranoia and persecution complex. 'Is it any wonder that I was driven mad', he wrote, 'by the intolerable sense of wrong?' Imagined harms were inflicted on him, while he called his inspiration a mental disease. 'The works of such genius are never sound in themselves and, in especial, always betray the general mental insanity.' Yet such imbalances enabled him to vault the hurdles of traditional tracks to reach the byways. Also the forked paths of human choices.

I claim merely to be the editor of the manuscript of Pons, left at his bizarre death. In a commentary, I write of the work:

It seems to deal freshly with some basic problems for biographers – the connection between the writer and the material, the limited understanding possible between the living and the dead and the impossibility of being both objective and entering into an understanding of the subject. By identifying himself wholly with Poe at the beginning of the work, then by divorcing himself from the poet's character, Mr Pons has provided a new solution to the process undergone by biographers during their long period of study – the initial attraction to, the following revulsion from, and the final synthetic verdict on another person, who may often impose his style and thought on the effort to describe him.

Set a Pons to catch a Poe, Dr Dupin said to his patient. Biography is autobiography, Dr Dupin also said. I believe that through his obsession that he was Poe, Ernest Albert Pons stumbled on an original way of translating the psyche of one age to a very different one, and of recreating a dead man's personality through his increasing awareness of his own. ... Still, in the words of his mentor and subject: 'To be appreciated you must be read and these things are invariably sought after with avidity.'

Now to the North Pole, to where Jack London was drawn in his quest for the gold of personal experience. Given the immediacy of his compulsive prose, I could not describe the man except in the present tense. In my biography, his past actions are told as happenings, not reminiscences. So the reader may be persuaded to enter under his skin and in the fists of the primary American macho writer before Hemingway, who lived his fiction and made a fiction of his living. By his doing, I sought to make him known again.

He had towered over his time before the Great War as a colossus. Yet his gargantuan self-projection produced an equally large reaction. Since the dominant schools of British and American critics were based in London and New York, and as the philosophic fashions changed from Social Darwinism to liberal reformism and Freudianism, a Californian upstart, whose racism was as blatant as his apocalyptic sense of social justice, was condemned to pinpricks and oblivion. To his more sympathetic critics, his obvious power and talent fell short of genius because of the tragic flaws in his thought. For them, the evolutionist too often dominated the mythologizer of the frontier. Jack London's brutal northland seemed vulgar and crude. When the doctrine of the Aryan race also became loathsome to the American public, Jack appeared to be the John the Baptist of the Nazi superman as well as of the Bolshevik revolutionary. Even if his books were burned in Hitler's Germany because of his socialism, his belief in white supremacy made him suspect at home, while his popularity in Stalinist Russia seemed to confirm that he was the enemy of liberty and individuality. His works were consigned to the shelves of nurseries. He was regarded by most of the literary critics as a misguided man, who had written a few good dog stories.

Such patronizing and misjudgement were ludicrous. Jack had

been such an individualist in his life, he had been so relentlessly modern, scientific, and prophetic in his works. A trend in intellectual fashion came to his rescue, the increasing emphasis on the behavioural similarities between animals and human beings. He was certainly the prophet of the correspondences between beasts and men; *The Call of the Wild* and *White Fang* will always howl to us. And he despised critics as a breed. 'What's it all worth?' he asked. 'Cavil, and carp, and criticize, bark and snap, and what does it amount to? You're none the better for it. The world is not.' He declared his rebel *credo*:

> My kind kicks authority out of the path. Your kind puts mine in jail for violent assault on authority. My kind makes the living language. Your kind preserves the language my kind makes. Your kind and mine are always at war. We have been so in the past, and we shall be so in the future as long as languages live upon the planet. This is not sophistry; it is clubbing home the science of language, and is deeper than the deepest generalisations of the purist and the vulgarist. Think it over.

He strove to realize his dreams, not to analyse them. As he thought himself larger than life, he tried to do more than other men did. For a man, who has a heroic vision, can do more than a man, who knows himself too well and is afraid to move. To deny weakness, to insist on excess and success is to live at full stretch. Jack London lived nine lives and wrote more than fifty books and founded a ranch and died at forty. A man like that was worth his own myths.

Of course, the fable was too great for the person of one man. At times, he seemed to be trying to live out the history of the whole of mankind as well as to personify the American or the Californian dream. He had the vaunting ambition of the self-taught; he was always the poor boy in the public library, who determines to read every book on every shelf in order to add up the whole sum of human knowledge. This was a noble and futile aspiration, and a tragic one, which condemned a finite mind and body to an infinite dissatisfaction. Even in legend, Jack was not the American Adam, the innocent in the wilderness, nor the spirit of Huckleberry Finn, the savage fleeing civilization, nor even the Horatio Alger hero, the assiduous kid determined to make good. Although he had elements of these three stereotypes, he was more of the incessant Western pilgrim. However great his self-destruction and his corruption, his mind ranged on to a new vision of a new earth.

In writing his biography, after two full years of research mainly at the Huntington Library while based in a hired cabin on the Holly-wood Hills, I believed that I solved the mystery of whether Jack had committed suicide or not. I had become close to the heir, Milo Shepard, on the Jack London Ranch by Glen Ellen. I knew that Jack had taken an overdose of morphine and atropine against the pains of his overworked body and blocked intestines. Yet he had been taking too many painkillers for years. He had merely miscalculated the daily dose, when his weakened body could no longer stand the injections. When I put this theory of death by misadventure to Milo, he left the room and returned with a small case, containing the two hypodermic syringes, which Jack used all the time to quiet his ailments. He never meant to kill himself, but to drug himself to sleep.

He was already a walking corpse, only kept from collapse by the strength of his will and his constitution. His myth of himself was that he could put any amount of drink and drugs into his body and get away with it. Supermen do not die, even from an overdose. He had certainly made no preparations for dying, no last letters, no winding up of his affairs, no provision for tomorrow. There was a Colt .44 revolver beside his bed. He did not use it on himself like *The Little Lady in the Big House* in one of his lesser novels. His large injection before dawn seems to have been an impulse, not intended to be terminal. A needle-thrust at brief oblivion rather than a snatch at death, a quick remedy for a sudden agony. To the maker of his own myth, taking the remnants of two bottles of morphine and atropine capsules rather than two capsules might seem no more drastic than swallowing two bottles of whisky rather than two glasses in his drinking days. His body had always stood it so far.

This time, it did not. In his coma, his will to die seemed stronger than his will to live. As he had written in *Martin Eden* of his hero's drowning: 'Death did not hurt. It was life, the pangs of life, this awful, suffocating feeling; it was the last blow life could deal him.' Once he had lapsed into his coma, he intended to see his death through as he had seen his life through. He did not even think that willing one's death was a bad thing. He supported the right to suicide and euthanasia and cremation. In that, he was a true Californian. He believed that the body should be always young and that, if it betrayed its owner, it should be scattered to dust and ashes. He believed in risking himself and working as if he could live for ever.

I married again, a younger English woman, fresh from the counties, apparently the sort of debutante that I had pilloried in *The Breaking of Bumbo*. Unlike myself, who appeared to be privileged though well-educated, Miranda Seymour came from a grand background and was poorly educated. She was brought up to be a debutante and marry well, for she was a Howard de Walden on her mother's side. Her grandmother, the splendid Margharita, was the only one in that extended family who admired me for my wit. Once asked by one of her numerous cousins at a county ball what I thought they needed to stop breeding like rabbits, I replied, 'Myxamatosis.'

I made matters worse at the wedding reception at the Berkeley Hotel. There I piled gaffe on indiscretion. Ill at ease among the glitter and formal attire of hordes of unknown people, I was unaware that I was meant as the bridegroom to praise the hosts at length for the celebration. Hauled to a microphone, I found myself coming out with an unpardonable and never-forgotten one-liner. I merely thanked Mr and Mrs George Seymour 'for an extraordinary occasion'.

So I was disliked in Nottinghamshire as much as I had been at Cambridge, when an undergraduate. I rarely visited Miranda's stately home at Thrumpton, a Jacobean mansion beside a dark Trent tarn. The problem was her rather mean and very snobbish father George, who mistook egocentricity for eccentricity. He once took me aside in his lowering and unread library of leather-bound books with gold spines, and said to me:

'Here are *you*, Andrew, who went to Eton and the Brigade of Guards. I was only at Westminster and in the Green Jackets. Isn't life strange?'

Yes, isn't life strange, particularly for those who have inherited rather than merited anything? In our ten years of marriage, Miranda began to show an application and a capacity for reinvention worthy of Proteus. She had met me as an interviewer for a tabloid newspaper. With some home tuition, she managed to secure enough A-levels to get a place at Bedford College, where she took an indifferent degree. She wrote some historical romances, the best about Lord Byron, meant to be a kind of ancestor, and much later a fine biography of

Mary Shelley. Our marriage foundered in her disastrous affair with an immoral philosopher from University College, where I had once taught American history and political philosophy.

But then, escaped from my enveloping shadow as a sort of Count Frankenstein, Miranda showed her brilliance and resourcefulness. She wanted to become the subject of her biography of Lady Ottoline Morrell, the doyenne of the ripe Bloomsberries. For Garsington, read Thrumpton. And she succeeded magnificently as a tireless author and reviewer and literary networker. She rose and rose with many traces to become a Professor at a local university and an authority on English society from the 18th to the 20th century. Ironically, her real *grandeur* worked in her favour; my false one was somewhat my down-fall. But *chapeau bas, madame*. May our marriage Rest In Peace, and be blessed by Merlin, our splendid son.

Before our wedding, we had gone to Corfu to spend the summer in a hired haunted country house, meant to be cursed because of the honour killing by brothers of a wayward sister. Looking for a paradise of our own, we came across, at the village of Kombitsi on a hill, a mouldering stone ruin with a decrepit orchard and olive trees overlooking a Venetian fountain with the purest water on the island, and a two-mile view across a wooded valley towards a pair of bell-tolling ancient hamlets, a white foresight across a forest of Eden. The place was again held to be cursed. A Venetian Count of old name had built our farmhouse and an olive-press and had started on a monastery, when his only son fell ill. He had promised God that if his boy recovered, he would complete the holy place. If not, he would have his revenge. The child died. The three places were smashed.

To this day, the Greeks often desert the houses, where their mothers and fathers have died. The decision of one Greek and two British gay intelligence officers to rebuild the ruins of Kombitsi after the Second World War was locally held to be the kisses of death. We bought the half-restored farmhouse down the hill from one of the officers who had transferred his lover from Greece to Umbria, and so his choice of a holiday home. A donkey was then grazing in our sitting-room, but the work was eventually done while the village waited for the inevitable doom.

A trio of the owner and his heirs at the renewed olive press were brought down. At the monastery, the buyer died of asthma on a flight, while his sister departed in a car crash near Athens. We were nearly eliminated by a thunderbolt from Zeus, as we rose from the runway in an Airbus during an electrical storm. The plane was named *Odysseus*, and the wise captain, with one engine knocked out, jettisoned his gasoline and landed us back on Corfu, where a replacement craft, called *Nestor*, eventually returned us to England.

I reckoned that, even facing the Homeric wrath of the Greek gods, I had beaten the curse of our place. Yet the villagers were unconvinced, because they had not seen our escape. So many years later, with my bare hands I slowly built a stone shrine under the stairs for my beautiful 14th century Spanish wooden statue of the Madonna and Child. When it was done, I asked the local papas to arrive with our neighbours to bless our house. At the climax of the ceremony, my son Merlin had recovered from oversleeping and began descending, naked down the marble steps. Some angel, he. But then, how are curses lifted, unless the future is brought along to hallow the past?

A while before, I had broken the peace of our house by recommending to J. Lee Thompson the filming of *The Greek Tycoon* on and off Corfu. I had refused to be an extra during the luxury yacht scenes, although the lure of the movies persuaded many of the local gentry to spend a sultry day for little purpose or fame. I had, however, agreed to hold an end-of-shoot party at our country villa. Excitements and preparations were intense, as before Battle of Marathon. Contrary to etiquette, I invited the villagers along with the aristocratic families in a muddle without much of a mingle.

A kid and a lamb were roasted on spits over charcoal pits on the lawn, hand-turned for eight hours. On this occasion, I was not asked to eat their shorn testicles to prove that I was truly a man. A small cacophony of musicians was also present to greet their hero, Anthony Quinn, the supreme celluloid Zorba the Greek, although he was rather Mexican, actually.

I had met Quinn before, having a drink with the director. He was surly at the intrusion of a stranger, but when J. Lee praised him on his performance as the Greek Tycoon, he expanded, telling tales about being directed by Raoul Walsh, the inventor of the John Ford manner down to a black patch over one eye and a laconic wit. Walsh would pretend not even to look at an actor's performance during a take. He was rolling a cigarette, which he only removed from his lips to say, 'Roll 'em' and 'Cut.'

Walsh would only speak to the Script Girl to ask, 'Did the actors say all their words?' If she said they had, he would say, 'Print it – next shot over there.'

Once a posh New York actress arrived to make her first film. Errol Flynn was operating on a body in the foreground. She was playing a nurse, so Walsh told her to go to the background.

'And what do I do there, Mr Walsh?'

'Do what nurses do – screw with the bottles.'

Later in the shoot, Quinn himself didn't know what to do, when he ran down some steps to greet Flynn emotionally, after a successful operation. So Walsh said, 'You know, Tony – give him the garlic in the mouth!' And so Tony did, and they both looked close and tender, short of a kiss between men.

Quinn also told us of Marty Ritt, directing him and Sophia Loren. Whenever he spoke his lines, Ritt always said, 'That was great, Tony. Print it – but would you cut it in half?' Quinn hacked down his words on each of four takes until a long speech became a mumbled sentence. And for the actor, this was his best scene in all the picture.

Later, waiting for the cast to arrive at our party in the gloaming, I mused on the presence of the film stars. Their secret lay in their unpredictability. Would we see an electric smile or a temper tantrum? Two hours too late, four black limousines made the perilous journey to the hilltop *taverna*. Then the troupe staggered down the dusty path through the olive trees. Huge and dominant, Quinn strode in.

'*Kirios*!' they shouted, 'what eat?' Carving knives were waving as banners. 'Meat? Lamb bit? Goat?'

True to Zorba, Quinn growled, 'Gimme the whole leg.'

A haunch was hacked off a lamb. Quinn held it between his two hands and took a ferocious chomp down between his teeth. Then he howled. A sliver of tooth flew out as a piece of shrapnel, striking the luminary Jacqueline Bisset of *Bullitt* fame on the cheek. Quinn squatted, clutching his jaw.

'A dentist,' he moaned.

Consternation did not quite reign. I went to my Byronic lawyer and fixer. For in Corfu, all was impossible, certainly on Saturday at midnight. Yet I knew all was possible, too, through the right channels.

'There is a problem,' I said.

'No problem,' he said, 'for Zorba. Merely an advertisement.'

The lawyer walked up to the *taverna*, for we had no telephone. He threatened and honied some dentist, who opened up his torture chair. Assisted under the hoots of the Skeops owls in the olive grove, Quinn was transported into town and repaired and returned with another gold tooth to join in the feast.

I was dancing with the baby Merlin on my shoulders, and the whole world was giddy with the human stars, who, as the ancient gods when they came to earth, settled all our divisions and our woes. Towards dawn, we went our various ways. And I stood under the galaxies in their pinbright patterns in the heavens with the flung chiffon of the Milky Way, and I blessed the fact that somehow we could get away with our follies down here, occasionally.

The last novel of William Golding was called the *Pythia*. The book described the life of the priestess of Apollo's oracle at Delphi, where she gave her inspired prophecies. She spoke in the name of the giant python of inspiration, which can still be seen in friezes in Ephesos, curling up the rod or alchemic wand of the Greek gods of wisdom, such as Hermes. This was the legend, for pythons appeared to be long gone in Greece. At our stone farmhouse at Kombitsi, however, myth became fact. We seemed to have a phantom killer on the baked tiles. At night, there were the sounds of dragging and screeching, as though Jack the Ripper was pulling a dying dockside tart across the roof. The only traces in the morning were coils of smashed yellow clay coverings above our home.

Just before we left the house for ever, the gardener Taki came to me with his shotgun over his shoulder. For the local village of exiled Albanians murdered any living thing which flew or moved or squirmed. '*Kirios*,' he said, 'look what is near the fountain.' And he took me down the path under the burned oak and the pine trees to see a miracle. A great red and green and creamy snake lay coiled across the dust, as high as an anthill. He was the monster, who had climbed our wisteria pergola and consumed the squalling tree squirrels above our bedroom. Yet he was also the Pythia of the oracle and the past, perhaps the last one to survive in the wilderness valley, which we could view from our window. He drank from the water of life, which nourished us all.

I thrust down Taki's gun.

'You will not have him,' I said in my ancient incomprehensible Greek. 'He has more *nous* or intelligence than you and I.'

The python slowly uncoiled and curled away in splendour, almost as long as a cricket pitch. I was glad to preserve such a proof of myth.

When I had finished *Under Milk Wood* in 1971, the British film industry was in the doldrums. We were not making more than a dozen pictures a year. I was writing savage pieces for the *New Statesman* called *Who Killed the Film?* 'More than half the film technicians are now out of work and the future of the film industry is being left to the bloody hands of Hammer and to the blue jokes of Carry on Regardless. There is no immediate prospect of a new infusion of American risk capital to resurrect the corpse. Since the Scots are necrophiliacs, I would like to sing you a song over the body:

Who killed the film?
I said the producer
Playing faster and looser.
I killed the film.

Incredibly, I appeared to have raised the money for another film, called *Rider*, backed by Associated Newspapers and the Greek government. To begin at the ending, two of the bigger actors in size in all the world made me the filling in a split bun. Squashed between them at the best restaurant in Athens for fourteen hours, we had eaten everything good to eat in the place and drunk twenty-two bottles of wine. We were celebrating our latest film disaster, which was not called *A Funny Thing Happened To Me On My Way To The Acropolis Last Night*. My guests were Orson Welles and Oliver Reed. They were large men. Orson needed three chairs to sit on my left: Oliver needed two on my right: I was spread thin as meat paste between them. The feast was all being paid for on my American Express card, which Oliver had fished out of my breast pocket.

'Stars don't carry credit cards,' he said.

This was another lesson in how some make money without making a film. While Orson and I had left our contracts to our lawyers to get signed by our English financiers, Oliver had insisted that his contract was signed before he left for Athens. There was a stock market crash and Associated Newspapers withdrew in the first week of shooting. Oliver threatened to sue and received an out-of-court settlement of two hundred thousand dollars plus interest for not playing in the film. Orson and I, without the vital signature on the final piece of paper, received nothing. We could have sued and perhaps won. But if we had sued a newspaper group, we would have been guaranteed bad publicity for the rest of our lives. And as they who live by the cinema need good publicity, so those who live by the hacks can die by it.

My film had begun in Athens, where a producer called Finos, the proprietor of the best studio there, had offered me a co-production deal on a subject, which I called *Rider*. I wrote it as a modern version of Faust. A motorcycle rider on the Wall of Death, to be played by Oliver Reed, is offered a few thousand dollars for his heart by Orson Welles, the owner of a transplant hospital. He sells his heart to make money for his greedy mistress, played by Orson's mistress Oja Kadar, then he sells off the rest of his organs. Rich patients are waiting for these vital parts. Like Mephistopheles at midnight, thugs move in to kill Rider and collect the parts that he has sold. He eludes them, until a final great stunt leap to freedom or death.

The two main parts were written for Oliver and Orson: the two stars immediately accepted them. I had heard that the English press group wanted to try its hand in backing films: the subject, the stars, and the co-financing from Greece were attractive. The total budget of the film was less than one million dollars. Although I had developed it as far as packaging it, I gave way to a producer nominated by the newspaper company, an ex-actor, who should have stayed that way, playing minor roles minimally, and without conviction.

I had first seen and heard the huge Welles in *L'Ami de Louis* in Paris with its red-squared tablecloths and service of whole legs of lamb. He was booming away at his faithful follower, Peter Bogdanovich, who was tracking him as well as John Ford. Two remarks reverberated in thunder across the restaurant. 'Fellini is just riding from whore to whore.' And another story about the meanness of young women. He had picked one up at a party, and had been asked to take her home. Once he had done this, flattered as an older man and rather excited, she leapt out of the automobile, saying, 'Thank you so much for taking me home.'

'Very literal,' Welles remarked. 'And thrifty.'

When accepting his part in *Rider*, Welles used his usual insincere flattery over my telephone.

'Let me begin by saying that yours is the best script I have been sent all year and I shall be delighted to play in it. Of course, the fee you have offered me is one-third of what I have ever accepted for playing for eight days. If you were to offer me King Lear, naturally I would play for one dollar. But as it is, I do notice that your partner Mr Finos has a studio in Athens. I need to complete my last picture *Othello* with certain Greek sequences. Perhaps we can work something out.'

That would not be. Meeting Orson at the Carlton Towers in London, I saw him sitting in a brown suit, his trousers nearly up to his armpits to contain his belly, with a white beard and eyes as quick as mice in the pretence of jocularity in his face. A certain *rapport* built up between us, as we exchanged film buccaneering stories. I said, 'Everybody is moderately criminal in films,' and he said, 'Yes, but *moderately* criminal – within the limits. I hope that applies to your Mr Finos.' Later my cameraman Walter Lassally told me a splendid story about Welles. Christopher Plummer was fawning upon him in *Oedipus* and he offered to give Orson an eye-line for his close-ups in scenes between the two of them, only to hear, 'Dear boy, it's very kind of you to offer your help, but when I say my lines, I am speaking only to myself.'

Contracts were signed with Oliver Reed, and agreed for Orson Welles and for me. My production company, Timon Films, received some money from the newspaper group and entered into various agreements with a few British actors and technicians, especially Walter Lassally, who knew Finos, spoke the language, and had won an Oscar for his work on *Zorba the Greek*. I flew out to Athens to prepare the film, leaving my lawyer to have my contract signed by the newspaper group and my fee put in the bank. Then all began to happen. Finos pulled out of the co-production deal, but brought in the Greek government Film Board in his place: *Rider* was to be the first major co-production in Greece; new democracy had been restored after the long night of the generals. My producer took over the final financial negotiations, while I prepared to start shooting. Walter Lassally appeared, and photography began, before Orson and Oliver flew to Athens. Particularly funny was the fact that the last remaining Wall of Death rider in Greece was a gypsy in a skirt on an old Norton. She had to be bulked out to play Oliver in the circus sequences – the only time that mighty male was doubled by a small woman.

When Alexander the Great asked the Greeks what they feared most, he expected them to say, 'Alexander the Great.' In fact, they replied they were afraid of the sky cracking open, and a piece of blue brick falling on their heads. In Athens that December, the sky did crack open. The English stock market collapsed. It dropped to 150 points, losing 60 per cent of its previous value. Technically, many of Britain's larger companies and smaller banks became insolvent. Even my large newspaper group was sailing close to the rocks. The order went out: 'Abandon all projects.' That paper ship was saved, we were scuppered.

We were nearing Christmas. No rescue operation could be mounted, as everybody was on their knees at home, or inebriated until the New Year. The producer fled Athens, leaving me and the production accountant to face the storm. I paid off most of the technicians with cheques for two weeks' wages, hoping the Season of Good Will would make my bank honour them. Orson cooked up a plot with Oliver Reed, who had viewed this sort of havoc before, to lay waste to the Grand-Bretagne hotel and cause the maximum scandal possible and call a Press Conference to say that the English newspaper bastards had stranded them. I managed to stop the mayhem by pointing out that the Greek government was still backing us, and it was not to blame.

Orson was awesome. He fixed me with his baleful eye. 'I only came here because of you, Andrew,' he boomed, exaggerating. 'I have men in London, and I cannot pay their bills. I have women in Paris, and I cannot pay their hills. I have persons of doubtful gender in Rome, and I cannot pay their bills. I only came here in order to pay their bills, and now I cannot pay my bills here. You will not leave this city, until you have paid my bills.' I said I would, my credit card cracking from overuse in my hand. I left Orson on the sight of his imperious shape, discovering on the telephone that his lawyer had failed to have his contract signed and was avoiding him. 'I do not care,' Orson declared to the secretary, 'if your master is in bed, in court, or in jail. He will speak to Orson Welles.'

Later, Orson collapsed and deflated into a grey-faced, limping, tired and sympathetic old man, before I saw him and Oja Kadar off at the airport. He told me that the secret vice of W.C. Fields was not alcohol and squirreling away money, but collecting books. The literary flair of the lines of the comic came from his wide reading; but he feared that knowledge of his library would harm his screen image. I was reminded of that, when later talking to Barry Humphries of Dame Edna Everage fame, who confessed to me that he was a bibliophile. The 15,000 books in his apartment were buckling the floorboards, so he had to buy the flat below, in case they crashed through its ceiling.

As I saw Orson waddle away towards his plane, I was reminded of the first time I had seen him in the flesh, performing *Moby Dick* in a London theatre. His presence and genius were overpowering. With five supporting actors, he conjured up, from a packing case and a swinging rope, the pursuit of the great white whale. But, as one of my surreal French postcards used to declare, *tout casse, tout lasse, tout passe.*

Now it was my turn to flee to London and confront the minions of the newspaper group. They tried to avoid me, but ended by seeing me with their lawyers. When I threatened to sue them, they taught me one of the many lessons I was to learn from my Athenian adventure.

'Sue us, sue us,' they said. 'It suits our cash flow.' They intended to fight the case to the House of Lords, they said, which would cost me at least another hundred thousand dollars and three years. Did I have that amount of money and time to burn? I decided I did not and took back my screenplay. Another year, another decade, it might be made again, and I would be paid. So I was. As Orson had told me, I would render all my life in six letters, before R.I.P.

'What letters, awesome Orson?"

'M.P.; Y.P.; H.P.: *My* problem; *Your* problem; *His/Her* problem.'

Indeed, the downfall of *Rider* was *My* problem.

Oliver Reed made a lot of money for not working, Orson Welles broke even, and I was skinned alive. Most of the people engaged on the film were paid a little, but far less than they had hoped. I should not have left London until all the documents had been completed, but then the film could never have been prepared in time to meet the dates when the two stars were available for shooting. It had seemed a safe project, a good script, a small budget, backed by a Greek government body and a major English communications company. Who should know that the London stock market would collapse and the sky fall in?

Making an independent movie is a high-risk business. Those who always get money from it are those who take a fee while preparing it and are not liable for anything, if all goes wrong. I once asked Evelyn de Rothschild for money to back my film again, and he replied. 'If I want to gamble, I prefer racehorses.' Thinking about the black farce in which *Rider* hardly left the post, I could only reply, 'I agree.' Racehorses are already there and are beautiful. To gamble on them is not necessary.

Curiously enough, after this debacle, I did finish a film with that gentle bruiser, Oliver Reed. My old friend Alexander Weymouth, heir to Longleat, had given me his first novel, *The Carrycot*. Its subject was the owner of a stately home, who was drugged and did not know whether or not he had battered his baby. Borrowing from *The Turn of the Screw* and from the Losey and Pinter, *The Servant*, played with sinuous malevolence by Dirk Bogarde, I constructed a part for Oliver as the dominant butler who took over the Elizabethan mansion and the child heir. The only film money in London, apparently, was in the pockets of four young producers with Canadian resources, or lack of them. Did I have a project? Yes, Alexander's novel. The budget was only £75,000. The schedule was three weeks. Mission impossible. But then, there was no other game in town.

Oliver was briefly unemployed. His brother David said he liked the part. He would play for a percentage and all of Italy, where he had a deal. I cast Derek Jacobi as the weak owner of the ancient pile, Fiona Lewis because she was the most beautiful woman in all London, and the French actress Anna Gaël, as she was Alexander Weymouth's true wife among his many wifelets. My cameraman was Harry Waxman, who was meant to have the fastest hand on the lens in the west. The whole of Longleat came for free, nobody received more than £200 a week, what an opportunity for, as the Americans put it, a crap shoot.

First, I had to pass the test of Oliver. I had to drive down to his Gothic monstrosity of a Victorian folly in Surrey, where we consumed a cellar of wine and fields of grass, smoking out of our nostrils. Then Oliver announced he would not play, unless I rowed him across a muddy lake on his property. Arriving there, two large fellows were fishing along with a vast black dog. 'Poachers,' Oliver yelled and started at them, only to think thrice and end by inviting them to the village pub that evening. He still, however, had to provoke me. Going down a small bank towards a wood, he picked up a fallen branch and tossed it to me. 'Quarterstaffs,' he said. 'You wanker.' Then he picked up a branch himself.

I had had enough. Also I had the slope. I charged down and smote the surprised Oliver to the ground. As he tried to rise, I struck him again. Another Bannockburn, I thought. Then he bellowed as the Minotaur, and he knocked me flat. I looked up at the raging bull, and I began laughing, and so did he. We had achieved mutual respect. In the years to come, when we rarely met, he would always give me a wet kiss and say, 'Beware Andrew when his blue eyes lock.' That was the lesson of the stars, which I had learned from O'Toole. 'Get this shot,' he would say and then do something unscripted and unexpected. I had surprised Oliver by a sudden quick action that is the hallmark of a great actor, which he was.

In a remarkable scene of recognition, Lady Bath looked at Oliver, and he looked at her. Two hooded blue glares. She laughed and said, 'Cousin.' 'What,' Oliver said. 'I'm a Tree,' she said. 'Beerbohm Tree – the old actor, you know – my grandfather.' And Oliver Reed really began laughing. 'And Mrs Reed – Mrs Broken Reed – my grandmother.' Yes, it was so. Beerbohm Tree had an official family by his wife, and an unofficial one by his mistress. As she had to have a married name, with his usual wit, Beerbohm Tree called her Mrs 'Broken' Reed, and both the director Carol Reed and Oliver were her descendants.

I was sleeping in Alexander's decorated Kama Sutra bedroom in Longleat, so for the love-scene, I lay Derek Jacobi on his back in a loincloth with the naked Fiona Lewis, bumping and grinding down on him, trying not to get pierced by the many plaster-and- sawdust protuberances, sticking out from the erotic Indian scenes on the walls. Fiona had been very funny about working with Oliver in *The Devils*. 'There I was starkers on a swing,' she said, 'flashing my beaver at all below.' She was even more amusing about a day of bestriding the recumbent and rather single Jacobi, and riding him barefront as her mount. 'A bloody triumph, darling,' she said, 'after all that effort. I felt a tiny bump beneath me, late in the afternoon.'

What was I thinking when I cast the adorable Timon, a blond

angel only four years old, as the heir of Longleat, sacrificed by his *outré* father Derek Jacobi and menaced by Oliver Reed, the satanic butler? My ex-wife Marianne had to stay in the mansion to look after the little boy, and Miranda insisted on coming down as well, only to tell me that she was pregnant. Such a far-out *ménage* of two wives and a golden child hardly disturbed Alexander, who had there his own wife Anna Gaël and mother of his two children, despite his scores of wifelets. She was to become in Paris a close friend of Marianne in the future.

Yet with crass insensitivity and total concentration on the making of the film, I hardly considered the effect on Miranda, who hid any pain from me. The melodrama of the screen had spilled over into our private lives, and we did not seem to care. Only Timon struck back. When he wasn't skipping through the daffodils outside with his favourite woollen rabbit, he was shrieking in protest at a naked bath scene. During the evening rushes, however, he would creep through the chairlegs and bite Oliver Reed in the ankles. And Oliver did not resist. He knew he had earned it.

At the end of the film, Alexander hosted a minor *louche* party. I remember the jazz singer George Melly climbing a bookcase to lick the cock of a marble cherub and my friend Henry, Lord Pembroke, dancing wildly. I had advised him not to make his soft-porn film *Emily* with Koo Stark, but he had not listened. Looking for film money, he invited me back to Wilton on my journey home. I had just been bilked of my quarter share of the profits of *Blue Blood* because the Canadian mob said they would remove me from finishing the cut of the film, unless I signed a new contract, giving them everything. So I did. They always said of me I cared too much about making a film at any price. That night, we played Don Maclean, singing 'Bronco Bill's Lament' in the vast Double Cube Room, as large as a studio. In the end, all the foyers and the lawyers, who could pull a fountain pen, did always end up, even with your saddle and your horse. One man's work was another man's play.

Blue Blood was not long enough, so I wrapped by shooting Oliver for an extra five minutes in the basement of my house in Hanover Terrace in Regent's Park. He had grown a moustache and a beard for *The Four Musketeers*, but necessity is the godfather of improvisation. I had Oliver polishing a huge silver platter, which hid the thicket under his nose. Only those twin lasers of his eyes expressed his searching ferocity. This was the best scene in the picture. The less the great stars do between bursts of sudden action, the more they dominate.

Lurid sequences were inserted in the film in an orgy scene. I removed my name from the picture, although I fear it is still there. One good review was received from *Harpers & Queen*: 'Whatever anyone has said or is about to say about it, Andrew Sinclair's film *Blue Blood*, shot entirely at Longleat, must rank as quite the most bizarre and beautiful upper-class social document of our times. Oliver Reed plays the butler with unique inimitable inferior-person accent, Fiona Lewis confronts with *breathtaking nakedness*, Alexander Weymouth wanders in undisguised as himself.' If later the film was to be praised as almost as worthy of Buñuel's assaults on the sad charms of the bourgeoisie, I did not deserve such a fate.

The Wonder of Children and Movies

I never saw my son, who was not quite my son, until he was two. But I had also made a music-box behind the bluntish spires of Notre-Dame. The Hunchback rose in dark and silhouette against the moon and brilliant firmament. *La Vie en Rose* played in a far tinkle. *Ma mie*, his grandmother, made him kiss it every night. So when we met by the Métro Raspail, she put his hand in mine and walked away. He looked up past my face towards the stars and said, '*Boîte à musique au papa.*'

The quick confidence of boys and girls revives again in what we have lost so long. Dreamday and trust and love without a doubt. And music-boxes are more sure with time than any taste of *petite madeleine*. Proust was transported back by sense and smell. But tunes and eyes rehearse the magic world of children, making infinities of instants. The now was then in ceaseless repetitions, matching the sounding metal pins that sent old airs to float in puffs of dandelions. I still wish to be so small again in wonderland.

We all will end in boxes anyway. If we can place in them our little lives and make our visions turn on paradise and hitch a lift on hearing *Memories* to play again in Eden endlessly, then my son's words are true. A very heaven may be no larger than a tiny thing. I followed Joseph Cornell, the last of the Surreal makers of collages and small things on framed shelves, and I made a series of music boxes for the Redfern Gallery in Cork Street – a toy history of the 20th century. I have always believed that, as long as we can live our lives with a flick of wonder, we are not wholly lost souls. Yes, the child does make the man, but only if the man allows the child to be within him.

In the days when the Seine-side kiosk book vendors were still selling Edwardian *papeterie* and fantasy postcards, I built up a collection, which I would use in my own *automates*, for those of the period were too dear to buy. I also collected old tin toys for the wonder and brightness of them – early lunch-tins of Superman and Star Wars, flashing space guns and rocket ships and robots, even a Japanese businessman rolling on wheels of the globe with his briefcase to conquer the world. One shop in Paris still sold the little tinkling machines. And in East End markets, I bought broken watchpieces and battered Second World War model aeroplanes to bolster my childhood collection.

From these materials, I constructed a personal history of my century, ranging from the Battle of the Somme through Hitler and Hiroshima to Bill Clinton smoking a cigar beside a painted Russian Lewinsky wooden doll. This was satire through the eye of a child. For as tiny Timon, who saw the galaxies in a music box, small ones view the world as it appears to them, and they speak the truth about what is in front of their eyes.

I suppose I have always been with the rogue Autolycus in *The Winter's Tale*, 'a snapper-up of unconsidered trifles.' And in his wondrous book on the art of Joseph Cornell, Charles Simic appreciated the collection of the *bric-à-brac* of our time to make a statement of who we were. 'The disorder of the city is sacred. All things are interrelated. As above, so below. We are fragments of an unutterable whole. Meaning is always in search of itself. Unsuspected revelations await us around the next corner.'

Moreover, Simic compared Cornell with my cherished American poet, Emily Dickinson. Their biographies explained nothing. The pair of them were without precedent, eccentric and original, and they lived within the riddle. 'If her poems are like his boxes, a place where secrets are kept, his boxes are like her poems, the place of unlikely things coming together.' Another poet W.H. Auden wished for his godchildren 'a sense of theatre', if they want to go far. So they will know the difference between what they do and say, and who they really are. I will wish my godson 'a sense of wonder', if he wants to reach far. So he will never know the difference between what he says and sees, or who he really is. Infinite curiosity about the cabinet of curiosities, the *wunderkammer* which is the world.

The mission of my life was to bring up Timon and Merlin as brothers. Always a solitary boy, I had become divided from my brother Ian, even in our school playground. We both played together without understanding each other. He had married a *corps de ballet* wife and had three daughters, and they had lived for a decade in early hippie Ibiza. They had returned for education to Totnes in Devon, and all had rather fallen apart for them, when Ian's wife died early of cancer. Now I was determined to bring up together Merlin and Timon, as far as I could, given society and its conventions. Not that I cared for these confines too much. For I believed that no child was in any way responsible for the sins of the father. No matter the parent of any child who has no choice on who's the daddy, so must be loved. Innocence is all.

After the death of the great American film director John Ford, I found myself called in by his widow Mary and his daughter to write his biography. This had been attempted shortly before by a couple other directors, Peter Bogdanovich and Lindsay Anderson, but Ford hated pryers and probers. 'The truth about my life,' he said, 'is nobody's damn business but my own.' He even gave inquirers a false name, as a reformed drunkard at a bar. He was actually baptized John Augustine Feeney, one of the surviving seven of eleven children, born to an Irish-American family in Maine. Ford loathed producers even more than interviewers. He would take the iron viewfinder off the old Mitchell camera, stick it to his blind eye as Admiral Nelson at Copenhagen, then pretend to be deaf and ask the studio Honcho to come closer, then cry out 'Pan left!' and swing about and brain the poor fellow, who would never come on location again. A penchant for clandestinity does protect one's identity, and see off any interference. He was my chosen film-maker for his style, also as the only one to screen all American history from the Revolution through the Civil War up to the Battle of Midway in person, and even the Korean intervention.

So in my obsession for bringing up the two little boys, I took out with me to California as to Longleat, Marianne and Miranda and their two sons and an elegant nanny with a hash habit or so. After a spell in a friend's vineyard, we ended on the beach in Malibu in a hired house. Oblivious to any tensions between my two wives or what the Hollywood therapists might think of my actions, I found the small boys engaged and entranced, especially when they went to Disneyland and were hugged by Mickey Mouse, whom they still thought might be real in his wondrous way.

I was also writing a five-part serial show for Italian television of *Martin Eden*, Jack London's fictional autobiography, ending in his willed death. Its charismatic director, Giacomo Battiato, stayed with us and would put on screen *Orlando Furioso* and other classics of his country. While in our house on the shore, a storm raged in from the Pacific, and my lower room collapsed onto the shingles. The scene on the star-studded beach was apocalyptic.

- The dark surfers rode as Hell's Angels on the crests of the revving waves
- The hippies moved in from the canyons to make smoking teepees from the piled Asian driftwood
- The squad cars squirted by, horns blaring and headlights glaring
- The chained prison gangs were trucked in to clear the mast-high debris
- In a week or sand dust and screaming the strand is restored to a jogtrack
- The stars in their courses and trainers trot to the pier again
- Bashed by the surge, a battered seal lives on a washed boulder for three days
- My small boys try to feed him fishes but he will not stir
- Then he is gone in the night tide

When *Martin Eden* would appear on European television, it would be a blinder. But in Malibu, Jack London's passage to suicide and the storm and the lone sea on the rock seemed to comment on my own confusion. I was not committed to upheaval, but I could not escape it on any project in my wilfulness. The way I chose to go would lead to little disasters round the corner. As I hardly consulted anyone, I deserved what I got, the opprobrium and the mayhem.

We all try to deny our defects. The subject of my book and film researches, John Ford, could hardly see. His disability became his cinematic vision and his contribution to his country. With 4F eyesight, and a black patch over one peeper, he created the panorama and ritual of the shifting American frontier. With his Low Level Oblique photographic techniques, he helped to make possible the largest sea invasion of Europe in human history. Weighed down with Oscars and medals, he died a Rear-Admiral as well as a film legend. Rarely have so many owed so much to the far-seeing insight of one man.

Ford stitched an Irish realism into his embroidery of the past. He presented his first star, Harry Carey, as a 'sort of bum, a saddle tramp, instead of a great bold gun-fighting hero.' He said he liked 'fresh air, the wide open spaces, the mountains, the desert.' Sex, obscenity, and degeneration did not interest him. He also learned most everything, while directing in the silent cinema. Motive and plot were revealed in action and expression. 'That's when pictures and not words had to tell the story,' he said. 'Sound wasn't the revolution most people imagine it was.'

Ford insisted that producers stay off the set while he was actually shooting. His bad treatment of them was legendary. When one producer told him he was behind schedule, he tore ten pages from the script and said, 'Now we are three days ahead of schedule.' To teach that producer a lesson, he never shot the missing sequences. On another occasion, the associate producer of *The Informer* came on set to say that the rushes of the previous day's shooting were great. Ford then declared that there must be something wrong with the scenes if the front office liked them, so he reshot them for the next two days at an additional cost of $25,000 on the budget. The intruder should have remembered what Ford had done to him, when he had dared to appear on set for the first day of shooting. Then Ford had seized his chin, turned his face into profile, and declared to the assembled technicians and cast, 'This is an associate producer. Take a good look at him, because you will not see him again on the set...'

Ford would not tolerate anyone who tried to interfere with his total control during principal photography. To him, the finance was the producer's only role during shooting, and to show his contempt of money, he would not even carry it. He would leave his bills for his friends to pick up, and they would have to be repaid by his business manager.

To those who dared to say how they thought a scene should be done, Ford's reaction was immediate. When one actress tried to tell him how to play her part, he assured her that he was paid to direct and asked, 'Honey, what do they pay you for?' When an assistant cameraman said he reckoned a shot would look good from a neighbouring hilltop, Ford agreed and made him manhandle all the camera gear up there.

So Ford achieved total command and the fidelity of his people. He was taciturn, only explaining what was absolutely necessary, so that everyone hung on his least word. He created tension and then exploded it, never explaining his motives, any more than a priest or an admiral would. He took full responsibility, keeping the producers and the studio from intervening. Once he had chosen his group, he allowed them initiative, but he never forgave any negligence or incompetence.

Through his mastery of the medium and refusal to explain his art, he knew how to create an atmosphere of complete dependence and trust in him. Yet strategy and organization won only half of his battle, for much of his genius lay in his pictorial sense, in his understanding of pacing and playing his scenes, in his special view from his private tower, and in his scenes of the rhythm of human life set against his instinct for the seasons of nature and the tides of the sea.

In *Stagecoach*, Ford created the archetypes and myths of the West. The picture was mostly filmed in Monument Valley in Arizona – an ancient salt seabed surrounded by eroded crimson and scarlet buttes and bluffs, the gigantic sculptures of time and weather, which make the efforts of mankind appear irrelevant and vain. By setting the wheels of transport and the uniforms of an official army against these prehistoric masses, Ford reduced the image of human progress to a few insects crawling beneath the indifferent stone faces of the ages.

The Apaches, however, were never presented as intruders upon the majesty of the landscape, but as its true inhabitants, painted like the rocks and the desert and the eagles and the wildcats, a part of the scale and ferocity and liberty of the place. They were as large as their own land or they vanished within it. When once their scouts were seen on the rim of the crevasse through which the stagecoach passed as into the entrance to hell, they seemed a distant warning to the eye of the intruder upon their space, as the danger signal a ship might fly in the vast expanse of the ocean.

Ford not only pictured most of American history, but he helped to forge it. He did not become a Rear Admiral in the American Navy for no service; his rank was hardly an honorary degree. In the 'thirties, he had used his ketch, the *Araner*, to look out for submarines off California and to photograph Japanese installations in the Pacific Ocean. With a cameraman, he flew to record the enemy assault on the Midway Islands. His true shot of the raising of the flag during the air assault became an icon of war documentary cinema, and a symbol of patriotism. His sense of the dramatic had taken him into surveillance for the Navy. Now he had actually been wounded in combat, while filming a scene of courage under attack that would have seemed excessive in one of his own movies. In these, he had already taught his country's soldiers and sailors the stance of brave acts. If they now performed and Ford recorded them in actual war, they had been inspired and he had learned his skills from Hollywood artifice. At *The Battle of Midway*, illusion and fact were one.

Through an assistant, Mark Armistead, Ford developed an aerial reconnaissance technique, Low Level Oblique, which provided the D-Day data for the invasion of the Normandy beaches. Five hundred clockwork Eyemo cameras were also mounted on the front of the landing craft; these were triggered by the ramp thumping down on the beach. With this device, five hundred takes of the troops charging into France could be shot, rather outdoing later pastiches like Spielberg's *Saving Private Ryan*. Such was the real stuff, indeed.

The finale of Ford's confusion with actual warfare and a cinematic effect took place, when he was seconded to the Seventh Fleet to make *This Is Korea!* Emulating Conrad in *Heart of Darkness*, in which a French cruiser loosed a useless barrage onto West Africa, Ford asked the Vice-Admiral in charge of the battleship *Missouri* to provide a climax for his movie. He demanded whether the 'Mighty Mo' had ever fired all of her sixteen-inch guns in one broadside and in one direction. The Vice-Admiral replied that no American battleship had ever done that, for fear that the recoil would make the ship turn turtle.

'How much longer have you got in the Navy before you retire?' Ford asked. When the answer was a mere six months, he said, 'Wouldn't you like to know anyway?'

'We'll try it,' the Vice-Admiral said.

The next day a target was selected somewhere on the mainland of Asia, and all the huge guns of the 'Mighty Mo' were trained on it. Ford and his cameraman wisely rose from the battleship in a helicopter and turned their cameras on the target below. 'Roll 'em,' Ford said on the radio.

The *Missouri* fired her thundering broadside into Korea. The battleship rocked sideways on the recoil, keeling nearly halfway over, until her starboard decks were awash. Then she righted herself, shaking off the water like the leviathan she was. Ford got the shot and had a crescendo for his film, the Vice-Admiral settled a Navy puzzle, and somewhere in Asia, there was a series of vast and pointless explosions.

Ford was always in love with confrontation. A secret supporter of the Irish Republican Army, he could only be roused by patriotic calls to duty, whether subversive or not. When I first visited his retreat in Palm Desert, his widow, Mary Smith Ford, was too comatose to see me. When I last left, I had gingered her up a wee bit. In recall of past glories, she sat up, blazing in emeralds in her bed, and telling me about how she used to waken her husband to get him to work, in the early days of their long marriage. She would open the bedroom windows noisily, then put 'The Battle Hymn of the Republic' on the gramophone. A full chorus would chant the patriotic words, *Mine eyes have seen the glory of the coming of the Lord*. If Ford still refused to move on the crashing sound of *The grapes of wrath are stored*, his wife would change records to army bugle calls, sounding reveille to taps and finally to hillbilly music, which usually sent him swearing out of bed.

Ford was always a family man, who loved his home and his cronies. He had little to do with the mob of young actresses, who tried to involve him personally in their careers. Mary Ford remembered 'a lot of contention' from the actresses, particularly Madeleine Carroll, but she refused to listen to any Hollywood gossip during their marriage. 'Believe nothing you hear,' she always said, 'and only half of what you see.' On the only occasion that she threatened to leave her husband, he started the car and stood on the horn to hurry her departure. She did not try that tactic again.

Their daughter Barbara told me of an affair with Katharine Hepburn, during the filming of *Mary, Queen of Scots*. But then, the divine and electric lady was always a soft touch for the Irish rough man, as Spencer Tracy. She adored a flick of the domination, which Ford always demonstrated to his actors. John Wayne was certainly aware of that, when he was herding geese as a prop boy on *Mother Machree*. Ford always chose his patsies for the day, to be hazed and to keep the tension high. 'They were all scared shitless of him,' Wayne boasted, 'all except me and the geese.'

I was privileged to have many interviews with the old Ford factory players. Doing so many films with him made Wayne an angry admirer. 'He would do everything but hit an actor with a club. I said, if he got an Academy Award, I'd cut my throat.' Ford got many, and Wayne did not slash his necktie. Inviting his habitual screenwriter Dudley Nichols to board his yacht *Araner*, where he was having a prolonged drinking party night and day, Ford balanced a heavy script of *The Long*

Voyage Home on the palm of his hand, and he asked Nichols, 'Is this your only copy?' When the reply was 'Yes,' Ford said, 'Too long,' and threw the scenario through a porthole into the ocean. 'You write it right,' he said. 'Then I'll direct it.'

'That was one of the great things about Ford,' Henry Fonda asserted. 'The things that weren't in the script.' In *My Darling Clementine*, there was a sudden smell of desert flowers, and the Sheriff Fonda simply kicked his legs and said, 'That's me.' For Ford was the ultimate professional. He drank between films, not on them. As he reported of *The Quiet Man*, 'That's how I shoot movies – straight between the eyes.' On another occasion, he declared to Lord Killanin: 'Thank God, I am the Irish peasant of the peasants, and they never stop working till the potatos are all out.' And yet, as he said of his spare last Western, pared to the Shinbone, *The Man Who Shot Liberty Valance*: 'You build a legend, and it becomes a fact.'

I met John Wayne in his heavy days, when he was paying his respects to John Ford's widow. I answered the door at the house at Palm Desert, and there he was, old and fat and familiar. With all the manners of his roles, he pretended to presume I did not know him. 'I am John Wayne,' he said, 'and I come to call upon Mrs Mary Smith Ford.'

As I ushered him inside, I noticed his extraordinary gait. He had small feet on a large body. And so, as Agag, he walked delicately. Like a centaur, he always seemed the upper part of any horse he bestrode. But in his boots, he always appeared unsure of his ground. 'He walks like a fairy,' William Wellman once said of him. 'He's the only man in the world who can do it.' This was the walk of a loner permanently at risk out of the saddle, waiting for the next threat from his own unkind kind. He stalled and teetered, until he could sense the danger and blast at our secret fears with the terrible execution of his carbine or his fist.

There is an evil in the grace of violent action. When murder seems a glory, then power may become a philosophy. Only in a just war, if there are any, can an apology be made for killing other men as a necessary duty. Yet if that killing is done with the ferocity and style of a beast unleashed, then there is a horrific ambiguity between the pleasure of the lethal sight and the merit of the cause. Wayne never killed extravagantly or gladly, but only as a service, which often he did not particularly like.

The man on horseback used to be a general. In complex times, he would ride up, as the Duke of Wellington or Andrew Jackson, and step from his charger into the House of Lords or the White House. His presence solved our difficulties. He inspired mass confidence. In his image lay our safety. Now that most Western democracies prefer economists to military men, and even in Latin America the general rides up to the presidential palace in a tank, the man on horseback is an actor. His screen role still makes our difficulties seem simple for the moment. His decisions resolve our self-doubts. Usually set back in time, he revives our forgotten wishes for heroes and clear choices. And while his image lasts before and behind our eyes, he is our fantasy leader. He remains John Wayne in our unconscious eye.

John Ford used Wayne's natural ease of movement and shyly vulnerable bulk to suggest the archetype of the western outsider, withdrawn with women and only comfortable in action with men, better than the system and the people who misjudge him. 'Well,' he says to Dallas, when they are ostracised in *Stagecoach* at dinner at Dry Fork, 'I guess you can't break out of prison and into society in the same week.' As Walker Percy wrote in his novel *The Moviegoer*, other people might treasure climbing the Parthenon at sunrise or meeting a girl on a summer night in Central Park, but his own memorable moment was the time when John Wayne, again in *Stagecoach*, killed three men with a carbine as he was falling to the dusty street.

In his private life, Wayne was to marry three Spanish-American women and sire many children and grandchildren. Despite his apparent embodiment of the Anglo-Saxon myth of superiority and dominance, he had the Border fantasy about the women of the South, somehow forbidden, somehow sweeter, somehow more animal. He showed that in his understanding of the scene of his greatest compassion, when the racist Ethan Edwards finally takes the 'tainted' Natalie Wood in his arms in *The Searchers*; Wayne was a man capable of hidden passion and eroticism, which Ford once more revealed in him.

Still working with the ageing Wayne, Howard Hawks found that his actor was losing his grace of action. He was no longer like a big cat, but a heavy man, who sat like a sack on his horse. But as Wayne lost the beauty of swift movement, he acquired a distance from his performance. He relaxed into his own weathering, until he could at last perform his most comic role, Rooster Cogburn in *True Grit*, and win his only Oscar for such a wry and robust role, a man with a patch over one eye, slouching on his big mount like a sagging Colossus.

The Man Who Shot Liberty Valance begins with Wayne already in his coffin. The film is the revelation of his relationship with James Stewart, who takes away his woman and depends falsely for his reputation on Wayne's cold-blooded killing of a hired gunman. In his final angry speech to Stewart, Wayne shouts out that he will take the responsibility for the murder. He is a loner of the frontier, where action solves the problem of moral doubt. So he will die alone, while Stewart will marry and breed and make the wilderness sprout like a cornfield. His time is done and Stewart's is come. The film is a bare epitaph and a requiem for the passing of the great days of the West and for those who died in the passing.

Their masterworks have added poignancy, because Ford and Wayne both fought against cancer in the last years of their lives. Ford's fight was as heroic and unsung as Nathan Brittles' campaign in *She Wore a Yellow Ribbon*, but Wayne had to go public. He often boasted in his way of 'licking the Big C', until it finally ate him away. Even so, he was uncomplaining and magnificent in his going down.

To our eyes, he will always be the outlaw as Galahad, the just war hero, the professional soldier, the laconic man of violence, and the mythic figure, brave and lasting unto death. His record will disappear in the witch-hunts of yesterday, which in a few centuries will seem no more real than Salem. Yes, he was gung-ho about the Vietnam War, and he had backed Senator McCarthy's paranoiac 'Reds under the Bed' anti-Communist crusade, while Ford had battled against it, telling Cecil B. DeMille to forget everyone signing a loyalty oath, and to get on with making films.

As for Wayne, the final private face of the man, who learned courage and some grace of tongue by imposing his many good parts on his behaviour, should not be forgotten. I will always remember the honour and dignity of his last 'political' speech during President Carter's inauguration, when he praised the occasion and declared himself a member of the 'loyal opposition'. Finally, he did respect democracy in his beloved country. He didn't agree with the Russian, who said that the trouble with free elections was that you didn't know who was going to win. In some ways, the characters he played had become himself.

The image abides, while politics subside. Wayne had a young riposte, a middle- aged authority, an old man's legendary quality that will transcend his reactionary beliefs, although it will never deny them. The image is finally greater than the man, which is the mystery of a true star. His good luck was to have John Ford to teach him how to picture the messages of the roles he played. If Ford was not his Svengali, he was his example, until Wayne could at last match off-screen his master's compassionate strength. When, on set at the scene of the Crucifixion, Wayne was asked to show more reverence and awe, he added to his lines. 'Aw!' he said, 'this is the greatest scene in all the world.' Awe, he still provokes in us in many of the greater scenes in all the world cinema.

John Ford created the myth of the American West and the rituals of the US Cavalry and Navy. In searching for his identity, I received my greatest compliment from James Stewart, who looked up at my long lugubrious Scots Viking face as I was coming in, and said, 'Ah, I see a dead ringer.' He also wrote to me, when he read my published biography: 'I think this fine book pays great and deserved tribute to John Ford and should be required reading for young directors who desire to direct pictures in the correct meaningful way.' Ford's example had certainly directed me behind the camera. All those, who served him, were his troop of horse soldiers or his crew. His films created an enduring memory of a past that abides, although we were never there, as if there were no other places, where we would rather be.

In my scrimshaw Hollywood days, I had long admired those legendary actors of malignancy and wit. Tallulah Bankhead was the wickedest lady on screen and stage of the nineteen-twenties and thirties. She received her guests in her bath for champagne breakfasts at noon. She caused a riot at Eton while trying to seduce royal heirs to the throne. She made Noël Coward look like the provincial hick he had once been.

Born in 1902, the child of a leading politician, Tallulah never lived to the manner born, but to excess. She burned the candle at four ends – booze, drugs, bad men and women. Her film titles reflected her reputation – *Thirty a Week*, *Tarnished Lady*, *My Sin*, *The Cheat*, *Thunder Below*, *Devil and the Deep*, *Faithless*, and *A Royal Scandal*. She claimed to have had five hundred lovers of both sexes, and even the third one, the sexless. She was addicted to the 'working-class simplicity' of cocaine. 'It isn't habit-forming, darling,' she said. 'I've been taking it for years.' When found *in flagrante* with a married person, she would dismiss the affair with the remark, 'There's less to this than meets the eye.' But she would provoke the issue, when she caught the wife of an adulterous Member of Parliament giving her the cold stare, while her husband looked anywhere else. She drifted over and cooed to him, 'What's the matter, darling? Don't you recognise me with my clothes on?'

Only one actress, playing Southern belles such as *Jezebel* along with Tallulah, was more waspish. But then who could equal Bette Davis with her tart tongue? Of her rival's notorious love life, Bette observed: 'She was the good time everybody had. And those who didn't, didn't miss it much.' She was, after all, the original lady, who was as pure as the driven slush. As with Mae West, Tallulah liked her lovers to be well-hung and always on tap. Her advice to other women was: 'Cars are like men. It's much better to have two on standby in case one breaks down.' She was the Helen of her time, whose bad taste launched a thousand quips. We miss her, but thank God, I never had to meet her.

The man I wanted to see was George Sanders. In his role as a charming villain, he was matchless. If Erich von Stroheim was the man you loved to hate, Sanders was the man you hated to love. Before Beckett and Pinter, he was the maestro of brevity and the put-down. In *All About Eve* he commented that she made the minutes fly like hours. 'He was,' as Rebecca West wrote, 'every other inch a gentleman.' And as Spike Milligan, he could have answered the query, 'Why does everyone take an instant dislike to you?' with the reply, 'It saves time.'

His only rival in insouciance and brief wit was Robert Mitchum, who claimed to have only two acting styles 'with and without a horse.' He also said of himself, 'Whatever you do, don't get caught. No one's ever caught me acting.' And on a release from prison after a two months' sentence for disorderly conduct, he declared that jail was 'like Palm Springs, without the riff-raff.' His gait, he called 'The Goose', no shuffle as Wayne on small feet, but a waddle forward, chest pouting, eye-lids drooping, to his next grumble and mumble, or booze and bar.

Yet of all the Hollywood miscreants, few could exceed Howard Hughes. He had a pimp deliver nightly to his Beverly Hills Hotel bungalow a different broad. One time of dark, the woman arrived dead. There are three versions of the end of the story. Some say that he was so egocentric that he never noticed. Some say he liked the experience and bought a mortuary. Others say he had the pimp delivered the same way the next day. Possibly, all the tales are true, and if not, characteristic. But there's Tinseltown for you.

SILENCE OR SPEAKING OUT

Power may corrupt, but an accommodation with power and its loss may corrupt absolutely. At Hanover Terrace, I watched the speedy breakdown of a Labour life peeress after she lost office and its paraphernalia, the limousines and the briefings and the meetings with those who think they manage the nation without being able to realize that they are almost superfluous and easily replaceable. In a sequel to *Gog*, I chronicled the postwar history of Britain until the 'seventies through the deeds of the giant rebel's half-brother *Magog*, a supreme civil servant and later the Master of a Cambridge College.

The style of the novel was described as 'simple and honed – bitter, despairing, blackly humorous…' Outwardly the idealistic public servant, inwardly the unscrupulous hypocrite, Magog showed that 'if politics was the art of the possible, then principles were the patina of the pragmatic.' As a whole, the work was described as 'a brilliant, terrifying, almost vicious exposé and sequel to the memorable earlier *Gog* …with linguistic verve and a twisted humour to match the wit of that other modern English madman Anthony Burgess'. It shared one characteristic with *Gog*, as Bernard Bergonzi noted in *The Situation of the Novel*. As in epics and sagas, there was no psychological motivation. The language, incidents, and characters making up the action fused into a people's self-discovery as well as a few personal insights. Through what they did, Gog and his antithesis Magog managed to get to know something of themselves and their grandiose failures.

I also wrote two biographies of men of power, who never questioned or lost their vision of their self-importance. The first dealt with the American financier J.P. Morgan, who was the last tycoon able to prevent a Wall Street crisis by the exercise of his apparent dominance. His weapon and his beacon was his monstrous red nose, like Etna erupting. His visitors could only stare at this volcano. Struck dumb by the fiery outburst, newcomers were awed by Morgan's bulk and height. Their pity for the flaming nose weakened them, so that he could easily exploit their feeling with his abrupt demands. Small eyes under heavy brows blazed in twin laser beams. Meeting Morgan was running into an irresistible force, and he used his awful presence to break down resistance in business, women and art dealers. He had no need of encounter manuals or management techniques. He appalled people into instant agreement.

The young men, who worked for J.P. Morgan, were called his Angels. They were the first of the Yuppies, rising by insider trading in Morgan syndicates, but they had to be beautiful, too. The Harvard football hero Robert Bacon was the original Angel. Morgan seemed to take a perverse pleasure in surrounding his diseased nose and portly body with the vigour and good looks of the young. He liked his Yuppies to appear as brilliant as his works of art. At the time when the angels of God took wives among the daughters of men, Wall Street stated that the result was the Morgan partners.

Unlike modern financiers, his discretion was total. He never flaunted his many mistresses and actresses, only the bishops whose company he loved to parade. When Charles M. Schwab, then president of the Morgan steel trust, went on a junket to Monte Carlo, Morgan dressed him down like a choirboy for tarnishing the name of Morgan by association with his foreign affairs.

'But all I did,' Schwab said, 'was what you have been doing behind locked doors for years.'

'That, sir,' Morgan replied, 'is what doors are for.'

The causes of the Crash of 1907 are still contemporary – the flight of capital abroad, the issue of watered bonds at prices far above their true value, rampant speculation, overextended and misused state banks and trust companies, and economic pressure from the government. The Knickerbocker Trust closed after backing an early speculator called Heinze, who was trying to make a corner in copper rather than derivatives on tatty real estate. The National Bank of America followed suit, and there were runs on all the trust companies and marginal banks. Morgan imposed his will on the crisis. He made President Teddy Roosevelt deposit government surplus funds in the banks and suspend borrowing regulations, so that the lending institutions could procure loans wherever they wished. He acted to all the leading bankers as ruthlessly as he did to his own syndicates and investors. If they would not produce funds to bail out the stock market and protect people's savings, then they would never participate in a Morgan deal again.

The run went on. Crowds besieged the trust companies. Cash haemorrhaged. Morgan threatened any bear, who profited from the panic and spread alarm, that he would be 'properly attended to' once the crisis was over. And Morgan was always vindictive in his enforcement of his edicts. People still feared for their savings and demanded payment in cash. Morgan sent for gold bullion to be shipped from Europe and pledged all the liquid funds he had been accumulating since the last 'rich men's panic'. The City of New York itself was threatened with default and needed $30 million to meet its payrolls and short-term debts. Morgan summoned a final all-night conference in his Library to deal with the insolvency of the city and the collapse of the trust companies. Losses had to be taken, the last resources of the financiers used. That was the only way to end the panic with a show of complete confidence and contempt for the speculators.

He left the bankers together, surrounded by his medieval illuminated manuscripts and Early Renaissance master paintings, while he retired to another room to play solitaire through the night. He knew that fatigue and anxiety were the right instruments of persuasion. At dawn, he appeared and said he wanted a simple signature from the bankers that they would pledge an amount of cash based on their remaining resources and calculated by Morgan experts. He waved his hand towards a piece of paper. 'There you are, gentlemen,' he said. Nobody moved. He put his hand on the shoulder of a banker called King. 'There's the place, King,' he said softly, 'and here's the pen.' He put a gold pen in the banker's fingers. King signed, and all the other bankers signed. The Crash was stalled.

Morgan's success in the panic proved that the financial health of the United States could not be left in the hands of one man. His triumph saw the actual defeat of his power. The Federal Reserve Act of 1913 was the consequence of Morgan's victory, and government backing for banks in trouble should have put an end to future emergencies, although it did not. Trust companies were not fully insured and the stock market was still exposed. All the regulations at the start of this century have not cured the abuses, on which Morgan and his partners flourished. The lending of insurance and savings money from companies under Morgan's control to finance his speculations was declared illegal, but it continued. Insider trading, which made the fortunes of Morgan's fallen Angels, was merely recreated on the grand scale. No law has been able to stop stock watering since the first cattle were led to the drinking trough before being sent to market. The Junk Bond is merely the Morgan steel or shipping trust bond magnified. Wall Street does not reform much any more than the City of London. The ways of dealing remain rather the same, and government regulations that seek to modify the moneychanging always end up circumvented or sold short.

As for the film producer Sam Spiegel, he turned the illusions of the screen into a fortune he loved to flaunt. When I first met him, I was on his radar as a possible screenwriter for one of his projects. Behind his desk in Mayfair, he had a painting of a wild mammal with markings. Looking forward, he said: 'A leopard can't change his stripes.' Alas, I replied: 'Spots, Sam. A leopard has spots, not stripes.' His answer was: 'When I say a leopard has stripes, it does.' Even with the evidence staring him in the back, Spiegel had to dominate. I lost the job. The animal was evidently not a zebra.

By his interferences in the making of his pictures, Spiegel did not endear himself to his stars. During the filming of *The Bridge on the River Kwai,* at a party at the Japanese embassy in Colombo, William Holden wrapped a performing king cobra round Sam's neck. He then tried to buy the cobra to put into Sam's bed. Spiegel would die of a heart attack, even if the snake did not bite him. The head of overseas Columbia Pictures did not agree, saying, 'I don't think it would even penetrate Spiegel's skin.'

After *Suddenly, Last Summer,* directed by Joseph Mankiewicz, was a wrap, Katharine Hepburn asked him if he was sure that he did not need her services any more. 'Yes,' he said, 'I'm sure.' She put her face close to his and spat in his eye. Then she strode into Spiegel's office in Shepperton Studios and asked him the same question. She received the same answer and spat again in Spiegel's other eye. 'It's rather a rude gesture,' she admitted later, 'but at least it's clear what you mean.' Spiegel took out a sixteen-inch monogrammed handkerchief, wiped the spit off, smiled 'and went on tracking. That's the way he was.' He did not work with Hepburn again.

For *Lawrence of Arabia,* Spiegel was quite thrifty, saying that he never used 'a thousand camels when only a couple of hundred will do.' When filming in the Casa Paladaz in Seville, an electrical cable was wrapped round a marble statue, which shattered on the floor. The Duchess of Medinacelli forgave Spiegel with the words: 'And, after all, it was only Roman.' In early days, when hustling money to back *The African Queen*, he had been rather withering about the English aristocrats, who had failed to cough up. 'What do you expect,' he told Lady Cook, 'from these shabby gentiles?'

When riches flowed into his coffers, Spiegel bought a yacht, the *Malahne*, on which he entertained the celebrated and the powerful. 'He embellished everything,' his designer Tessa Kennedy said, 'with his impeccable taste for suits, wine, food and cigars. But he screamed at fools.' He hardly ever swam. 'He could float,' Lady Keith noted, 'but very little progress was made.' He became more and more tyrannical with an increasing desire to make sumptuous pictures, such as the failed *Nicholas and Alexandra* about the last Tsar of Russia. The film included the immortal line: 'Stalin, I'm Lenin, and I want you to meet Trotsky.'

At his first screen test for Spiegel, Peter O'Toole was asked to pretend to be a doctor performing an operation. O'Toole turned to face the camera, before ad-libbing: 'It's all right, Mrs Spiegel, your son will never play the violin again.' Spiegel's rage was incandescent, but O'Toole later got the lead in *Lawrence of Arabia*, where he complained that Spiegel treated him as if he was Rin-Tin-Tin. Asked by the screenwriter Robert Bolt how he thought Spiegel would die, O'Toole had replied with Celtic insight: 'Sam will die in two inches of bathwater.' And indeed, on New Year's Eve alone in a hotel room in Saint Martin in the Virgin Islands, Spiegel had a heart attack and fell into the tub. Peter Ustinov was present, while a young American doctor tried to revive the dead man by pummelling his great chest. 'Give him the kiss of life,' the doctor told Ustinov, who demurred from doing the useless act. 'Alive or dead,' he said, 'I would not kiss Sam Spiegel.'

Harold Pinter knew Spiegel as well as any man at the end. He seemed almost a father as well as the commissioner of two screenplays, *The Last Tycoon* and *Betrayal*. 'He was a man of strongly-held views, passionate about the human spirit overcoming adversity. How it flowers. How it blooms. Survival. I think he knew about that.' He was the ultimate film czar, but also the final great individual producer. The last time I saw him was three months before his death, dispensing champagne and generosity in his Park Avenue apartment. He was particularly proud of a Soutine hung on a wire. He pulled it aside to reveal a television screen, which could show on video all of his major films. Behind the paintings and the display was the survivor, who made the pictures, and put his life into the creation of celluloid illusions.

My last show of having some influence on the American historical scene emerged as another comic *film noir*. Ironically, defeat was turned into a hollow victory. What I lost, I was to win. Nothing collapsed except, as usual, my reputation, depending on the voyeur's point of view. After leaving and refusing some university jobs because I knew I was too restless to see the tenure through, I would finally bury any academic career during the bicentennial celebrations of the American Revolution. Still recommended by my old glorious tutors, Oscar Handlin and Richard Hofstadter, I was asked to give a seminar on Women's Rights at a vast gathering of historians of America in a mysterious *schloss* outside Salzburg. All expenses paid, of course. But by whom, and from where? Very broke and tired, I drove overnight from London to Austria, and so Childe Andrew to the Dark Tower came.

In the glittering hall with several hundred other historians, I found my obscure seat. A cheque for $350 lay on my plate; a carafe of red wine stood near my glass. Some courses of whatever were served, and I began to drink. Time for speeches arrived, and a distinguished recent professor from Brown University rose to inaugurate our strange meeting. As my diary noted, he delivered his speech badly as though he had not worked on it. He was stumbling over his high-speed reading as if ashamed, refashioning the whole of American history to present the United States as the misguided helper of other people's Revolutions, a role it could no longer play, having matured. Demeaning it was, to send on a young hand to paint over ineptly a political mistake before a large group of trained people who had come here to challenge history, not to support American governmental errors.

I felt my gorge rising, my bent legs as well. My hands clutched the underside of the table to prevent me bobbing up. I sat down and stared at the necessary cheque on the plate. The professor droned on, that the Vietnam War was also about freedom. I tore the cheque into little pieces, so that I might rise again, if I could not stop myself. I could not. I heard myself shouting:

'We came here about the American Revolution. Not to justify the War in Vietnam. This is a disgrace, and I am leaving.'

Some five hundred shocked faces stared at me, as I lurched out. A tall and handsome fellow in a blue blazer and striped military tie, met my unsteady progress and took me to the *schloss* bar and bought me a drink or three. I must say, the CIA is always impeccable in its coverage.

'Andrew,' he said, with the familiarity of strangers, who know precisely who you are, 'I absolutely understand your outrage. But, as you were in the Brigade of Guards, you must know I was also in the 14th/20th Hussars. And we must, as old soldiers, justify the wars of our countries.'

Such aplomb, such logic. He persuaded me to stay for my seminar the next day, which I did. How could I run away from my obligation and my duty, even if unpaid? Other historians approached me, and I recorded that 'I was accused of seeking notoriety. Perhaps. Protest is certainly bad manners – the essence is not to be paid for it. I simply could not stand the jockeying of all the academics for international places and funding. After all, I had been taught by Cambridge professors, high in British Intelligence in the Second World War. The CIA, which is funding this event, was certainly making a few connections behind the façade of real history seminars going on.

'As I told their man, my protest was less a moral one, but more an attack on their ineptitude. They claimed not to have checked the keynote speech (a new inefficiency to me). Bumblers all – I wonder. I said that to spend all this money to keep this extraordinary *schloss* together, and not to open a conference with more care, was highly stupid – no film man would be guilty of such bad logistics. Of course, I was making a moral protest, but I am so suspicious of giving myself a moral reason for such an act, I would rather give a technical one. At any rate, I have knocked the nail in my coffin finally as an academic; it is impossible to employ me now formally.' My diary concluded:

Next day, after the debacle, I feel I have overdone it. I have not slept much for four nights, too long on the road to Salzburg, perhaps protest is merely a matter of being overstrained. Then I hear that my sympathetic friend from the CIA and the American Embassy has been spreading around that the only reason I exploded was that I heard Britain called 'old and corrupt' in the

18th century. Well, it was among two hundred reasons, but let that pass ... What I watched was the reason I could never go back to academics – the calculated ass-licking to advantage of the top mandarins, the refusal to recognize their bought role by the US government, their judicious rebuke to my outburst ('there were *points* in that speech ... the speaker is a good man ... he really *thinks* that ...). And I suddenly felt glad that I had divorced myself from them.

They, after all, were party to the Tom Sawyer principle. Tom goes out to whitewash an old grotty picket fence (shall we call it Vietnam). He does it so thoroughly and historically, filling in all the cracks and knots in the woodwork, and stands back, persuading all his friends and acquaintances to whitewash the fence even more thoroughly than him – they even pay for the privilege – but in this *schloss* case they get paid.

I left this Kafka's Castle of Intelligence and Revisionism, and I eventually returned home to London. Six months later, out of the ether on my unlisted telephone, a voice sounded in my ear:

'Andrew, I am Richard Wade. I'm over here at Balliol. You know, they put up visiting Professors of American History from time to time. I much admired your book on Prohibition.'

'Well, sir,' I replied, 'I much admired your works on city and country conflicts in the West.'

'May we meet? I would like to talk to you.'

And so I invited him to dinner in Regent's Park. And he informed me of the thoroughness of American Intelligence. After my tirade at the *schloss*, a poll of all present had been taken. Should the American Revolutionary War be linked to Vietnam? Four in five historians agreed with me that it should not.

'Oh, yes,' Richard Wade said, 'you were right to protest. Our policy changed in all our future celebrations.'

'But,' I said, 'that does mean that, in future, I am unemployable.'
'Exactly.'

And so it turned out to be. Academically speaking, although an ex-Marxist professor from Ohio had resigned from the advisory board after my intervention, and he later wrote to me that I was 'the spirit of the 'sixties' in speaking out as I had against the whole American historical establishment. Too great a role for me, as impulsive and as instinctive as Gog in opposing the lies of authority. Only once would I be reinstated by Malcolm Bradbury to teach American history in the 'twenties to his graduate students at East Anglia. Fellow novelists as well as professors in literature and creative writing, he and David Lodge had stuck to their tenure and their departments, the career that I had shunned. But as so many transatlantic academics, their fiction rarely strayed from the college and the comic psychology of *The History Man*, while mine veered towards the saga and black farce. I was paid a pittance, and the commuting from London was exhausting, ending in a trek back through a sudden Norfolk blizzard, late for dinner with the American ambassador in Regent's Park. Then Malcolm asked me to dine at his home, when my classroom agenda was over.

'And what important research were you doing?' I asked him.

'Television,' he said. 'A series. Blott on the Landscape.'

And so it was, my final recall, a blot on the campus.

In my other encounters, the Hanoverian cold blue eye was only excelled in ice by the glacial glance of Lauren Bacall. In my single years, Kenneth Tynan used occasionally to lob me in as a walker or a clown for formidable women. In the case of Bogart's widow, I so quailed at her look that I stuttered. Her withering frigidity made me feel as Captain Scott, waiting to be frozen in the Antarctic. As for sitting at dinner in the cool seat next to Princess Margaret, I tried, I tried, I damn near died in dredging up a *bon mot* or two; but my jokes were frogs in my throat. I had once seen a man swallow the reptiles live in the Boulevard du Montparnasse. I had hoped he brought them up squidgy and later, but I brought not a smile to the royal face. With an azure gaze of twin turquoise pebbles, I was dismissed. Just another bore, really. Andrew, glare off.

At another dinner party, given by Kathleen Tynan, I was again given the bare seat next to Princess Margaret, after Ned Sherrin had to leave early to cobble together a production on Ziegfeld and his Follies. Indeed, I noticed that she did not refer to herself with the royal 'We', but was detached from privilege. She called herself 'It'. When the novelist Angela Huth commented on a disaster during a royal visit to Oxford, where the College vicar had preached a Socialist sermon at Evensong, the Princess forgave the *lese majesté* with the remark, 'It was greatly amusing.' Rather better than her great-grandmother's 'We are not amused.'

She was most interesting on the selection of the Poet Laureate. 'My sister chose Ted Hughes. Everyone else wanted Philip Larkin. Hughes wrote a poem for my Mother. She had it framed. It's bigger than the dinner table. I read it. Didn't understand a word of it. Poets, they should rhyme. AB. AB. CC. Why don't they? I wrote a poem the other day. It was a letter, but I wrote it out like modern poetry. It sounded very good.'

So she went on with her rude humour and false philistinism, disguising her intelligence and a sort of vulnerability. The whisky-and-ice was untouched in the tumbler, she lit the cigarettes in the holder from her own gold lighter. Despite the royal poise, her fingers were mice on the tablecloth. When I last saw her at a distance, I thought I was losing my wife-to-be Sonia to a rival at a large party, where Princess Margaret was in her element, singing Cockney songs at the piano until dawn broke, before it broke her.

As for the other grave occasions, they vary in my experience between black farce and deep grief. Coasting towards the tomb, I find the terms are changing. While there is no insurance against life, it is actuarial. Where my friends meet each successive year, or those who survive of them, are at Four Funerals and a Wedding. I recollect a tale of Colonel Jacques, a Free French officer left over in Beirut at the close of the Second World War. His comrades began to die on an annual basis. After several graveside ceremonies, he refused to attend another one on his crutch. When asked why not, the reply was: 'He cannot come to my burial.'

Lately, I have attended too many memorial services for those I knew in the arts. Their final rites were performances rather than sacraments. The London churches, which usually commemorate such celebrities, tolerate both show business and the divine. They range from the Actors' Church of St Paul's at Covent Garden near the Garrick Club through the liberal St James's in Piccadilly and St Martin's in Trafalgar Square to Westminster Abbey with its Poets' Corner and thespian reliefs. Not since the Greeks have the muses and the gods been so confounded.

At St Paul's, a memorial was held for the songsmith, Alan Jay Lerner. At a certain moment in the ceremony, the late Daniel Massey trilled a trifle from 'Gigi' and clasped the altar in his finale. We left the church with an anathema from the resident Father Michael. Unless we put many a tenner into the contribution box to stop the roof falling down, we were doomed by our caterwaul-ings. Quite right, too.

At the Piccadilly church, the service for the gay media commenta-tor Russell Harty ruffled the Georgian harmony of the place. Prob-ably the most retiring and relaxed of Northern English humorists, Alan Bennett, also a don at the University of Oxford, gave the ad-dress. After a music-hall song about 'The Biggest Aspidistra in the World', he declared that while he was shy at their mutual *alma mater* on the Isis, Russell didn't get it from Proust, he went straight across the allotments to get it, whatever it was. 'Cheek is not one of the virtues,' Alan declared, 'but it is on the limits of courage.' Russell's mother beamed in the front pew, while her son was given his coming out in the pulpit.

None of these odd rituals approached the dark comedy of Kingsley Amis's passing- out charade at Covent Garden. There was nothing sacred about it, only the profane. Its melancholy came from its lack of sanctity. What was the point of the glum wake, except for the backchat of the bystanders? How remember the author of *The Old Devils*, when he did not even hope for a transition to Dante's *Inferno*? A belief in dust and ashes only leaves behind dust and ashes and fud-dled memoirs. In his recollections, I was the writer of Scots name, the butt of the old barroom joke. I had offered him a round of drinks in the pub, and I had left my wallet behind. In fact, I never went to a pub with Kingsley in my life, although we were both Fellows at Cam-bridge at the time, and his son Martin was then tall enough to be knee-high to a foxglove. Kingsley just had to tell a sneering hoary beery story, and he was too fuddled to put another Scots name on it: he could only think of mine. Once, I saw an elderly Kingsley stag-gering away from a late lunch, and we asked him to our table for a last drink. 'Another drink,' he mused. 'But it's never the last one!' Yet he lurched on, but not too far or too long, to the last one, in the end.

If we are to remember the glory of great memorial services, let us recall the ceremony for the late Poet Laureate, Ted Hughes, in West-minster Abbey, as tragic and incantatory as the plays of Aeschylus and Racine, which Ted had translated. The cross of the great nave in front of the choir, the high lights of the sun breaking through the soar of the windows in promise and illumination were met by the flights of angel voices from The Tallis Scholars singing *Spem in Alium*. Descants darting as swallows affirmed, 'I have never placed

my hope in any other than you, O God...' And Ted's voice spoke
in a recording he had made from a song in *Cymbeline*. We were no
more to fear the heat of the sun, nor the furious winter rages. I
could see the Prince of Wales seated opposite me with The Queen
Mother trembling on the verge of her last century, and Ted Hughes
and Shakespeare were reminding them:

> The sceptre, learning, physic, must
> All follow this and come to dust.

Yet it was not the dust of mockery or disrespect, it was the dust of
dry soil before the rain, which fell on the land from the spirits of
the few such as Hughes, who turned their country into the good
earth. So the song from *Cymbeline* ended:

> Quiet consummation have;
> And renowned be thy grave!

Then Seamus Heaney celebrated his peer and lost friend, as part of
the tapestry of England, of the rivers of its life. He had been at Ted's
burial, when his daughter Freida and son Nicholas with four family
friends had carried the coffin low on handles. Heaney saw it as the
dark barge burdened on the water, which bore King Arthur to
Avalon. Two crows, indeed, had risen from the trees and circled
Ted's bier on its passing. Heaney also saw Hughes at home with
Caedmon, the first English poet, in his monastery, as he would have
been with Wilfred Owen in the trenches, which his father had just
survived. 'Part of him recognised that the body was born to ecstasy
as well as extinction.'

Hughes was conjured as a Merlin in his wizard casting of a fly in
the trout rivers of Devon. And as another witness averred, Ted had
wondered at the intricacy of the head of the last fish he caught, a
barracuda off Cuba. He hymned the cruelty as well as the majesty
of creation. He knew of the ordeal of survival, as any sheep farmer
would. One of his poems read aloud was about a new-born Marsh
calf, quiffed and glossy, destined for the butcher, but quivering to
live, and learning to moo.

I had heard another disembodied voice at a Service of Thanksgiving in Westminster Abbey, that of Laurence Olivier. Yet the words

had not been prophetic, but stage-managed. In a procession, that was no coronation, Olivier's theatrical crowns and laurel wreaths had been carried on red cushions by leading actors, such as Michael Caine and Maggie Smith and Ian McKellen, to be laid on the High Altar as if they were Her Majesty's regalia. These appearances had reduced the ritual to a role. And though I was sitting beneath the memorial to Garrick himself, where Olivier would lie beside him and Irving beneath the bust of Shakespeare – as The Bidding of the Dean declared – I found this last tribute in the Abbey as trumpery as the gilt and glass and paste props of drama on Shaftesbury Avenue. Surely the soul of Olivier had deserved more from us, i'faith and by God.

Back now at Westminster, I was listening to Seamus Heaney reading Ted's poem to his dead mother. The day of his memorial service was the date of her passing. His 'Anniversary' would commemorate her and now himself. Every May 13th, he used to see her on the torn-off diary page where his brother had jotted 'Ma died today'. In his remembrance of her, she was telling her sister Miriam about her children in the afterlife.

> Now my mother
> Shows her the rosary prayers of unending worry,
> Like pairs of shoes, or one dress after another,
> 'This is the sort of thing,' she is saying,
> 'I liked to wear best.' And 'Much of it,
> You know, was simply sitting at the window
> Watching the horizon. Truly
> Wonderful it was, day after day,
> Knowing they were somewhere. It still is.
> Look.'

As the Prince of Wales held out the Order of Service to his grandmother, Her Very Old Majesty pushed his helping hand away. Sitting on her curved small throne, she could still look after herself, thank you very much. So small and so enduring, like a blue urn, she was the image of my mother, who had died before at the age of eighty-seven, independent to the end, plunging forward from a sudden clot in the brain into my remembrance. I was not allowed to see her after the *post mortem*, only to watch her cremated and scatter her ashes on samphire growing by a Devon sea-shore cliff garden. I had spent hours trying to remove the last trace of her, the stain on the carpet, but like Lady Macbeth, I could never sweeten that dark spot on my hand.

Yet our Queen Mother still lived and would see in the Millennium. And Ted had written eulogies to her and her family, particularly of the River of the Water of Life mentioned in the Lesson in the Abbey, the crystal flow in the Book of Revelation, which proceeds out of the throne of God and nourishes the Tree of Life with its fruits for the healing of the nations. Ted believed enough in myth to know that every nation needed a Queen Mother in symbol, if not in reality. And so in his 'Anniversary', he brought all our mothers to our minds, while we could regard the frail Ancient of Days on Her throne chair.

Standing there, Seamus Heaney, in the marvel of his reading of the poem, was our choice to follow Ted as the Poet Laureate. Yet even the far reach of his own understanding of the struggle of the land and the ordeal of all existence would not allow him to forget the woes of Northern Ireland and its bloody history. He could not take the royal post because of the hod and the peat of the heavy past.

Memorial services are unpredictable, and we are not as wise as Hughes or Heaney in their incarnations of ancient mysteries. A magical ceremony such as this conjures up a country's history as well as the memory of dead family and friends. Anecdote and awe associate. Past fragments fly about. Yet in this instance, a common humanity made us weep and rejoice and value the tradition of our land, which still had a rare voice or two to sing it forever. As the Bach prelude and fugue played at the end of the service in Westminster Abbey, and The Queen Mother moved slowly away on her stick and grandson's arm, again a spell of time took me back fifty years. She was young then, and fair, with that milk-pink Scottish complexion of perpetual youth, and her daughter Margaret appeared as a Shirley Temple doll snatched from a cradle. They had come from Windsor Castle to hear some of us boys reciting poems and Saying Lessons at the Eton College Literary Society. In my boldness and casualness, it seemed nothing much to declaim Wilfred Owen and the killing of his enemy, his friend – or Dylan Thomas declaring that death had no dominion against the dying of the light.

Now in the Abbey, after half a century, the worlds I had dispraised rose again in honour of the dead of the Two World Wars and the poets, who took me so long to understand. Young faces were old maps now, some erased for ever, yet as long as I had eyes and ears, I might recollect them, as Ted had resurrected his own wounded father in 'For the Duration' with his scars and silences and night-mares, wading back from the trenches into the glare to carry his children to safety.

SONIA

⁕

Another climacteric in my life was a separation from my second wife and two years of solitude in rebuilding the Nash terrace house in order to sell it. I lived in the gutted ruin in one habitable room, feeling like the hero of Robert Louis Stevenson's *Kidnapped*. I would walk up a stair to find it ended in nothing. I was desperate and unable to write, in debt and without inspiration.

Then, at the only cocktail party I had attended in a year, I had what I call a recognition. I looked at a woman of extraordinary beauty and intelligence and sympathy and grace, and she looked at me. She had been widowed ten years before and courted by dozens of desirable men as Lady Melchett for a decade. But our recognition was total and absolute. We had rather given up the idea of commitment, or sharing, or living closely together. On her sofa in Chelsea, we touched hands and made love. I asked her to come to Paris to see me, but I was not sure that she would arrive. A flight to me, or a flight from me?

- When you walked into
- *La Closerie des Lilas*
- With your little bag of tricks
- I was not sitting at the bar
- You were not certain
- I would be there at all
- You looked up at me
- And then that one smile
- Fearful relief, a shy future
- The Mona Lisa shut her lips
- No question the now
- Your strange pucker
- Seals us for ever
- Then our bed burns
- And over that October
- A scatter of chestnut leaves.

I always gave Sonia the name of Lethe, that river, which led Dante behind Virgil from the Inferno through Purgatory to Paradise. This was the needful stream of oblivion for all I had known or loved before her. The Norse God Odin had two ravens. One was Thought and the other was Memory. They flew out every evening over the world. Their master and men feared that Thought would not return at morning. And if the bird did not, a greater fear was the loss of memory.

I did not see any foreshadow of tragedy when I asked Sonia to wed me at a table by the bar at the top of the Twin Towers, more than a hundred stories tall in Manhattan. This was hardly the place to commit ourselves to each other for the rest of our lives, as Helen to Paris in Troy. The eyrie of out tryst would also be reduced to fire and dust. We were pledged to be two as one. We did not know that three thousand would die up there. How be Cassandra in our prophecy?

We spun on from New York to Los Angeles and Bali, where all the right roads pointed to the centre of the world, the sacred mountain of lava, away from the South Seas. Then on to Pagan in Burma, where the Irrawaddy paved a shining way, a Buddha's path past a thousand flaking golden stupas on a yellow plain. Then by car horn and one-track mountain train to where Sonia was born, in the hill-station of Nainital, seven thousand foot high in the Himalayas. I had often told Sonia that her only worry was worry itself, as the only fear is fear. And yet I was fearing the loss of love. A mob was on strike in the steep streets – food prices rising, the usual story. But we were the alien stricken. The sun was chill on the foot hills, the Himalayas were far and indifferent.

'I was born in Nainital,' Sonia said, 'But I did not come to die here.'

In the graveyard of St John in the Wilderness by a headless fallen angel, we stopped by a mossy stone ark, still stating: JAMES GIDEON DREW *Killed in the Landslip*. One hundred and six years before, thirty-three inches of rain fell in twenty-four hours (how the Raj builders loved numbers even in their disasters). The mountainside dropped down on the Queen Victoria Hotel, burying guests and soldiers in a living tomb.

So cold was the night at the Swiss Hotel, a crumbling fretwork tin chalet, a period piece older than mammoths in glaciers, that we envied those, who were warmer in earth. Yet we had come to see the full moon at Nainital, and the steps of the hospital where she was born. Somewhere here was her horoscope, the telling of what would be, and what had already been. How two souls met in some despair, who might have never met except for those steps and the mother in jodhpurs riding out too late with the subalterns, then delivering Sonia in front of the hospital.

We found the birth certificate, which certified a Female Infant and was mixed with the certificates of death, on old wooden shelves. So the legends and the records declared. We had waited too long to meet each other, but we had come again to Nainital to declare the crescent of our love until the coming of our death. This would be at the same hour, in the same place, together. And somewhere later in Udaipur, we were reborn in the cauldron of our passion.

Although Merlin loved running up and down its six flights of stairs, I had to sell my Nash mansion in Hanover Terrace. This was done badly, a million pounds short of its potential. Yet I had never cared for money very much, unless I could use it in the pursuit of my arts. But I needed now to be free to pay off the divorce settlement and to be with Sonia. The problem was my collection of 15,000 volumes. Books are extensions of memory, and I still might have to refer to them. The choice was simple. Would I read these books again or could I borrow them easily from the London Library? Half of them went, as would happen to the remnants again, when Sonia and I were to leave Tite Street for a river apartment in Pimlico, where one didn't need a passport to arrive. The American novelist Thomas Wolfe of *Look Homeward, Angel* fame declared that travelling with half-a-ton of books was very hard. They may furnish a room, but they tend to be burdensome.

My new family were my inherited grace and favourites. For I have little time for babies, and there were none as yet. But children from three to ten years old do love and believe you totally, also they have the sense of wonder which may see them through. Puberty and adolescence are very tiresome times, but at college level, I can maintain anybody with devotion. Sonia's eldest child, Peter Mond, Lord Melchett, was noble without his title, a leader in Greenpeace and the Soil Association. Sonia disagreed with him, when he would not marry his superb partner Cassandra Wedd, and thus would disinherit his son. For Sonia had lost her title to her son with the death of her first husband, and she had lost it twice by her marriage to me. Her elder daughter Kerena would also have two husbands, the second the veteran television presenter, Adam Boulton. Her three splendid daughters would find careers in the arts, the law, and even the police force. As for her younger sister, the adorable Pandora, she would study art at Ruskin College at Oxford and become an excellent painter, able to instil motion onto a canvas. I had to ease her out of her nest with Sonia and find her a place elsewhere. Luckily, we seemed to love one another, and she would find an enduring marriage and two brilliant sons, whose careers at university I hoped to aid.

At Sonia's home in 16 Tite Street, a gloomy terrace house facing north and south, we found that this was the false address of Oscar Wilde. During the annual Chelsea Flower Shows, green carnations would be posted through our iron gates, and our front garden blooms were stripped by his followers, who did not know that Oscar had actually lived down the street. Later, we were to stay in a glass-mirrored bed at L'Hôtel de Paris, where Wilde had died, saying that the wallpaper did him in.

Sonia and I, however, were very happy to be where we were in London. The drawing room had been the scene of so many of her parties, when she had been known as the Merry Widow, holding fiestas for admiring peers and politicians and the theatrical movers and shakers. For she was on the Boards of the Royal Court and National Theatres. I added the writers, and both of us, old friends. I loved her choices of who was to be invited. She always picked a mixture of those who were falling to meet those who had risen. In these encounters, fortunes were reversed and even marriages were made. On the great Wheel of Chance of society, she knew that the spinning of the numbers could change anyone's luck in the game.

I gave Sonia a Georgian mourning ring which had not been filled in. The ebony enamel band that overlaid the gold was only inscribed 'IN MEMORY OF'. A black blank awaited the initials of the dead person to be. My wife believed that the ring symbolised our union, which would always be in her memory, and never die. Ten years after our wedding day, I would have the inside of the ring inscribed with our initials and the Latin X ANNI. From that time, there were doldrums in our love. Perhaps I could not do what I wanted to do, perhaps she worried too much about what might have been done.

And then one day, the incised outer band of the ring split away from the enamel. She took it as an omen. Her first platinum wedding ring given to her by her previous husband had broken the week before she married me, and platinum does not break.

I said that I would repair the ring. It was difficult to remove over the joints of her long finger. I put the two pieces in a pocket and forgot about it. After some weeks, Sonia asked about the ring. I said that I would find it. I searched for day after day through all my clothes with increasing fear. I could not find the ring that said IN MEMORY OF. Sonia said that I must have thrown it away or left it in a dirty suit. I hunted through my wardrobe again. I inquired at the cleaners. The two parts of the separated ring were not to be found.

Months passed, and things drifted between us. Then Sonia chose the shirts that I might wear on our summer holiday. As I packed a white one, the two halves of the mourning ring rolled out of its pocket. I made them whole and gave the ring to her as she was lying in the Chelsea sun of that hot July. 'Look,' I said. 'I told you. I could never lose that ring.' She could hardly believe it. Yet she put on the ring below the second joint of her long finger. It would never leave her hand again. IN MEMORY OF, and our two initials inscribed within the gold and the enamel.

Apparently back on the London social scene, my literary reputation was taking the same knocks as at Cambridge with the publication of *The Breaking of Bumbo*. I was climbing the ladder of success wrong by golden wrong. Again, little could be farther from the truth. Sonia's father had been a poor Army doctor in India. She and her sister Bunty Graham had been brought up in England as I had been, during the Blitz and the rationing and the stringencies of the Second World War. When she had married Julian Melchett, he had been disinherited from the Mond fortune for marrying somebody as obscure as she was. Before meeting him, she had even worked in a watch factory before going out to Germany as a secretary in the Control Commission. He had earned his own way from a bankrupt Norfolk venture in growing grass seed to become the head of nationalized British Steel; so he was able to leave Sonia some properties, which she developed and was to sell.

She and I had married because we shared most of the same tastes and values, acquired at a time of national stress and demand on the individual. Our duties then had seemed to us as important as our rights, which had nothing to do with our forced low standard of living. And Sonia and I needed each other. She was magnificently without pretension or pretence, rather shy really, and she wanted me in company as a close shadow on her shoulder.

At one of Sonia's parties, the newscaster Anna Ford was accused of hurling a glass of red wine in the face of Jonathan Aitken, then a Member of Parliament. Actually, her hand was trembling so much that it affected her aim. Some other gentleman was splattered, while Jonathan, for the time being, remained unspotted. But the incident, wrongly reported, made a better story and provided a staple for the gossip columns, which stated that Anna was as straight a shooter as any Calamity Jane. Old slurs never die, they only feed the media. Anna was brilliant in her beauty and her discrimination. But at a dinner party of hers, I was sat next to the journalist Polly Toynbee, whose frequent television appearances seemed to have honed her prejudices. Anna's splendid brother, who taught theology at St Paul's Girls' School, was wearing a small crucifix round his neck.

'That's like wearing a gas chamber,' Polly told us. And why? Because the Christians loved torture – they were the biggest torturers of all – although I kindly didn't point out comparisons to the Mongols and Stalin and Pol Pot. For Polly, the belief in the Crucifixion was an approval of Belsen. When I did protest that Christ suffered for us, and that the worship of Him was against pain, I was stabbed with the worst glare of my life. Its blade pierced my soul, if I had one, that is.

Once I had a conversation with the author Salman Rushdie about the writers who had most influenced us in our bardic novels. Kindly, he mentioned my *Gog* which came out before his *Midnight's Children*. After the Alpha of all, *The Odyssey* of Homer, we agreed on Cervantes in *Don Quixote*, then on to Laurence Sterne and Franz Kafka, James Joyce and Thomas Pynchon, a contemporary inspiration from his *V* and *Gravity's Rainbow*. To that list, I would add, for my sake, the names of Jonathan Swift and Edgar Allan Poe, Céline and Calvino and Borges, the master of the modern stories of mystery and the imagination. All of these have informed all I have tried to do.

Although I had been on both sides of the barricades, yet because of the World War when we were young, we seemed to be old-fashioned in some ways. We had both seen the Coronation of The

Queen, she in Westminster Abbey as the youngest peeress, I standing overnight on the street behind the Guardsmen in their finery. Their ranks I was shortly to join in my National Service, to watch again the Golden Coach roll by. Yet such was the good fortune of our characters and choices, nothing to do with our colonial heredity or any bought opportunity. We were happy to fight for free speech and democracy under a constitutional monarchy, which had answers as well as traditions in playing its role so well.

Picked from my little private bunch of stories, I remember a lunch with Edward Heath in his house in the close of Salisbury Cathedral. His shoulders heaving with mirth at his own wit, he spoke of when he was Prime Minister and being asked to conduct an orchestra in Spain. Unable to resist this unlikely appreciation of his musical talents, he found himself in Barcelona, a baton in his hand. The Queen and Prince Philip were staying with the King of Spain; but when He suggested that they attended the Heath concert, Her Majesty was said to say: 'I never go to concerts. Can't abide them.'

'Then,' Heath went on, 'most graciously to make up, they asked me aboard the *Britannia*, which was moored nearby. And as I walked up the gangway, Philip met me, waving his hands. 'Diddle, diddle, diddle with your fingers, Heath – can't you find anything better to do?'

When the composer Tippett was knighted at Buckingham Palace, The Queen said to him, 'I am sorry, Sir Michael, not to have heard any of your music. But you see, all my sister and I heard here was the D'Oyly Carte people, who came in specially to sing for us. We never heard anything else.' And on her Jubilee, with Her usual honesty, She saw a more aged portrait of Herself on the new £5 note. And so She remarked, 'It makes me look older. But then I am older.' On another occasion at Buckingham Palace when She was dishing out honours, a bewildered lady from Africa asked Her, 'What do you do?' She answered the question, when she praised Prunella Scales for playing Her to the life in the National Theatre, while talking to the traitor Anthony Blunt, the Master of Her Pictures: 'I think,' She said to the actress, 'you'd quite like to do what I'm doing.'

At the opening of the new Faculty of Law at Cambridge, with the other gowned Doctors of Philosophy, I stood next to a Welsh Professor, who described a previous encounter with royalty, while receiving some sort of an award. He had heard that Her Majesty never listened to what was said to Her, when She gave out the gongs. So he piped up, 'I murdered, ma'am, my mother-in-law at breakfast over the Rice Krispies.' And Her unsmiling Majesty replied, 'What a good idea.' On this university occasion, She led the royal procession with Prince Philip behind Herself. Looking up at the glassy front of the modern Faculty, he said with relish: 'What a good place to grow tomatoes in.'

When I talked about The Queen to the incredible Irish tycoon and rugby player, Tony O'Reilly, he said that he mentioned the great kidnapped Derby-winner Shergar to Herself. Prince Philip had dubbed the local Irish CID Inspector as O'Clouzot, when the policeman, after two months of investigation could positively announce that the interior of the rustler's horsebox was blue or green. When I suggested to O'Reilly that his stud of twenty-nine horses were all Shergar's colts, he laughed and replied that he had told The Queen that Shergar was probably now mincemeat – a frightened stablelad did in the stallion and had to hide the crime.

O'Reilly now asked The Queen what she most wanted. And She answered, 'To race at the Curragh.'

'Indeed,' O'Reilly said. 'With a minor territorial adjustment, you would be most welcome.'

'Not in my lifetime,' was the response. O'Reilly did also point out that the Irish did not always agree among themselves. When the President of the Republic de Valera died, the Honour Guard were Sinn Féin to a man. So they fired *into* the coffin. They were rather like the Irish firing squad in a circle around a condemned man. On the command, 'About turn,' they did so and all killed each other. Lying low, only the victim escaped. So it might be for Her Majesty.

When Douglas Bader, the legless pilot hero, was asked why The Queen had taken so long to knight him, he replied that She had not taken too long. A general telephoned him about the ceremony in Buckingham Palace.

'How are you,' a voice said, 'about kneeling?'

And the double amputee replied, roaring with laughter: 'Flat on my face.'

So he was permitted to stand for the tap on the shoulder by the sword of Her Majesty.

I met Princess Diana twice. Once, we were trying to film the

Prince of Wales at Kensington Palace, when she popped her head round the door of a waiting-room, and when she was told what we were doing, she laughed and said, 'This is His Life,' meaning it was her husband's brief reign on a television show, but not her own. At a charity *première*, I was placed next to her, and she said, 'I hear you're awfully clever. I am as thick as a brick.' And she laughed again. What could I say? 'Yes, ma'am. No, ma'am. *I don't think so*, ma'am.' Pronounced 'ma'am' as in 'jam' or 'marm' as in 'charm'? I didn't know, so I said nothing. As for Prince Charles, when I thanked him for his television performance for charity, he smiled and said, 'I told you, I do twitter on a bit.'

Yet as a requiem, my favourite remark came from Prince Philip, when at a banquet at Buckingham Palace, the High Commissioner to Swaziland dropped stone dead. The Prince merely observed: 'Now I wonder what he means by that.'

The Royal Archives are stored securely in the Round Tower of Windsor Castle, where I spent many months on the research of a biography of Vicky, the eldest daughter of Queen Victoria and later the Empress of Germany for only ninety-nine days before her husband, the Crown Prince, died. My climb up the winding stone stairway was pinnacle high, before I might read the letters between the Princess Royal and her mother, often written criss-cross to save paper, the ink sometimes smeared with tears. As always, the path to my book forked in amazing directions. There was a shagreen leather case on a table containing the letters of the Duke 'Butcher' Cumberland, instructing his cavalry to hunt down the broken Highlanders after Culloden like savages and put their homes to the torch. There was also the question of how The Queen's correspondence had been retrieved from the widowed Vicky's retirement castle, the Friedrichshof, after the Second World War. The courier had been Anthony Blunt, the Keeper of the Royal Pictures at the time, but also loyal to the Kremlin as well as to his royal mistress.

Later accused of treason himself, Blunt had been sent out to retrieve the letters between Vicky and her mother, occasionally revealing Prussian military manoeuvres in wartime. His other duty was to bring back the abdicated Duke of Windsor's highly dangerous messages to his cousins, the Hesse family, so close to Hitler on the eve of the Second World War. Of course, when I asked to see these missives as well, I was told that they were missing, because of so many of British bombing missions over Bavaria in the conflict. This evidence was never to be disclosed, although my biography was allowed to appear, entitled: *The Other Victoria: The Princess Royal and the Great Game of Europe*, in which she played and lost, leaving her son the Kaiser William the Second to involve her country in a global struggle with scores of millions dead.

My neighbour in Hanover Terrace was Harold Pinter, and I had put his wife Vivien Merchant in my film, *Under Milk Wood*, where she played Mrs Pugh to the harsh housewife made. At the time, Harold was writing *No Man's Land* which, I realised much later, when I saw him playing the lead in it, was about the isolation of fame. The hero, indeed, lived in a park attended by a strange duo of unease. Pinter also solved the problem of acknowledging the words that he had once written and how they should be played. I visited him with a horror picture producer, who had also produced the film of Pinter's *The Birthday Party* in earlier days, when art meant as much as gore. It was a fraught meeting at which, in the producer's words, Pinter was like 'a flung knife, quivering in the wood of the door'. At the rushes of *The Birthday Party*, the producer had begun to ask, 'Isn't that the scene when… ?' And Pinter had interrupted. 'I said – or rather – I was heard to say – I know – I wrote it.'

I know, I wrote it. Neither Descartes nor Beckett ever made more conclusive a Statement. But in knowing Harold for so long, we never reached any conclusions about our affairs. When he left Vivien to an early dying and went off with Lady Antonia Fraser with her six children, we became estranged. I had known Antonia Pakenham since we were both at the Dragon School. Even at twelve years old in blue shorts, she was a formidable figure and used to clobber me on the rugby field. When her husband, the distinguished Hugh Fraser, had visited Harold to complain about losing his wife, the playwright was watching a Test Match on television. Both were cricket-mad and shared a bottle of champagne. And by the time 'stumps' were called and Hugh left, he realized that he had forgotten why he had come round in the first place.

The later problem was that, when I met Sonia, she was having a fling with Hugh, who wanted to marry her. All of Antonia's children expected Sonia to become their stepmother, just as Harold would become their stepfather – and unexpectedly, a very good stepfather he was. He seemed to have been missing a large family all of his life. He could not rage, rage against the living of the young. But alas, Sonia preferred me as a husband, and Hugh was soon taken ill and died. Such cross-stitched lives could hardly be put straight. And indeed, on one of the last occasions that Sonia and I were to see the Pinters, they invited us to their table at Le Caprice.

'Don't you think,' Antonia said, 'it is time we talked about things?'

And Sonia said with her wise diplomacy:

'It is still too soon, Antonia.'

For there could be no resolution of anything, only the uneasy remembrance of past occurrences. And Harold bore grudges bitterly. Once he swore at Norman Lamont at a party of ours, because the ex-Chancellor had backed General Pinochet in Chile.

'What is that fucking Fascist doing in this room? I'm leaving.'

'No,' I replied, 'I am leaving, instead. It's only my party, and I've got it wrong.'

He gave a rare laugh, and stayed.

I once wrote a denunciation of the European intervention in Kosovo, and I pointed out that nobody had been able to control the tribal and internecine Balkans since Roman occupation, and that every conqueror or peace-keeper had lost out there for nearly two thousand years. I sent it to Harold, who had blasted the intervention on television; he came to a party afterwards. Incredibly, most of us opposed the folly, even Simon Jenkins. Harold only blew up against the President of Magdalen College, Anthony Smith, who smiled and asked Harold, 'Why do you care?'

'Care?' Harold shouted. 'People are dying there, you liberal smirking fool!'

Harold's arm was caught, before he waved it. He stayed to talk of the War Decade of the arts in the 1940s with the playwright Hugh Whitemore and the director Anthony Page. All had read my book on the period, *War Like A Wasp*. I was flattered by their attention. I hardly ever heed my critics, but I do drink in the rare praise of my peers. We all survived the conflict, although we all might have agreed with the social escaper from prison camps, Bill Ash, when he said, 'This is the only war I'd be seen dead in.'

At Scarborough, when another actor-playwright, Alan Ayckbourn, approached Pinter about how to play his role in *The Birthday Party*, Harold replied: 'Mind your own fucking business. Concentrate on what's there.' And when much later, he was asked why he had stopped writing plays, he replied, 'A play isn't a sausage machine – if they still have sausage machines.'

I fearfully offended Harold, when I was congratulating him on his reading of the poems of Philip Larkin, particularly on death. I said I'd met Larkin once at a party at All Souls, and he was dressed in a dickey and black evening suit, appearing rather portly. 'He looked just like Jeeves,' was my comment. Harold growled, 'I don't understand a word you're saying,' and walked away. Later, he wrote a play of eight lines on one of the best slip catches ever taken. He had done it, and saved the game. He sent the printed work out to his closer friends. It was called 'Catch'. He had remarked at his 60th Birthday Party, 'Did you know that cricket was the only "Good Thing" God created on earth?'

At lunch with the Freddie Forsyths, Lizzie Spender told me another cricket story. Harold had written a great poem of exquisite brevity.

Leonard Hutton is dead.
Is dead. Is dead.

Then he sent it to his best twenty cricketing friends, who played in the special Pinter team. In a lather, having no response, he rang up the playwright Simon Gray.

PINTER: What did you think of my poem, Grey?
GREY: I haven't finished reading it yet, Pinter.

At Harold's 70th Birthday Party for P.E.N., he made a few confessions. He told of two tribunals in 1948, which let him off National Service as a conscientious objector – his father paid the fine. He apologized for not marching with the Campaign for Nuclear Disarmament. 'I had a defect of character – too much privacy.' What the evening of extracts made clear, with Harold himself playing in *The Dumb Waiter*, was that his plays and his political and his moral stance were one. Yet so many of the distinguished guests praised him for so many different aspects of his personality that he had to come on stage at the end to state that he hardly recognised himself in what these speakers said he was – but it did persuade him that he did exist.

At dinner later with the actress Rowena McCullough and Hugh

Whitemore, we heard more of Harold's rages. When Rowena asked him when his new play was being put on, there was an eruption. 'What do you mean, put on? It has actors! They put on a play. What do you mean?' Another time when Harold was on a tirade over the telephone, Rowena yelled back, 'I'm just having a row with Hugh. Don't interrupt me.' That shut him up. But Hugh's story was best. In writing a BBC script, Harold demanded *(slight pause)*, *(pause)*, *(long pause)*, then *(SILENT PAUSE)*. The terrified director called Harold. *SILENT PAUSE*? For once Harold admitted an error. 'Typed it wrong,' he said. 'Change back to slight pause'

Having known Harold for more than thirty years, ever since we were neighbours at Hanover Terrace, I had always wondered at his switch to visceral anti-Americanism. The genius of our age in stage-craft and screenplay, he followed the disastrous example of the French and the ex-Marxists – my first wife Marianne, a host of friends, even Graham Greene – who saw Yanks as gun-toting murderous imperialist cowboys. The public face of George W. Bush was made for this caricature. Perhaps only Samantha Cameron, the wife of the Tory leader, could ask, while sitting next to Harold at dinner, 'Tell me, Mr Pinter, are you interested in politics?'

Anyway, the only thing was to treat this everlasting anger with humour. Outside Westminster Cathedral at Elizabeth Longford's memorial service, where it was agreed that all the Pakenhams talked too much, the coatless Harold rejected the offer of my umbrella to shiver in his own reveries. And at Paddy Pakenham's funeral, Harold backed growling against a wall at the Wake in the Rembrandt Hotel – as I often do at gatherings, waiting to see who may come and talk to me, or rather not.

The divine Sonia dared to approach and entrance him for ten minutes, all smiles and almost flirting. I also ventured an approach, after talking to his brother-in-law Kevin Billington about the splendid priest at Brompton Oratory, who sternly declared that only Roman Catholics 'in a state of grace' could come up and take communion – but then Kevin was watching at the Mass all the old Catholic reprobates stagger up for their bread and wine.

Kevin rightly observed that it was rather presumptuous of those bygone sinners to think they were in a state of grace. When I told this to Harold, he began his usual effing and blinding about people who said prayers to the dead. What use were they? Then I said I

thought he was in 'a state of grace'. 'WHAT?' 'A state of W. G. Grace
–' and even Harold laughed at such a cricket joke. Then he asked,
if we prayed. Yes, Sonia said, traditionally, for those we loved. It did
us good, even if not them. And Harold said, he respected that. Sonia
could make Medusa blink.

After the Catholic wedding in Farm Street of Rebecca, one of
Antonia's daughters, we all regressed for lunch beneath the marble
pillars of the House of Lords. The bridegroom, an irrepressible
Irish barrister, thanked us for deserting the grouse moors for this
August function. 'Let the widgeon fly free,' he declared. 'Let the
woodcock, snipe and quail roam. We are all for the underdog. I pro-
pose a toast to the happy life of the grouse.' Even Harold had to
drink to that, although not his preferred description of the under-
privileged of the earth.

Among friends, Harold was almost mellow. I had sent him a copy
of another book of mine, *An Anatomy of Terror*, which he said he was
dipping into with great interest. 'Oh,' I said, 'use the index. You can
pick out the anti-American bits.' This got a smile from him. Then
I dared to say, quite truthfully after his throat-cancer operation,
'Speaking to you as an actor, Harold, how do you continue to look
so young and handsome?' This made him laugh at last, and he forgot his fury. Praise is the opium of the thespian.

Unable to travel to Sweden, in a wheelchair under a plaid blanket,
frail and skeletal, Harold delivered his Nobel Prize speech on television. His opening was brilliant about his plays.

- They begin with a phrase or a word, as 'dark'.
- Three characters are called a. and b. and c.
- They talk, and Harold visualizes them.
- They put on flesh and blood and get away from him.

Harold didn't know how he wrote as he did, or had done what he
had done. Then the speech changed to the sad old rant about the
'Evil Empire' of the USA, preaching lies of liberty and democracy.
Even Tony Blair should be tried over the war in Iraq as a war crim-
inal. Harold should have stuck to his line about his early plays. 'As
I said before, our beginnings never know our ends.'

When I reproached his stately wife Antonia about his rabid Nobel
Prize acceptance speech, she squashed me flat. Moving majestically

away, she said: 'He does believe it, you know.' Yet I had not quite worked out his reasons for accepting the prize from such a donor, although he had joked that he would give Antonia £300,000 of it to buy a dress. He was admirably brave about his cancer of the throat, but he and Antonia hated any questions on the matter. At the swan-song of George Weidenfeld's career, celebrating sixty years of publishing in the National Portrait Gallery, Harold excelled himself with the precision of his language.

HAROLD: Hello.
MAN: Hello. How are you?
HAROLD: I didn't say, 'How are you?' I said, 'Hello'.
MAN: Well, how are you anyway?
HAROLD: That is the fucking disease of modern society. Everybody wants to know how you are. I just say I'm fucking awful. Fucking awful.

As the genius of brevity, how could Harold have put it better? Except with a double pause.

His finest, and almost final performance was in *Krapp's Last Tape*. He said of Beckett that he was 'the most courageous, remorseless writer going – and the more he grinds my nose in the shit, the more I am grateful to him.' Playing Krapp, sitting in an electric wheelchair, fiddling with the spools of recorded memories or sweeping them to the floor, pounding the table in anger, grimacing or sneering or briefly yearning for a lost girl on a punt to 'Let me in,' Pinter gave a meaning to Krapp's life without meaning, his 'last fancies … drowned in dreams and burning to be gone.' What Harold has written and done will burn always within us, even though he is gone. Such a genius feels he has a licence to free speech. As with the electric artist Lucian Freud, mere manners were a gag, a torture to their mouths. Expletives are the essence.

Ironically, Sonia and I have gotten on well together for thirty years, because during the day, as Harold and Antonia, we give each other a wide space out, a room or two apart. And our love for far travels has always brought us more together. For Sonia was always a creature of the weather. Once she was bathed by a warm South Wind in a dhow off Africa. The languorous air flowed into her veins, as if a blood infusion. Sea and breeze, water and air, were her thermometer. And emulating Einstein in my Sonia formula, I had to do better than:–

$e = me^2$

The velocity of light was less to me than the speed of love. And the sight of her so transcendent gave me an equation:-

$t/a = s^2$

Temperature/Atmosphere = Sonia squared.

A fond hand on the wheel was steering the passage between generations. She refused to accept the reefs of age. Once in a villa near the irregular towers of San Gimignano, she had entertained Edna O'Brien and her own daughter Pandora, when out of the dust, weary in sandals and knapsacks, and impromptu, arrived Craig Brown and Nicholas Coleridge and Buccleuch's son, John Scott, all looking for Pandora and a good summertime. Charades and laughter rocked the tiles. All of them would become humorists or artists or magazine editors, who would always treat Sonia as one of them.

A couple of decades later, I would meet the glamorous Hugh Grant, who had known Pandora at Oxford. He declared: 'We were all in love with her there. She was so beautiful and so unapproachable. We didn't dare get near her. What has happened to her?'

When I told him of her country existence with two boys, he added: 'Riding with the staghounds across Exmoor. How perfect. I do wish I had dared.'

THE FABULOUS PORTANOVAS

Sonia and I often dared to prolong our trips to Yucatán and the Mayan temples by staying over with the Portanovas at Acapulco in a layered ziggurat of a palace, set on a cliffside above the Pacific Ocean. I had first heard of Ricky from the malice of gossip columns. He was represented as a creature of excessive extravagance with a slipping toupée and behaviour. But he himself was to tell me of far voyages, more curious than those of Sinbad the Sailor. He had to make his way in the world, before the death of his unseen grandfather and his divorced mother uncorked a vast inheritance like the genie from the magic lamp. He had tried to corner all the sapphires and rubies in India and Burma and Ceylon.

'I had a Jeep and three Sikh guards with the old Lee-Enfields. The three-o-threes you could Rapid Fire until the linseed oil boiled out of the woodwork and burned your hands. We only needed them in the hills sometimes. The rest was bargaining. And the pay was in gold guineas and rupees. We went beyond the Brahmaputra as far as Mandalay.'

Back in Rome, Ricky did well in the gem trade, although he also modelled for the *fumetti*. These were cartoon romances, illustrated by balloons of dialogue floating in sexy still photographs. And when Ricky's grandfather died in 1957, Ricky found himself with a monthly check of five thousand dollars from the Trust Fund of the estate, and a golden ticket to Monte Carlo, both for social and tax reasons. He loved the famous and escorted everybody from Greta Garbo to Errol Flynn on various escapades. He gave and gave flamboyantly, until he had to borrow ten thousand dollars to fly to Houston and begin a long lawsuit against the Cullen trustees to give him his due. He slowly increased his share of the take to a million dollars a month. He married Sandra Hovas from a struggling family in Houston, whose wholesale furniture business was often on the edge. She was seventeen years younger than him with an electric attraction and a large bosom – she was called 'Buckets' at High School. And she would save his lifestyle and his life. He then managed to turn the extravagances of the screen into a series of true romances. Even more than the newspaper proprietor William Randolph Hearst of Citizen Kane fame for his Californian extravaganza of Xanadu, Ricky created a world of social fantasy at his Arabesque in Acapulco. This was such stuff as hallucinations are made of, but it was real, although hardly credible.

Ricky's dream palace was not the West Egg of Jay Gatsby's parties in Scott Fitzgerald's masterpiece. Behind the security gates a herd of concrete camels safely grazed above the five giant palettes connected by a tented trolley railway up the cliff face. Down the rocks tumbled many a waterfall past a vast pool into the Pacific. In the twenty-eight guest suites, tigers in lacquer and mother-of-pearl burst through the bedroom walls.

There were no corners or straight lines wherever. All was curved or arched in the Moorish fashion. A pastel fretwork pervaded throughout, a style I had only seen once before in Cairo in the grottos of its last Egyptian monarch – and so I called it Faroque. And, indeed, in the past it turned out that Ricky had been an intimate friend of King Farouk's sister. And so he had created a mirage so serpentine that all his guests were entwined within the elaborations of its djinn.

The guests could walk up or down beside 'Sandra's River', flowing over blue mosaic to arrive at the tented top of the main room, a wobbly oval some two hundred yards about. Half of that was a swimming pool which made a second gulf above Acapulco Bay, as if the ocean had tossed up an azure pancake. Under the arches, candles blazed taller than grenadiers, and gold cloths hid the round tables. Tuberoses drenched the air, while among the nacreous bric-a-brac, a papier-mâché Madonna took away her false face from her real one.

So the Portanovas captured their fantasies in their palace by the sea. The flow and curves of the scrollwork were nets for parrots and leopards. The pools and rock crannies were traps for silver turtles and mother-of-pearl doves. Fables reigned in the rainbow curtains of the suites with their giant brass tortoises and birds of paradise and circular stone bathtubs, big enough to bathe a baby hippopotamus. The doors of the cupboards and rooms were all keyholes painted with candy-coloured stripes and mirrored, so that we were always looking into a spell of selves. All that was alive was woven into that cliff place, the grasses and the serpents, the lilacs and the

lions, the termites and the lizards, the humming birds and the drag-
ons.

The Portanovas knew their visitors better than Gatsby did – a
Texan blonde with three oil wells and four husbands, arms dealers
and ladies from Monterrey and the Chase Manhattan Bank,
Hollywood superagents and Simon of Castle Howard, where
Brideshead was Revisited in the film of it, Mexican plutocrats and
Cuban refugees. Two of them were found coupling in Scheherezade
Two. Ever courteous to her guests, Sandra asked them, 'Can I help
you?'

One of her friends was married to a businessman from over the
Border, whose favourite story after dinner was to tell of taking a
rival on a high ride in his helicopter. Pushing his competitor out of
the door, he heard his victim ask as he fell to earth, 'WHY? Why?
Weee…' Then thump.

Such questions were never asked at Arabesque. Living and dying
seemed suspended in this lotus-land. Acceptance was all. Of course,
the screen stars came, to check that their celluloid roles were no
make-believe. There were Tony Curtis and Michael York, both as
ageless as Rider Haggard's She, stepping from the flame of eternal
youth. Kirk Douglas and Sylvester Stallone looked in, the muscles
of past and present time. Also in evidence were Barbara Walters and
Plácido Domingo and Roger Moore, playing a skit as James Bond
for a charity show. Indeed, some scenes from *Licence to Kill* were
filmed in Arabesque, as 007 found his perfect location.

While we were there, Joan Collins came in her confection, and
the blue glaze of Frank Sinatra, who fortunately did not recollect
my rudeness at Limehouse, on the Thames. He was sent for by
Sandra to solve the problem of Ricky's new friend, who had come
to call, a small basking shark. Pools had been built in the rocks to
catch the deluge down the cliff. Pumps lifted the sea on high to cascade down to the beach, by the flick of a switch.

'Just like life,' Ricky used to say. 'An endless treadmill. We use
too much energy to come back to where we started from.'

He was then talking to the shark, not to me. A fisherman had
caught it in his net and had sold it along with his catch. Ricky had
put it in his rock pool and fed it with steaks and cutlets. Now the
shark was a better companion than I was. It stayed up till dawn and
never answered back.

'You do not mean to scare people,' Ricky used to say, as the shark nuzzled at his fingers to snap down a hot dog *à la moutarde*. 'You merely have to bite. God made you so. He gave you all those teeth. What else should you do with them except eat things?'

Then Ricky sneezed. He always took a sneeze as a personal attack by heaven. So the ancient Greeks had thought thunderbolts and lightning were the assault weapons of the gods.

'Damn you up there,' he cursed. 'You get up my nose.' He turned back to give the shark some kidneys *en brochette*. The shark ate the skewer as well. 'I do not hate you, my friend. You are as you are. Exactly what you should be in creation. No frills, no nonsense. All you want is breakfast.'

Late that night, Sandra came down the steps cut in the rock between the concrete joists, which supported the palettes of Arabesque. She knelt by Ricky, as he fed the shark. The dark round her eyes was not kohl, but lack of sleep.

'Come to bed, my love,' she said. 'Perhaps I am softer than your shark.'

'You are,' Ricky said. 'But he is more truthful than you. He only loves me because I feed him. And he listens to everything I say. He never contradicts me.'

'A wise shark.' I saw Sandra take Ricky's hand and softly bite the tips of his fingers one by one. 'Do I – really – eat you – because – I don't – get enough – to eat?'

Ricky laughed.

'You and my shark,' he said, 'you are my best friends.'

'I'm not jealous,' Sandra said. 'But perhaps your shark would be better off in the sea, where his friends and family are.'

'He is my guest, too,' Ricky said, waving towards me. 'I have checked on his background, and he is admirable for what he is. A shark of honour. You can trust his teeth. A pedigree pal. And as you know, I never turn away a guest unless he is rude to the cook.'

'But he might be happier back in the sea.'

'Not as long as he wishes to stay.'

Sandra left Ricky with his friend the shark, and myself. For she was dropping with sleep. For days, she brooded on how to separate the new companions. Then she telephoned her friend Conchita in the Land of the Stars and heard that Ol' Blue Eyes Himself was coming down their way.

Nobody could make a dinner for forty better than Sandra; if the Roman Emperors served larks' tongues, she served ceviche with shrimp and clams and conch marinated in lime or scooped avocado with the spawn of Sargasso Sea eels or langoustines as soft as the garlic butter. The quails to follow were marshmallows on the tongue, the curried chicken hotter than the seven spices of sin, the mango sorbet as sweet as a lick of paradise. At the end of the dinner, Ricky took Sinatra to meet his friend in the rock pool. The basking shark smiled as best it could, given the dentures donated by creation, and it gobbled down a quart of chopped steak.

'You will not meet a better type in Hollywood,' Ricky said. 'Always turns up on time. Straight as a die. Never says no to a good deal. You can count on him in a crisis.'

'He reminds me of my old agent,' Sinatra said. 'The one who did nothing and took the dough. Why don't you turn him loose?'

'But he is my guest.'

'Not by choice. Tell you what – ?'

'What?'

'What would you take to turn him loose?'

Now Ricky knew that there was one thing that Sinatra would never do. He would not sing at private parties. He guarded his voice like the gold in Fort Knox.

'Sing for your supper,' Ricky said. 'And the shark goes free.'

Sinatra scowled. Then he looked at the shark, now floating like a tea-tray with a carving-knife on top. Round and round and round it skimmed the small pool with nowhere to go. The eternal return without getting on. Or maybe like a mobster trying to leave Alcatraz.

'You've got it,' he said. 'I sing and he swims.'

So Sinatra sang to the dinner guests that night. And when the songs were done, Ricky turned on the pumps until a flood swilled on the cliff top. Then he pressed the switch for the release gate, and a cascade flushed out the nooks and the pools, scooping the shark down to the sea inlet below.

There were tears in Ricky's eyes.

'I know he will come back,' he said. 'He is my friend.'

'No,' Sinatra said. 'He needs the sea and the other sharks. We don't.'

For three days the few swimmers in the sea paddled back to the beach because a small shark came up to put its nose in their hands, as if they had something to give. But on the fourth day, the shark did not reappear, and never again. And I heard Sandra ask, 'How long does one remember a free lunch?'

The following day in the swimming pool, Sonia learned that the old bank of Barings had collapsed because of a rogue trader in the Far East. What money she had was invested by the firm, which also looked after the portfolio of The Queen of England. From their lounging chairs, the other guests wondered how Sonia would cope with the crisis. She swam slowly up to Sandra and said, 'Well, The Queen and I will just have to take in lodgers, though she has rather more space.'

Great wealth creates parasites. Lawyers intervene to deal with trustees and bankers and even family. Ricky began to slip into the paranoia of his younger brother. He had cause. There was a mysterious fire at his mock-Regency mansion in Houston. And there, his groom, mistaken for him, had the back of his head blown off by a rifle shot through the window. There was a poisoning attempt at a major London hotel. And when Sonia and I were at Arabesque, we were both struck down by a brief paralysis from toxic food or water. Soon after our stay, we heard that many of the staff of seventy had been fired.

Ricky's growing mistrust could well refer to his and Sandra's dying. She had suffered for many years from the nervous illness called MS, which is generally debilitating with periods of remission. She had been diagnosed at the Mayo Clinic, but they could find no reason for the continuing pains in her arms and her legs. In the New Year, the suffering moved into her skull. At the end of January, she flew to a hospital in Houston, where she was told that she had an inoperable brain tumour. She had only three or four weeks to live. Ricky felt sick himself and would not eat and chain-smoked in spite of his damaged throat. A friend told me, 'He let himself go and died.' And Sandra lapsed into a coma and passed away on a Good Friday, though not for her.

I was never more than a bystander in these affairs, as Nick Carraway was to Tom and Daisy Buchanan and the flawed hero of *The Great Gatsby*. Scott Fitzgerald had already put my observations in the mouth of his narrator. Nick had an unaffected scorn for everything which Jay Gatsby represented. Yet 'if personality is an unbroken series of successful gestures, then there was something gorgeous about him … it was an extraordinary gift for hope, a romantic readiness such as I have never found in any other person.'

That was what I thought, when I knew Ricky. Even so, he was more real than Gatsby. Yes, he had been a jewel-smuggler as Gatsby was a dealer in forged bonds. Yet his title did come from Naples and not from a false and hinted genealogy. He did not claim a spurious Oxford degree, as Gatsby had in his doctored photograph. His wealth did derive from the Cullen Trust Fund in Texas, although its value and sources were always an oil-well for lawyers and more mysterious than the Styx. Fortune had blessed him as it did the lesser Gatsby. He used it with equal flamboyance and stranger taste. However, he and Sandra, as Jay and Daisy, were condemned by the mischance of their extravagance to a bitter end.

Unlike Daisy and her husband Tom Buchanan, the Portanovas did not smash up things and creatures and then retreat back into their money or their vast carelessness. They used the money to build up their illusions and their friendships with more than gifts of good cheer. Five thousand dollars to a broken-down spear-fisherman, a whole toyshop to village children in Sri Lanka, an incredible largesse of impulse.

Most of the rich are rich because they are mean. They never have a million enough. They break their wrists, reaching from the cheque. Not so the Portanovas, who had a generosity of spirit, which matched their hospitality. Ricky once had a bar in Naples which went bust, but was named after Bogart's Rick's Place in the film of *Casablanca*. He and Sandra were always romantics with a sense of wonder and a finesse, which could turn dream and fantasy into fact. I wish I could say, 'Play it again, Portanovas. Play it again.'

FORGIVEN IF NOT QUITE FORGOTTEN

The cinema was now a wrap for me, and so I ended my long involvement in publishing classic screenplays. I was clearing the holds to write *King Ludd*, for the time had come historically to tell about the Luddites, who first wrecked the new textile machines. My story was of the printers like Francis Place who defended liberty, on to the sad end of the print unions through new technology, locked out by barriers of barbed wire while journalists set their own copy for *The Times* at Wapping. Contemporary events had given *King Ludd* its shape. I thought that it would complete what I called *The Albion Triptych*, from mythology through history to the present day. Even so, I still flirt with a fourth book, *Melchizedek*, to make up a quartet, not from Alexandria, but which would reveal the secrets of the military-industrial complex that has ruled since the killing of Abel by Cain, until the final Apocalypse by nuclear missile.

For once, I appeared to have outlasted my English critics for my better work. The reviews for *Gog* from my peers were incredible. I could even bear to quote some of them:

Frank Kermode:
The energy and the funniness of the book yield to sadness and anger … I hope it will wake up reviewers and novelists, perhaps even the political left. And may you continue to prophesy.

Ian Rankin:
The Albion Triptych is full of a bawdy humour and a love of exaggeration reminiscent of those found in *Tom Jones* and *Tristram Shandy*. However, for all the allusions, echoes and arch references, Sinclair's vision is singular, and his triptych is sure to prove a lasting monument on the landscape of modern British literature.

Edmund Fuller:
The best tribute to Gog is the fact that we must evoke weighty

names for its best qualities. Inevitably one turns to Cervantes and Swift... laughter, horror, violence and lust all... are facts of Gog's unclouded quest-journey, which may be long remembered.

And on *King Ludd*:

Hilary Mantel:
No moderate opinion is possible; it is a work of genius.

After Homer, my most pervasive influence in writing novels had been Cervantes with his sword of irony. He had invented Don Quixote in the 17th century to end old notions of the passages to the dead. Once the Don and his squire Sancho Panza encountered Death riding on a cart with a human face, an angel with painted wings, an emperor and a Cupid and an armoured knight with a feathered hat. They represented the strolling play of *The Parliament of Death*. 'Being a demon,' the leader of the troupe said, 'I am capable of anything.' Although an imp with bladders frightened Quixote's horse Rocinante so that he was thrown to the ground, Sancho persuaded his master not to combat Death and fallen angels and emperors, even in show. There was not a real knight among them.

Such charades came to their apogee when Don Quixote was lowered into the Cave of Montesinos, where marvels were said to happen. He was guided there by a student of works of chivalry, and he returned after three days and nights in a coma of beatific visions. On awakening, he declared that he had seen the Elysian Fields and a Grail Castle with walls of crystal. From it emerged the robed wizard Montesinos, who swore that he was held under a spell by the enchanter Merlin.

Quixote then told of the speaking corpse of Charlemagne's nephew who died at Roncesvalles and was laid out on a slab. His salted heart was carried in a Grail procession by black-robed women with white turbans. Other guests in the castle included Queen Guinevere and her maid, who poured the wine for Lancelot 'when from Britain he came'. Sancho laughed at the Don's testimony, but here Cervantes mixed credibility with fantasy, citing a Cide Hamete as the actual author of this episode. Hamete was made to declare that he could not believe in everything which had happened to the valiant Don Quixote. Until now, all the adventures were possible. But the one in the cavern was beyond reason. Yet Quixote could not lie. Therefore, the wise reader must decide for himself. However, it was reported that Quixote retracted his vision on his deathbed, confessing that he had made up the Arthurian pieces because of what he had read in other romances.

Here Cervantes appeared to invent the modern novel of deconstruction. He would not declare that he did not believe in the legends of chivalry and the hereafter. He would only write that a scribe doubted them, also that the fictitious Don Quixote had denied at his dying one particular adventure. The reader himself had to decide on the value of the text. In another episode in *Don Quixote*, Cervantes had his knight encounter the bronze speaking head from the Grail legends. It was set on a jasper table and said to be cast by an enchanter, Escotillo. When the Don asked the head whether the happenings in the Cave of Montesinos were a dream, it replied, 'There is much to be said on both sides.' The head was revealed to be mechanical and was broken up by orders of the Inquisition, 'the sentinels of our faith'.

Attacked by a canon of the Church for believing in the chivalric romances such as *Amadis*, Quixote said that his questioner, not he, was bewitched. To try and persuade anybody that Amadis and the other knights had never lived was the same as saying that the sun did not shine, ice was not cold and the earth did not bear fruit. If all the romances were lies, 'there was no Hector nor Achilles, nor Trojan War nor Twelve Peers of France nor King Arthur of England who still goes about in the shape of a raven and is expected to reappear in his kingdom at any time.'

He then described another vision of a Grail Castle, in which he was the Knight of the Lake. Plunging into a seething cauldron of water, he found himself again in the Elysian Fields of paradise in front of a jewelled castle made of diamonds, rubies, pearls, gold and emeralds. There beautiful maidens bathed and fed him and told him they were held under a magic spell, until a knight would release them. This perception, Quixote said, made him a better man, brave, polite, generous, courteous and bold. If the Arthurian legends were the stuff of dreams, they became actual in the change of character of their believers. This was another way of saying that the romantic search for the divine was still a valid way to God, a moral journey in its own right. Even if the knight, still on his quest in Spain, was out of date and a figure of fun, his trials were real enough, as were his sufferings, and these purified his spirit. When illusions became deeds, they made a better man.

These arguments could not survive the final verdict of Cervantes, when he killed off his glorious character. The deluded knight was received back into the Christian faith. Chivalry and the crusades were finished, although not the inward quest for a life after death, which the novel achieved in its serial publications. The enduring popularity of the work put Don Quixote among the immortals. Cervantes' mockery of actual pilgrimages on earth concentrated the search for revelation on the interior journey towards the soul. The Cave of Montesinos would become the analysis of dream. The quest for life after death would come to be found in the individual imagination and faith and even experience.

Anniversaries may prescribe our choices. After fifty years, some remembrance of 1939 and the Second World War was looming by the end of the century. I had been a child then. How would I assess it now from an odd corner? That angle would have to be British culture, now that I appeared to be one of its minor representatives. To my delight and surprise, I discovered a vibrant and brave blossoming of the arts, almost another Renaissance in a war-torn country. If it was not quite the produce of the old conflicts between Milan and Florence and the Holy See, it was still engendered by the war against Berlin and Tokyo and modern Rome.

So I researched and wrote a book, *War Like a Wasp*. For the Second World War gave Britain a sting, a stimulus and an endurance. On the Home Front or on service abroad, there was action and the fear of death. The Blitz concentrated the mind wonderfully. The arts flowered, poetry and painting, cinema and dancing. 'I would rather have been in London under siege between 1940 and 1945 than anywhere else,' the editor John Lehmann said, 'except perhaps Troy in the time that Homer celebrated.'

Then came a terrible victory with the knowledge of atom bomb and concentration camp. The postwar years of austerity prolonged rationing and deprivation until the end of the 'forties. The arts that had bloomed now withered and dispersed. A myth grew of a far decade, when we had won a war, lost a peace and not done much else and not much good. In fact, these were the years of the best work of Henry Moore and Francis Bacon, of T. S. Eliot and George Orwell, of Noël Coward and Laurence Olivier. This was a decade of miraculous invention.

I was trying to recreate the world of the 1940s with its encounters and its characters, its conflicts and its discoveries, its hopes and its disillusions, the scene of pubs and clubs, where scarce drink could be found and the fighting forgot. This was the time of the short piece, the poem, the story and the sketch. Anyone who knew someone in the loose coterie of Fitzrovia that took over from Blooms-bury could have anything published. Everything printed was read by a nation, avid for learning and waiting for action.

This was also a feverish and democratic time, using the language of the period in small magazines. For even paper was rationed. Those who served in the Armed Forces or on the Home Front had a short attention span. Conflict and orders were always calling them to duty. They read in fits and starts in an age made for anthology. So I edited *The War Decade*, the first home collection to view the global struggle and the postwar years as a whole. My selection told the national story from the outbreak of hostilities until the Festival of Britain in 1951, which signalled the end of austerity. Many of the pieces were by little-known writers, some of whom were ultimately killed in action. I tried to capture the feel and shock of these years, to show how everyone from all walks of life reacted to sudden attack and long waiting, to blackout and rationing, and so I endeavoured to recreate the pains and the fears and the hopes of that exceptional time, in which I had grown from a child into a very young man.

Of the leading magazine editors in the war, I did not know Cyril Connolly at *Horizon*, but once I witnessed a wonderful scene on an evening with the epicene John Lehmann at his home. He was proudly showing off a Canaletto of Venice hanging above his chimneypiece, when his young Italian toyboy leapt forward, stuck a vermilion fore-finger nail right through the canvas where a palazzo was painted fronting the Rialto, and shouted: '*Io habito quà!*', not mentioning his stay with my host. I did, however, become friends with Lehmann's successor on *The London Magazine*, Alan Ross, also the painter Patrick Procktor, whose flair and repartee were also works of art.

'I am the Red Queen,' Patrick once said to me. 'And why? Because I am the only artist who ever had tea with Mrs Khrushchev, the Divine Mother of the Kremlin.' And on another occasion, he declared, 'I am a screaming Communist dyke out of *The Rocky Horror Show*.'

Witty and extravagant, taller than a rickety scarecrow, with the shrill bray of a whistling donkey, Patrick was the best company and a dab hand with a brush. He shared his first show with David Hockney and somewhat resented the success of his fellow painter. He had a more delicate touch than his rival, and he drew more out of his subjects than a bright surface. He painted me in the Colony Room with an oily champagne glass in my hand, and with a wasp, crawling towards a circular bowl of cherries. In the background, caricatures of Muriel Belcher and her favourite 'cunty', Francis Bacon.

I suppose this was Patrick's way of courting me with his predatory act. He once sighed at lunch and said, 'Andrew, what a loss you are to the gay world.' He was a little more delicate than Daniel Farson, who saw me eating with the handsome young Timon, who bore my name.

'Who's your friend, Andrew?' Daniel asked.

'My son,' I replied.

'That's what they all say,' the laughing Farson said and gave me such a pat on the back that my face was knocked into my raspberries and *crème fraîche*.

Patrick used to give Princess Margaret takeaway Indian meals, wrapped in tinfoil, when she visited him at his home. She forgave him for the wit and fun of his company. A great friend was the drunken Peter Langan of the Brasserie fame, where Patrick painted some of the murals. Peter also acquired Odin's restaurant in Marylebone after its proprietor died. He engaged in a close relationship with the widow Kirsten, and then burned himself to death. Patrick then officially married Kirsten and adopted her two children, an act of magnanimity and long-suffering. The boy became something of an explosives expert, which led to certain detonations. Yet Patrick, with his endless grace and tolerance, put up with every provocation from his boy-friends and family, the ultimate gentleman in his rag-tag artist's clothing.

At my final lunch at the Garrick with Alan Ross, the emaciated Patrick came over to our table.

'Ah,' Alan said, 'you remind me of the last time I saw Harold Nicolson here.'

'Do I?' Patrick said.

'I asked,' Alan said, 'whether he was dieting. He said he was dying.'

Actually, Alan would be the first to go. I was reminded of Swann talking to the Duchesse de Guermantes, when she was rushing off in her carriage. She asked whether they would see each other soon. No, Swann replied, he was dying. Oh, the lady replied, you must be mistaken. Anyway, she had to leave with the Duke for dinner. He would not be kept waiting.

Patrick telephoned the next day to say that he had escorted Alan to the Underground at Piccadilly, although he very much disapproved of that way home. He thought that Alan had 'taken a powder', because of his melancholia, and had expired on the Tube. In fact, he had reached home and died of a stroke, as his tragic wife Jane told me. He had spoken at lunch of his numerous treatments for depression, based on his war experience of being consigned to the flooded hold of a destroyer with a hose to put out a blaze, while surrounded by floating corpses. There was no recovery from that.

Of all my Soho friends, Alan was the only noble one, a great heart, a good poet, a wise and witty talker, an elegant editor of *The London Magazine*, which he financed mainly on his winnings on the horses. With him died the best of Fitzrovia in its warmth and welcome to all strangers and artists of any style. As for Patrick, he was finally elected into the Royal Academy. This recognition was his ultimate satisfaction. His house and much of his past work had burned down, and now he was honoured for the excellent painter that he truly was. Too often, too few are known well for their worth, until they are dead.

My unlikely biography of Elisabeth, Empress of Austria, was engineered by the absorbing Marie Christine, the Princess of Kent, from the old Habsburg domains herself. At a dinner party, I was elected by her as her 'literary guru', which she announced to all the other guests. And who can refuse a royal command? Her first book was accused of plagiarism, so I gave her the old adage against the charges laid against her: 'Taking from one source is plagiarism, taking from ten is research, taking from twenty is genius.' And she did take from more than twenty sources.

I found her a Valkyrie princess, energetic and compulsive, witty and magnificently indiscreet. At a dinner at Kensington Palace, she told me a wonderful story of being in the family way, and also hounded by *Private Eye*, which declared that her marriage to Prince Michael was forced because of a pregnancy. She was determined that the baby would not be premature. She was seven months gone, when she rode her Arab in Richmond Park. Then she lent her mount to one of the progeny of Elisabeth, Empress of Austria. The horse threw the Habsburg girl and bolted and ran into a car, breaking both of its front legs.

Seeing it in its agony, Princess Michael went and sat on its head. Covered with blood and jolting up and down, she waited for help. Three vets refused to appear on that Saturday afternoon – and she wanted them struck off. Prince Michael set off on his motorcycle to the nearest hospital and police station. The coppers, alas, were controlling a football match and had no guns, while the hospital could only supply syringes and tranquillisers. And a reptile photographer appeared to take shocking shots of the gory swollen Princess, squatting on the thrashing head of dying horse.

Eventually Prince Michael came back with the syringes, which he gave to his wife. She injected them by the dozen into the horse's neck, until it was knocked out. Eventually, a man came along with a gun and shot the beast dead. She went back to her Richmond house and began two-hour labour contractions, while lying on the sofa. She rang Dr Pinker, the royal obstetrician, who was then on a shoot in Scotland. The baby could not arrive so early without disgracing the Royal Family. So Pinker gave her the immortal advice: 'Ma'am, cross your legs and think of England.'

Such was her will and courage that the Princess did just that. She fought down the labour pains, and she did not deliver her first-born until six weeks later. Telling me the tale, she fixed me with her glittering blue-green stare.

'And Andrew,' she said, 'the baby was born ten months after my marriage. Six pounds. And yet, it was still premature for some.'

For the tabloid press had always hounded her. Then we nearly co-operated, indeed, on a biography of Elizabeth, Empress of Austria, but I ended by doing it on my own. I always thought that Marie-Christine would have made a better Empress for her homeland Austria than had the Bavarian Elizabeth, who was less determined, but superb in the saddle. And certainly, if Prince Michael were ever recalled to serve as the Tsar of Russia, for he was the image of the last unfortunate one Nicholas, then she would have been superior in beauty and intelligence to the Empress Catherine the Great, and perhaps even greater in her presence.

The malign crash which killed Diana, Princess of Wales, provided a theme for my biography, which was called *Death by Fame*. Assassins and accidents stalk beautiful notoriety. Murdered by an Anarchist with a rusty sharpened file, Elisabeth of Austria lived in retirement, as she thought an Empress, separated from her husband, should for her reputation. Diana fanned the blaze of publicity in a confusion of charity with celebrity. At many a fashionable occasion to raise money for good causes, even the clearing of landmines, there were all the icons of wealth and screen and song, pursuing the illusion of a headline tomorrow. Diana could not preserve her privacy and her mystique against this disparate and competitive group of stars.

Both Elisabeth and Diana fell victim to the frenzy of their admirers and the press, although the Princess of Wales had more insidious assassins, the thousand thousand pricks and soundbytes of modern networks. She had milked the media for her own purposes, but she hated their intrusion on her intimacy with the few she loved. The least detail of her doings was broadcast to every green screen on the globe. At her death, the Internet made it possible for anyone with access and a computer to intrude on the mass mourning for this royal stranger. Although the million million viewers never knew her, they felt they did because of the incessant reportage of her life. *She was more than a royal*, a website read, *she was real*.

Of course, she was not. Her car smash in Paris coincided with the passing away of Mother Teresa in Calcutta, where the nun had worked for fifty years in the streets for the poor and the lepers of society. She would be beatified, but Diana eclipsed her in their dying. Communication had won the final victory. Celebrity is worth more than sanctity. And so now say all of us.

Fame is a posthumous perk. But because of the newshounds on the scent of politics, celebrity can easily be turned into notoriety. At a dinner party given by the *Time* correspondent, Frank Melville, Willy, Lord Whitelaw talked of his crucifixion by the British press. He was accused of causing a constitutional crisis between The Queen and Mrs Thatcher about sanctions on South Africa and the break-up of the Commonwealth. When asked whether The Queen was worried about Mrs Thatcher's behaviour, Whitelaw replied, 'Who isn't?'

He also declared that all, who remembered American aid in the Second World War, were for the air strike against Colonel Gaddafi in Libya. Yet again, Mrs Thatcher did not consult The Queen, the Head of the Armed Forces, on the use of British airfields by the American fighter-bombers. And The Queen was again furious.

Willy told Sonia why Mrs Thatcher had kept on losing male members of her Cabinet. She would talk 'man to man' in private, then at the next Cabinet meeting, she would forget any compact, go her own way, never stop talking and hectoring, and brook no opposition. She ruled capriciously and firmly – and the men could not trust their one- to-one deals with her.

Before she was handbagged by her own party, Mrs Thatcher declared at her last Tory Conference as leader that she wanted an open, classless England. But she had hardly abolished We and They, Us and Them. The Conservatives and the Labour Party had existed on that division, although it became more South vs North. And the irony was that Mrs Thatcher was ousted by the man without appearance, John Major, whose pride lay in his nonentity and lack of background in education. He was the Cheshire Cat of politics – his wide smile with its ambiguous reassurance and hidden ruthlessness was still fading away, long after he had vanished from the scene.

In a cartoon, I read: 'We are the future, alas.' The later Prime Minister David Cameron began the slow puncture of his predecessor Tony Blair with the prick: 'You were the future – once.' He had agreed with the Buddhists that past and present and future are all the same. In politics, however, a day is enough for damnation. A Black Wednesday, or the sacked minister Norman Lamont remarking of John Major, 'In office, but not in power.'

Tony Blair dragged on beyond the lease of his lodgings in Downing Street, only to be dismissed by Denis Healey, who himself fulfilled the adage that all political lives end in failure. Of Blair wanting to be remembered for his tenure of ten years as Prime Minister, Healey replied: 'Bugger history. And sod 'em, or Gomorrah, if you prefer it.'

The problem of Blair was that, as he spoke in his own justification, he more and more believed in what he was spouting out. He was scuppered by his own rhetoric. He was convinced by his very statements. 'I wish to make this absolutely clear' meant that 'I will make this even more obscure,' except to his intent. He turned his hopes into matters of future deliverance.

If we are to be remembered by what we have done in any office, Blair will be recalled by what he said he would do, and never did. He would never be redeemed by his wit, but only condemned by his greed and his gaffes. To intervene in Afghanistan and Iraq, and to support Israel against Lebanon, was to cheer on old imperial howlers. As the Romans and Shakespeare knew, the belief in one's speeches led to the death of Julius Caesar. Blair reminded me of one of the Triumvirate, who tried to rule Rome thereafter. He was Lepidus, condemned by Mark Antony Brown as 'a slight, unmeritable man, meant to be sent on errands.' Alas, Blair's errands were of his own choosing, and most of them, fiascos. Never trust what you can say. Only do as you do. And fame will judge him for that.

Je ne regrette rien. So Piaf sang, or such. Perhaps I have regretted one thing in my prolonged and misspent life. Yet it was only an introduction to a man who would be celebrated at all costs. For my wife Sonia and I had met Murdo McLean. 'There were only three of us,' he said with his usual accuracy and modest charm. If not quite a member of the Trinity or the patronage committee, he certainly knew what he was.

Lloyd George had found that he could not fix parliamentary business in advance without a civil servant in 12 Downing Street. A referee was needed to sort out the differences between the government and the opposition. He would deal with the Whips directly. His job was to prepare answers to inquiries before they were put. Prime Minister's Questions in the House of Commons was a serial and superior pantomime. As another civil servant has said, 'We can always provide the answers, if we can set the questions.' Forewarned is disarmed.

Indeed, any reasonable response could be provided, if the problem was known. Yet should one have an Agriculture Minister, who put his foot in his mouth along with some five million cattle destroyed, or a Transport Minister, whose vowels sounded like coals shovelled into a boiler, which had a leak and precious little plumbing. The minister would be pursued by the Tory Furies, until the next election.

To explain Murdo Maclean. There had been three bachelors in service, since the original appointment by Lloyd George. They had all lived in 12 Downing Street with its connecting doors to Numbers 11 and 10, a throughway to power. They had fixed Question Time for nearly eighty years, by advising the Whips before that rigged horse race, so winning replies could be saddled in advance. When he said he was one of three, Murdo had also hinted that he was the third most powerful civil servant after the Secretary to the Cabinet. Completely unknown, he oiled the wheels of the great engine of our government. What was done was done, by his infinite sagacity.

Back to my sole regret, I found myself at the wedding reception in the Polish Club of my divine step-daughter Pandora. I usually don't know where I am or what I am doing, but this time I had a reason. Murdo knew, as he knew everything, that a friend of the family, Lord Shackleton, would also be in attendance. He sat on the other Trinity, the patronage committee, which might deny peerages to some, also lesser awards. There could be doubts about a few of the entries, given sleaze and a party loan or two.

While the band at the reception was blaring out salsa and not mazurkas, Murdo arrived blithely through the chic scrum. 'I hope you don't mind,' he said, 'but I have brought along my chauffeur.' I looked beyond him to see the grinning Jeffrey Archer.

Actually, I did mind for three reasons, and none of them were literary. We all write what we can, and good luck to those who make a bomb out of it. I had first seen Jeffrey, auctioning off the House of Commons and Lords Swimming Race for a charity in Ulster, and shouting, 'Who'll give me another hundred quid for this noble Earl?,' shivering in his pink trunks. In terms of human dignity, I would rather have seen a knacker knocking off a diseased bull at an *abattoir*. Why would Jeffrey want to join them, if he did not value them?

The second quibble was social. Jeffrey never tolerated gatecrashers to his Krug champagne and Shepherd's Pie parties at Tory conferences or on New Year's Eve in London. Intruders were slung out. Luckily, we had never knocked. But as I have occasionally been credited for old-fashioned Highland hospitality, I said I didn't mind if the chauffeur called unasked at Pandora's party, whatever his destination might be.

Thirdly, there was the problem of Dame Edna Everage. One should never ask for too much, even for publicity. I had seen Jeffrey begging twice with a parcel at Dame Edna's television door, only not to be admitted by Her Grace and Favour. He was not good enough yet for Her, obviously, even though She had ennobled Herself as a Royal Dame. I now wondered if Jeffrey had not come to our wedding reception in pursuit of a more official title.

Murdo was waiting like Macbeth to slip in the dirk. 'Isn't Eddie Shackleton here?,' he asked. 'Jeffrey would so like to meet him.' As I had just been chatting to our noble friend, I replied that this was a private occasion, Pandora's wedding. 'Oh, please,' Murdo said, 'do bring him across to talk to Jeffrey.'

With a heavy heart, I walked back to the table. One must be courteous at one's own gatherings, even if a request is outrageous. Obviously, Lord Shackleton had blocked Jeffrey Archer's last application to become a peer, although it was supported by Margaret Thatcher herself. Sitting down, I said most unhappily, 'I'm afraid a gatecrasher has arrived, called Jeffrey Archer. He wants desperately to talk to you. I don't know why. Would you mind too much?'

I could see that Lord Shackleton did mind. Yet as I was the host, and we were bound by the courtesies of a social occasion, he sadly pushed back his seat and toddled off to talk to Murdo and Jeffrey. After introducing them to him, I lurched away. What passed between them, I don't know. With all the din, they were out of earshot.

The next thing I heard, Jeffrey was Lord Archer. I suppose that is how things still occur in this country. Between arranged contacts and serious politics and abused friendship, something happens. I wish it were not that way. But I only regret that introduction now. From when l was a don at Cambridge, I remembered the admirable and fragrant and constant Mary Archer. In my simplicity, I now was used by a conniving system. I think Murdo Maclean was the best person in his job he could possibly be, but only Dr Pangloss would agree with me. I regret that I helped to get Jeffrey Archer his peerage by his being a chauffeur, for once, rather than hiring others to drive him.

And yet I admire him, too, and he will always return, as General MacArthur once vowed to do to the Philippines. I am always a friend to anyone, whose wily pride pre-empts their downfall. Nobody can deny Jeffrey's dread ability to entertain us all most dramatically. The plots in his thrillers have always been worthy of Machiavelli, and more. Even after a prison sentence, served for perjury, his title re-

With Joanna Lumley and John Bird during the filming of The Breaking of Bumbo

Peter O'Toole and the author on the set of Under Milk Wood

The author directing Elizabeth Taylor in Under Milk Wood

Richard Burton and the author during the filming of Under Milk Wood

(l to r) *Timon and Andrew Sinclair, Derek Lindsay*

Sonia Graham, Lady Melchett

Sonia and Andrew at the top of the World Trade Center

Andrew and his film boxes

mained with him, as did a fearsome object – the elephant's foot, which served me as an umbrella stand, when I was young. Brought back from Africa by my parents, this amputated and hollowed hide leg was impervious to all the dirt and wet flung upon it. The Archer is dead, long live the new Jeffrey, whatever he presents himself to be. As Barry Humphries, playing Dame Edna Everage, asked the noble old lag: 'Is there no beginning to your talents?' Or ending.

TERROR AND RESISTANCE

In an effort at understanding by historical examples, I wrote *An Anatomy of Terror*, a popular diagnosis of our time of troubles. Held to be unprincipled, I found ten principles in all that skulduggery:

Terror is warfare by extreme means.
Terror is the lifeblood of tyranny.
Terror is the weapon of the outlaw against the oppressor.
Terror is murder on the cheap.
Terror is the lash on the back of the refugee.
Terror is victory by stealth for the few.
Terror is defeat by cowardice for the crowd.
If we are terrorized, we may become terrible to those who make us fear.
Terror is measured by the scale of its victims, not the merit of its cause.
Tolerance of terror is no virtue.

My own experience of what was defined as 'terror' in Western countries lay less in the past, more in present Cuba. Two centuries ago, the *sans culottes* in the French Revolution were terrorists to the Bourbon defenders, but when those without trousers succeeded in overthrowing the throne and beheading the monarch, their slogan of *liberté, égalité, fraternité* became the *oriflamme* of France, although succeeding despotisms, as that of the Emperor Napoleon, had little to do with these admirable aims.

Later, the 'freedom fighters', who sought independence by any larcenous means, appeared to be bandits without a cause in the eyes of the ruling governments. Stalin robbed banks for the Bolsheviks before tyrannizing Russia after the Revolution. The proletariat needed a dictator before it could be freed. But when? And for what? Would Al-Qaeda be justified in raising its finance from the heroin trade in order to release people to drift off on a high everywhere? Yet had not an Opium War put China under Western domination?

If each person was free to do as he or she pleased, the result would be anarchy. As Hobbes declared in his phased approval of *Leviathan*, without discipline life would be brutish, nasty, solitary and short. Society demands the restriction of personal liberty. The questions are, how much? For how long? And how acceptable are such fetters and an iron hand? My answers from 3,000 years of burrowing into the bygone were none. Struggles for secular or religious independence still rack the globe, even if a Third World War and the near destruction of the human race are postponed until the next instalment.

In my Cuban encounters, the hijacking Black Panthers declared that they were fighting for the freedom of the black American people. Their white rulers had put them in prison for crimes against the law, which had nothing to do with politics. So they confused resistance against the state with the human rights, which they asserted. The reason for their new revolution was not so much *No Taxation Without Representation* as *No Coercion Without Empowerment*. As small Napoleons or Stalins, they wished to dictate the terms of giving freedom to their black brothers, who might do only what they were told. Liberty was a sentence to obey.

Personally, I met two extraordinary people among those in control, who managed to resist acts of terror and religious conflicts for many decades. One remarkable man, Theodor or Teddy Kollek, born near Budapest and the founder of a kibbutz on the Sea of Galilee, kept the peace in Jerusalem for twenty-eight years. This Mayor was driven by an extraordinary energy, allied with a genius for diplomacy and a passion for the Holy City. He knew of its divisions. As he testified, there were in Jerusalem one hundred and four groups of Jews with cultural differences. There were forty groups of Christians, while the Protestants had only been there for one hundred and fifty years. There were many Muslim sects, all differing over the religious law of the Koran, the Shariah, as against the common law, which was also opposed by the Torah of certain Jewish groups. Of the Jews, Kollek said, 'We were all minorities everywhere against the Government. Now we are the majority.' The only solution in Jerusalem between the differing sects was long-term education. Jerusalem would otherwise become 'a mixture between Beirut and Belfast,' a fate which it may still await.

Without too much offence to the Muslim and Christian minorities, one hundred thousand people out of five hundred thousand in the city, Kollek would ring the walls with new apartment buildings and monuments, film institutes and music centres and parks, museums and colleges and convention halls and tourist hotels. Aided by a Jerusalem Foundation, heavily subsidised from Europe and the United States, he modernised Jerusalem while retaining the aura of the ancient religious sites. He respected the Muslim shrines on the Temple Mount, which were restored by their keeper, King Hussein of Jordan, from the proceeds of the sale for more than eight million pounds of his London mansion on Palace Green.

Although Kollek considered the unity of Jerusalem 'an irreversible historic fact', he testified to the resilience and continuity of his people over the millennia. Even if the Holy City were divided again, 'We are like ants building the most beautiful ant hill that was ever created, and we hope it will continue to exist undisturbed. But who knows? Maybe a man with a stick will come along, poke into our masterpiece, and part of it will be destroyed. If so, here we are, like ants. And we will build it again and again as well and as beautifully as we know how.'

Teddy visited the Chelsea home of Sonia and myself in London. So we were aware of what was going on in Jerusalem. Sonia's previous husband had been Julian Mond, later Lord Melchett. Although ennobled because of the explosives industry of the First World War, the first Lord Melchett had become an important backer of the Israel-to-be, with avenues to be named after him in Haifa and an institute by Lake Tiberias. I even wrote a book about Jerusalem, after I had often visited the city. The first time was under Jordanian occupation, with the police officers dressed as blue bobbies in shorts. I recorded it as a Shangri-La of tranquillity. After many other visits to Jerusalem, soon held in Israel's stern hands, I ended by advocating a divided international city, split between the three conflicting religions of the Torah and the Bible and the Koran, rather as Vienna was partitioned after the Second World War between four quarrelsome powers. Let us hope that such an improbable solution will come in time to prevent an Armageddon around that sacred Mount.

Through the assassination of the previous ruler, the young Hussein became the King of Jordan. His situation was grave with the influx of some million Palestinian refugees into his Bedouin realm. Somehow he kept a balance between the incomers and the tribal peoples. There could be no reconciliation with Israel, after the expulsion of so many Arabs from their properties. When I was younger, on my first visit to what had been Palestine, I had a conversation with an embittered teacher. From our perch, he could see his expropriated house and patch of earth.

'I am a dead man already,' he said. 'I have no land. I live in camp. What care I if the whole world dead, if I dead already.'

He was waiting interminably against the day of the next war against Israel, when the Jews would be swept into the sea, and Arab refugees would occupy their restored places. When I asked him what and where more than a million Jews were to go and do, he answered: 'Not we responsible. Go where they come from.' But when I pointed out that many Jews could not now go back where they came from, he only shrugged and fluttered his hands as doves.

In the future, however, the next war would lead to the Israeli occupation of Jerusalem and the West Bank of Jordan. The situation would become well-nigh untenable for King Hussein to keep the peace in the rump of his domain. Yet he still pursued a policy of moderation, only using his Bedouin forces to quash a Palestinian rebellion. And when Sonia and I visited Petra in Jordan, Queen Noor heard of our coming, when we reached there. The dominant colour of the ancient rock city was mullet, but we never expected to find blue and coral, purple and yellow sandstone, making fantastic abstract ceilings and facades in the shapes of waves or wings. The first shock of coming out of the black gorge of the Sig to the definition of the pink Treasury was the lesson of the medieval *Le Roman de la Rose* – the vast cleft was vaginal and Satanic, the pink flower, carved in cliff, the Rose. The centuries had melted the edges of the other rock temples, until they fused in stone. Time makes the scratchings of mankind bearable, for millennia merge them slowly back into nature. Our handiwork erodes into mute traces. Nothing is more moving than the evidence of human striving against its littleness over the ages.

The Royal Family now insisted that we were their guests, although we had made previous private arrangements. On a dicey voyage from Aqaba on the royal launch to view a Crusader castle in Sinai, we were intercepted in the Red Sea by an Israeli gunboat, trying to spot who was aboard. Our captain sent us down to the cabin, before he took off. A flying table-top nearly sliced off Sonia's left leg. The predatory craft was left in our wake, and when we reached Petra, even a lethal cocktail in the Catacomb Bar was not quite enough to do us in. *Sic transit pax in terris.* If the noblest Arab and the noblest Jew had had their way in Jerusalem, I feel that they would have filled the many fissures of the Holy City with the tears and mortar of their wise diplomacy.

As a publisher, George Weidenfeld was a man of infinite guile and international connections. His mind seemed to rival Dr Johnson's, a dictionary of the twentieth century. He described himself as an agnostic, but tribal Jew, rather as I see myself as somewhat of a Highland Scot. His service was for the future of Israel and for the genes in his family. As I do, he preferred loyalty to integrity and the chattering Hampstead classes. The world scene remained a battle between good and evil, the democracies against Hitler and Saddam. No government could yet cope with the Computer Revolution or the Internet, the rise of China and India, or the Armageddon scenario in the Middle East.

In his own remarkable role, however, he hosted private seminars with the Vatican, funded by the Rothschild and Ford Foundations. He aimed for the great reconciliation between Catholicism and Germany with Israel, also Israel with Palestine. Such was the secret diplomacy, striving to save a world with a bleak future, by a man of consummate charm and volubility, memory and imagination. His overt diplomacy was evident at his extraordinary dinner parties. He brought the culture of Central Europe to an insular London society. Under voluptuous Italian paintings and those of Klimt in the hall, the brighter and the better met in adept conversation. If any *spiegelmeister* put together the sense and sensibility of postwar Europe, that man in literature was Weidenfeld. Personally, I was overawed by those I met at these celebrations over forty years, the wealth of knowledge and people there. Sometimes I felt that all the movers and scribblers in the world were shrunk into his drawing-room.

One of his parties seemed the most dramatic to me. We were not looking at a screaming Pope by Francis Bacon, but over the black River Thames towards a new Buddhist pagoda, which George thought rather spoilt the view. A former head of the Jewish Agency entered, Louis Fischer, to tell of the rescue of twelve thousand Falusha from Ethiopia – the black Jews, the lost tribe of Dan and the Queen of Sheba. He praised the Presidents Eisenhower and

Nixon for helping in this salvage. Sixty million dollars had been raised in the United States for the airlifts on the slogan:

SIX THOUSAND DOLLARS TO SAVE A JEWISH LIFE –
ONE HUNDRED AND FORTY LIVES FOR A MILLION.

To cap the occasion with his political wit, George recounted a story about Harold Wilson, who was visited in 1968 by four of the American presidential candidates, seeking support in the forthcoming election. Hubert Humphrey came in with one aide; he burbled on and was generally liked. Nelson Rockefeller strode in with two aides; when questions were asked, he pointed to the one aide or the other, and never said a word. When Teddy Kennedy entered with three aides, he asked fatuous queries or sat down in long silences. Yet Richard Nixon appeared alone with his yellow pad and probed with searching questions to which nobody had the answers. He impressed everybody, whatever his future policies might be.

On a birthday party for George at the National Portrait Gallery, the television guru Robin Day heard me say that I felt uneasy with the great and the good, staring down on me. It was as though we were *passé* already.

'I'm not,' Day said. 'My portrait's already hanging in the next gallery.'

In his white suit, Bernard Levin was going to find out who wasn't there. He would print a list of the unasked, those who had lost out over the last decades. He was soon to lose out with life himself. At his memorial services, two of his greater lines were spoken.

The pen is mightier than the sword – and easier to write with. The future is not what it was – and the past isn't any better either.'

Another remark I heard at the Gallery of the distinguished departed, looking down at George as if they were preparing to greet him, came from the wise journalist, Bryan Appleyard. He was retelling an observation of one American film producer, John Hayman, about another, Elliott Kastner, who was 'a man, who lets failure go to his head.' More a commentary on my life than that of the wonderful Weidenfeld, who enhanced the lives and aided the success of all who met him. On his 88th birthday, indeed, he was honoured in Berlin as an architect of a renaissance of feeling between Germany and England, the Catholic Church and the Jewish community. As the German leader Angela Merkel declared of the ever-talkative and diplomatic publisher: 'George always gives me his advice. And if I don't take it, he gives it to me again.'

In terms of giving advice, Samuel Beckett was supreme. Once, I sat next to Billie Whitelaw at dinner. Her generous expressive lips told me of how she used her mouth under Beckett's own direction. He was incredibly meticulous, as he told her how to play.

'Ah, Billie, on page 4, line 10, please say 'Oh yes', not 'Ah yes' – and on page 22, line 7, it should be 'Ah yes', not 'Oh yes'.'

On one occasion, Beckett exploded.

'No, no, no .. I put 2 dots in that pause … not 3 dots.' (as, indeed, had Céline).

When I acted the part that way, Billie commented, I saw that he was right. And when she was in *Not I* – a monologue with a luminous mouth – the stress was so great that she dislocated a vertebra and still went on stage, strapped up. She explained to me:

'I was too much a coward not to play.'

Oh, the courage of actors! Ah, meticulous authors! And when later in a play in the National Theatre about Bertolt Brecht in Hollywood, Billie appeared in an apron at a dinner party and turned round to reveal a bare bum, I did consider what performers will do to get a good part, or parts, whatever the show, or they show. Or what those will do when trying to write an autobiography, which can only be a *mise-en-scène*, full of trickery and gaps and costume changes.

PAST AND PLAY

From the North bank of the Thames, we could see the sun rise in the morning and the moon at night. I was writing in an octagonal tower room, the sacred shape of the Templars, the Knights of the Grail books I was researching. After being intrigued about my heredity in several visits to the St Clair chapel and castle at Rosslyn, I had become involved in their building. In a series of books on the Arthurian romances and on a medieval Orkney scroll and the broken Border tombstones which I continued to find, I believed that I had discovered many of the Templar secrets and the design of Rosslyn as a Chapel of the Grail in this quest for the thousand years of the genealogy of my family.

The first work, *The Sword and the Grail*, became 'The Book' for the Sinclair clan, now spread in hundreds of thousands from Lothian through Fife to Canada and beyond. They were descended from a Norse freebooter called Rögnvald, who became the ruler of Orkney and the Shetland Isles. After invading France with the fleet of Rollo the marauder, they had adopted the name of St Clair, the Latin for Holy Light and a blessed martyr reputed to cure blindness. Later, the Norman Conquest saw them established in England and Scotland, where they acquired the legendary lands of Rosslyn. Earls there for over seven centuries, they sailed on crusades and became Lord High Admirals of Scotland, dominating the Flanders and North Atlantic trade routes in the 15th century. To paraphrase Hobbes, my research consisted of the right ordering of family names in my affirmations.

The story began with my discovery of a Templar gravestone split into three pieces in Rosslyn chapel, then mildewed and neglected. This proved to be the St Clair cover of the bones of a Templar Master, who had been killed fighting the Moors in Spain, while trying to take the Heart of Bruce for burial in Jerusalem. Over the following twenty years, I came upon more than a hundred Templar tombs, shattered and forgotten after the Reformation. Then I chronicled the family's voyages to Palestine and Greenland and North America with the Zen captains from Venice. The final curiosity lay in the Masonic Lodge in Orkney, the vast Kirkwall Scroll, the uttermost medieval map in the North of Europe, which proved that the Knights Templars left their heritage to the Masons of the world through the Ancient Scottish Rite.

These findings were printed in *The Secret Scroll* and *Rosslyn* and a comprehensive work, *The Discovery of the Grail*. I was much criticized by literary pundits for embarking on such a quest despite their veneration for Arthurian romances and Norse sagas, beloved by my mentor Jorge Luis Borges. I had always written in a factual and epic style, modelled on Homer and Cervantes as well as on Swift and Joyce, but somehow my critics confused me with the ridiculous and grotesque thrillers of Dan Brown and his ilk, the purveyors of cod fantasies such as the *Holy Blood and the Holy Grail*. My Grail was never attainable, and I described only the search for the sacred vessel, as for the wisdom of God. *The Independent* did note: 'Andrew Sinclair guides us through this romantic story that has preoccupied poets, priests and pilgrims from Zeus to Jung to Indiana Jones. This is an absorbing history which transcends the frontiers and creeds of culture and religion.'

Closer to home, I wrote a factual novel of the Sinclairs, *Blood & Kin*. As Rudyard Kipling celebrated, the Scots had been the soldiers and the engineers and the officials and the servants of the British Empire – my father being the last of several generations. Published at a time when the Scots were feeling more nationalistic, such an inquiry was not always acceptable to the old and forthcoming country. The noted novelist Allan Massie, however, compared the work in *The Times Literary Supplement* to a northern *War and Peace*, and the author to Tolstoy and Proust, the Norse sagas and John Buchan.

When a sequel to my book on wartime culture was requested, I turned a cultural history of the 1960s into something of an autobiography of that decade. *In Love and Anger* chronicled my perceptions, and my mistakes. The problem with looking back in one's own life is that remembrance is spiced. The *petites madeleines* of Proust were hardly the fare in the Co-existence Bagel Shop and City Lights in the San Francisco of the Beat era. One also must avoid self-excuse, although that is hardly my way. I judge myself merely by what I have done. I would rather condemn myself than redeem. This is not masochism, but an effort to straighten the road.

The work dealt with the fall of the revolutionary rainbow into a chic red tinge, as delusionary as Mao's handbook. That was the consequence of an urban culture, passing from a desire to change the world into a *fricassée* of instant celebrities. The menu was now the message. Commitment was being replaced by public relations. If we were not seen, we were has-been. Fluency was more important than integrity, and religion was no longer the opium of the people. The drug itself was the delight of the intellectual.

I tried to praise the older ways of civilisations in two works, *The Need to Give*, about the patrons of the arts through the ages, and *Arts and Cultures*, a retrospect of the Arts Council of Great Britain on its fiftieth anniversary. Over four years, I had the opportunity of meeting most of the great and the good in the funding of our culture, although their fine intentions were often limited by the avarice of governments. Yet the creation of a National Theatre, in which my wife Sonia sat on the board, and a vibrant network of dance and drama and festival, spread over the whole land, was a grand achievement, in contrast to the increasing dumbing down in broadcasting and television and the cinema. Particularly in language and literature. I felt with a few friends that we were standing on the bridge with Horatius, facing a howling mob, determined to muzzle our tongues and blunt our pens.

I had always found more truth in myth than in recent history, which soon passes from memory while folklore abides. And so I had pursued old ruins and legends over the globe. Most of the relics had been destroyed in wars, the self-inflicted folly of the human species. Its palliatives lay in games and play. The masterpiece, *Homo Ludens* by Huizinga, hymned the luxury and pageants of the late courts of the Grand Duchy of Burgundy, itself vanished through war and the lust of other monarchs.

And I found that the wonder and play of small children also induce healing and lasting love. Depending on how she thought we should be behaving, my mother would forever be threatening to change her will or her bequest of pieces of furniture to my brother and me. And depending on who was visiting her, she would shift around the framed photographs of her family from prominence to full back position. But her tiny grandchild Merlin seduced her back to hugging and kissing and fondling and forgiving all of the supposed sins of my sins. She even accepted my young Timon at last and left him a side-table, despite the question of who his father really was. And so, in her last decade, we all loved one another. Or we tried to do so, and believed it.

LIFE LINES

⎯⎯◦∞◦⎯⎯

Other than herself, the amazing grace of Sonia was the gift of her family. Over thirty years, I would watch her mould two generations of children and grandchildren, of nephews and nieces and their progeny, into a honeycomb.

In Norfolk, at Courtyard Farm of a thousand acres, which had gone on her first husband's death to her son Peter, I would be fortunate to sit at *the* supreme family dinner party I had ever known in all my eighty years. This was no Dylan Thomas Christmas do with fat drunken uncles and snoring dogs, but an occasion of teasing and fun and merriment and intimacy. From my natural solitude, I had been plucked at long last by the velvet whip and subtle diplomacy of Sonia, this mother of all mothers. Her everlasting beauty and her example had pressed vegetarians and stag-hunters, atheists and believers, small boys and a retiring pilgrim, into a sweet pot of mutual love and trust and humour. In this fresh version of the play, *The Man Who Came to Dinner,* I could no longer act my usual curmudgeonly role of the Angry Old Boy. I was overwhelmed by the closeness of the family I had never had, and had missed all my life – and now was mine.

A long while ago, a friend of mine, Joe Ryan, was given a tour of the morgue at *The Times*. He was asked whether he would care to see the obituary of anyone he knew. He chose mine. When he next came round, he spoke of what he had done.

'So what was your verdict, Joe?'

'Better die now,' he commented. 'It'll never get any better.'

He would have been right, except I met Sonia and have had thirty years of engagement with periods of delight. I was not tempted to follow the example of a lady novelist I knew, who used her newspaper friends to review her obsequies and her age in both *The Times* and *The Telegraph*. While I am all for those who compose their own Memorial Service before they pass over, I don't approve of those who diddle and fiddle with their requiem. One's life needs to be dusted off by other hands – or even polished; with luck I bless the time in my overdue existence to pen these topsy-turvy memoirs, which may amuse, or maybe not.

At my advanced age, I was shocked into more survival by a fond menace from Sonia:

'Don't you dare to die before me.'

I was quite frightened back to life. So we do go on a bit, because of love. My devils were turned into phantasmagoria. My eighty years had also taught me how impossible it was to describe them. Except for the admirable Thucydides, all historical writing was a form of autobiography, at least a revelation of the current prejudices, which informed the writer. I had been trying to express this thinking by interweaving social history with my existence. Occasionally and often unwillingly, we do find ourselves briefly a part of what has gone by. At the end of many thousands of days, what was the result of my incoherent performance?

Growing older, because I could not avoid it. Feeling more, which was equally inevitable. Becoming the grit of the past in William Blake's terms, when he claimed that eternity was in a grain of sand – and so suggested that the doings of each of us might contribute to some moments, which might endure in the smallest of ways. Taking some responsibility, because of the needs of the few I loved. And above all, surviving the cruel disillusions of middle age to pan into a golden sunset and a surmise that if most actions were useless, some printed words and graven images might cause quite a few people to consider and to make a difference.

We can only be a shallow trickle into the ocean of history, but we are accountable to it. Few of us wish to be. But when history impinges on us – a threatened invasion of our land, the moral choice of betraying a country or a friend – we cannot avoid what to do. We have coasted through the past most of our lives, but sometimes we have been in the rapids. We discuss our times, but then we are plunged into them. Social history is a million million biographies of different lives, from which we make a small selection. What happened to each one of us individually may have affected some or many of us. In the little may lie the larger.

Burials, though, may be a good business for the grave-digger, but also for the filcher. When my stepmother Phyllis died, she appointed me as her executor. Viewing what happened after her passing, I felt more like her executioner. When I reached her final bed in a care home, I found a tweed-clad lady rifling the chest of drawers.

'What are you doing here?' I said. 'Stealing?'

Before scuttling off empty-handed, she said:

'She left it to me before she died.'

Indeed, dying leads to looting. The carrion seekers fly in. A relation of mine and magistrate was known as the vulture of the shires. Pretending compassion, he would swoop down on the expiring wealthy. Removing a select object or two for his stately home before the last gasp, he would aver: 'Well, she left it to me.' And who could possibly say him nay?

Twice in India, I had seen what vultures are designed to do. Once in a car, I had passed a carpet of wings heaving as surf – the feral birds were beaking a rotting holy cow. Then when playing on the Parsee golf course in Mumbai, the sole green meadow of grass in the whole reeking city, I hooked my drive high into an open round tower, which turned out to be a funeral ghat. The corpses there and my ball would be carried off to an afterlife by the sacred scavengers.

Such is the crime of some of those in modern medicine, who rival the vultures and the body-snatchers in their quest for research and the removal of human bits and pieces. And what is the point of prolonging the lives of men who have deliberately done in their livers and lights like drunken footballers, and who can pay for the gut and kidney operation and don't deserve it? None of this should happen without the consent of the victim and the family. But that is the sorry state of modern medicine, short of organ donors, and the crematoria, which reduce the evidence of cutting up corpses to ash in an urn. A funeral is worthy of Asian and Greek myth and faith. Look again at King Priam of Troy, begging Achilles to return the ravaged Hector for a proper funeral. Otherwise, the vulture which pecked daily at the guts of Prometheus, still torments me in the memory of the passing of my mother, for I could not lay her properly to rest.

An assumption has been made by human beings that they should live as long as possible at the expense of all other species and even the planet. Why? What happened to the old idea of 'a natural span'? We lived out our life, as we were born into it. Only recently, with the improvement in medicine and diet in advanced countries, have 'the natural span' and 'life expectancy' more than doubled. They are now seen as 'rights', and so people demand that their societies keep them going for as long as humanly or inhumanly possible.

But why? Actually, as in *Sinbad the Sailor*, an old person now sits on a young man's back, burdening him with the weight of debt. The ageing are slowly killing off the working and the living. As in *The Merchant of Venice*, a dowager is long withering out a young man's revenue. But it is worse than that. In a ravaged and exploited terrain and ocean, and under a fouled atmosphere, the young and the poor must toil to prolong the existences and pensions of the old and the privileged.

Such conditions cannot hold: they will burst. Rather than Herod massacring the Innocents, we shall have a mass children's crusade against their bloated forefathers, who will not pass on. For what is 'a natural span'? Probably, what your organs will give you. Yet now British doctors are proposing that they may take away, to transplant into the just-alive, the organs of the nearly-dead, if not expressly denied this undue dissection.

Most societies for thousands of years have insisted that bodies are buried in one piece. The ceremonies around the washed and dressed corpse, and its consignment to a resting-place, eventually to make the ground fertile, are a celebration of the complicity of the living and the dead. To break such sacred links is a sad suggestion. For remembrance with dignity is for the human spirit more worthwhile than ten thousand scalpels, used with impunity and impiety.

For those, who want to die when they sense that their time has come, and for those, who desire to be carried out according to the procedures of their ancestors, no intrusion should be allowed on their private faith. Not all of us wish to live too long or to be condemned to unrest on earth without peace. As each life, so each death is the private business of each of us. Let the state or the surgeon never seek to remove that final choice. It is one's own, the legacy of tradition and the family. Dying particularly deserves respect.

In my own case, I kissed the cold cheek of my father on his bier, and I signed his death certificate before he was cremated. This was the same for my stepmother and my only aunt, an identification before the final fire. Yet when my mother died at the age of eighty-seven, the local hospital removed her and refused to let me see her. I was too shocked to protest, although I said that I had to identify her and sign her death certificate. What had been done with her? In what state was she kept until I failed to see her in her closed coffin at the crematorium? At her age, her organs would have been useless. Later, the Bath hospitals garnered a bad reputation in the mortuary treatment of the dead. Whatever happened to her body was heartless, a show of that impersonality which modern medicine had dropped as a screen between the patient and the family, rather as the Manichees believed in the veil between an evil earth and a caring heaven. Later, I scattered my mother's ashes over a sea garden in Devon, and I found with her a seed of peace as the sustainer of samphire.

What we are in danger of losing is our sense of place and heritage, which depended on living near the tombs of our ancestors. Indeed, all our epic literature through Homer and Virgil and Dante has spoken of the necessity of the proper burial of the dead, without which no afterlife in the Elysian Fields or Hades, in the Inferno or Paradise, was possible. The ritual mourning of all societies was a necessary relief from grief and a release into the hope of resurrection. Even now, nothing can describe the anguish of Argentinian mothers, whose lost children were among the *desaparacidos* of the time of the rule of the Generals. Where are their bodies now?

Advances in medicine have largely killed off caring in the home. In the modern age of hygiene, the smells and stenches from the sick and the terminal cases have become too nauseous for most families to stomach. Outside Greece and Southern Italy, in Western Europe the ancient and the incontinent are usually shifted from their beds to 'old people's homes', where they are bereft of their younger beloved, who are waiting for their inheritance. The stricken end in hospital wards and single rooms. They are among strangers or stranded alone. They are stuck with intravenous tubes, they are pricked by syringes, they are doctored by alien bureaucrats. There is nothing they know in their wandering elsewhere, if anywhere else exists. The nurses are not their daughters, the orderlies are no sons. The dying have little dignity and less hope in any future. The suffering are abandoned to the drug and the clipsheet, to the forsaken here and now, without much hope of a hereafter.

In his seminal work, *The Hour of Our Death*, Philippe Ariès wrote about the invisible death, which has appeared in the modern world. 'Society no longer observes a pause; the disappearance of an individual no longer affects its continuity. Everything in town goes on as if no-body died anymore.' Where are the funeral processions of yester-year? If the black hearses now coast along the highway, they are honked on horns because they delay the traffic. Few are allowed to die at home any more in doubt and pain and odours as in Tolstoy's 'Ivan Illyich', passing away among his close companions. Instead, they shout as Father de Dainville did in 1973, abandoned in a unit called intensive care, with little caring in it: 'They are cheating me out of my own death.' As Ariès noted: 'The time of death can be lengthened to suit the doctor. The doctor cannot eliminate death, but he can control its duration, from the few hours it once was, to several days, weeks, months, or even years. It has become possible to delay the fatal moment; the measures taken to soothe pain have the secondary effect of prolonging life.'

The doctor has now claimed that the control of death is a mission. Yet he is a mere lip-servant of society. Before him, the priest spoke up for a fair or a good term of survival, which may well have been ordained. The pretence of hospitals is to tell people that they are not going to die yet. They are not informed that they should pre-pare to meet their Maker – a phrase used by one of my doctors, when an elderly patient would not swallow her prescription. Unas-sisted or sudden death remains the horror of our times, because it does not have the benefit of medication and of cosmetic funeral parlours. The unexpected loss of life has become the stuff of sus-pense movies, the shock of *Psycho* rather than the placebo of eternal quiet.

Yet there is no refuge from dying. It is inevitable and implacable. It has no cloaks or shrouds. To rend the veil between the naked and the dead requires a messenger. This is the good news of the history of all societies upon earth, and we should not ignore that inspira-tion. For life is no more a virtue than death is a blessing. Once born, we must accept both existence and the end of it with the hope of more to come.

Personally, I have had a variant of the after-life experience on earth, which led me to survive into light from the Channel Tunnel. A terrible tempest at Christmas blew down a quarter of the forests of France, also the slate roof off my farmhouse in Normandy. In a howling blizzard and a gale, I rescued what tossed goods and fur-niture I could, before returning on a Eurotunnel train beneath the sea. Halfway across and submerged, a fire was announced. Everybody was evacuated to the front two rail compartments, where my vehicle was. When we emerged into the murk of Kent, the cars in the leading carriage were allowed to drive away. I never looked back. That is the lesson of all those who have been briefly in a tube to the Inferno.

Culture and social ritual have been the messengers between heaven and this world, even if Christ and the angels appear to many as mere symbols. The gone are always being seen again in art as souls, images, voices, masks, heroes, ancestors, founders and family. As long as we continue to care for the dead, their existence in this world for now and the hereafter will persist. Religion and marriage and burial, as the Italian philosopher Giambattista Vico stated, will continue to promise an unearthly life to come. *The Dominion of the Dead* by Robert Pogue Harrison is worthy in its elegant concerns to rank beside the *Essays of Montaigne*. In treating of the afterlife, the heroes of Harrison are Vico and Martin Heidegger, two philosophers in a rare linking. Vico is praised for believing that through our dying since ancestral times, the dead return or proceed to some realm whence we and the unborn draw life. Heidegger appeals for his emphasis on the bequest of any life to the future, the handing on and repeating and enhancing of a personal history for the good of those to come. Legacies from the past run ahead of us. *Being and Time* states that 'man dies constantly until the moment of his decease,' while the short piece, *The Thing*, declares: 'Only man dies. The animal perishes. It has death neither ahead of itself nor behind it.'

Harrison goes further than Edmund Burke's claim of the great chain of the living and the dead by relating the living to the earth, where the dead lie. The departed were the first to have a dwelling in a cave or a cairn, while most cities were constructed around the tombs of heroes or saints, and they were surrounded by necropolei. The Romans particularly built their villas about the worship of their ancestral spirits, the *lares* and the *manes*, while there were also household gods, the *penates*. Our culture derived from the dead and we pass it on to the future. Like it or not, we perform the will of our ancestors. We live in their old homes and walk their streets, and in a sense, they are the neighbours who have merely passed by another way.

Over the last fifty years, the love of a few true and other women and particularly children has saved me from pursuing a solitary career in too many directions simultaneously. I was lucky in writing some good books and making one good film, but I was the world's worst businessman and failed at academia and publishing. I never found making money very interesting. I had, however done a few things and met a few people, the excuse for telling these stories.

Who am I? Or rather, who I am. I never agreed with my Proustian friends, who thought we were defined by the opinions of society. I had no truck with the Freudians with their motivations and complexes. I remained stuck on Camus, Existentialism and a doubting Gnostic faith. By their deeds, ye shall know them. If you watch your own behaviour, you will see who you are. I used to shock those who loved me by saying, 'A man is the measure of his enemies.' By observing how they behaved, I did the opposite. When they were mean, I was generous. When they defrauded me, I told them kindly what I thought of them over a lavish lunch. As I well know, we are all frail and prone to error and need a speck of forgiveness. So if I did not judge others, why judge me? I always treated my many foes with tolerance and smiles, knowing that they would change their minds the very day that they needed me again. Success leads to redress.

Mercy is a terrible swift sword. It leaves conscience as a dirk in the vitals of the aggressors and increases the sting of their envy of any magnanimity. Yes, the bad behaviour of those set against us induces better behaviour by ourselves. Our defence is our merit, their attack is their *hari-kari*. I have tried to define myself by what I have done and how I have behaved in this world. Within this frail wicker armour, I abide. My inner demons, pride and wrath and recklessness, are mainly my lapdogs now, given thirty marvellous years of an unexpected and extended family life. At least, three generations of some people respect me, even if they may not all love me. Out of the enduring, with good fortune, may come forth sweetness. We are what we have done and will do.

I am short on a trio of the seven sins. Sloth, envy and jealousy are not my bag. I have always worked hard at trying to be original. I shout with Cocteau – There can be no School of Art or Anyone. However derivative they are, other academics or authors or filmmakers do things their own way, each to his last. Otherwise, they are in the dock for plagiarism. Whether they make too much money with indifferent offerings or manipulate fond criticism from their cabals, is no concern of mine.

Four creators of genius made me their friend and follower – Bacon and Golding, Hughes and Pinter, all gone before, but timeless in their work. They suggested that the personal lives of artists were more important than public affairs because the future would salvage their works and not those of the rulers and the statesmen, who were held to be significant. What was admirable in that disparate quartet was their fierce retirement from cliques of opinion, their private opinion in defiance of current trend, the incandescence of their inner vision which they imposed upon millions of readers as seers with an insight into the human condition. These were the very few in our time who stated: I AM AN ARTIST. THIS IS WHAT I THINK AND SEE. I DO, THEREFORE WE ARE. Even if we do not know who we are, we will be judged by what we have done.

Afterdeath and *If*

Nearing my end, I wrote a book on *Afterdeath*. Shown to Harold Bloom, the Professor Emeritus of Literature at Yale and author of *The Western Canon*, he replied:

> Your book I find both sublime and ultimately a survivor. You know annihilation waits, and that our desire for the transcendental and extraordinary is like our love for Hamlet, who does not love us. Gnosis abides, because there is a *spark* in the Ruck.

After praising my 'superbly baroque prose', Bloom told me of coming back from being 'one of the undead' after losing another seven pints of blood and suffering triple open-heart by-pass surgery. He declared that Valentinus was right. '*First* we resurrect and *then* we die.' I was reminded of the man who declared to Voltaire that he worked too hard and drank too much coffee and was killing himself, only to hear Voltaire say, 'I was born killed.'

In my own case, I only passed through the lighted cave on two occasions, when I was examined within a bright mechanical coffin to see if my prostate cancer had spread to my lymph glands. Beethoven's *Pastoral Symphony* was played through my earphones to mitigate the hellish thunder and howling of this purgatory of the radiological process, which reminded me of the euthanasia of Edward G. Robinson before he was converted into edible pellets in the film of *Soylent Green*. My operation consisted of a photographic intrusion into my arse rather worse than a gang rape in Sing-Sing, although I had resisted sodomy all my life long. This assault was followed by another invasion of my rear end, this time soothed by an anaesthesia taken from the waters of Lethe. I awoke to be shown an internal map of a galaxy, the picture of ninety pellets of radium which had been pumped by thirty hollow needles into my prostate to kill the cancers before they slowly killed me. I staggered away, an atomic man for a year, who did not quite believe that these fiery particles represented the vital sparks within me, trying to heal and then escape my pained flesh.

I had always been interested in the hereafter. During the Second World War, at the age of eight at my School in Oxford, I had fallen under the spell of a mystic poem in *The Dragon Book of Verse*. The psalmist of the British Empire, Rudyard Kipling, had written a Song to Mithras, which he also called 'A Hymn of the 30th Legion', posted in the 4th century on Hadrian's Wall. The verses testified to a divine warrior cult, which worshipped the fertility of the bull and the celestial voyage to the sun:

Mithras, God of the Sunset, low on the Western main,
Thou descending immortal, immortal to rise again!
Now when the watch is ended, now when the wine is drawn,
Mithras, also a soldier, keep us pure till the dawn!

Mithras, God of the Midnight, here where the great bull dies,
Look on thy children in darkness. Oh take our sacrifice!
Many roads Thou hast fashioned, all of them lead to the Light,
Mithras, also a soldier, teach us to die aright!

Later, archaeology would confirm the inspiration of Kipling. As the early Christians, the followers of Mithras were organized in cells. Their widespread chapels in the Roman Empire were often built underground or in caves with the signs of the zodiac set on mosaic floors. Part of the service was a communion with a consecrated cup and a loaf, symbols of the holy supper which Mithras had taken with the sun after his time on earth. The Christians claimed that the followers of Mithras had stolen their Eucharist, although the reverse might have been true. The pagans also believed in the survival of the divine essence in humanity, and in rewards and punishments in an afterlife. Mithras would descend on the warring world as Christ at the Last Judgement. Then he would awaken the dead, separate the virtuous from the sinners and rule over a heaven on earth.

The Mithraic celestial journey was Gnostic, for the individual could directly reach the divine intelligence without a state church. In the mosaic ceiling decoration of the small tomb of the Iulii in the Vatican cemetery, I once saw a Christ or Helios or Mithras shown in his sun-chariot among a design of vines on a radiant gold background. In Roman funeral art, many gods were invoked in a hope for an afterlife in some pleasant paradise. Dionysos and Herakles were particularly popular on tombstones as demi-god conductors to another existence, while scenes of Tritons and Nereids conducting a ship of souls through the sea demonstrated a desire to reach the Elysian Fields or the Islands of the Blessed.

The Druids were the priestly caste of the Celts. To Julius Caesar and early Roman historians, they appeared as barbarians, who used the entrails of their human enemies as pointers to the future and even burned their captives in an immense wicker man. The grave goods and slaves cremated with their chiefs merely showed a belief in a hereafter very much the same as existence in this world. Caesar noted how splendid were the Gallic funerals, in which everything the dead man was supposed to have loved was destroyed. As in ancient Greece, chariot burials were also part of these primitive concepts of a life beyond the grave.

Later classical historians from the school of Alexandria used Posidonius to elevate the Druids into followers of Plato and Pythagoras with a faith in the immortality of souls. Dio Chrysostom even considered the Druids as superior in ancient wisdom to the priests of Egypt and the Magi of Persia and the Brahmins of India. They were seen as philosophers and prophets and bards, the peace-makers among the warring warrior chieftains. Although they had no literature, their learning had been passed on through memory and verse, as were Homer's works, but in forest clearings and wooden and stone temples. For Strabo, the Druids held that 'men's souls and the universe are indestructible, although at times fire and water may prevail.'

With Jung, I believe that our ancestral instincts and myths are inherited. For instance, I never knew that my lifelong passion for seeing old stones would mean that I was looking for a hereafter. In a sense, our living is a pilgrimage. We seek for an answer to dying. Even those who think we are utterly extinguished along with our corpse try to leave something behind them – a family, a memory, a work, often a tomb.

Ranging world-wide over forty years, I had often stared at the carved rocks of the stone dead. I had never thought why the peoples of history had left these memorials until I came to Filitosa in Corsica.

I had not popped the lethal question to my own dull mind. Why did we ever scrape on granite with a flint to honour the departed? Why did we bury our dead in sarcophagi? How could a marble tomb be a passage to immortality? The body had to perish. No monument could endure. Herostratus became famous for burning down the Temple of Diana in Ephesos, while the original great Mausoleum at Halicarnassus was plundered for the British Museum. Stones and statues might abide in ruins, but corpses hardly did, even as mummies.

So why did we inter our dead in stone? Looking at the smooth and scoured rocks at Filitosa, I remembered that we were cave-dwellers. Our ancestors had lived in the rock. They had buried the bones of their families in the back of these recesses to protect the remains from the live beasts, the bear and the mammoth, which they were hunting. With this insight, I could review all my long travels. They might be a series of searches for the mystery of a life after death, if there was one.

Studying the ancient classics at Eton College informed the rest of my life. In Plato's *The Republic*, Socrates had invited his pupil Glaucon to imagine 'an underground cave-dwelling, with a long entrance leading to the light.' In the cave were prisoners in irons, who saw the shadows cast by a fire and the things other prisoners carried across the mouth of the cave. They thought this appearance was the real world. This was false for the free philosopher, who could approach the source of the creative light, and who would know of the phantoms which represented life on earth. The voyages of the soul were traverses into the cavern. The way into the dark was a ticket to the realm of the spirits. As Jung declared, 'There is no trouble about time in the unconscious. Part of our psyche is not in time and not in space.' So the Gnostics would speak of a veil between heaven and earth, which could only be rent by Christ and the angels, who were the messengers. Otherwise, on hands and knees, we had to make the hard passages for ourselves in our journeys.

Crawling up the narrows to the burial chamber of Cheops in the Great Pyramid in Egypt was almost as painful as a baby struggling out of the womb, though I hardly remembered that labour. Never had my young thighs become such tangled knots of pain. Sweat started from my body in a Nile flood. Later I learned that the royal funeral barge of the Pharaoh had docked at the stone Gates of

Heaven at the river end of the Causeway of the Giants leading to the royal tomb. There was also a shaft from the resting place of the Pharaoh through the stepped stones. This allowed his spirit to escape to the Transpolar Stars. Such was my first vision of the entrances to other existences.

Surrounded by jets of burning gas from oil refineries, Eleusis was an abscess on the highway between Athens and Corinth. For the classical world, it was the ultimate place of ritual of the passage to the afterlife. Each year, thousands of initiates were led through nine days of the cycle of birth and death and regeneration. 'When a man dies,' Plutarch wrote, 'he is as those who undergo the Mysteries. All our lives are journeys by twisting paths with no ways out. The moment we end, we are overcome with terror and shuddering and wonder. Then a light welcomes us and pure meadows, songs and dances and sacred appearances.'

This afterdeath experience was enacted annually at Eleusis, based on the myth of the earth goddess Demeter going down to the lower world to rescue her daughter Persephone from its ruler Pluto. Symbolizing the seasonal rotation of crops, Persephone could remain on earth from spring to autumn, only to return to her husband and Hades in winter, because she had tasted the seeds of the pomegranate, the food of the dead. For twelve hundred years, this celebration of the traverse from the underground to the sunlight illuminated those who were anxious about an afterlife, if there was one. For had not the poet Callimachus reported a conversation with the dead Charidas?

> QUESTION: Charidas, what is below?
> ANSWER: Great darkness.
> QUESTION: What about resurrection?
> ANSWER: A lie.
> QUESTION: And the God of the Dead?
> ANSWER: A myth. We perish utterly.

The fragments of huge pillars and broken blue mosaics at Eleusis led me towards underground chambers and a circular well of rebirth. The ruins faced the sunrise below an old tower crowning the hill. The vast statue of Demeter or Ceres, the earth mother, had been plundered by British scholars, who had bribed the Turkish governor to haul away the carved stone to the Fitzwilliam Museum at Cambridge, where it was still presiding when I was learning a little at that university.

Another voyage to the underworld was the one which inspired Virgil. By the Appian Way south of Rome, the oracle of Nemi and the ancient Temple of Diana near the hilltop village overlooked a lake in a cradle of lava. Only an overgrown arched wall now fronted some hollows in the rock, although in the small museum there, stone anchors recalled the ferry to the underworld, as those at Delos and Delphi, Crete and Malta, where there were also carvings of the voyage of spirits over the waters. This was the site of Sir James Frazer's pioneering work in anthropology, which he called *The Golden Bough*, the branch which Virgil plucked to see him through his journey across Lake Avernus that still fills the crater of an extinct volcano.

The Latin poet's guide was the Sibyl of Cumae. When I reached there, a tunnel more than a thousand yards long took me from the black lake to her cave. Outside, the green valleys and marshes by Lake Miseno were still held to be the Elysian Fields and the Stygian swamps. The burrow to the Sibyl's cave was a mighty vaulted hewn entrance with clefts and rooms carved into its sides. The echoes of the heels of my boots sounded as the drumbeats of a knell. Yet in the vacuum of the final chamber, there was no oracle now to give me a pass to Charon's boat, which might take me to the far side of human experience.

These were my original quests on my feet. Then I began to read more of epic voyages to the underworld. In ancient civilizations, there were three ways to depart for the spirits of the dead. They might go by sea or in a cave or a grave. River and delta and island people took to the waves and the far ocean which lapped the limits of the world. Mountain people sought the entrance to Hades in watery recesses, where an underground ferryman carried them to their terminal unrest. Forest and steppe people trusted to fire or passages from tombs or urns to transport their ancestors in ashes or decay to the beyond. Our everlasting quest for the afterlife was given a geography in the epics which have shaped all of our literature. They were the guidebooks for our souls in passing.

Because of the tragedies of the house of Atreus, I could not approach the nine burial chambers at Mycenae without fear and trembling. The doorway to the great tomb was seventeen feet high with a stone lintel weighing more than a hundred tons. The vast Cyclopean walls of the citadel overlooked a golden plain streaked with grey-green olive trees running down towards Troy to the east, but a bleak limestone hillside blocked the south and the sun from my view. Beehive and shaft graves from about 1350 BC had yielded golden masks and inlaid bronze swords and armour and shaped shields of pre-Homeric hero kings, also clay models of ships and chariots as carriers to the afterlife. But the Mycenaeans were long departed before the woes of Agamemnon began. Perhaps their way to the underworld was the covered stairway to an underground spring within the stronghold. In the inscrutability of history, only the plays of the supreme Greek tragedians have remained to commemorate the ancient royal house. As Euripides asked:

> Who knows whether to live is but to die,
> And to die is to live?

Yet other carriers to the afterlife were being interred in the courtyard tombs of Salamis in Crete. These horses and chariots of the sun supplemented the ivory and terracotta boats excavated at Knossos in the palace. The largest of the Cretan tombs of the seventh century BC had two chariots and six horses sacrificed before its stone temple door. Inside the war vehicles were iron-tipped arrows, a quiver and a shield and a sword. They suggested the need for another battle to reach the hereafter. Other carvings or monuments or vase paintings within the ancient Greek sphere of influence showed the connection between boat and water, chariot and sun. The Episkopi sarcophagus depicted a funeral chariot gliding over waves as if a boat. At Kalochorafiti in the Messara, a memorial displayed a ship with fish below, while above a horse-drawn chariot was descending, lit by sun-discs and rays. Such symbols would be paralleled by Nordic rock carvings as at Trundholm in Denmark, where I saw a Bronze Age sun drawn by horses inscribed on a stone sky.

Those who wished for vainglory had large monuments built for their remains. About 350 BC in Asia Minor, the Satrap of Caria, Mausolus, built so huge a memorial with a crowning chariot frieze that he gave the genre his name, Mausoleum. His plundered statue stands in the British Museum, but destruction overtook his funeral structure, although the foundations still survey the harbour of Hali-carnassus or Bodrum. The Military Knights of Rhodes used its blocks and pillars to build a castle, even though it had been described as one of the Seven Wonders of the World.

Alexander the Great besieged Halicarnassos during his advance into Persia, and he devastated the city. But he stopped at Pasargadae by the tomb of Cyrus the Great, which was surrounded by a grove of trees and fruits, flowers and herbs, an earthly paradise which the dead emperor could not expect in the underworld. He had wished for no desecration of his memorial, leaving an inscription:

> O man, I am Cyrus
> Who acquired the Empire for the Persians
> And was King of Asia:
> Do not grudge me, then, my monument.

While shuffling off this mortal coil as Hamlet, I am mindful of these traces of other journeys to that undiscovered country, from which no man returns.

BEING OR SEEING

Of the three great revolutions since the 18th century, the agricultural and the industrial and the digital ones, the last is the most far-reaching. Instant global communication by the stroke of a fingertip is science fiction, now fact, beyond our wildest dream. In the case of the sales of artworks, most of them are now by website, also by bids from afar. The question is how to engage the attention of the quick-browsing young with an attention span of eight seconds, rather less than a goldfish.

Modelled on the supreme pop videos of David Bowie, I made four short films, to tell the surreal stories of my Art Boxes. One was personal, one was about the history of transport from the balloon to outer space, the third dealt with the cinema from Nadar through Buñuel to sci-fi and galactic travel. No more than 6 minutes long, each film consisted of a montage of some 40 entertaining shots, telling a witty story. To engage the fickle viewer, with an attention span less than a goldfish in a bowl, onto YouTube went 'The Magical World of Andrew Sinclair'. The fourth short was about my Film Boxes, which were many glances into the history of the cinema, as well as memories of the movies I had made.

As Rudolf Arnheim noted in his *Film as Art*, 'The art of the moving image is as old as the other arts, it is as old as humanity itself, and the motion picture is but its most recent manifestation.' The Russian director Pudovkin had written, 'The lens of the camera replaces the eye of the observer.' Yet the brain behind the retina selects the scenes in your sightline, while in the cinema, you see the images that the director chose for you to see. The same is true of mental pictures, after reading the work of a great author.

Joseph Conrad observed that, through the power of the written word, he wanted to 'make you hear, to make you feel – it is, before all, to make you see.' And so too, the film-maker for over fifty years, John Ford: 'I believe movies are primarily pictures, so I play them that way. Let the pictures do the talking for you.'

The first universal language was the silent film. The incredible movements of Charlie Chaplin were instantly translated across the world, whether he was making boots or bread rolls dance on forks, or getting magic tricks wrong in a pantomime, or unbalancing on a trapeze in a circus. With the talkies, however, film joined literature. For many of its creators, from Eisenstein to Orson Welles, their influences ranged from Homer and Shakespeare to James Joyce. As if in the theatre, their art was to make the mind see an acted scene within a frame rather than on a stage set. All were shows of the imagination. To the critic Herbert Read, the film as a work of art ranked with great drama, great literature and great painting.

'What really comes before our mind when we *understand* a word?' So Wittgenstein asked in his primary *Philosophical Investigations*. 'Isn't it something like a picture? Can't it be a picture?' He then mentions the word 'cube', and concludes. 'People in general apply *this* picture like *this* … we have here a *normal* case, and abnormal cases.' As in the word 'cubist', indeed, when applied to paintings, which are distorted cubes. The young Picasso, however, wandering round Paris with Georges Braque before the First World War, was mad about cowboy and Chaplin films. As cubists, they both saw the value of superimposition and montage to alter time and change vision.

If Wittgenstein used 'cube', I'd like to consider a picture in a 'frame'. Whether we understand it or not, the picture is contained in the frame of our understanding and seeing. So we may interpret it ourselves and even remember it for later use. And yet, the 'frame' cannot contain the picture, which may run off the edges, in sight-lines which mutate with the flicker of our vision.

Following the photo-collages of Man Ray, David Hockney's inspiration dated back to the *camera obscura*, used by Renaissance painters for putting proportions and perspective into their art. In 1982, he made up his 'Life Story' from collages and montages of Polaroid snapshots. He had 'no idea of where the edge of this is going to be.' One pair of hands was seen five times, as in a film strip. People were 'looking at the picture … and looking at something like a picture.' These were 'the first pictures which could confuse the viewer.' And though they were still, yet because of the restless eye, they were 'moving pictures'.

That is where film met art. Photo-collages included the watcher within the picture. As Hockney later added, 'It's all about looking, looking, looking.' His Polaroid assembly of the Grand Canyon could not compete with John Ford's movie landscapes and montages of the Arizona desertland, but the composition of many illustrations was often an inspiration to film-makers. The rounded Chatsworth landscapes of Turner resembled the vision of the eyeball, large at the edges, curving into a distant focus. The triptychs of Francis Bacon ran in lines off the sides of the canvas as did those on Japanese porcelain saucers. The space could not contain the design. Bacon even wanted his viewers to be reflected in the thick glass over his paintings, so that they were within the frame as in a room.

Eisenstein noted in 'The Dynamic Square', the sketches by Degas of *modistes* and ballet dancers trapped motion, as if in a cinematic still of a performance. He dwelt on the size of the frame, from square to widescreen, from the vertical to the horizontal. A pioneer culture of discovery, as in the American Western, demanded the spread horizons of prairies and mesas and painted pinnacles, while an industrial revolution looked to the straight upward lines of smokestack and skyscraper.

Even so, cinema was the only art based on dynamic and speed phenomena, and yet *everlasting* as a cathedral or a temple, because it remained always as it was made in time. It existed, free from the creative effort that gave it birth, unlike the theatre or the dance or music, the other dynamic arts, which were subject to new interpretations throughout the ages. Cinema was also a synthetic art, built from the collaboration of a group, comprising the screenwriter and the director, the cameraman and the sound-recordist, the composer of the musical score, the art director and the location manager, and the inspired manoeuvres of the actors. Technique was the basis of film production.

For me, montage and cutting and camera action are as the mounting and hanging of paintings or collages in an exhibition. Eisenstein also found the principles of film composition, the linking of three or four sequences, to be the same as the joining of scenes within an Act in a drama. Indeed, cinemas were originally called theatres, and that is what museums and some pioneer galleries are now presenting in their art shows – brief tasters about the creators.

In the Tate and the Louvre and the Museum of Modern Art, a short trailer explains the life of the artist, be it Rembrandt or Picasso, also why he painted that way at that time. These are the newsreels and biopics of the world of images. They inform and educate the viewers. They make the mind see more intently. The artists may also be discovered and marketed on iPhone and YouTube and website, broadcasting their messages and images to all who want to know across the whole world.

The digital revolution has put an end to pilgrimage. The moving picture is the modern transporter across space and time. Why visit, in choked and controlled crowds, the supreme painting of Genesis in the Sistine Chapel, when the Vatican has recorded its minute details in crystal-bright photography? And the various genres of fantasy cinema, from monsters to vampires, from robots to aliens, have recalled the ancient myths and demons, which once infused our thinking – Cyclops and Grendel, and on to Frankenstein and Dracula and King Kong. From our couches we easily wander the wildernesses of our dreams and nightmares. Now we travel by stroking a small screen, not by trekking through a jungle or surviving on a motorway. Yet the original work of art still seduces us into a far journey. To begin at the beginning, that is the craft of the creator, and may it ever be so.

My craft of odds and ends in frames had begun as a hobby and as gifts to friends and children, the *Wunderschränke* of the original Cabinets of Curiosities. Thirty years later, these little Boxes were considered as works of art. After all, had not the young Michelangelo been rated only as a mason? I write this, not in comparison, but to point out the ridicule and irrelevance of much art criticism. For me, the makers are their own better commentators, and only Dr Johnson and John Ruskin have excelled as critics, because they defined our language as well as our insights. Those who can, write; those who can't, are critics: few combine.

Hazard plays a large role in our destiny. Genetic luck forms our intelligence, geography gives us a place and an opportunity, while any success depends on being born at the right time. Nothing is further from achievement than to show promise in the wrong environment. My later craft coincided with a cultural trend in galleries and museums, responding to the digital revolution in perception.

Many artworks had to be recorded on film, because they were perishable or invisible. The fat and the fur of Joseph Beuys, the pickled shark and live flies and rotten meat of Damien Hirst, this ordure would not last. Without a camera eye, what remained of Performance or Conceptual Art, which misled the vision in displays in museums? The media had become the message, because it could fix the passing scenes forever.

My forthcoming book on our mind and insight, *Being or Seeing: From Homer to Hollywood*, is a study linking most of the forms of culture and thought. It deals with philosophy from Plato to Wittgenstein; with mythology and literature from Homer to Borges; with painting from the cavemen to modern abstract artists; with optical illusions through the origins of cinema to the digital age; with psychiatry and neurobiology and how to take in images. *To be is to perceive*, and these pages explain how we have to review what we do to be what we are. The most important factor is that authors and artists, film directors and cameramen, talk directly to the readers, who are their own critics. In their academy, they learn their craft and make up their ideas about seeing the past on their own.

We talk of framing a thought, putting it into context, licking it into shape, drawing a line under it. These are the metaphors of the arts, which we use to describe the processes of the mind. And with our eyes shut, we view in our dreams the moving pictures of our hidden selves. The interpretation of what we see derives from the culture of our countries. Imprinted on our insight is what we were taught about where we live. Tradition is the arbiter of our vision, even in our rebellion. Usually, I am retroactive or prophetic in what I do. I fail nine times out of ten, and I can only try to emulate Samuel Beckett, who hoped his next failure would be better than his last one. But miraculously, I seize the day, and the apple may fall gravely from the tree.

This autobiography is as that of Mark Twain, who wrote: 'This Autobiography of mine is a mirror, and I am looking at myself in it all the time. Incidentally I notice the people that pass along at my back – I get glimpses of them in the mirror…' His life was a passing show, seen as if on an identity parade.

THE DYING WORD

Rage, rage, against the dying of the light. All authors should rage now. In this complaint, I must join the French critics in distinguishing the *auteurs* of personal and original films from other studio directors, who make vehicles for public consumption. An author to me is somebody who submits a manuscript to a good publisher, who agrees to publish it in the refined form the author intended. Many a writer, however, has become somebody who accepts a large advance not to write a desired book. There may be a contract to develop a commercial outline into a popular product, and then to sell it through the writer's celebrity or personality or human interest story, if there is any interest, that is.

The draft, which reaches the publisher, is not in its final form or always by the writer's hand. Whether ghosted or dictated or tapped incoherently onto a laptop computer, this wraith of a book is then 'Englished', an immortal term from Bob Gottlieb, that doyen of American editors. When Random House refused to 'English' the recent work of Joan Collins and demanded the return of her advance, the dispute reached a court of law. Both sides should have been judged for failing to carry out the due process of literature.

The great editors and champions of their authors are dead or out of a job. Charles Monteith has gone from Faber & Faber. When my first Bumbo novel was accepted by him, he never tried to alter the curious style of his undergraduate author. He suggested that I cut the first chapter to reach the meat sooner, and that I deleted the rape of the hero on the regimental flag. When I protested that the scandal had taken place, he replied that fiction was stranger than truth. I would not be believed. The telling of that incident would destroy the credibility of the whole book. My inexperience gave way to his wisdom. The novel was published successfully in his suggested form.

There were some editors almost of his class, who survived, unlike Tony Godwin, in the smaller English publishing houses and the university presses. But then came the invasions of the body snatchers, the conglomerates who gobbled them up. In my fifty years as an author, these Hengist and Horsa raids have occurred three times, but the third has been far the worst for authors and serious publishing.

The process of assimilation was always the same. Small and middling publishers promoted respectable authors, who occasionally sold very well. They were ingested by international conglomerates representing the new media. These pursued the alloy of all the elements, by which the same firm owned the book that made the merchandise that made the television and cable series that made the electronic discs, which could be spun off until the end of the laws of copyright, now extended to seventy years beyond the death of the author.

Accountants always took over these flabby corporations, which could only swallow and never digest. The publishers could not talk to the film people, who could not convince the tape wizards, who were the despair of the trivia merchants, who were meaningless to the computer freaks. And trade books rarely made more than five per cent, which was derisory for the bankers and the balance sheet. So stripped of its few assets, usually hallowed nursery stories, the book list was spat out for the next shark. Its authors were ignored, except for their market value.

Their guardians, the grand old editors, had been retired. This sacking was called 'downsizing', presented as a necessity for surviving economically and continuing to pay dividends to directors and shareholders. The wise and the experienced, who fought for their authors, were replaced on half the salary by the young and the fearful, who wanted to keep their jobs at all costs except to themselves. Greater output was demanded from the workforce and the authors, as if the pigs were still running *Animal Farm*. Editors had to see through the presses twice as many books, on which they could spend half the time and care. Many posts were eliminated, so that authors were made to do their own editing, write their jacket copy, buy their own illustrations and ensure adequate publicity, should they wish their books to sell at all.

The collapse of serious mass publishing in the face of international market pressures was accelerated by the growth of the chain bookstores in the United States and Britain. Salesmen now ruled the roost with statistics, culled from ratings on Amazon, which was mainly to replace the chain bookstores. Its brilliant device was overnight delivery and banking the proceeds before it paid its bills. There was also a celebrity culture, in which the famously illiterate, as soccer and pop stars, were assigned ghost writers to fill the best-seller lists with gossip about their notorious and insignificant brief careers. Recently, a younger publisher of two of my more successful books, liked a third one. He was head of his imprint within a con-glomerate. Yet he could not publish this fresh work. As he wrote to me, it was not in his gift.

In whose gift was it, then? My old publishers generally put out the books I wrote, because I was their author. My new publisher did not choose to fight for his taste, or he could not. The truth is now, committees usually select or commission books, and these are dominated by salesmen and accountants. To oppose them is to risk dismissal. The good and the marginal is condemned for the popular and the venal. *Sic transit gloria scripti.*

Technology has contributed to the fatigue as well as the suicide of the author. Since the invention of electronics, the publisher may demand more from the poor scribe. He wishes the work to be pre-sented on a floppy disc, ready for instant printing. It may be flawed, but it looks fine on the page. The presentation is the content, and there is no costly editorial process at all. However literate they are, all authors still need the devoted attention of their publishing house, if the best possible book may be achieved. The radical printer Francis Place used to rewrite the texts of his authors. Balzac and even early Evelyn Waugh relied on their printers to correct their grammar and spelling. Very few word processors will do that, and precious few editors, either.

Not only are the traditional energies of publishing in atrophy, but also the working methods of many authors and writers degenerate the text. Through electronics, the economies of the publishers are made possible by the print-outs of the tappers of keyboards. I hope to illustrate my point further by citing Heine, who stated that sec-ond only in importance to remembering was forgetting. In writing a paragraph of some style, selection is all. Oblivion helps, too. Once extensive research is stored in a computer, the temptation is to spew it onto the pages verbatim. If faulty memory has to serve, at least an induced brevity may become the handmaid of elegance.

The Book is Dead, Long Live the Book. I am no Palinurus look-ing into my unquiet grave in these sad depths of serious publishing.

For after the storm, Italy is in sight. The conglomerates are disgorging their unwanted lists, to which the good editors may return. A few small independent houses and university presses and poetry magazines such as *PN News* still fly the tattered banners of excellence, while others are founded. And Barnes and Boyd and Byatt, to name a few, yet write the works of quality that even the salesmen cannot keep from fame and prosperity.

I had intended to rearrange a sacred epitaph to suit the state of serious publishing: IT LIVETH NOT, BUT IS DEAD. Untrue. IT LINGERS, TO RISE AGAIN. The great Westerner, Larry McMurtry, wrote on the death of the luminous Barbara Epstein, whom I did not know well enough to describe, these words about her editing over many decades in the old and revered manner in the *New York Review of Books*, which still maintains, as Dr Johnson's Dictionary, the best style in our writing:

> My typescripts probably looked like what all typescripts must have looked like when Barbara was a young and sprightly editor about town. Writers were just messier then – not everybody likes neat.

> Probably the deepest conviction that Barbara and I shared – a conviction we at once recognized in one another – was the belief, common in the Fifties, that the highest possible aspiration was to somehow connect with literature, and then to live for it, in it, near it.

> That conviction has lost none of its potency. One big thing Barbara and I had in common was that we belonged to an age before spell check – this, in itself, makes for a kind of bond.

> Barbara Epstein's death means the loss of a great order – an order, needless to say, that we literates have benefited from and cherished these last forty years.

'You are lucky, Andrew,' a relative of mine recently observed. 'Most people are only rediscovered after they are dead.'

Indeed, fame is usually a posthumous thing, if at all. A roll of the dice in the press or the market dictate a contemporary masterpiece, let us say the unmade bed of Tracey Emin, which will be displaced by another grubby earner after a succession of rejections. In my own lack of career, given the swings and hurdygurdys of the publishing circus, I had been a celebrity during my twenties and forties and somewhat in my seventies, then dismissed as beyond bookshelf life. Along with my peers, we were too old, too literate and unable to guarantee minimum sales of ten thousand copies, before the pulpers gobbled up our print. Most authors drown the third time, but I have gulped up for a fourth and final breath.

Copyrights were to save me, not of my own books, but of those I had published during my movie excursions. By the quirk of fortune and a change of law, I found myself holding in private hands, exempt from film studios or national institutes, not only most of the media rights in *Under Milk Wood*, but in the seventy-five classic screenplays I put out during my Lorrimer years. A stubborn and losing game had become a winning play. As in my case, Érik Satie had taught his friend Cocteau 'the perspective of time, and the absurdity of attaching the slightest importance to either praise or insults. Intentionally to seek to give pleasure, or the reverse, seemed to him an incomprehensible attitude. Without hesitation he would take up an untenable position.'

In Europe, literary copyrights lapsed seventy years after the author's death. Such was not true of printed screenplays, which ran on for seventy years after the date of publication. In one instance, I had saved the screen rights of *The Third Man* by having the scenario appear in America, where the British studio had forgotten to renew its claims. Moreover, the United States was to make my two decades of furthering film education most significant. Under pressure from Hollywood and the pop song industry, George W. Bush and Congress extended movie and music rights to 95 years. Suddenly, much of the wealth of the opening decades of the world cinema lay in my hands for the next thirty years in Europe and fifty years in the United States. The fortune should not be mine. I would restore this cornucopia to the Film Institutes and Libraries for mass education, but only keep pension from a lost and lonely, dear and dedicated cause.

Another change in publishing and film-making altered my possibilities. I made the first film biography of Dylan Thomas, *Dylan on Dylan*, using his own words. The digital revolution reduced my film crew from forty on *Under Milk Wood*, to four, and the finishing processes from twenty to three by computer. Anyone could make a cheap movie now, as anyone could have a book printed in a small run for very little. The problem was always distribution, but with the rise of the Internet and payment on line, we might create a thousand Eisensteins or Hemingways, where we had only had one or two. But, of course, the question of true talent would remain.

I had been a professional historian of the United States, a Fellow of Cambridge and Columbia Universities, of Stanford and University College, London. On my way from Harvard to Hollywood, I had never found the right direction, so I used to say in Tinseltown that I was the only Don there not from Corleone. But I had also studied the Classics until I was seventeen years old, and then I had taught Political Philosophy to students from the London School of Economics – *Plato to Mao* in ten easy lessons. So from the example of our first democracy in Ancient Athens, I believed that if we were citizens, we should serve the state and our society, in recompense for our rights. And from Immanuel Kant and the later Existentialists, I thought that we had moral duties, also that we would only be credited for our acts.

I began in satire and I end in irony. He, who remembers, forgets. A single recall deletes the other happenings of the time. As in the film of *Rashomon*, that was not always the case. Another sponge on the slate blackboard, I wipe out what I do not choose to chalk about the past.

In his 'Cock and Harlequin' of 1924, Cocteau stated that everybody in Paris wanted to be an actor or a writer. Those who were artists only heard:

'Why do you do these things?' asks the public.
'Because you would not do them,' answers the creator.

Since the digital revolution and the coming of the smart phone, which can take tolerable photographs using something the size of a powder compact, everyone wants to be a film director without any knowledge of how to perform. The results are slapdash and inconsequential, without a dram of cutting and editing. The imposition of hope and ignorance over craft and application. Outside a news flash, there is little chance of paid distribution or even viewing for the amateur, who depends on the superfluous choices of unseen browsers, clicking by happenstance onto his offering.

As for writing biography, let alone an impossible autobiography, such a quest is more than a discovery of another person, for it is also a matter of self-discovery. If the subject of the biography is not too alien or repugnant, the writer goes through a painful process of immersion in another's life, a baptism by research. There is the following process of separation and definition, painful and discriminatory. He or she, the subject, is not I, the author. I am not he or she. Even if I do understand another fairly well, I must not pardon, but explain and judge.

For me, both literary and historical biography are an identification, and a divorce. I try to choose subjects with whom I have sympathy and whose society I have considered. The process begins by an inquiry, whether there are papers and what are the terms of access to them. Biographers may not always have the troubles detailed in *The Aspern Papers*, but they do have the problems of family or state censorship. If and when I am given entry on reasonable terms to material and witnesses, then I plunge. But how now? Perhaps religion was once the opium of the people. But presently, Twitter is the hash of the masses. Where is the handwritten letter, the basis of the records of a life? Those inked words from past good pens are fetching astronomical prices in auctions, because they are still in our sights. Will this be the future of the e-mails of the great? Most improbable, although the graffiti of Banksy are scraped from walls for auction to the credulous.

As a historian and a writer, I can only view our social traditions as the arbiters of our lives, and not the mechanistic gene or the class war or the deterministic apologies of any age. I am also a democrat, who values free choice, however limited that may be. In those terms, evidently the majority of humankind has always opted for a faith, which has offered a life of some kind beyond the dust of death. Some religions make this promise most difficult to keep, particularly the Christian one. The Resurrection of the Body in Jesus does contradict the senses. Even He said, *Noli Me Tangere, Do Not Touch Me*. Another palisade against probability is the Islamic Paradise, with its maidens and its palms and its cool rivers, where we live again in our old forms. Yet such delusions produced the Christian martyrs and the Muslim suicide bombers. These sacrificers of self evidently preferred another world to the one down here. They denied their flesh and reproductive future. And if their brains were washed, they acted with their feet. By their deeds, we do know them.

Given the balance of time, religion has been the muzzle of ambition, the brake of brutality, the curb of cupidity, the rein of pride, the halter of tyranny. If its message has often been a compromise with oppression, an offering of a better hereafter set against a poor present, that salve was necessary for multitudes, in order to bind up their wounds in a rotten social system. They were enabled to limp ahead. If throughout the ages, Faith had not always been the nurse of human suffering and endeavour, then it would have died out with its billions of victims. Its endurance is more convincing than the Darwinian theory of the struggle for the survival of the fittest.

What of the admirable continuance of the weak? To persist over here, we need to believe in more than the random flicks of quarks and genomes and other infinitesimal and perhaps irrelevant sparks of existence. As Sir Peter Ustinov so elegantly put it, he did not wish to die 'before the end of a sentence.' And when serving as the Chancellor of Durham University, where some 30,000 degrees were conferred during his tenure, he did observe to the graduates, 'education ends with death – or slightly later, according to your beliefs.' Indeed, it is so. In the beginning was the Word, and so we may speak and write. And even if the Word is not God, we seek to complete our sentence here – at our own ending, that is and was and may be. Or perhaps, we should follow the example of Monsieur de Fontenelle, then ninety-five years old, who was accosted by a woman of ninety.

'Death has forgotten us,' she said.

The older man put his finger to his lips and answered, 'Shush.'

Or even better, perhaps, to agree with Charles Lamb, disputing with William Godwin and Coleridge about which was the best – *Man as he was*, or *Man as he is to be*. And Lamb said, 'Give me Man as he is *not* to be.'

The time of praise is gone. And yet no blame,
Only the sniper and the ricochet,
The dagger in the back, the snide hearsay,
He isn't what he was, ain't that a shame.

He can't write what he wants or how he meant,
So young, so brilliant! Yet the way he took
Was too much writing, book on book on book.
He will not stop till he is excrement.

Don't count him out. The bell that tolls for him
Is just Round Eighty in the greater game.
Come back for more and take it on the chin –
Who knows the score of referees of fame?
The three-timer loser clears the final bar –
The once forgotten now familiar.

Finally, the University Library at Cambridge has taken over my literary papers for the benefit of future research. Back to my *alma mater*. I am its first and only post-Modern author on file, whatever that means. My contemporary polymath and don, Alan Bennett, has given his papers to the Bodleian, also for free, and not for a fortune to Texas. This is the apotheosis of my decades of struggle against the erratic fashions of literary criticism. To use my Rabelaisian and Swiftian jargon, I have outlasted the Scrutiny of the Leavishites and the Semidiotologists and the Derridadadumdumbs, and the followers of Foukault and Lacan't and other mugwumps.

Posterity will now be the judge on their judgements. I have had enough of the Societies and Institutes and Arts Councils and their *apparatchiks*, who rise by committee to become cardboard Knights and pantomime Dames in their self-promoting careers. As I have said, we are all original. Criticism is often bigotry, the belief in one style of writing at odds with many others. As elephants, older literary generations, if still alive, never forget. Fortunately, younger generations cannot remember, until given the reminders. And power passes by. Culled are the cults and fashions of yesteryear. As Ozymandias, sand scatters over their ruins. Where is the grandiose gone? Into the footnotes of forgotten texts. Apt words endure. And Irony is my best obsequy, even if it is an evasion of the truth.

NOTHING IS SO

'Who wrote it? Did I Another? Probably. Are we not become others the moment after we've done writing. A posthumous book? That too is possible; are we not today yesterday's dead?'

So Cocteau wrote in a preface to *Le Livre blanc*, first published in 1957 in England, where homosexuality was still a criminal offence. His rather autobiographical account treated the port city of Toulon as the Sodom of the South of France, where sailors never refused a hired offer of love. The book was claimed to be by an unknown author, who did not specialise in a taste for his own sex – not the role that Cocteau displayed in his famous art and other works. And yet, he did highlight the abyss between honesty and autobiography, between omission and confession, memory and fact, a sense of theatre or of vengeance, his acting and his acts. And he posed the ultimate question, how describe yourself, if you don't know who you are, even in disguise. As Hoss said in Sam Shepard's *The Tooth of Crime*:

> Ya know, you'd be OK, Becky, if you had a self. So would I. Something to fall back on in a moment of doubt or terror or even surprise.

In the absence of a strong sense of self, which may be a delusion, autobiography is an exercise in futility. For Cocteau, 'words have no sense. All right, Granted. Then have they any when you explain to me at length why I do wrong to use them? Accept the game, master it, arrange it as you please, but let there be a chance of give or take…'

Although language is a labyrinth of sidelines, in my own way, I have started in satire, tried to write some sagas, and ended in black farce as I aim to resurrect some of the things I have done. My example was the conclusion of two sublime authors, Mark Twain and Thomas Mann. To follow *Huckleberry Finn* in his voyage down the Mississippi River, Twain invented a *Confidence Man* on a steamboat, up to every trick of chicanery and masquerade, devilry and superstition. And after *Buddenbrooks* and *The Magic Mountain*, Mann looked back on the artifices of his literature in *Confessions of the Confidence Trickster Felix Krull*. These masterpieces of declining age appeared to be reappraised as scenes on a manipulated stage, written by supreme stylists who did accept the game of words, master it, and arrange it as a theatre of sardonic laughter, as did Evelyn Waugh in *The Loved One*, that elegy to the crematorium of the Happier Hunting Ground.

My great terror was the thought of meeting myself. Every mirror is a shock of recognition. Is that the image of me? Or is that really me? Will the glass stop my hand as I reach out to touch my face, or will I touch my own flesh opposite me? Alice Through the Looking Glass may meet Alice or Andrew in Reverse. As Rilke wrote:

> Now it was stronger, and it was I who was the mirror. I stared at this great, terrifying, unknown personage before me, and it seemed appalling to me that I should be alone with him. But at the very moment that I thought this, the worst befell: I lost all knowledge of myself, I simply ceased to exist.

The fear of the double is, of course, common to all. A split personality in the same body, Dr Jekyll and Mr Hyde. A spirit leaving the body while asleep, the *doppelgänger*. The vampire coming out of the dead body and having no shadow. The shadow divorcing itself from its maker to wander darkly on its own. Only Groucho Marx got the better of this primitive fear in *Duck Soup*. His brothers, dressed as himself in moustache and nightgown, imitated the other side of the broken mirror till Groucho grabbed one by the shirt-tail.

I always thought this obsession of mine was superstitious before I ran into an old friend of mine Jim Watson a few years ago. Jim with Francis Crick had discovered the secret of life. Like a twin Frankenstein, the two biologists had worked out the structure of the DNA molecule, the basis of our chromosomes. After receiving his Nobel Prize, Jim became worried. He knew that we were only a few years away from genetic tinkering. And when I ran into him, he was off to see the American President's advisers. His own discovery had been developed. New researchers had almost reached the point where they could cut off a piece of a man's skin and reproduce from it *without benefit* of woman a thousand perfect replicas of the man.

My horror had nearly become actual and was equalled by that of Jim Watson. What if some new Hitler in power decided that he was the perfection of humanity and had himself reproduced one million times over? Aldous Huxley's *Brave New World* was a leap closer to us. People could be produced for determined grades of society to conform with standards thought to be desirable. No luck of the genes was left to catapult somebody from a poor family to join the technocrats or the diplomats.

Yet the social consequences of this disastrous genetic breakthrough were nothing to my personal horror. What if an enemy took a fingernail clipping – enough for a witch's spell? What if he reproduced me twenty times over so that, when I was old and failing, twenty perfect likenesses came up to taunt me and mock me with my old age? Why, I would have to pursue every copy of myself and gun him down. And then, could I be put on trial for murder, when I had only killed the twenty duplicates of myself, and yet remained alive, ready for more duplication?

As Frankenstein knew, the monster of the dream can be made flesh. Obsessions are the far side of the mirror. My technique of only trying to tell anecdotes to defer my immediate execution was modelled on that of Scheherazade, entertaining the Sultan in *The 1001 Nights*. And my deductions about my series of tall stories were these:

- Appearances are clouds of flies.
- Presumptions squawk as parrots.
- Only deeds count.
- So I tell stories about a little of what I have done or seem to have done. Also tales of what other people said or did, as I remember these, obscurely.
- As with Céline and Pinter, the dots and the pauses are more significant than the words. So much to write, so sparse the pages.
- Leaving out and running yourself down may be seeking the praise of others.
- We chuck our sins in the bin of omission. Our virtues may flicker in our acts, but these should rarely be put on show.
- Motive is no excuse for our mistakes, good intention is no refuge from blame.

– Fame is no spur, but the bridle on our pace. Our luck is if we are on any record.
– And when we are gone, we may only Rest In Proof.
– Yet irony is finally a failure of belief.
– So what if I believe falsely that nothing in this book is true?

And at last?

Illumination – that was our sight –
A spark, a flash, a burst of sun,
Radiance when the day was done,
No evening or dead of night,
Yet here the dimming of the light.

In comets, stars and shining bright,
Our spurts and starts at sound of gun
Shot out kaleidoscopes of fun,
And now we move to dull and fright –
It is the dimming of the light.

In age there is no blast or fight.
Only accept there's nothing won,
No leap, no stretch, and choice is none,
Only the dimming of the light,
Yes, the dimming of the light.

This book is only an assertion, with not so many witnesses left alive to check these tales. Identity is the alias by which we seek to conform. Character is shown by what we have done. I am not I, until my acts are facts. I am, therefore, I think. No one may know who I thought I was, until death ends my manifestations.

Q.E.D. [*Quis Est Demonstratum?*]

NEAR THE END

INDEX